Lecture Notes in Artificial Intelligence 2990

Edited by J. G. Carbonell and J. Siekmann

Subseries of Lecture Notes in Computer Science

T0280296

João Leite   Andrea Omicini
Leon Sterling   Paolo Torroni (Eds.)

Declarative Agent Languages and Technologies

First International Workshop, DALT 2003
Melbourne, Australia, July 15, 2003
Revised Selected and Invited Papers

 Springer

Series Editors

Jaime G. Carbonell, Carnegie Mellon University, Pittsburgh, PA, USA
Jörg Siekmann, University of Saarland, Saarbrücken, Germany

Volume Editors

João Leite
Universidade Nova de Lisboa
Faculdade de Ciências e Tecnologia, Departamento de Informática
2829-516 Caparica, Portugal
E-mail: jleite@di.fct.unl.pt

Andrea Omicini
Università di Bologna
Dipartimento di Elettronica, Informatica e Sistemistica
Via Venezia 52, 47023 Cesena, Italy
E-mail: andrea.omicini@unibo.it

Leon Sterling
University of Melbourne
Department of Computer Science and Software Engineering
Victoria 3010, Australia
E-mail: leon@cs.mu.oz.au

Paolo Torroni
Università di Bologna
Dipartimento di Elettronica, Informatica e Sistemistica
Viale Risorgimento 2, 40136 Bologna, Italy
E-mail: paolo.torroni@unibo.it

Library of Congress Control Number: 2004106089

CR Subject Classification (1998): I.2.11, C.2.4, D.2.4, D.2, D.3

ISSN 0302-9743
ISBN 3-540-22124-7 Springer-Verlag Berlin Heidelberg New York

Springer-Verlag is a part of Springer Science+Business Media

springeronline.com

© Springer-Verlag Berlin Heidelberg 2004
Printed in Germany

Typesetting: Camera-ready by author, data conversion by Olgun Computergrafik
Printed on acid-free paper   SPIN: 11008521   06/3142   5 4 3 2 1 0

Preface

Agent metaphors and technologies are increasingly adopted to harness and govern the complexity of today's systems. As a consequence, the growing complexity of agent systems calls for models and technologies that promote system predictability and enable feature discovery and verification. Formal methods and declarative technologies have recently attracted a growing interest as a means to address such issues.

The aim of the DALT 2003 workshop was two-fold. On the one hand, we wanted to foster a discussion forum to export such techniques into the broader community of agent researchers and practitioners. On the other hand, we wanted to bring in the issues of real-world, complex, and possibly large-scale agent system design in the perspective of formal methods and declarative technologies.

Thanks to the very high quality of our program committee, we managed to put together a rich program, including three technical sessions and two panel sessions: *The Use of Declarative Programming for Agent-Oriented Software Engineering*, moderated by Leon Sterling and Andrea Omicini, and *Declarative and Logic-Based Technology for Agent Reasoning and Interactions*, organized and moderated by Rafael Bordini and Wiebe van der Hoek, with the participation of five invited panelists.

This book contains the revised and extended versions of the papers presented at the workshop, as well as three invited contributions by leading researchers of the field. It is composed of three parts: (*i*) software engineering and multi-agent system prototyping, (*ii*) agent reasoning, BDI logics and extensions, and (*iii*) social aspects of multi-agent systems.

As an introduction to this first part (and in some sense, to the whole book), Omicini and Zambonelli suggest a new view of MAS as complex systems, inspired by some of the recent results in evolutionary biology, and discuss the many different roles that declarative models and technologies can play in the engineering of complex software systems and of MAS in particular.

Castaldi, Costantini, Gentile and Tocchio discuss how a suitably-designed logic-based agent infrastructure (Lira), combined with a logic-based agent-oriented development framework (DALI), makes it possible to supervise and possibly reconfigure the global behavior of a MAS in a dynamic way.

Bergenti, Rimassa, and Viroli provide a framework for the formalization of autonomous agents, that promotes multiple and layered views over social agent features such as ACL, ontology, and social role.

Clark and McCabe present Go!, a multi-paradigm programming language aimed at agent-based applications. By showing how it can be used to build a simple but nontrivial MAS, they face a wide range of issues, from intra-agent to inter-agent ones.

In the last paper of the first part, Son, Pontelli, Ranjan, Milligan, and Gupta present a brief overview of an agent-based framework for rapid application prototyping, called ϕ-log, which is rooted in the specific field of evolutionary biology, and is meant to exploit the power of declarative programming to free evolutionary biologist from the burden of directly managing the mess of the many heterogeneous bio-informatic tools and data available today for her/his work.

The second part of this book is devoted to models of agent rationality. Traditionally, declarative technologies have always played a key role in capturing the notion of a rational agency, and in defining it in a formal and intuitive way. Notably, modal logic has proved to be a very powerful formalism to express classic agent mental categories, such as beliefs, commitments, goals, and intentions, and to extend them with, and reason about, other notions such as interaction, cooperativity, expectations, and ignorance.

This part starts with an invited contribution by van der Hoek and Lomuscio, in which the authors explore the unknown, promoting ignorance to a first class citizen when reasoning in Multi-Agent Systems. Arguing that being able to reason about what agents *ignore* is just as important as reasoning about what agents know, they motivate and define a non-standard multi-modal logic, by means of a sound and complete axiomatization, to represent and reason about ignorance in Multi-Agent Systems.

Ancona and Mascardi define Coo-BDI, an extension of the BDI architecture with the notion of cooperativity. The proposed ability of having agents collaborate by exchanging and sharing plans in a flexible way has great potential in the implementation of interpreters of BDI programming language.

Moreira, Vieiera, and Bordini build on their previously presented structural operational semantics to AgentSpeak(L) – a BDI, agent-oriented, logic programming language – with an extension to account for inter-agent communication. While doing so, the authors touch upon the long-lasting problem of the semantics of speech acts.

Trân, Harland and Hamilton take the challenge of extending BDI theories to multi-agent systems in an interactive, dynamic environment, and attempt to readdress the computational grounding problem. They provide a formalism for observations – the only connection between mind and worlds – and expectations – the mental states associated with observations.

Flax offers a domain-based approach to the problem of computationally limited deduction and reasoning. The notion of *restricted entailment*, together with the corresponding modal logic interpretation, is presented to model resource-bounded reasoning of agents.

The third and last part of this book focusses on agent interaction. Since the early days of agent research, great attention has been devoted to the study of interactions. This has been done at various levels: by adopting a coordination perspective, by trying to standardize agent communication languages and protocols, and defining a semantics for them, and at a higher level of abstraction, by defining agent teams, societies, organizations, institutions, possibly incorporating organizational notions such as roles and hierarchies, and deontic notions such as norms and obligations.

In this, declarative and logic-based approaches have often been used to define communication language semantics and interaction protocols, both in mentalistic approaches and in social approaches. Also, logic has often been used to define and give an operational semantics to the coordination of reasoning in multi-agent systems.

This third part is started by an invited contribution, in which Colombetti, Fornara, and Verdicchio discuss the use of commitments to give a social semantics to agent interaction, defining the semantics of Agent Communication Languages in terms of changes in the social relationships between agents. The *social commitments*, which represent such relationships, are taken to be primitive concepts, underlying the social dimension of Multi-Agent Systems.

Vasconcelos focusses on communication among the components of a multi-agent system, proposing a logic to describe global protocols. A simple notation is employed, based on first-order logic and set theory to represent an expressive class of electronic institutions. The paper provides a formal semantics for the constructs introduced and presents a distributed implementation of a platform to enact electronic institutions specified in such a formalism.

Alberti, Gavanelli, Lamma, Mello, and Torroni take a resource sharing problem as a case study to present and analyze a social semantics for agent interaction. The formalism introduced is an extension of logic programming with an abductive interpretation, and it allows one to formally define, in a simple and declarative way, concepts such as fulfillment, violation, and social expectation. The authors show how to use these concepts to verify the correct behavior of agents interacting in a society that defines the interaction protocols allowed.

Finally, Küngas and Matskin present a model of cooperative problem solving. Linear logic is used for encoding agents' states, goals, and capabilities. Linear logic theorem proving is applied by each agent to determine whether the particular agent is capable of solving the problem alone. If no individual solution can be constructed, then the agent may start negotiation with other agents in order to find a cooperative solution. Partial deduction in linear logic is used to derive a possible deal, and plans are extracted from the proofs, determining agents' responsibilities in cooperative solutions.

We would like to take this opportunity to thank the authors who answered our call with high quality contributions, the invited panelists, the panel organizers, and all the workshop attendants, for the deep and stimulating discussions, and the authors of the three invited papers. Finally, we would like to thank the members of the Program Committee for ensuring the quality of the workshop program by kindly offering their time and expertise so that each paper could undergo quadruple reviewing.

March 2004

João Leite
Andrea Omicini
Leon Sterling
Paolo Torroni

Organization

DALT 2003 was held in conjunction with AAMAS 2003, the Second International Joint Conference on Autonomous Agents and Multi-Agent Systems, and in cooperation with the ITC Melbourne.

Workshop Organizers

João A. Leite, Universidade Nova de Lisboa, Portugal
Andrea Omicini, Università di Bologna / Cesena, Italy
Leon Sterling, University of Melbourne, Australia
Paolo Torroni, Università di Bologna, Italy

Program Committee

Rafael H. Bordini (The University of Liverpool, UK)
Jeff Bradshaw (The University of West Florida, FL, USA)
Antonio Brogi (Università di Pisa, Italy)
Stefania Costantini (Università degli Studi di L'Aquila, Italy)
Yves Demazeau (Institut IMAG, Grenoble, France)
Jürgen Dix (The University of Manchester, UK)
Toru Ishida (Kyoto University, Japan)
Catholijn Jonker (Vrije Universiteit Amsterdam, NL)
Antonis Kakas (University of Cyprus, Lefkosia, Cyprus)
Daniel Kudenko (University of York, UK)
Alessio Lomuscio (King's College, London, UK)
Viviana Mascardi (Università degli Studi di Genova, Italy)
Paola Mello (Università di Bologna, Italy)
John Jules Ch. Meyer (Universiteit Utrecht, NL)
Charles L. Ortiz (SRI International, Menlo Park, CA, USA)
Sascha Ossowski (Universidad Rey Juan Carlos, Madrid, Spain)
Luís Moniz Pereira (Universidade Nova de Lisboa, Portugal)
Jeremy Pitt (Imperial College, London, UK)
Ken Satoh (National Institute of Informatics, Tokyo, Japan)
Michael Schroeder (City University, London, UK)
Onn Shehory (IBM Research Lab in Haifa, Israel)
Carles Sierra (Spanish Research Council, Barcelona, Spain)
V.S. Subrahmanian (University of Maryland, MD, USA)
Francesca Toni (Imperial College, London, UK)
Wiebe van der Hoek (The University of Liverpool, UK)
Franco Zambonelli (Università di Modena e Reggio Emilia, Italy)

Additional Referees

Álvaro Freitas Moreira
Pavlos Moraïtis
Josep Puyol-Gruart
Sarvapali Ramchurn
Juan A. Rodríguez-Aguilar
Ralf Schweimeier

Marek Sergot
Arnon Sturm
Hans van Ditmarsch
Pınar Yolum

Table of Contents

MAS as Complex Systems:
A View on the Role of Declarative Approaches

Andrea Omicini[1] and Franco Zambonelli[2]

[1] DEIS, Università degli Studi di Bologna a Cesena
via Venezia 52, 47023 Cesena, Italy
andrea.omicini@unibo.it
[2] DISMI, Università degli Studi di Modena e Reggio Emilia
via Allegri 13, 42100 Reggio Emilia, Italy
franco.zambonelli@unimore.it

Abstract. The ever growing complexity of software systems calls for new forms of understanding and conceptual tools. It has been argued that some "Laws of Complexity" exist, which govern the behaviour of complex systems of any sort, from natural to artificial ones.

Along this line, in this paper we draw from the most recent findings of evolutionary biology to develop an original view over Multiagent Systems (MAS). A schema for a "layered", hierarchical view of MAS is introduced, aimed at providing computer scientists and engineers with a powerful conceptual framework for MAS observation / modelling / construction. We first introduce the three levels of the hierarchy in general, and then show how they impact on current proposals for methodologies of agent-oriented analysis and design. Finally, we exploit the hierarchy to provide an overall organised view over declarative approaches to MAS, by using as a reference those presented in the other contributions in this book.

On the one hand, a hierarchical view allows the many different approaches to be distinguished, classified and possibly compared. On the other hand, it makes it possible to reveal the richness and diversity of declarative models and technologies for MAS, as well as to show the multiplicity of ways in which they impact on MAS modelling and engineering.

1 Introduction

In the context of computer science, complexity is everyday more claiming for its own space among the main issues to address. Today computer-based systems are undeniably complex to design, complex to develop, and complex to maintain. The very promise of agent-oriented computing, indeed, is in fact to help computer scientists and engineers to envision and build complex artificial systems that they can manage. It is not commonly agreed, to some extent, whether agent abstractions and technologies are either another source of complexity – with respect to current mainstream object technologies, they surely are –, or rather the conceptual and practical tools required to harness the intrinsic complexity of today artificial systems. Indeed, they are likely to be both, and maybe

J. Leite et al. (Eds.): DALT 2003, LNAI 2990, pp. 1–16, 2004.

this is also a condition that they share with any newer and more sophisticated theory or technology making its appearance in any field, not only in computer science. For our purposes here, however, it suffices to agree on the fact that Multiagent Systems (MAS henceforth) can be generally seen as a class of complex software systems, wide and meaningful enough to legitimate in principle some sort of conceptual association between complex system in general, and MAS in particular.

Even though a satisfactory and shared definition of the very notion of complexity is not available, yet there is a common understanding that complexity raises the same sorts of problems within many diverse and heterogeneous areas of human knowledge. From this perspective, it has been argued [1] that some "Laws of complexity" exist, that cross the strict boundaries of traditional separations between distinct scientific disciplines. As a result, rather than useful or merely inspiring, exploiting inter- and trans-disciplinary approaches in order to understand complex system comes to be almost mandatory.

Accordingly, if some Laws of Complexity exist, they should apply to artificial systems, and to MAS in particular. On the one hand, this is likely to be why so many different techniques or theories coming from many different disciplines (biology, social sciences, organisational sciences, economics, politics, philosophy) are currently brought to agent-based models and systems [2,3,4,5]. On the other hand, this apparently legitimates extrapolation and adaptation of general results about complexity from heterogeneous research fields to computer science: or, at least, it makes it worth a try.

Under this perspective, evolutionary biology is surely one of the most intriguing related fields. There, in fact, the interest of the scientists lays not only in understanding the behaviour of complex biological systems, but also (and mainly) in modelling and motivating their evolution over time, their history – how they came to reach such a level of complexity from the very simple systems that marked the appearance of life on the Earth. In some sense, software systems are undergoing their own form of "evolution" too, moving from quite simple (algorithm-based) systems to intricate (interaction-based) systems [6] – e.g., from computer programs to MAS. Even though here we do not need to give too much meaning to such a transition, this fact indeed makes the parallel seem even more suggestive.

According to the *theory of hierarchies* [7], biological systems are amenable to be represented as organised on different layers: from genes and cells up to organisms, species and clades. On the one hand, each layer exhibits its own characteristic behaviour and dynamics, and it is governed by its own set of independent laws and rules. On the other hand, each layer is inextricably blended with the others, and strictly depends on both upper and lower layers. According to this view, every attempt to explain any non-trivial behaviour of biological systems – such as, of course, their evolution over time – has to be rooted in at least one of the layers, as well as in its interaction with the others along the whole hierarchy.

In this article, we start (Section 2) by taking as our reference the three levels devised out by Eldredge [8] (microevolutionary, intermediate, and macroevolutionary – see Subsection 2.1), and elaborate on how and to which extent this view can apply to software systems. So, in Subsection 2.2 we first essay the construction of a hierarchical view over complex software systems, by using MASs as our case study. Then, in order to demonstrate the potential of such a view, we critically discuss some key features of current agent-oriented analysis and design methodologies (Section 3), by showing how a hierarchical view is indeed necessary toward an effective approach to MAS modelling, engineering, and development. Finally, as the main aim of this article, we exploit the hierarchical view of MAS (Section 4) to recast the many different declarative approaches to MAS – as they emerge from this volume in particular – , so as to reveal the multiplicity of the levels at which declarative models and technologies can impact on the modelling and engineering of agents and MAS.

2   A Theory of Hierarchies for MAS

Indeed, evolutionary biology deals with one of the most difficult and articulated issues in the wide scope of human knowledge: not only how biological systems (possibly the most complex systems we have direct experience of) work, but also (and mainly) how they did come to work like they do during and after millions of years of evolution. As a result, once recognised that complexity has its own patterns that traverse the boundaries of traditional disciplines, drawing from the findings of evolutionary biology seems a quite natural way to try better understanding the ever growing complexity of software systems – and of MAS in particular – both in terms of its current state, and of its possibly otherwise unforeseeable directions.

2.1   Hierarchies for Complex Biological Systems

Broadly speaking, complex systems do not allow for simple explanations. A recasting of this apparently trivial observation in terms of the most recent results in evolutionary biology, is that complex systems call for "layered", hierarchical explanations. A first fundamental result is the so-called *theory of the hierarchies* [7]: in order to understand biological systems, and their evolution over time as well, several different "layers" has to be accounted for – from genes, to cells, up to organisms, species and higher taxa. While each layer is in some sense autonomous, and exhibit its own independent laws and dynamics, at the same time layers are organised in a hierarchy, each one strictly connected with the upper and lower levels, each parts of bigger totalities, each also wholeness composed of smaller parts. When observing / understanding / explaining a biological system, then, many different levels of abstraction can be adopted – which in the case of biological systems may correspond, for instance, to the gene, cell, organism, or species levels – and provide different but equally meaningful views over the systems.

Along this line, Eldredge [8] interprets evolution of biological systems as occurring at (at least) three levels: the microevolutionary (genes), the macroevolutionary (demes/species/clades), and the intermediate (organisms) one. In accordance with the theory of hierarchies, each level is essential to the general understanding of the system's wholeness, it is autonomous with its own laws, patterns and behaviours, but it can not be understood in isolation independently of all the other levels. For instance, while Dawkins [9] seems to ascribe the whole dynamics of biological evolution to the dynamics of (selfish) gene reproduction[1], Eldredge [8] and Gould [11] clearly show how the dynamics of individual organisms, demes, species, etc., as well as their interactions with the ever changing environment where they live and reproduce, irreducibly affect the process of biological evolution, which cannot be simplistically imputed to the genetic mechanisms alone.

Even though further works [11] argues that a higher number of different levels may befit a hierarchical view over biological systems, we do not proceed along this path any further: the three levels individuated by Eldredge already seem detailed enough to formulate a first hierarchical view of complex software systems, and of MAS in particular.

2.2 Hierarchies for Software Systems & MAS

Correspondingly, there are at least three levels of a potential hierarchy that we can use to observe / interpret / build complex software systems in general, and MAS in particular.

At the lower level, corresponding to the microevolutionary level of genes in biological systems, software systems exhibit what we can call the *mechanism* level, where the basic mechanisms for building system components are in place, and play the most relevant role. Things like programming languages, basic network protocols, and the corresponding mechanisms and abstractions have a deep influence on the sorts of systems that programmers and engineers can put together. Mechanisms and abstractions like parameter passing in C, closure in Lisp or ML, sockets in Java, anchors in HTML pages, or records in a DB system, provide the basic expressive power that is required for building any software system today, including MAS. It is quite obvious that no complex system could be either represented or built by focusing solely on the mechanism level – in the same way as no history of biological evolution could be fully understood at the microevolutionary level alone, that is, by adopting the genetic mechanisms as the only forces for evolution. Analogously, then, further upper levels are required other than the mechanism one for complex software systems: however, this level is essential indeed, since it provides the basic bricks for complex system observation and construction.

---

[1] Even though some recent work seems to minimise the "reductionist attitude" of Dawkins [10], his work is taken here as a frequently cited example of the widespread attitude of scientists to disregard complexity as a sort of implicit threat to the role and power of human science – and of human scientists, as well.

At this very first level, also, some of the main differences between biological and computer-based systems come out clearly – which are basically reducible to the differences between natural and artificial systems. First of all, the microevolutionary level and the corresponding genetic mechanisms are given once and for all (to some extent), and the work of biologists is to understand them fully, and devise out their influence on biological systems and their evolution as well. Instead, the understanding of the basic mechanisms and laws that regulate software systems at the mechanism level typically leads as a secondary effect to the selection of some mechanisms and to the definition of new ones. For instance, the long history of programming languages and of their specific linguistic mechanisms, shows how tools at the mechanism level are invented, then spread and used widely, and then accompanied / surpassed by new ones, meant to address either the limitations of the existing ones or newly emerged issues. Secondly, given that software systems are built by humans, differently from biological systems, they come along with the tools that are used to build them. Very simple tools such as code debuggers, profiling tools, or JavaDoc, provide computer scientists and engineers with a sort of embedded view over software systems that allow them to check, monitor and verify the system behaviour at the mechanism level. The same embedded view is obviously not available in the context of biological system – which is likely to be one reason why a lot of the genetic research is currently devoted to observe and represent exhaustively biological systems at the microevolutionary level.

At the highest level, by focusing now on MAS as our software systems for the sake of simplicity, we find notions like agent societies, organisations, teams, groups, and the very notion of MAS itself: we call this level the *social* one. This clearly matches the macroevolutionary level of biological systems, where demes, species, clades, and possibly phyla come into play. The first and main point here is that entities at the social level are to be interpreted as individual first-class entities, despite their apparent "plurality". In the same way as single populations or species exhibit their own dynamics, and either survive or die depending on their success as a whole in interacting with their environment (and with other populations or species, in particular), a MAS displays at the social level a global behaviour, whose conformance to the application requirements, for instance, determines its success as a whole. Social abstractions such as coordination media [12] or e-institutions [13] work as the basic bricks at this level – which is also the one where extra-agent notions, such as the agent infrastructure, become relevant, if not prevalent.

At the intermediate level, software components (agents, in MAS) obviously play the role of the individual entities of the system – basically, the same as the organisms in the biological setting. Focusing on MAS, we can easily name *agent level* such an intermediate level. What we conceptually see at this level of abstraction are things like agent architecture and inner dynamics, agent communication language and individual protocols, and the corresponding abstractions and mechanisms. BDI architecture, FIPA speech acts, agent semantics specifications – all come into play at the agent level, along with the troublesome (and boring, in the end) issue of "what an agent really is". The dynamics of this level of the hierarchy is quite obvious in some sense: a good deal of the agent literature struggles at this level, actually. However, what we learn from the theory of hierarchy is that each level is autonomous and independent in the laws that rule its behaviours, but that no satisfactory view of the whole can be given at one level alone. This comes to say that any view of complex software systems, and of MAS in particular, should account for all the three levels – the mechanism, the social, and the component/agent levels – and that failure to do so may result in a global failure of any attempt to observe / model / build such systems. As a paradigmatic example, in the next section we will focus on Agent-oriented Software Engineering (AOSE) techniques, tools and methods, to show how the different views over a complex software system like a MAS affect the way in which such system is conceived, designed and engineered.

3   A Hierarchical View of AOSE

In the context of AOSE research, it is seemingly easy to devise out the three levels of the MAS hierarchy depicted above. So, even though typically they are not distinguished, nor are they explicitly revealed in current AOSE practice as well as in recently proposed agent-oriented analysis and design methodologies, nevertheless such three levels are to be identified, so as to clearly point out how they affect the way in which complex MASs are modelled and designed.

3.1   The Mechanism Level

What are the basic "ingredients" to build an agent? That is, the basic bricks required to build a computational organism capable of autonomous actions and decision making? Although such a question seems to be of paramount importance, as also outlined in the discussion of the previous section, current AOSE practice seems to mostly disregard it.

In the area of agent-oriented methodologies, the basic assumption underlying most proposal (sometimes implicit, as in TROPOS [14], or explicit, as in [15]) is that the mechanism level does not influence at all the way a MAS is modelled and designed. The mechanism level is assumed to influence the implementation phase only, and the modelling and design can proceed independently of it.

Other specific proposals for agent-oriented analysis and design methodology assume a totally different, and possibly more radical position, by stating that the basic underlying mechanisms will be that of, say, specific programming environments or paradigms. This is the case, for instance, of most mobile agent methodologies [16], which always consider Java (and related technologies and middleware) as the target development technology.

Both endeavours have advantages and drawbacks.

On the one hand, assuming a technology-neutral perspective enables designers to adopt a more modular approach to system design, and at the same time frees them from having to deal with low level implementation details. However, this may also lead to troubles during the following implementation phases, where the required commitment to a specific technology could force developers to adopt tricky and ineffective solutions to match the design requirements against the technology constraints. In other words, with reference to what we stated in Subsection 2.2, such an endeavour misses in explicitly considering the reciprocal influences of the mechanisms, agent, and social levels.

On the other hand, assuming the presence of a specific technology allows for very efficient designs, that can be subsequently implemented without any mismatch. However, this makes it very hard to produce a general understanding of the characteristics of a complex MAS and to produce re-usable and modular model and design.

In our personal perspectives, some sort of intermediate approach should be enforced, so as to preserve the clear separation between the different layers of the hierarchy, but at the same time to take into account the influence of the underlying mechanisms over both the agent and the social level.

3.2   The Agent Level

Mechanisms are used to build agents and societies where agents live. As far as agents are concerned, the discussion about what an agent really is and how it should be modelled has been around for several years, and a considerable amount of research work still struggles about such an issue. Such a discussion appears dramatically important in the modelling and design of complex MASs, in that it implies defining the essential features of the organisms, that is, of the individuals, that will populate such MASs. Nevertheless, the discussion could become more constructive by simply recognising the fact that defining exactly what an agent is is indeed a matter of modelling and design choices, rather than an absolute truth about the agent-oriented paradigm.

It is clearly possible to identify different classes of entities, all exhibiting different degrees of situatedness, autonomy and decision-making capabilities, that we could call agents with some good reasons. For instance, according to the taxonomy introduced by Maja Mataric [17], one can identify the following classes:

- reactive agents, which are basically capable of perceiving events and, based on an internal state, perform some sort of reactive autonomous action in direct reaction to events or to inter-agent communications;
- deliberative agents, which are capable of internal planning and internal decision-making aimed at achieving specific goals, and which can dynamically change their plan based on the perceived events or the occurred inter-agent communications;
- behavioural agents, which locates somewhere in between reactive and deliberative agents. As deliberative agents, behavioural agents are capable of autonomous goal-oriented decisions making. However, as in reactive agents, their overall activity (i.e., the goals they have to achieve) is strictly related to their interaction / communication history.

The first class typically includes most mobile agent systems and embedded agents [16], the second one includes BDI agents [18], while the third class is typical of situated robots [19].

In the area of agent-oriented methodologies, agents are definitely the main focus of the design activity. That is, unlike the mechanism level, the agent level is always explicitly taken into account. Still, most methodologies fail in specifying what an agent is to them, and why the defined methodology suits that specific class of agent. In other words, most methodologies propose guidelines for building complex societies of agents without actually saying what types of agents they are considering. This is the case, for instance, of Gaia [15] and MASE [20], where all that is said is that an agent is an entity capable of autonomous actions, of communicating with other agents, and of sensing events in the environment, three features that all the three classes of agents introduced have to exhibit, and that makes such a characterisation of an agent non-informative at all.

The consequence of this missing specifications at the agent level is that several important aspects are left unspecified, that are likely to somewhat influence both the mechanism and the societal level. As a result, first of all such missing specifications may be the sources of further mismatches between design and implementation (besides those identified in the previous subsection) when it comes to implementing agents. Even more, specific assumptions about agent capabilities (thus belonging to the agent level) may somewhat affect the global design of a MAS (that is, the social level). For example, the capability of agents of sensing events and re-forging their goals on the basis of such events, is an individual agent feature that clearly influences the overall behaviour of the system.

In some cases, the specification of the reference agent type is indirectly suggested by the methodology itself. For instance, most methodologies for mobile agent systems assume a reactive agent model [21]. Only in a very few cases, such a specification is made explicit. One of these cases is that of the Prometheus methodology [22], which is explicitly conceived for MASs made of of BDI (that is, deliberative) agents.

Summarising, the construction of a complex system, as a MAS is, and the full modelling of its structure and dynamic behaviour, requires a precise and unambiguous definition of the features considered as essential at the agent level.

3.3   The Social Level

The ultimate goal of the process of an agent-oriented methodology analysis and design is that of building a MAS as a whole, capable of achieving a given application goal in an efficient and reliable way within a target operational environment. The resulting MAS will of course include a (possibly varying) number of agents and, thus, agents are the primary necessary components of it.

However, agents alone do not represent the full picture in MASs. On the one hand, a MAS may exhibit collective behaviours that cannot easily be modelled in terms of the behaviour of its individual components. On the other hand, a MAS may involve more components than agents and may require the explicit modelling of such additional components. As a simple example, consider the case of an agent-based Web information system, or of an agent-mediated marketplace. In both cases, in addition to agents, the overall MASs include a computational environment made up of digital information and digital goods, and may include some sort of security infrastructure influencing the actions of the agents by, e.g., inhibiting malicious opportunistic behaviours. In general terms, the proper modelling and engineering of a MAS requires an explicit modelling of the societal aspects, i.e., of the environment in which the MAS situates and of the social laws to which the agents of the MAS must obey.

Most methodologies for agent-oriented analysis and design proposed so far plainly disregard the social level, and consider the specification of a MAS as complete for the only fact of having accurately specified the set of agents that are part of it. This is the case, for example, of the first version of the Gaia methodology [23] and of the MASE methodology [20], where neither the MAS environment nor any type of social laws are taken into any account.

The authors of this paper have been pioneering the adoption of explicit social abstractions in MAS analysis and design since several years ago [24], and have proposed and implemented several effective mechanisms (e.g., tuple-based social interaction spaces [25]) to support the development and execution of socially enriched MASs, i.e., of MAS explicitly dived in an environment and explicitly obeying a set of social laws. Also, they have contributed at enriching the Gaia methodology with the necessary set of environmental and social abstractions [26,15].

Recently, several other proposals have started recognising the need for an explicitly modelling of the social level. For instance, it is now acknowledged that the design of open MASs where multitudes of self-interested agents interact in an opportunistic way, requires modelling the "social laws" that rule agent interactions. This has led to the general concept of "agent institutions" [13], intended as societies of agents interacting in accord to an explicitly modelled set of "institutionalised" rules.

The explicit modelling of the social level in the engineering of a MAS is very important, and may influence both the agent level and the mechanism level. At the agent level, it is important to recognise that the autonomous decision-making capabilities of an agent are likely to be somewhat limited by the social level (e.g., by the super-imposition of social laws), and to model agents and their capabilities accordingly. At the mechanism level, it has to be acknowledged that the super-imposition of social laws may require specific mechanism as, e.g., programmable interaction media to mediate and rule interactions [27]. Therefore, the appropriate modelling of the social level cannot abstract from the societal mechanisms available, and vice versa. In addition, as a general consideration to be accounted for at every level, it is important to outline that the environment in which a MAS situates (specifically, the dynamics of such an environment) may affect the global behaviour of a MAS in unpredictable ways, and that the actual effectiveness of a MAS strictly depends on its capabilities of preserving an acceptable behaviour independently of environmental factors.

4   A Hierarchical View of Declarative Approaches to MAS

The old, silly question "Why should I use Prolog to program?" has become "Why should I use Prolog for my agents?" in the agent age – and it is possibly even sillier than it was then. On the one hand, the range of the declarative and logic-based models and technologies developed in the last ten years is so wide that talking of Prolog only is simply non-sense. On the other hand, moving from simple programs and algorithms to the elaborate structure of MASs makes the space for logic-based approaches even larger than it was before. Along this line, the multi-layer, hierarchical view over agent systems introduced in this paper is exactly meant to provide a well-defined conceptual framework where to classify and evaluate the potential contributions of declarative and logic-based approaches to the modelling and engineering of MAS.

   In order to avoid excessive spreading of this paper scope, and also to promote a unitary view of this book, we will draw our cases and examples from the papers that follow this one, discussing and framing them accordingly. So, in the rest of this section, we will exploit the hierarchy for MASs devised out in the previous sections in order to illustrate the many levels of contributions that may come from declarative approaches to MAS, by taking as our main reference the remaining contributions of this book.

4.1   The Mechanism Level

The shift from current mainstream object/component-based technology to agent technology could not be more evident when taking into account programming languages at the mechanism level. Take, for instance, Java as the mainstream reference technology for the mechanism level, and consider on the one hand the intermediate (component) level in component-based approaches, on the other hand the intermediate (agent) level in agent-based approaches. Intuitively, the distance between the mechanism level and the component level in component-based approaches is all but large. Think, for instance, of the small conceptual distance between the Java language, at the mechanism level, and a JavaBeans component, at the component level: few lines of properly written yet simple Java code make a working JavaBeans. On the other hand, the incredible amount of the efforts to build up a suitable support for agents upon Java-based technology in the last years (see JADE as a fundamental example of this [28]) witnesses the much larger distance between the mechanism and the agent levels in agent-based approaches. Whichever non-trivial acceptation of an agent one may adopt, a Java agent will easily not be a simple chunk of Java code: think, for instance, of the mere implementation of agent social abilities in term of properly handling a fully-fledged agent communication language.

   Such a distance is the main reason why declarative technologies and logic-based languages come so strongly into play in the agent arena: abstractions and metaphors at the agent level require mechanisms that directly support them – and embedding an agent knowledge base or a BDI architecture upon, say,

Prolog, is clearly much easier than doing the same upon, say, Java. It is not by chance, then, that most declarative approaches to MAS place themselves to the mechanism level, but in such a way to clearly head toward the agent level, by either implicitly or explicitly incorporating agent-level abstractions and models. Picking up the examples from this book, ϕ-log and GOLOG [29] are first of all logic-based languages, but the whole ϕ-log project (that by the way is concerned with evolutionary biology) promotes an agent architecture that clearly belongs to the agent level. Analogously, [30] basically introduces the multi-paradigm programming language Go!, which incorporates a series of (quite heterogeneous) linguistic mechanisms, but also provides a blackboard-based agent architecture that should be more properly placed at the agent level. Logic-based mechanisms are introduced by [31] (the mechanisms of Restricted Entailment) and [32] (a non-standard multi-modal logic) to support abstractions and models at the agent level – such as agent reasoning about its own ignorance. Finally, [33] defines an agent-oriented logic language, clearly belonging to the mechanism level, that takes into account the agent-level (embodying the agent level with the BDI) and looks at the social level, through Speech-Act Communications.

In the end, applying the hierarchical view to declarative approaches to MAS makes a couple of relevant things clear at the mechanism level. Firstly, current object-oriented mainstream languages (such as Java and C++) implicitly define a mechanism level that is too poor for MASs: a simple logic language like Prolog intrinsically provides a more expressive support for agent-based models and abstractions. Secondly, Prolog itself does not directly endorse any agent level metaphor: this explains why most of the research at this level (as demonstrated by the contributions in this book, too) concerns the definition of a technological platform at the mechanism level to adequately support and promote suitably expressive declarative models at the agent level.

4.2   The Agent Level

At the agent level, the same problems pointed out in Subsection 3.2 seem to be evident in the literature on declarative and logic-based approaches. That is, on the one hand, the virtual absence of a plain and unambiguous discussion about the notion of agent supported (and the motivations behind it, as well) affects many of the research works in this area, too. On the other hand, the power of declarative approaches as an expressive means to denote and model architectures and behaviours of systems is clearly fundamental for MASs at the agent level.

As a first example of this, [34] introduces a formal framework for agent specification, that promotes a layered description (in terms of multiple "tiers") of agent architecture and behaviour. Also, BDI-based approaches clearly belongs to the agent level, since they explicitly define the inner structure and dynamics of an agent. In this perspective, [35] generalises BDI logics to encompass the notions of observation / expectation for an agent, while Coo-BDI [36] extends the original BDI model with the notion of agent cooperativity – which builds a bridge toward the upper social level. Analogously, the social issue of cooperative problem solving is one of the main target of [37]: there, Linear Logic is basically used to model agents as social entities.

More generally, it easy to see that, at the agent level, declarative and logic-based models work well both as formal tools for the description and definition of agent architectures and behaviours, and as sources of metaphors and abstractions to enrich and empower the individual agent model. So, in the same way as in the case of AOSE literature, the fact that a good deal of the literature on declarative approaches to MAS is concerned with the agent level, but anyway disregards the central point of the precise and exhaustive definition of what an agent is, does not prevent relevant results and promising directions to emerge.

For instance, as it comes out from some of the examples in this book, one of the most frequent "implicit definitions" for agents is the BDI one: in short, one agent is such if it is built around a BDI architecture [35,36]. On the one hand, the BDI model constitutes a conceptual bridge between the mechanism and the agent level, since it provides an architectural principle for agents that can be supported by suitably designed languages at the mechanism level. On the other hand, it is not by chance that BDI is essentially a logic-based model. In fact, whenever features like deliberative capabilities, intelligence, and sociality are taken as defining agent traits, declarative and logic-based approaches are typically the most suitable ones at the agent level, since they provide the adequate expressive power as well as the required level of abstraction – as obvious, for instance, in the case of knowledge-based agents. Less obvious, but manifest from works like [36], is that expressiveness of declarative models is such that not only it helps in bridging between the mechanism and the agent levels, but also enables the agent level to encapsulate and promote abstractions that directly refer to the upper, social level.

4.3   The Social Level

Intuitively, the social level is where the complexity of MAS is going to explode. Handling a MAS composed by possibly hundreds or thousands of agents, as an open system where both known and unknown agents coexist and interact in an unpredictable way, is obviously more than a challenge to MAS engineers. For this very reason, the social level promises to be the one where declarative models and technologies have the potential to provide the most relevant contribution: for instance, by allowing system properties to be assessed at design time, and then enforced at run time by suitable declarative technologies, independently of the MAS dynamics, and of the MAS environment as well.

This is exactly the case of the notion of social integrity constraints [38], which formalises within a logic-based framework social concepts such as violation, fulfilment, social expectation, that can be enforced at run-time through a suitably-defined logic-based infrastructure. The infrastructural concept of institution is then endorsed by other two papers of this book: the notion of Basic Institution is formally defined in [39], founded on the social interpretation of agent communicative acts, while Logic-based Electronic Institutions [40] are first-order logic tools aimed at the specification of open agent organisations. Finally, the integration of DALI and Lira [41] shows a very interesting example of an agent technology vertically spanning the whole MAS hierarchy. While DALI is a logic language (at the mechanism level) that implicitly embeds an agent model (at the agent level), Lira works at the social level – and their integration definitely aims at providing a complete declarative framework for MAS engineering.

Even though there are already several interesting applications of declarative models and technologies at the social level (such as the ones included in this book and just cited above), the potential of such approaches in taming the complexity of MAS is seemingly so high that in the near future the authors expect to see many other works pursuing this very promising direction. XML was maybe the first declarative technology to become mainstream: along this line, while artificial systems grow everyday more complex and intricate, many others of this sort are likely to follow.

5   Final Remarks

Drawing from the field of evolutionary biology to computer science does not imply that we endorse a view of software systems as biological systems – not so plainly, at least. Instead, it simply means that, at the current stage of technology and human knowledge, there are similarities and commonalities enough between the two sorts of systems that an interdisciplinary approach to complexity in software systems seems worth to explore.

Indeed, the undisciplined use of interdisciplinarity is generally dangerous: for its obvious fascination, as well as for the virtual absence of shared and well-defined "operating instructions". The risk of unfruitful speculations, led just for the seek of scientific curiosity, but basically unpurposefully, is surely high and never to be underestimated. However, apart from the obvious consideration that *a priori* undirected speculation is part of the "normal" scientific activity [42], there are several manifest good reasons to adopt the interdisciplinary path we followed along this paper.

First of all, as discussed at the beginning of this article, complexity has its own ways, that prescind from the strict boundaries of individual scientific disciplines. This makes monodisciplinary approaches surely myopic and potentially sterile, and calls for a broader view over the fields of interest that should not be limited any longer to computer science and artificial intelligence, and possibly even trespass the boundaries of cognitive sciences.

Also, the ever growing intricacy of software systems, and of MASs in particular, ask computer scientists to provide their own vision of future problems and solutions, and their own view of the possible directions. Otherwise, the evolution of pervasive artificial systems like MASs is going to be driven mostly by the urgency of (possibly non consistent) market or societal pressures, rather than by a clear understanding of the system's potential benefits and dangers. Such a vision is unlikely to be found now within computer science – too young and immature is the field, today, from a scientific viewpoint, to provide such deep insights over future evolutions of computer-based systems. It is then natural to look for conceptual contributions toward more mature fields, where complexity spreads its wide wings both over space and over time – evolutionary biology being obviously one of such fields, and one of the most intriguing and stimulating, by far: from there, some inspiring and unfathomed visions of the directions that artificial systems like MASs are going to take are more likely to come.

Within the field of computer science, agent models and technologies promise to provide the conceptual and practical tools to face the ever increasing complexity of computer-based systems. On the one hand, research on AOSE straightforwardly deals with the complexity issue. In fact, AOSE abstractions and technologies aim at enabling software engineers to build increasingly complex MAS (thus addressing a form of "spatial" complexity, related to MAS dimension), whereas AOSE processes and methodologies are meant to harness the intricacies of MAS engineering from analysis to deployment (thus addressing a form of complexity "over time", related to the MAS development history). On the other hand, declarative models and technologies are by their very nature made to face complexity. In fact, roughly speaking, declarativeness allows properties of systems to be denoted / imposed while transcending the system dynamics.

However, a consideration like the one above seems obviously too generic to actually promote declarative approaches in the MAS context: a more precise and articulated vision is required, of all the many benefits that declarative, logic-based models and technologies may bring to the agent field, and to AOSE in particular. Under this perspective, the approach based on the Theory of Hierarchies presented in this article, and applied first to AOSE in general, then to declarative models and technologies, may well represent a first, meaningful step along this direction.

Acknowledgements

The authors are grateful to the many people whose work and remarks have helped in conceiving and shaping the material that has been used in this paper. In particular, we are deeply indebted to Paolo Torroni, for his persistence in trying to convince us to write this article, as well as for his continuous support and enduring patience that have made this work possible. Also, we would like to thank all the authors that contributed to the DALT 2003 workshop, and to this book in particular, which provided us with such a vast amount of relevant material that we could use to build up this article.

This work has been partially supported by MIUR, Project COFIN 2003 (ex 40%) "Fiducia e diritto nella società dell'informazione", by MIPAF, Project SIPEAA "Strumenti Integrati per la Pianificazione Eco-compatibile dell'Azienda Agricola", and by the EC FP6 Coordination Action "AgentLink III".

References

1. Kauffman, S.A.: Investigations. Oxford University Press (2001)
2. Calmet, J., Daemi, A., Endsuleit, R., Mie, T.: A liberal approach to openess in societies of agents. [43]

3. Tolksdorf, R., Menezes, R.: Using Swarm intelligence in Linda systems. [43]
4. Feltovich, P.J., Bradshaw, J.M., Jeffers, R., Suri, N., Uszok, A.: Social order and adaptability in animal and human cultures as analogues for agent communities: Toward a policy-based approach. [43]
5. McBurney, P., Parsons, S.: Engineering democracy in open agent systems. [43]
6. Wegner, P.: Why interaction is more powerful than computing. Communications of the ACM **40** (1997) 80–91
7. Grene, M.J.: Hierarchies in biology. American Scientist **75** (1987) 504–510
8. Eldredge, N.: Unfinished Synthesis: Biological Hierarchies and Modern Evolutionary Thought. Oxford University Press (1985)
9. Dawkins, R.: The Selfish Gene. Oxford University Press (1989)
10. Sterelny, K.: Dawkins vs. Gould. Survival of the Fittest. Revolutions in Science. Icon Books Ltd., Cambridge, UK (2001)
11. Gould, S.J.: The Structure of Evolutionary Theory. The Belknap Press of Harvard University Press (2002)
12. Omicini, A., Ossowski, S.: Objective versus subjective coordination in the engineering of agent systems. In Klusch, M., Bergamaschi, S., Edwards, P., Petta, P., eds.: Intelligent Information Agents: An AgentLink Perspective. Volume 2586 of LNAI: State-of-the-Art Survey. Springer-Verlag (2003) 179–202
13. Noriega, P., Sierra, C.: Electronic institutions: Future trends and challenges. In Klusch, M., Ossowski, S., Shehory, O., eds.: Cooperative Information Agents VI. Volume 2446 of Lecture Notes in Computer Science. Springer Verlag (2002) 6th International Workshop (CIA 2002), Madrid, Spain, September 18-20, 2002. Proceedings.
14. Bresciani, P., Perini, A., Giorgini, P., Giunchiglia, F., Mylopoulos, J.: A knowledge level software engineering methodology for agent oriented programming. In: 5th International Conference on Autonomous Agents (Agents 2001). ACM Press, Montreal, Canada (2001) 648–655
15. Zambonelli, F., Jennings, N.R., Wooldridge, M.J.: Developing multiagent systems: The Gaia methodology. ACM Transactions on Software Engineering and Methodology **12** (2003) 417–470
16. Karnik, N.M., Tripathi, A.R.: Design issues in mobile-agent programming systems. IEEE Concurrency **6** (1998) 52–61
17. Mataric, M.J.: Situated robotics. Encyclopedia of Cognitive Science (2002)
18. Kinny, D., Georgeff, M., Rao, A.: A methodology and modelling technique for systems of BDI agents. In Van de Velde, W., Perram, J.W., eds.: Modelling Autonomous Agents in a Multi-Agent World. Volume 1038 of LNAI. Springer-Verlag (1996) 56–71 7th International Workshop (MAAMAW'96), 22–25 January 1996, Eindhoven, The Netherlands.
19. Mataric, M.J.: Integration of representation into goal-driven behaviour-based robots. IEEE Transactions on Robotics and Automation **8** (1992) 59–69
20. Wood, M.F., DeLoach, S.A., Sparkman, C.H.: Multiagent system engineering. International Journal of Software Engineering and Knowledge Engineering **11** (2001) 231–258
21. Cabri, G., Leonardi, L., Zambonelli, F.: Engineering mobile agent applications via context-dependent coordination. IEEE Transactions on Software Engineering **28** (2002) 1034–1051
22. Padgham, L., Winikoff, M.: Prometheus: A methodology for developing intelligent agents. In: 1st International Conference on Autonomous Agents and Multi-Agent Systems (AAMAS 2002). ACM Press, Bologna, Italy (2002)

23. Wooldridge, M.J., Jennings, N.R., Kinny, D.: The Gaia methodology for agent-oriented analysis and design. Autonomous Agents and Multi-Agent Systems **3** (2000) 285–312
24. Ciancarini, P., Omicini, A., Zambonelli, F.: Multiagent system engineering: The coordination viewpoint. In Jennings, N.R., Lespérance, Y., eds.: Intelligent Agents VI. Agent Theories, Architectures, and Languages. Volume 1757 of LNAI., Springer-Verlag (2000) 250–259 6th International Workshop (ATAL'99), Orlando, FL, USA, 15–17 July 1999. Proceedings.
25. Omicini, A., Zambonelli, F.: Coordination for Internet application development. Autonomous Agents and Multi-Agent Systems **2** (1999) 251–269 Special Issue: Coordination Mechanisms for Web Agents.
26. Zambonelli, F., Jennings, N.R., Omicini, A., Wooldridge, M.J.: Agent-oriented software engineering for Internet applications. In Omicini, A., Zambonelli, F., Klusch, M., Tolksdorf, R., eds.: Coordination of Internet Agents: Models, Technologies, and Applications. Springer-Verlag (2001) 326–346
27. Omicini, A., Denti, E.: From tuple spaces to tuple centres. Science of Computer Programming **41** (2001) 277–294
28. Bellifemine, F., Poggi, A., Rimassa, G.: JADE – a FIPA-compliant agent framework. In: 4th International Conference and Exhibition on The Practical Application of Intelligent Agents and Multi-Agent Technology (PAAM'99). (1999) 97–108
29. Son, T.C., Pontelli, E., Ranjan, D., Milligan, B., Gupta, G.: An agent-based domain specific framework for rapid prototyping of applications in evolutionary biology. In this volume.
30. Clark, K.L., McCabe, F.G.: Go! for multi-threaded deliberative agents. In this volume.
31. Flax, L.: A proposal for reasoning in agents: Restricted entailment. In this volume.
32. van der Hoek, W., Lomuscio, A.: A logic for ignorance. In this volume.
33. Moreira, Á.F., Vieira, R., Bordini, R.H.: Extending the operational semantics of a BDI agent-oriented programming language for introducing speech-act based communication. In this volume.
34. Bergenti, F., Rimassa, G., Viroli, M.: Operational semantics for agents by iterated refinement. In this volume.
35. Tran, B.V., Harland, J., Hamilton, M.: A combined logic of expectations and observation (a generalisation of BDI logics). In this volume.
36. Ancona, D., Mascardi, V.: Coo-BDI: Extending the BDI model with cooperativity. In this volume.
37. Küngas, P., Matskin, M.: Linear logic, partial deduction and cooperative problem solving. In this volume.
38. Alberti, M., Gavanelli, M., Lamma, E., Mello, P., Torroni, P.: Modeling interaction using *Social Integrity Constraints*: A resource sharing case study. In this volume.
39. Colombetti, M., Fornara, N., Verdicchio, M.: A social approach to communication in multiagent systems. In this volume.
40. Vasconcelos, W.W.: Logic-based electronic institutions. In this volume.
41. Castaldi, M., Costantini, S., Gentile, S., Tocchio, A.: A logic-based infrastructure for reconfiguring applications. In this volume.
42. Kuhn, T.S.: The Structure of Scientific Revolutions. The University of Chicago Press, Chicago (1962)
43. Omicini, A., Petta, P., Pitt, J., eds.: Engineering Societies in the Agents World IV. LNAI. Springer-Verlag (2004) 4th International Workshop (ESAW 2003), London, UK, 29–31 October 2003. Post-proceedings.

A Logic-Based Infrastructure
for Reconfiguring Applications*

Marco Castaldi, Stefania Costantini, Stefano Gentile, and Arianna Tocchio

Università degli Studi di L'Aquila
Dipartimento di Informatica
Via Vetoio, Loc. Coppito, I-67010 L'Aquila, Italy
{castaldi,stefcost,gentile,tocchio}@di.univaq.it

Abstract. This paper proposes the DALI Multiagent System, which is a
logic programming environment for developing agent-based applications,
as a tool for component-based software management based on coordination. In particular, we show the usefulness of the integration between
DALI and the agent-based Lira system, which is a Light-weight Infrastructure for Reconfiguring Applications. We argue that using intelligent
agents for managing component-based software systems makes it possible to: (i) perform monitoring and supervision upon complex properties
of a system, such as for instance performance; (ii) perform global reconfigurations dynamically, through the cooperation of intelligent agents.

1 Introduction

After a long predominance of imperative and object oriented languages in the
software development process, declarative languages, thanks to new efficient implementations, have recently regained attention as an attractive programming
paradigm for the development of complex applications, in particular related to
the Internet, or more generally to distributed application contexts. Declarative
methods exhibit important well known advantages: (i) the reduction, also in
terms of "lines of code", of the effort required for solving a problem, (ii) the actual reduction of errors introduced in the application, (iii) the fast prototyping
of complex applications, that reduces "time to market" and development costs of
business applications. In many cases, these applications are better implemented
by using agents technology: declarative languages make the implementation of
intelligent agents easier and effective. In our opinion, agent-based distributed
applications give really a chance to Artificial Intelligence to show its usefulness
in practical contexts.

* We acknowledge the support of MIUR 40% project *Aggregate- and number-reasoning
for computing: from decision algorithms to constraint programming with multisets,
sets, and maps* and by the *Information Society Technologies programme of the European Commission, Future and Emerging Technologies* under the IST-2001-37004
WASP project.

J. Leite et al. (Eds.): DALT 2003, LNAI 2990, pp. 17–36, 2004.
© Springer-Verlag Berlin Heidelberg 2004

In this paper we show how DALI, a new logic-based declarative language for agents and multi-agent systems, supports the development of innovative agent-based applications. We consider the topic of distributed component management in the context of Large Scale Distributed Component Based Applications (LS-DCBA). The role of agents is that of monitoring and reconfiguring the system, in order to dynamically maintain some critical non-functional properties such as performance, high availability or security. The possibility of keeping a complex system under control while running is often a key factor for the success of complex and expensive systems. Several so-called "infrastructures" are being proposed to this purpose. In particular, as an interesting example we consider Lira, an agent-based infrastructure created for dynamic and automatic reconfigurations. As a case study, we have integrated Lira and DALI to create agents able to manage heterogeneous software components.

The DALI language [1,2,3] is a Prolog-like logic programming language, equipped with reactive and proactive capabilities. The definition of DALI formalizes in a declarative way different basic patterns for reactivity, proactivity, internal "thinking", and "memory". The language introduces different classes of events: external, internal, present and past. Like Prolog, DALI can be useful and effective for rapid prototyping of light applications.

Lira [4,5,6,7] has been recently defined (and fully implemented as a prototypical version in Java) to perform application reconfiguration in critical domains, such as for instance mobile and wireless systems and networks, risk management, e-government, environment supervision and monitoring. Each application/component of a complex system is managed by an attached agent, integrated into a hierarchy of agents performing different tasks. Reconfigurations are dynamic and automatic: they are performed while the application is running and as a reaction to some specified events. However, Lira only allows the agents to execute the orders of a Manager, without any kind of internal reasoning, preventing *a priori* any autonomous decision. Moreover, the hierarchical structure of Lira makes the coordination and cooperation among the agents difficult to implement, thus reducing the applicability in many real contexts.

The problems that we have found when trying to use Java for implementing agents in the context of a critical system (namely, for ensuring security of a bank application) suggested us the idea of using DALI instead of Java. In fact, the features of DALI are suitable for enhancing Lira by implementing forms of intelligent behavior in the agents. Thus enhanced, Lira may perform reconfigurations in a more flexible and adaptable fashion: not only under predefined conditions, but also proactively, in order to reach some kind of objective, for instance to enforce or verify properties of the managed system. To this aim, DALI agents managing different components can communicate and cooperate. The Intelligent agents (IAs), created by integrating DALI and Lira, are able to learn, interact and cooperate in order to: (i) perform monitoring and supervision upon complex properties of a system, such as performance; (ii) perform global reconfigurations through the cooperation of intelligent agents in order to fulfill the required properties.

We argue that Lira/DALI agents are easy to write, and independent of any specific agent architecture. We support our argument by presenting as a Case Study a practical experience of use of the enhanced infrastructure. In particular, we show how to implement in Lira+DALI the remote management of web sites in a web hosting provider that runs on a Windows 2000 Server. By using the features provided by Lira/DALI agents, the web sites management becomes easier, and it is possible to perform supervision and automatic reconfiguration in order to optimize bandwidth and space usage. The Case Study demonstrates how a declarative language like DALI has a significant impact in the developing process of complex applications in the practical and real context of LSDCBA. The agents created by the integration of DALI and Lira constitute in our opinion a significant advance in terms of supported functionalities, readability, modifiability and extensibility.

The paper is organized as follows: in Section 2 we motivate our work in the context of dynamic reconfiguration of component based applications, while Section 3 describes the DALI logic programming language. In Section 4 the Lira infrastructure is presented, eliciting in Section 4.5 some of the problems found when using Lira in particular contexts. Then, in Section 5 we introduce the general architecture of the Lira/DALI agents and in Section 6 we describe the Case Study. Section 7 summarizes the contributions of the work with respect to some existing approaches, and Section 8 presents the concluding remarks.

2 Motivations

Many approaches to dynamic reconfiguration for component based applications have been proposed in the last years. Dynamic reconfiguration comes in many forms, but two extreme approaches can be identified: *internal* and *external* [4].

Internal reconfiguration relies on the programmer to build into a component the facilities for its reconfiguration. For example, a component might observe its own performance and switch from one algorithm or data structure to another one when some performance threshold has been crossed. This form of reconfiguration is sometimes called "programmed" or "self-healing" reconfiguration [8,9].

External reconfiguration, by contrast, relies on some entity external to the component to determine when and how the component is reconfigured. For example, an external entity might monitor the performance of a component and perform a wholesale replacement of the component when a performance threshold has been crossed.

Any approach to critical resources management which uses internal reconfiguration presents different problems: firstly, since the reconfiguration policies are programmed within the components, they cannot be modified or extended without changing the component itself, thus reducing the reusability of such policies [10]. Secondly, in the presence of component-based applications with many heterogeneous components, each component is likely to have a different reconfiguration/adaptation policy, sometimes incompatible or conflicting with the policies of other components. The external approaches, instead, seem to be promising for self-adaptation of component based applications.

Even if external, the approaches of dynamic reconfiguration proposed in [11,12,13,14,15] rely on specific middlewares or component models such as OMG CORBA [16] or Enterprise Java Beans (EJB) in order to work: this is a problem in largely distributed component based applications, as the involved components are usually heterogeneous.

Finally, the *reconfiguration languages* proposed in [17,18] are not declarative, and they do not provide commands or functions for allowing internal reasoning, proactivity and reactivity.

The approach we propose here is meant to exploit the declarativity of the DALI language, and its ability to cope with different classes of events, for overcoming some of the limitations of the above-mentioned approach. In fact, intelligent component agents are able to cope with different reconfiguration/adaptation policies, in an heterogeneous environment. They can even change/adapt their policies either in response to external changes in the overall state of the system, or in reaction to local conditions that the agent detects. Then, our agents can join the advantages of internal reconfiguration by managing the component locally in a proactive way, and the advantages of external reconfiguration, being able to take orders from a manager. Moreover, the declarativity of the language allows to enhance this approach, by making easier to define agents that not only take orders, but also communicate and cooperate to reach overall objectives on the system state.

3   DALI Multiagent System

DALI [1,2,3] is an Active Logic Programming language, designed for executable specification of logical agents. DALI allows the programmer to define one or more agents, interacting either among themselves, or with an external environment, or with a user. A DALI agent is a logic program containing special rules and classes of events (represented by special atoms) which guarantee the *reactive* and *proactive* behavior of the agent. The kinds of events are: external, internal, present, past.

Proactivity makes an agent able to initiate a behavior according to its own internal reasoning, and not only as a reaction to some external event. Reactivity determines the reasoning and/or the actions that the agent will perform when some kind of event happens. Actions can be messages to other agents and/or interaction with the environment.

A DALI agent is able to manipulate its knowledge base, to have temporary memory, to perceive an environment and consequently to make actions. Moreover, the system provides a treatment of time: the events are kept or "forgotten" according to suitable conditions.

DALI provides a complete run-time support for development of Multiagent Systems. A DALI Multiagent System is composed by communicating environments, and each environment is composed by one server and more agents. Each agent is defined by a *.txt* file, containing the agent's code written in DALI.

The new approach proposed by DALI is compared to other existing logic programming languages and agent architectures such as ConGolog, 3APL, IM-

PACT, METATEM, BDI in [2]. However, it is useful to remark that DALI is a logic programming language for defining agents and multi-agent systems, and does not commit to any agent architecture. Differently from other significant approaches like, e.g., DESIRE [19], DALI agents do not have pre-defined sub-modules. Thus, different possible functionalities (problem-solving, cooperation, negotiation, etc.) and their interactions are specific to the particular application. DALI is in fact an "agent-oriented" general-purpose language that provides, as discussed below, a number of primitive mechanisms for supporting this paradigm, all of them within a precise logical semantics.

The declarative semantics of DALI is an *evolutionary semantics,* where the meaning of a given DALI program P is defined in terms of a modified program P_s, where reactive and proactive rules are reinterpreted in terms of standard Horn Clauses. The agent reception of an event is formalized as a program transformation step. The evolutionary semantics consists of a sequence of logic programs, resulting from these subsequent transformations, together with the sequence of the Least Herbrand Model of these programs. Therefore, this makes it possible to reason about the "state"of an agent, without introducing explicitly such a notion, and to reason about the conclusions reached and the actions performed at a certain stage. Procedurally, the interpreter simulates the program transformation steps, and applies an extended resolution which is correct with respect to the Least Herbrand Model of the program at each stage.

DALI is fully implemented in Sicstus Prolog [20]. The implementation, together with a set of examples, is available at the URL
http://gentile.dm.univaq.it/dali/dali.htm.

3.1   Events Classes

In DALI, events are represented as special atoms, called *events atoms.* The corresponding predicates are indicated by a particular prefix.

- **External Events.** When something happens in the "external world" in which the agent is situated, and the agent can perceive it, this is an *external event.* If an agent receives an external event, it can decide to react to it. In order to define rules that specify the reaction, the external event is syntactically indicated by the prefix *eve.* For instance, *eve(alarm_clock_rings)* represents an external event to which the agent is able to respond. When the event happens, the corresponding atom becomes true and, if in the DALI logical program that defines the agent there is a rule with this atom in the head, then the reaction defined in the body of the rule is triggered. The external events are recorded, in the arrival order, in a list called **EV** and are consumed whenever the correspondent reactive rule is activated (i.e., upon reaction the event is removed from **EV**).

  In the implementation, events are time-stamped, and the order in which they are "consumed" corresponds to the arrival order. The time-stamp can be useful for introducing into the language some (limited) possibility of reasoning about time. The head of a reactive rule can contain several events:

in order to trigger reaction, they must all happen within an amount of time that can be set by a directive.

Attached to each external event there is also the indication of the agent that has originated the event For events like *rainsE* there will be the default indication *environment*. Then, an event atom can be more precisely seen as a triple:

$$Sender : Event\_Atom : Timestamp$$

The *Sender* and *Timestamp* fields can be omitted whenever not needed.

- **Internal Events.** The internal events define a kind of "individuality" of a DALI agent, making it independent of the environment, of the user and of the other agents, and allowing it to manipulate and revise its knowledge. An internal event is indicated by the prefix *evi*. For instance, *evi(food_is_finished)* is a conclusion that the prefix *evi* interprets as an internal event, to which the agent may react, for instance by going to buy food. Internal events are attempted with some frequency (customizable by means of directives in an initialization file). Whenever one of them becomes true, it is inserted in a set **IV**. Similarly to external events, internal events are extracted from this set to trigger reaction. In more detail, the mechanism is the following: if goal G has been indicated to the interpreter as an internal event by means of a suitable directive, from time to time the agent attempts the goal (at the given frequency). If the goal succeeds, it is interpreted as an event, thus determining the corresponding reaction. I.e., internal events are events that do not come from the environment. Rather, they are goals defined in some other part of the program.

  There is a default frequency for attempting goals corresponding to internal events, that can be customized by the user when the agent is activated. Also, priorities among different internal events that could be attempted at the same time can be specified. At present, this frequency cannot be dynamically changed by the agent itself, but a future direction is that of providing this possibility, so as the agent will be able to adapt to evolving situations.

- **Present Events.** When an agent perceives an event from the "external world", it doesn't necessarily react immediately: it has the possibility of reasoning about the event, before (or instead of) triggering reaction. Reasoning also allows a *proactive* behavior. In this situation, the event is called *present event* and is indicated by the prefix *en*. For instance, *en(alarm_clock_ring)*, represents a present event to which the agent has not reacted yet.

- **Past Events.** Past events represent the agent's "memory", that makes it capable to perform its future activities while having experience of previous events, and of its own previous conclusions. A past event is indicated by the prefix *evp*. For instance, *evp(alarm_clock_ring)* is an event to which the agent has reacted and which remains in the agent's memory. The general form of a past event is *evp(E,T)*, where T is the timestamp indicating when the recorded event has happened. The shorthand *evp(E)* can be used, whenever the timestamp does not matter.

Memory of course is not unlimited, neither conceptually nor practically: it is possible to set, for each event, for how long it has to be kept in memory. The agent has the possibility to keep events in memory either forever or for some time or until something happens, based on directives. In fact, an agent cannot keep track of *every* event and action for an unlimited period of time. Moreover, sometimes subsequent events/actions can make former ones no more valid.

In the implementation, past events are kept for a certain default amount of time, that can be modified by the user through a suitable directive. The user can also express a condition of the form:

$$keep\ \ evp(A)\ \ until\ \ HH{:}MM.$$

The past event will be removed at the specified time. Alternatively, one can specify the terminating condition. As soon as the condition is fulfilled (i.e. the corresponding goal is proved) the event is removed.

$$keep\ \ evp(A)\ \ until\ \ Cond.$$

In particular cases, an event should never be dropped from the knowledge base, like in the example below:

$$keep\ \ evp(born(daniele))\ :\ 27/Aug/1993\ \ forever.$$

Implicitly, if a second version of the same past event arrives, with a more recent timestamp, the "older" event is overridden, unless this violates a directive.

It is interesting to notice that DALI management of past events allows the programmer to easily define *Event Calculus* expressions. The Event Calculus (EC) has been proposed by Kowalski and Sergot [21] as a system for reasoning about time and actions in the framework of Logic Programming. The essential idea is to have terms, called *fluents,* which are names of time-dependent relations. Kowalski and Sergot write $holds(r(x,y),t)$ which is understood as "fluent $r(x,y)$ is true at time t".

Take for instance the default inertia law formulated in the event calculus as follows:

$$
\begin{aligned}
holds(f,t)\ \leftarrow\ &happens(e),\\
&initiates(e,f),\\
&date(e,t_s),\\
&t_s < t,\\
&not\,clipped(t_s,f,t)
\end{aligned}
$$

where $clipped(t_s,f,t)$ is true when there is record of an event happening between t_s and t that terminates the validity of f. In other words, $holds(f,t)$ is derivable whenever in the interval between the initiation of the fluent and the time the query is about, no terminating events has happened.

In DALI, assuming that the program contains suitable assertion for *initiates* as well as the definition of *clipped*, this law could be immediately reformulated as follows, by just reinterpreting $happens(e), date(e, t_s)$ as a lookup in the knowledge base of past events, where we may find an event E that has happened, with its timestamp T_s, that initiates f:

$$holds(f, T) :\!- evp(E, T_s),$$
$$initiates(E, T),$$
$$T_s < t,$$
$$not\, clipped(T_s, f, T)$$

The representation can be enhanced by defining *holds* as an internal event. This means, the interpreter repeatedly attempt prove $holds(f, T)$. Upon success, a reactive rule can state what to do in consequence of this conclusion.

3.2   Actions: Reactivity in DALI

Actions constitute the agent's means of affecting its environment, possibly in reaction to an external or internal event. In DALI, actions may have *preconditions*, defined by *actions rules*. Actions without preconditions are represented by *action atoms*. In actions rules, success of preconditions determine the execution of the action: only if all preconditions are verified, then the corresponding action is performed. Preconditions are indicated by the prefix *cd*. In the case of **action atoms**, the actions always succeed (as DALI subgoals). If an action fails to properly affect the environment, the interpreter can generate a failure event, thus allowing the agent to cope with this situation.

Actions are indicated by prefix *a*. An example:

$$eve(saturday) :\!- a(go\_to\_the\_supermarket).$$
$$fridge\_full :\!- evp(go\_to\_the\_supermarket).$$
$$evi(fridge\_full) :\!- a(prepare\_a\_snack).$$
$$eve(child(I),\ we\_are\_hungry)) :\!- assert(children\_are\_hungry).$$
$$cd\ (prepare\_a\_snack) :\!- children\_are\_hungry..$$

Whenever the external event *eve(saturday)* occurs, the agent reacts by performing the action *go_to_the_supermarket*. Since the reaction is recorded as a past event (indicated by *evp(go_to_the_supermarket)*), the recollection triggers the proactive rule and allows the internal event *evi(fridge_full)*. The action *a(prepare_a_snack)* is executed if the precondition *cd(children_are_hungry)* is true. This is conditioned by the external event *eve(we_are_hungry)* coming from an agent *child(I)*. As soon as this event is observed, DALI executes the subgoal in the body of the rule, that consists in a predefined predicate (namely **assert**) that records the event.

Similarly to events, actions are recorded as *past actions*, with prefix *pa*. The following example illustrates how to exploit past actions. In particular, the action of opening (resp. closing) a door can be performed only if the door is closed (resp.

open). The window is closed if the agent remembers to have closed it previously. The window is open if the agent remembers to have opened it previously.

$$a(open\_the\_door) \; :- \; door\_is\_closed.$$
$$door\_is\_closed \; :- \; pa(close\_the\_door).$$
$$a(close\_the\_door) \; :- \; door\_is\_open.$$
$$door\_is\_open \; :- \; pa(open\_the\_door).$$

External events and actions are also used for expressing communication acts. An external event can be a message from another agent, and, symmetrically, an action can consist in sending a message. Presently we do not commit to any particular agent communication language, that we consider as a customizable choice that can be changed according to the application domain.

4   Lira

In the context of Large Scale Distributed Systems we usually deal with: (i) thousands of components that are part of one or more Applications; (ii) single Applications that are part of bigger systems, distributed over a wide area network. A basic objective of remote control is that of making the Java managed system flexible, highly modifiable at run time and stable with respect to many different faults. To these aims, remote (re)configuration should be dynamic: i.e., should be performed while a system is running, possibly as an automatic reaction when some event happens.

Lira (Light-weight Infrastructure for Reconfiguring Applications) [4,5,6,7] is a system that performs remote control and dynamic reconfigurations [11,12] over single components or applications. It uses and extends the approach of Network Management [22] architectures and protocols, where an agent controls directly the managed device and a Manager orders the reconfigurations. The decision maker could be an Administration Workbench with a graphical interface, or, in a more interesting case, a program that has the necessary knowledge to decide, when a specified precondition is verified, what kind of reconfigurations must be performed.

By component reconfiguration we mean any allowed change in the component's parameters (*component re-parametrization*): the addressed components are usually black-boxes, thus Lira must be able to dynamically change the values of the provided parameters. An Application reconfiguration [23] can be: (i) any change of the Application in terms of number and location of components; (ii) any kind of architectural modification [18].

Lira has been designed to be *light-weight* [4], given that components can be very small in size and might be run on limited-resource devices such as mobile phones or PDA. It provides a general interface for interacting with components and applications: this interface is realized using a specified architecture and a very simple protocol that allows one *to set and get variable values* and *to call functions*.

Lira has been created to provide the minimal amount of functionalities necessary to perform component reconfiguration and deployment. There are many others approaches of component reconfiguration, based on heavy weight infrastructures that manage also application dependencies and consistence. A complete description of the existing infrastructures with respect to the Lira approach is provided in [4].

The Lira architecture specifies three main actors: the **Reconfiguration Agent**, which performs the reconfiguration; the **MIB**, which is a list of variables and functions that an agent exports in order to reconfigure the component; the **Management Protocol**, that allows agents to communicate.

There are different kinds of agent, depending of their functionalities: the **Component Agent** is associated to the reconfigurable component; the **Host Agent** manages installation and activation of components and agents on the deployment host; the **Application Agent** is a higher-level agent able to monitor and reconfigure a set of components or a subsystem (for details see [7]); finally, the **Manager** is the particular agent providing the interface with the decision maker, having the role to order reconfigurations to other agents.

In the next subsections we will describe features of Lira that are relevant for the proposed integration.

4.1   Component Agent

The Component Agent (CompAgent) is the most important part of the Lira infrastructure: it directly controls and manages the component. To keep the system general, Lira does not specify how the component is attached to the agent, but it only assumes that the agent is able to act on the component. The CompAgent is composed by a generic part (called *Protocol Manager*) which manages the agent communication, and by a local part (called *Local Agent*) which is the actual interface between the agent and the component. This interface is component-specific and it implements the following functions for the component's life-cycle management:

- void start(compParams): starts the component.
- void stop(): stops the component.
- void suspend(): suspends the component.
- void resume(): resumes the component.
- void shutdown(): stops the component and kills the agent.

Moreover, each CompAgent exports the variables:

- STATUS: maintains the current status of the component. It can take one of the following values: **starting, started, stopping, stopped, suspending, suspended, resuming**.
- NOTIFYTO: contains the address of the agent that has to be notified when a specified event happens.

All the variables exported for the specific component must be declared in the MIB (Section 3.3).

A very important property of a Lira-based reconfiguration system is the *composability* of the agents: they may be composed in a hierarchical way [24], thus creating a higher level agent which performs reconfigurations at application level, by using variables and functions exported by lower level agents. The Application Agent is a Manager for the agents in the controlled components, but it is a reconfigurations actuator for the global (if present) Manager.

4.2   Manager

The Manager orders reconfigurations on the controlled components through the associated CompAgents. The top-level manager of the hierarchy constitutes the Lira interface with the Decision Maker. It exports the NOTIFYTO variable, like every other agent. The Manager is allowed to send Lira messages, but may also receive SET, GET, CALL messages: it means that different Managers can communicate with each other.

4.3   MIB

This description represents the agreement among agents that allows them to communicate in a consistent way.

The description provides the list of variables and functions exported by the agent. In particular, the MIB contains the variables and functions always exported by the agent, such as the STATUS or the start() ones, as well as variables and functions specific for the managed components, that are component dependent.

Finally, the MIB specifies constraints to bind declared variables and performed actions to obtain the specified behavior [6].

4.4   Management Protocol

The management protocol has been designed to be as simple as possible, in order to keep the system *light*. Based on TCP/IP, it specifies seven messages, of which six are synchronous, namely:

- SET(*variable_name, variable_value*) / ACK(*message_text*)
- GET(*variable_name*) / REPLY(*variable_name, variable_value*)
- CALL(*function_name, parameters_list*) / RETURN(*return_value*)

and one is asynchronous, namely:

- NOTIFY(*variable_name, variable_value, agent_name*)

4.5   Some Problems with Using Lira

The current Lira version specifies a very clean, powerful and effective architecture. The Java prototype works well in the test examples proposed in [25,4,5] [7].

Nevertheless, there are still problems to solve, related to both the specification and the implementation.

From the implementation point of view, an object-oriented language such as Java allows one to easily create every kind of Lira agent by inheritance from specified classes, thus encouraging agent's reuse. Also, it provides a direct interface with the managed component. However, it is not so immediate to implement in Java mechanisms to provide agents with some kind of intelligence, such as "internal thinking" or "memory". This is demonstrated by the fact that Java-based frameworks for agent development like JADE [26] have built-in reactive capabilities, but do not directly provide proactivity.

Moreover, the hierarchical structure of Lira inherited by the network management architecture model is useful and powerful but very strict. In fact, a hierarchical management is effective for rigidly structured domains, while however making the implementation of the agents very hard when coordination and cooperation is needed. With this limitation, the potential applicability of Lira is reduced.

5   The Integration

In this research, we have tried to overcome Lira problems by implementing a part of Lira agents in DALI.

There are several motivations for proposing DALI as a formalism for the implementation of intelligent reconfiguration Lira agents. Firstly, DALI's proactive capabilities allow the agents to timely supervise component -and application- behavior, by using *Internal events*. Secondly, by using *External events* the agents are able to communicate with each other so that they can synchronize and adapt their behavior in a changing environment (e.g., in case of applications oriented to mobile devices). Thirdly, by using *Past Events* the agents have a *memory* and can perform actions automatically whenever a well-known situation occurs. Therefore, the resulting infrastructure is flexible and allows run-time event-driven reconfiguration.

A good reason to keep a Java part of Lira agents is that the DALI infrastructure cannot act directly on the component to perform reconfiguration. In fact, DALI does not provide high level mechanisms to interact with the components, while Lira is specified with that purpose.

The agents created by integrating DALI and Lira, that we have called Intelligent Agents (IA) for dynamic reconfiguration, have an intelligent part provided by DALI and a managing part provided by Lira. In other words, we can say that DALI constitutes the "mind", and Lira the "hand" for performing reconfigurations.

The general architecture of the IA is shown in Figure 1. The interface between DALI and Lira is provided by a SICTUS Prolog library called *Jasper*, which allows one to call the specified Java method inside Prolog code.

Lira loses the TCP message management, but it still provides the access to the exported variables and functions through the following methods:

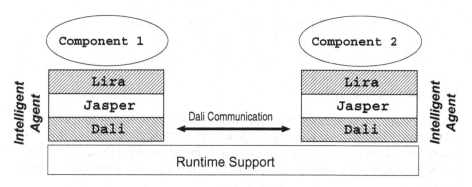

Fig. 1. The architecture of the Intelligent agents

$ACKmsg$ $\quad$ $msgSET(varName, varValue)$
$REPLYmsg$ $\quad$ $msgGET(varName)$
$RETURNmsg$ $msgCALL(funcName, parList)$

$void$ $\quad\quad\quad$ $msgNOTIFY(varName, varValue)$

The communication among IAs is implemented by using DALI messages, and is managed by its run time support. The Java methods are called by the DALI environment through the Jasper interface, whenever the corresponding DALI message is received.

In DALI, the reception of a Lira message is implemented by using an *external event*. When the event is received, the agent performs a specific action which hides the Jasper predicate. For example, the reception of the Lira message $CALL("STOP", "")$ is implemented as:

$eve(CALL("STOP", void) : -a(daliCALL(stop, void))$

where *daliCALL* is a macro which hides all the steps (objects creation, method call etc) necessary to actually invoke the Java method.

In the sample DALI code that we will present in the next subsections, all the operations for getting and setting values or more generally for affecting the supervised component are implemented in a similar way.

The reactive capabilities provided by DALI make the IA's able to dynamically perform reconfigurations either upon certain conditions, or upon occurrence of significant events. In some cases reconfigurations can be decided and performed locally (on the controlled component), whenever the managing agent has sufficient knowledge, otherwise they can be decided by means of a process of cooperation and negotiation among the different agents.

Also, the Lira/DALI IA's can manage and exchange meta-information about system configuration and functionality. In perspective, they may have knowledge and competence to detect critical situations, and to activate dynamic security processes in order to ensure system consistency also in presence of faults or attacks.

Finally, by using DALI primitives the agents are able to learn from past situations, for example to repeat the same kind of reconfiguration upon the same conditions, or to retry the same kind of negotiation.

6   The Case Study

The case study proposed here is remote management of web sites in a web hosting provider that runs on a Windows 2000 Server. This particular environment manages single web sites as independent components, allowing the administrator to start and stop web sites independently from the actual web server that hosts them.

The features of the example are the following: we have a general server W that manages the web sites W_i through the IAs IA_i. Each agent can communicate with the other agents and with the Manager. In particular, for each web site we are interested to supervise the disk space and the bandwidth.

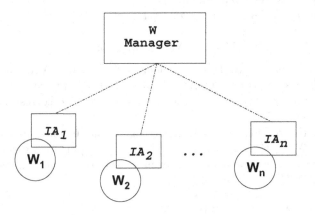

Fig. 2. The hosting web provider

In order to show the flexibility of these new IA's, we propose (a sketch of) the implementation of two different policies of reconfiguration, aimed at optimizing space and bandwidth usage.

The space is managed by using a hierarchical model, where a Manager maintains the global knowledge about the space usage, and when needed orders the reconfigurations to the agents.

A high quality of service for each web site is guaranteed through a dynamic distribution of the available bandwidth. To this purpose, we define a cooperative model, where an agent that needs more bandwidth asks other agents for obtaining the possibility to increase its own usage.

The details of these policies are described in the Sections 6.1 and 6.2.

In order to act on the managed component (a web site) and perform the reconfigurations, the IA exports the following variables and functions. USED_SPACE, that contains the used space; MAX_SPACE, i.e., the maximum space usage allowed; USED_BAND, i.e., the band used; MAX_BANDWIDTH, i.e., the maximum bandwidth allowed; STATUS, which is the state of the web site; NOTIFYTO, i.e., the agent that must be notified. ERASE(fileType, space) erases the specified files, thus freeing some space on the disk. COMPRESS(files, space) compresses the specified files thus making a larger space quota available on the disk.

6.1   Space Management

DALI Definition of the Manager Agent

Implementation of Site Maintenance. The manager starts the maintenance of a web site managed by an IA whenever a certain timeout has expired. The exact mechanism in DALI is that the predicate *activate_maintenance* is automatically attempted at a predefined (customizable) frequency, and succeeds as soon as the timeout is expired. Since this predicate is an internal event, its success triggers the proactive clause with head *evi(activate_maintenance(IA))*. As specified in the body of the rule, the manager sends a message to the IA to tell it to stop the web site, and perform the maintenance. When the manager receives by an IA (as an external event) the information that the maintenance has been performed, it orders to the IA to restart the site.

$activate\_maintenance(IA) : -timeout\_expired(IA).$
$evi(activate\_maintenance(IA)) : -a(message(IA, CALL("STOP", void))),$
$\qquad\qquad a(message(IA, perform\_maintenance(IA))).$
$eve(maintenance\_terminated(IA)) : -$
$\qquad\qquad a(message(IA, CALL("START", void))).$

Remote Reconfiguration. If an IA that manages a web site asks for more disk space, then the manager assigns more space to this web site if available. Only as *extrema ratio* the Manager eliminates old web sites with expired life time. The external event that starts the manager activity is *space_not_recovered(IA)* which means that the IA has tried (as illustrated below) to recover some space locally, but has not succeeded.

$eve(space\_not\_recovered(IA)) : -once(find\_space(IA)).$
$find\_space(IA) : -a(message(IA, SET(MAX\_SPACE, New\_space))).$
$cd(message(IA, SET(MAX\_SPACE, New\_space))) : -$
$\qquad\qquad space\_available(New\_space).$
$find\_space(IA) : -check\_accounts(IA).$
$check\_accounts(IA) : -a(erase\_expired\_web\_site, New\_space),$
$\qquad\qquad a(message(IA, SET(MAX\_SPACE, New\_space))).$
$cd(erase\_expired\_web\_site) : -expired\_web\_site\_exist.$

DALI Intelligent Agent Definition for the Web Sites

Site Maintenance. The following piece of code defines how IA copes with the orders by the manager of stopping/starting the site, and of performing maintenance. Notice that the IA becomes aware that maintenance is finished (i.e., becomes aware of its own internal state of affairs) as soon as *perform_maintenance* becomes a past event (prefix *evp*). This happens as soon as action *a(perform_maintenance)* has been performed. Then, *end_maintenance* becomes true, and, since it is an internal event, it triggers a reaction that sends a message to the manager to signal that maintenance is over.

$eve(CALL("STOP", void)) : -a(daliCALL(stop, void)).$
$eve(CALL("START", void)) : -a(daliCALL(start, void)).$
$eve(perform\_maintenance) : -a(perform\_maintenance).$
$end\_maintenance(IA) : -evp(perform\_maintenance).$
$evi(end\_maintenance(IA)) : -a(message(M, maintenance\_over(IA))).$

Managing Lack of Space. As an example of adaptive behavior, the following piece of code included in the definition of a local agent specifies that if the used space of the managed web site is close to *MAX_SPACE*, then the *IA* tries to find more space. First, the agent tries to recovery space locally, by either erasing or compressing files. If this is impossible, then it asks the manager. These local attempts of reconfigurations can be done only if they have not been performed recently, i.e., only if the corresponding past events (prefix *evp*) are not present (notice that the past events expire after a pre-set, customizable amount of time). Otherwise, the manager is informed by the message *space_not_recovered*.

$more\_space\_needed : -a(daliGET(MAX\_SPACE)),$
$\qquad\qquad\qquad a(daliGET(USED\_SPACE)),$
$\qquad\qquad\qquad MAX\_SPACE - USED\_SPACE \leq threshold.$
$evi(more\_space\_needed) : -recovery\_space(IA).$
$recovery\_space(IA) : -a(erase\_useless\_files(IA)).$
$cd(erase\_useless\_files) : -not(evp(erase\_useless\_files(IA))).$
$recovery\_space(IA) : -a(compress\_files(IA)).$
$cd(compress\_files) : -not(evp(compress\_files(IA))).$
$recovery\_space(IA) : -a(message(M, space\_not\_recovered(IA))).$

Updating Space Limit. If asked, the manager can give three different answers, corresponding to the following external events: (i) send an enlarged value *new_space* of *MAX_SPACE*; (ii) order to erase all files; (iii) stop the web site.

$eve(SET(MAX\_SPACE, new\_space)) : -$
$\qquad\qquad a(daliSET(MAX\_SPACE, new\_space)).$
$eve(CALL(ERASE, all\_files)) : -a(daliCALL(ERASE, all\_files)).$
$eve(CALL(KILL, void)) : -a(daliCALL(KILL, void)).$

6.2   Bandwidth Management

In order to exhibit a good performance to the end user, the Intelligent Agents cooperate for a dynamic band distribution according to the component needs. In particular, when an IA detects that the available band is less than the needed bandwidth, the internal event *seek_band* triggers a reaction: the agent checks which agents are present in the system and creates a list. Then it takes the first one and sends a request for a part of the band. If the agent receives the external event that indicates that more band is available, it sets the Lira variable MAX_BANDWIDTH, while the giving agent reduces its max bandwidth by taking off the given value. If the bandwidth is still insufficient, the agent keeps asking for band to the other agents are present in the system.

$seek\_band : - band\_insufficient.$
$band\_insufficient : -$
$\qquad a(daliGET(MAX\_BANDWIDTH)),$
$\qquad need\_band(B), B > MAX\_BANDWIDTH.$
$evi(seek\_band) : -$
$\qquad findallagents(Askable\_agents\_list),$
$\qquad askfb(Askable\_agents\_list).$
$askfb(Askable\_agents\_list) : -$
$\qquad member(IA1, Askable\_agents\_list),$
$\qquad\qquad a(message(IA1, ask\_for\_band(IA, IA1))).$

Symmetrically, if IA is asked for some band, it checks if it is actually in the condition to give it. When the external event ask_for_band arrives, the agent checks its bandwidth. If it has some unused band (the USED_BAND is minor of the MAX_BANDWIDTH) it keeps 80% of its band, and offers the remaining amount Bt to the other agent. Otherwise, the agent sends the message $impossible\_to\_transfer\_band.$

$eve(ask\_for\_band(IA, IA1)) : -$
$\qquad a(daliGET(MAX\_BANDWIDTH)), a(daliGET(USED\_BAND)),$
$\qquad Bt\ is(MAX\_BANDWIDTH - USED\_BAND) * 0.2,$
$\qquad once(check\_value(Bt)).$
$check\_value(Bt) : -a(message(IA, available\_band(IA1, Bt))).$
$cd(message(IA, available\_band(IA1, Bt))) : -Bt > 0, friend(IA).$
$check\_value(Bt) : -a(message(IA, impossible\_to\_transfer\_band(IA1, Bt))).$
$eve(available\_band(IA, Bt)) : -$
$\qquad a(message(IA1, accept\_band(Bt))),$
$\qquad a(daliGET(MAX\_BANDWIDTH)),$
$\qquad a(daliSET(MAX\_BANDWIDTH, MAX\_BANDWIDTH + Bt)).$
$eve(accept\_band(Bt)) : -$
$\qquad a(daliGET(MAX\_BANDWIDTH)),$
$\qquad a(daliSET(MAX\_BANDWIDTH, MAX\_BANDWIDTH - Bt))$

7   Discussion and Related Work

In [10], Garlan et al. proposed a methodology and a framework for performance optimization of a network component based application. In the proposed approach, the software architecture of the application plays a central role: the managed application is continuously monitored and, when necessary, it is reconfigured at the architectural level. The new configuration is chosen as a result of the online evaluation of a components-connectors models. Similarly to our intelligent agents, the *gauges* proposed in [10] communicate the monitored information to the manager, but, differently from the IAs, they are not provided with intelligence, and they cannot take any form of decision. The IAs, instead, have internal reasoning and memory, which allow the agents to activate whenever possible a *local* reconfiguration without asking the manager.

In [5], the decisions about reconfiguration are taken by using the feedback provided by the online evaluation of a Petri Nets model representing the system. Even if effective in the context of dependability provision, the impossibility for agents and manager to *remember* the previous decisions taken in similar situations forces an expensive model evaluation at every step. The memory mechanisms provided by DALI, instead, allows the agents to learn from the past configurations, adapting their behavior to the new situations.

In the current version of our framework, the Intelligent Agents and the Manager decide the best reconfiguration for the managed system by applying the defined reconfiguration policies, in a purely reactive way. Following the approach proposed by Son et al. in [27], the DALI/Lira framework can be modified so as to use planning mechanisms for the choice of the best reconfiguration. Each reconfiguration can be specified in terms of a plan to reach a specified goal, and the best one is chosen among the not failed plans. Currently, we are working on adding planning capabilities to the DALI language, and we foresee to upgrade the functionalities of the manager to have also this *plan-based* decision making.

The framework described in this paper is fully implemented, but it is a preliminary version. The current implementation suffers of many problems due to the technologies used for its development. Firstly, the Sictus prolog [20] used to implement DALI has a very heavy runtime support (a 10 Mbytes process for each agent), which creates many problems for the actual deployment of the Intelligent Agents within a limited resource device. Moreover, the library used for the integration between the Lira and the DALI agents, namely Jasper, does not provide a comfortable support for many Java types, thus making the implementation of the Prolog-Java interface not easy at all. Then, we are planning to use tuProlog [28] as the basic platform for DALI: tuProlog is characterized by a minimal yet efficient Prolog engine, created for infrastructures where software thickness and overloading is simply unacceptable [29]. tuProlog is written in Java, thus in allowing in perspective an easy interface with the Lira infrastructure.

8   Concluding Remarks

In this paper we have proposed our practical experience of using the logic programming language DALI for enriching the functionalities of Lira, an infrastructure for managing and reconfiguring Large Scale Component Based Applications.

The advantage of Lira is that of being lightweight, although able to perform both component-level reconfigurations and scalable application-level reconfigurations. The key design choice of Lira has been that of providing a minimal basic set of functionalities, while assuming that advanced capabilities are implemented in the agents, according to the application at hand. This has allowed us to gracefully integrate Lira with DALI, by replacing Java agents with DALI agents. To the best of our knowledge, this is the first running prototype of a logic-based infrastructure.

We have argued that DALI brings practical advantages under several respects. (i) The task of developing agents with memory and reasoning capabilities becomes easier, and the resulting agent programs are easier to understand, extend and modify. (ii) Reactivity, proactivity and learning capabilities of logical agents make the system more powerful through the intelligent cooperation among logical agents that can supervise and solve critical situations. (iii) Intelligent reasoning agents can cooperatively perform many tasks and reach overall objectives, also by means on suitable forms of delegation and learning. The coordination and cooperation among agents that are difficult to implement with Lira because of its hierarchical architecture can be easily realized by using Lira/DALI intelligent agents. This makes the resulting infrastructure powerful and effective, especially in real-time contexts.

Both DALI and Lira are fully implemented, and the Intelligent Agents have been successfully experimented. Future applications are being specified, in challenging contexts such as system security in critical applications.

References

1. Costantini, S.: Towards active logic programming. In Brogi, A., Hill, P., eds.: Proc. of 2nd International Workshop on component-based Software Development in Computational Logic (COCL'99), PLI'99, Paris, France. (1999)
2. Costantini, S., Tocchio, A.: A logic programming language for multi-agent systems. In: Proceedings of JELIA02, 8th European Conference on Logics in Artificial Intelligence, Cosenza, Italy. LNAI **2424**, Springer-Verlag (2002)
3. Costantini, S., Tocchio, A.: Context-based commmonsense reasoning in the dali logic programmming language. In Blackburn, P., Ghidini, C., Turner, R.M., Giunchiglia, F., eds.: Proceedings of the 4th International and Interdisciplinary Conference, Context 2003, Stanford, CA. LNCS **2680**, Springer-Verlag, Berlin (2003)
4. Castaldi, M., Carzaniga, A., Inverardi, P., Wolf, A.L.: A light-weight infrastructure for reconfiguring applications. In: Proceedings of 11th Software Configuration Management Workshop, Portland, USA. (2003)
5. Porcarelli, S., Castaldi, M., Di Giandomenico, F., Inverardi, P., Bondavalli, A.: An approach to manage reconfiguration in fault-tolerant distributed systems. In: Proceedings of ICSE Workshop on Software Architectures for Dependable Systems, Portland, USA. (2003)
6. Castaldi, M., Ryan, N.D.: Supporting component-based development by enriching the traditional api. In: Proceedings of 4th European GCSE Young Researchers Workshop 2002, in conjunction with NoDE, Erfurt, Germany. (2002)
7. Castaldi, M., Angelis, G.D., Inverardi, P.: A reconfiguration language for remote analysis and application adaptation. In: Proceedings of ICSE Workshop on Remote Analysis and Measurement of Software Systems, Portland, USA. (2003)
8. Oreizy, P., Gorlick, M., Taylor, R., Heimbigner, D., Johnson, G., Medvidovic, N., Quilici, A., Rosenblum, D., Wolf, A.: An architecture-based approach to self-adaptive software. IEEE Intelligent Systems **13** (1999) 54–62
9. Wermelinger, M.: Towards a chemical model for software architecture reconfiguration. In: Proceedings of the 4th International Conference on Configurable Distributed Systems. (1998)

10. Garlan, D., Schmerl, B., Chang, J.: Using gauges for architecture-based monitoring and adaptation. In: Proc. of Working Conference on Complex and Dynamic Systems Architecture, Brisbane, Australia. (2001)
11. Shrivastava, S.K., Wheater, S.M.: Architectural support for dynamic reconfiguration of large scale distributed applications. Technical Report 645, Department of Computing Science, University of Newcastle upon Tyne (1998)
12. Bidan, C., Issarny, V., Saridakis, T., Zarras, A.: A dynamic reconfiguration service for corba. In: Proc. of the 4th International Conference on Configurable Distributed Systems, Annapolis, Maryland, USA (1998) 35–42
13. Batista, T., Rodriguez, N.: Dynamic reconfiguration of component-based applications. In: Proceedings of Internation Symposium on Software Engineering for Parallel and Distributed Systems. (2000)
14. de La Rocque Rodriguez, N., Ierusalimschy, R.: Dynamic reconfiguration of CORBA-based applications. In: Proceedings of Conference on Current Trends in Theory and Practice of Informatics. (1999)
15. Almeida, J.P.A., Wegman, M., Pires, L.F., van Sinderen, M.: An approach to dynamic reconfiguration of distributed systems based on object-middleware. In: Proceedings of 19th Brasilian Symposium on Computer Networks. (2001)
16. The common object request broker: Architecture and specification. Omg official specification, Object Management Group (2002)
17. Endler, M.: A language for implementing generic dynamic reconfigurations of distributed programs. In: Proceedings of 12th Brazilian Symposium on Computer Networks. (1994)
18. Wermelinger, M., Lopes, A., Fiadeiro, J.: A graph based architectural (re)configuration language. In: Proc. of ESEC/FSE'01, ACM Press (2001)
19. Jonker, C.M., Lam, R.A., Treur, J.: A reusable multi-agent architecture for active intelligent websites. Journal of Applied Intelligence **15** (2001) 7–24
20. SISCtus home page: http://www.sics.se/sicstus/
21. Kowalski, R.A., Sergot, M.J.: A logic-based calculus of events. New Generation Computing **4** (1986) 67–95
22. Rose, M.T.: The Simple Book: An Introduction to Networking Management. Prentice Hall (1996)
23. Bellissard, L., de Palma, N., Riveill, M.: Dynamic reconfiguration of agent-based applications. In: Proceedings of European Research Seminar on Advances in Distributed Systems. (1999)
24. Wermelinger, M.: A hierarchical architecture model for dynamic reconfiguration. In: Proc. of the 2nd Intl. Workshop on Software Engineering for Parallel and Distributed Systems, IEEE Computer Society Press (1997) 243–254
25. Castaldi, M.: Lira: a practitioner approach. Technical report, University of L'Aquila (2002)
26. Bellifemine, F., Poggi, A., Rimassa, G.: Jade a fipa-compliant agent framework. In: Proceedings of PAAM'99, London, UK. (1999) 97–108 Project URL: http://sharon.cselt.it/projects/jade/
27. Son, C.T., Pontelli, E., Ranjan, D., Milligan, B., Gupta, G.: An agent-based domain specific framework for rapid prototyping of applications in evolutionary biology. In this volume.
28. Denti, E., Omicini, A., Ricci, A.: tuprolog: A light-weight prolog for internet applications and infrastructures. In: Proc. of Third International Symposium on Practical Aspects of Declarative Languages (PADL), Las Vegas, Nevada. (2001)
29. tuProlog web page: http://www.lia.deis.unibo.it/Research/2P/

Operational Semantics for Agents by Iterated Refinement

Federico Bergenti[1], Giovanni Rimassa[1], and Mirko Viroli[2]

[1] AOT Lab - Dipartimento di Ingegneria dell'Informazione
Parco Area delle Scienze 181/A, 43100 Parma, Italy
{bergenti,rimassa}@ce.unipr.it
[2] DEIS, Università degli Studi di Bologna a Cesena
via Venezia 52, 47023 Cesena, Italy
mviroli@deis.unibo.it

Abstract. In this paper we evaluate transition systems as a tool for providing a rule-based specification of the operational aspects of autonomous agents. By our technique, different aspects of an agent can be analyzed and designed in a loosely coupled way, enabling the possibility of studying their properties in isolation.
We take as a use case the ParADE framework for building intelligent agents, which leverages a FIPA-like ACL semantics to support semantic interoperability. Our grey-boxing technique is exploited to provide a specification where aspects related to the ACL, the adopted ontology, the agent social role, and the other agent internal details are described separately, in an incremental way.

1 Formalisms, Software Engineering, and Agents

This paper addresses the issue of sound multi-agent design trying to keep a system engineering perspective; that is, both when analyzing a problem and when synthesizing a solution the focus is kept on the whole, large-scale structure of the software artifact that is to be realized.

Striving for a sound design process naturally suggests to rely on some kind of mathematical tools: the precision and coherency afforded by formal and analytical reasoning holds great promises in terms of soundness. But, design is above all a creative process, and care has to be taken so as not to hamper it with too rigid a framework. In particular, formal methods during design activity should act as a tool to nurture an evolving idea, suggesting to the designer viable future choices while checking desirable properties of the current solution.

The formal tool we propose to provide effective assistance to the sound design of multi-agent systems (MAS) applies *labeled transition systems* to the description of interactive behaviors (of software abstractions) [1], as elaborated and promoted in the field of concurrency theory. When specifying a transition system semantics for an agent, a number of rules are given that describe in a quite declarative way the dynamics of the agent inner machinery, also providing insights on its internal architecture – expressed at a given level of abstraction.

J. Leite et al. (Eds.): DALT 2003, LNAI 2990, pp. 37–53, 2004.

We believe that this formalism is particularly well suited because of its calculus-like nature, which combines the description of a system with the prescription of its possible evolutions; this property buys designers some generativity, while remaining in a well grounded mathematical landscape.

In particular, in this paper we develop a formal framework that exploits basic features of labeled transition systems to address both composability and extensibility. Composability is obtained by dividing an agent model into several transition system specifications, that we call *tiers*; each tier captures the possible evolutions of the agent conceptual subpart dealing with a specific aspect. Beyond providing formal decoupling, tiers also mirror conceptually significant views over an agent behavior, thus easing the adjustable abstraction process. Moreover, starting from a partial specification of an agent behavior, namely a *grey-box model* [2,3,4], tiers are used to extend that specification by taking into account a new behavioral aspect, and leading to a new model that is a refinement of the former – according to the standard notion of refinement as "more deterministic implementation" introduced in the context of concurrency [1].

The tiers we use to describe an agent are more than a useful formal technique to us. They are closely related to the different levels of abstractions of an agent description.

The accepted scientific formalization of the idea of level of abstraction is the definition of *system level* [5]. A system level is a set of concepts that provides a means for modeling implementable systems. System levels abstract away from implementation details and are arranged in stack fashion so that higher levels provide concepts that are closer to human intuition and far away from implementation. System levels are structured in terms of the following elements: *(i)* Components, atomic building blocks for building systems at that level; *(ii)* Laws of compositions, laws that rule how components can be assembled into a system; *(iii)* a Medium, a set of atomic concepts that the system level processes; and *(iv)* Laws of behavior, laws that determine how the behavior of the system depends on the behavior of each component and on the structure of the system.

In the specific case of agent systems, a relevant application of this idea is the well-known Newell's *knowledge level* [5]. This level describes a single agent as structured in goals, actions, and a body, capable of processing knowledge and pursuing its goals according to the rationality principle. On the other hand, Jennings' proposal of the *social level* [6] moves from agents to MAS trying to raise the level of abstraction of the knowledge level. There, the system is an agent organization, that is, a group of agents with organizational relationships and dependencies on one another, which can interact through channels. Other alternative systems level have been described such as e.g. in [7], taking the benefits of both Newell's and Jennings' trying to provide a concrete and useful compromise.

The various system levels cited above (and all the other, lower abstraction levels that may actually concur to fully describe a real system) provide a conceptual framework that suggests how to meaningfully partition an agent formal model, so that each part expresses properties pertaining to a specific system level. In this paper we adhere to this very methodology, dividing the specification of an agent collaborative behavior into different tiers. In particular, due to the increased accuracy of a formal description with respect to a natural language one, these tiers are clearly finer than the usual conceptual system levels, but they can still be associated to a well defined system level.

As a use case for our approach we consider ParADE [8], a complete environment for the development of agents, taking into account social, agent and knowledge level issues, beyond of course interfacing itself with the lower system levels by means of its runtime support.

2 Outline

The remainder of the paper is organized as follows. Section 3 is devoted to describing the basic framework of labeled transition systems [1], which is exploited in this paper to formalize the behavior of agents and of their conceptual subparts.

Section 4 describes our novel approach to agent modeling. This is based on the idea of considering a partial specification of an agent behavior – namely, a grey-box model abstracting away from the agent inner details below a certain abstraction threshold [2] –, which can be refined by the specification of a *completion*. Such a refinement takes into account new aspects of the agent behavior, and leads to a new grey-box model that can be later refined again.

In order to show how our approach can be used to formalize an agent behavior in an incremental way, by separating different aspects of an agent design in different specification tiers, we take as a reference the ParADE framework for building agents [8], whose main characteristics are described in Section 5. ParADE exploits the formal semantics of a FIPA-like Agent Communication Language (ACL) to gain semantic interoperability, and provides *interaction laws* as a design mechanism to specify the agent social role. We chose to use this framework instead of others such as those based on the FIPA standard, the 3APL language [9], or Jack [10], since ParADE incorporates and keeps conceptually separated the many distinctive features that we believe are crucial when modeling MAS.

Section 6 provides a formalization of an agent behavior adhering to the main design choices of ParADE framework and considering five different tiers each dealing with a relevant aspect, namely, interaction, language, ontology, social role, and internal reasoning. Section 7 reports on related and future works, drawing concluding remarks.

3 Transition Systems

The semantic approach we describe in this paper is based on the framework of *(labeled) transition systems* (LTS) [1,11], which originated in the field of concurrency theory to provide an operational semantics for process algebras [12]. Here, LTS are used in a slightly different, yet common fashion: instead of focusing on the semantics of a language or algebra, we apply them to the description of the interactive behavior of a system, which in our case is an agent (or a subpart of it). This application of LTS is still referred to as an operational semantics, in that it describes the single-step capabilities of an agent to interact with the environment and to perform internal computations, resembling the idea of operational semantics in the context of programming languages.

A LTS is a triple $\langle X, \longrightarrow, Act \rangle$, where X is the set of states of the system of interest, Act is called the set of *actions*, and $\longrightarrow \subseteq X \times Act \times X$ is the *transition relation*. Let $x, x' \in X$ and $act \in Act$, then $\langle x, act, x' \rangle \in \longrightarrow$ is written $x \xrightarrow{act} x'$ for short, and means that the system may move from state x to state x' by way of action act.

Actions in a LTS can be given various interpretations. In the most abstract setting, they are meant to provide a high-level description of a system evolution, abstracting away from details of the inner system state change. In the sequence of transitions $x_0 \xrightarrow{a_0} x_1 \xrightarrow{a_1} x_2 \xrightarrow{a_2} \dots \xrightarrow{a_{n-1}} x_n$, the system evolution characterized by states $x_0, x_1, \dots x_n$ is associated to the actions sequence $a_0, \dots, a_{n-1}$, which can be though of as an abstract view of that evolution. In a sense, actions can be used to describe what an external, virtual entity is allowed to perceive of the system evolution, generally providing only a partial description. In the case where LTS are exploited to represent the behavior of interactive systems, actions typically represent the single interaction acts of the system.

Several remarkable concepts are promoted by LTS, such as the notions of system *observation* and *refinement* of specifications [13]. Since actions in a LTS can be interpreted as a view of the system transition from a state to another, it is then possible to characterize a whole system evolution in terms of the actions permitted at each step and the actions actually executed. This characterization is made according to a given *observation semantics*, which associates to each evolution a mathematical description called *observation*. For instance, according to observation semantics called *trace semantics* [1], an observation is simply made of an allowed sequence of actions. By nondeterminism, generally more observations are possible for a system – either because of the environment interacting in different ways, or because of different internal behaviors –, so that according to the given observation semantics the software component of interest can be characterized by the set of all its possible observations. The notion of refinement then naturally comes in: a system description is considered an "implementation" of another – i.e., it is more directly executable – if it is more deterministic, that is, if it allows for strictly fewer observations [1]. This notion is particularly crucial in the context of software engineering: when some safety property of interest is verified on a system specification, it continues to hold when the system is substituted with a refinement of it.

4   Grey-Box and Refinement

In [4], the rationale behind the grey-box modeling approach for agents is introduced. Its key idea is to represent an agent behavior by focusing on its part dealing with the interactions with the environment, called the *(agent) core*, while abstracting away from the complex inner details, namely, from the *(agent) internal machinery*. Clearly, deciding which aspects should be specified in the core and which should be abstracted away depends on the abstraction level of interest. In order to deal with agent proactiveness, one of the key notions introduced by this approach is that of *spontaneous move*, which is an event occurring within the internal machinery that may influence the agent interactions, thus affecting the behavior of the core. So, while complexity of agents can be harnessed by choosing the proper abstraction level, the internal machinery behavior can be anyway taken into account by supposing that spontaneous moves can nondeterministically occur.

In [4,2] a formal framework based on LTS is introduced to show that the grey-box modeling approach is particularly suitable for describing the agent abstraction. Based on this general idea, in this paper we go further developing this formal approach. We not only represent grey-box models as interactive abstractions, but also define a mechanism by which they can be refined by adding the specification of a new behavior, thus lowering the abstraction level and focusing on new details.

Notation. In the remainder of the paper, given any set X, this is automatically ranged over by the variable x and its decorations $x', x'', x_0, \ldots$ – and analogously, a set Any is ranged over by any, any', etcetera, and similarly for all sets. The set of multisets over X is denoted by $\overline{X}$ and ranged over by the variable $\overline{x}$ and its decorations; union of multisets $\overline{x}_1$ and $\overline{x}_2$ is denoted by symbol $\overline{x}_1 \| \overline{x}_2$; $\bullet$ is the empty multiset. Given any set X, symbol $\perp$ is used to denote an exception value in the set $X_\perp$ defined as $X \cup \{\perp\}$, which is ranged over by the variable $x_\perp$ and its decorations.

A Formal Framework for Grey-Box Modeling. Formally, an agent core is defined by a mathematical structure $\mathcal{A} = \langle I, O, P, X, E, U, \rightarrow_\mathcal{A} \rangle$. I is the set of acts that can be listened by the agent, O is the set of acts that the agent can perform on the environment. Both I and O can be *communicative acts*, involving the exchange of messages between agents, or *physical acts*, involving physical action in the agent environment, such as e.g. listening a stimulus from a sensor or moving a mechanical device by an actuator. P is the set of *place* states (or the set of *places* for short), which are the states of the agent core that can be observed by the agent internal machinery. X is the set of states of the remaining part of the agent core, so that $P \times X$ define the set of core states. E is the set of *events* occurring within the agent core and possibly affecting the internal machinery, while U is the set of *updates* notified by the internal machinery to the agent core, modeling the notion of spontaneous move. Relation $\rightarrow_\mathcal{A}$ is a transition relation of the kind $\rightarrow_\mathcal{A} \subseteq (P \times X) \times Act_\mathcal{A} \times (P \times X)$, defining how the agent core state evolves as actions in the set $Act_\mathcal{A}$ occur. These actions can be of five kinds according to the syntax $Act_\mathcal{A} ::= \tau \mid ?i \mid !o \mid \, \triangleright e \mid \, \triangleleft u$. Orderly, an action can represent the silent, internal computation τ, the agent listening act i, the agent executing act o, the event e occurring, and the update u being notified by the internal machinery.

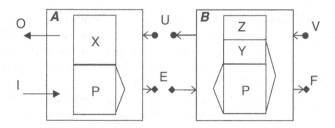

Fig. 1. Core and Completion

Refinement of a Grey-Box Model. It is common practice of system analysis and design to start considering a system at an high abstraction level, which is later lowered in order to consider much more details. Then, a key feature of our methodological approach is to refine the specification $\mathcal{A}$ by specifying some aspects of the internal machinery, that is, by conceptually moving them from the internal machinery to the agent core. This is done by composing the specification $\mathcal{A}$ by a new specification $\mathcal{B}$ called *completion*, so that the resulting system $\mathcal{C} = \mathcal{A} \otimes \mathcal{B}$ has still the structure of an agent core specification likewise $\mathcal{A}$ – hence it is still a grey-box model –, yet providing a number of additional details about the agent behavior.

A pictorial representation of our composition technique is shown in Figure 1. Formally, $\mathcal{B}$ is a structure of the kind $\langle Y, Z, F, V, \rightarrow_{\mathcal{B}} \rangle$. $W = Y \times Z$ is the set of local states added by $\mathcal{B}$ to the core state, Y is the part of it which is observable – along with P – to the new internal machinery, while Z is the local, hidden part of $\mathcal{B}$. $F \subseteq E$ and $V \subseteq U$ are respectively the new events and updates by which $\mathcal{C}$ interacts with its internal machinery. Transition relation $\rightarrow_{\mathcal{B}}$, describing the behavior of the completion, is of the kind $W \times Act_{\mathcal{B}} \times W$, with $Act_{\mathcal{B}}$ being defined by the syntax $Act_{\mathcal{B}} := p : \tau \mid p : e \triangleright f_{\perp} \mid p : u_{\perp} \triangleleft v$. Action $p : \tau$ is the silent action occurring when $\mathcal{A}$ is in place p. The action $p : e \triangleright f_{\perp}$ is executed when the place of $\mathcal{A}$ is p: event e occurs that causes f to be propagated towards the internal machinery. The subcase $p : e \triangleright \perp$ means that no event f is generated by event e. The action $p : u_{\perp} \triangleleft v$ means that when the update v is listened from $\mathcal{B}$ while $\mathcal{A}$ is in place p, then u is notified to $\mathcal{A}$ (or nothing if u is $\perp$). Notice that the occurrence of place p in these actions justifies the characterization of the place as the core's subpart observable by the internal machinery.

Given models $\mathcal{A}$ and $\mathcal{B}$, $\mathcal{C} = \mathcal{A} \otimes \mathcal{B}$ is defined as the agent core specification $\langle I, O, P \times Y, X \times Z, F, V, \rightarrow_{\mathcal{C}} \rangle$. The relation $\rightarrow_{\mathcal{C}}$, which is here of the kind $\rightarrow_{\mathcal{C}} \subseteq (P \times X \times W) \times Act_{\mathcal{C}} \times (P \times X \times W)$, is defined by the rules shown in Figure 2. Rules [I] and [O] state that input and output actions of the overall system $\mathcal{C}$ are executed on the agent core $\mathcal{A}$. Rules [AT] and [BT] say that a τ action in either $\mathcal{A}$ and $\mathcal{B}$ is executed in isolation, and makes $\mathcal{C}$ execute a τ action itself. Rules [AE] and [BE] describe the occurrence of an event in $\mathcal{A}$: in the first case no event f is generated by $\mathcal{B}$, in the second case $\mathcal{B}$ produces an event f. Analogously, [AU] and [BU] deal with updates, with [BU] considering the case where an update is propagated from the internal machinery to $\mathcal{A}$ and [AU] where no update is propagated to $\mathcal{A}$.

$$\frac{\langle p,x\rangle \xrightarrow{?i}_A \langle p',x'\rangle}{\langle p,x,w\rangle \xrightarrow{?i}_C \langle p',x',w\rangle} \quad [\mathrm{I}] \qquad\qquad \frac{\langle p,x\rangle \xrightarrow{!o}_A \langle p',x'\rangle}{\langle p,x,w\rangle \xrightarrow{!o}_C \langle p',x',w\rangle} \quad [\mathrm{O}]$$

$$\frac{\langle p,x\rangle \xrightarrow{\tau}_A \langle p',x'\rangle}{\langle p,x,w\rangle \xrightarrow{\tau}_C \langle p',x',w\rangle} \quad [\mathrm{AT}] \qquad \frac{\langle p,x\rangle \xrightarrow{\rhd e}_A \langle p',x'\rangle \qquad w \xrightarrow{p':e\rhd\bot}_B w'}{\langle p,x,w\rangle \xrightarrow{\tau}_C \langle p',x',w'\rangle} \quad [\mathrm{AE}]$$

$$\frac{w \xrightarrow{p:\tau}_B w'}{\langle p,x,w\rangle \xrightarrow{\tau}_C \langle p,x,w'\rangle} \quad [\mathrm{BT}] \qquad \frac{\langle p,x\rangle \xrightarrow{\rhd e}_A \langle p',x'\rangle \qquad w \xrightarrow{p':e\rhd f}_B w'}{\langle p,x,w\rangle \xrightarrow{\rhd f}_C \langle p',x',w'\rangle} \quad [\mathrm{BE}]$$

$$\frac{w \xrightarrow{p:\bot\lhd v}_B w'}{\langle p,x,w\rangle \xrightarrow{\lhd v}_C \langle p,x,w'\rangle} \quad [\mathrm{AU}] \qquad \frac{w \xrightarrow{p:u\lhd v}_B w' \qquad \langle p,x\rangle \xrightarrow{\lhd u}_A \langle p',x'\rangle}{\langle p,x,w\rangle \xrightarrow{\lhd v}_C \langle p',x',w'\rangle} \quad [\mathrm{BU}]$$

Fig. 2. Rules for composition of an agent core and its completion

Following an approach similar to the one reported in [3], which is not reported here for brevity, it is possible to prove that agent core C has a more refined behavior than agent core A in the sense specified e.g. by trace semantics [1]. Hence, our refinement technique can indeed be considered as a way of deepening a specification towards implementation issues.

5   ParADE

ParADE, the *Parma Agent Development Environment* [8], is a development framework that provides the agent developer with high-level abstractions like beliefs and goals, adhering to the general framework of BDI agent models [14] which is now a standard for autonomous agents – see [15,16] for examples of extensions to this framework. A hybrid agent architecture is implemented by ParADE which is capable of supporting autonomy and intelligent behaviors, exploiting the semantics of its ACL – resembling the FIPA ACL [17] but with a much lighter semantics. Such an architecture is basically goal-oriented but it also integrates reactive behaviors.

ParADE ACL provides an operational means for agents to exchange representations of beliefs, intentions, and capabilities. The semantics is modeled as the effect that the sender wishes to achieve when sending the message. We stick to a syntax similar to that of FIPA ACL: $\phi \in \Phi$ stands for any predicative formula, a and b for actions, s for the identifier of an agent sending a message, r for the receiver, $B_j\phi$ for "entity j believes ϕ", $I_j\phi$ for "entity j intends ϕ", and $done(a)$ for "action a has just happened". Each message is associated to a feasibility precondition (FP) that must hold in the sender and a rational effect (RE) that the send should intend: for instance $inform(s,r,\phi)$ has the precondition $B_s\phi$ – namely, the sender must believe ϕ – and $request(s,r,a)$ has the rational effect $done(a)$ – the sender should intend a to be executed. As a result, a precise semantics can be assigned to a message by its receiver, for example message $request(s,r,a)$ is associated to the semantics $B_r I_s done(a)$ (the receiver believes that the sender intends a to be executed) – see [8] for more details.

The ParADE ACL provides a means for exchanging complex logic formulae through simple messages as the receiver can assert what the sender is intending. Isolated messages are not sufficient to allow agents to communicate fruitfully. The classic example is the case of an agent requesting another agent to perform an action: in the case of asynchronous messages there is no guarantee that the receiver would act in response to a message. Moreover, the semantics of a single message might not be sufficient to express application-specific constraints. The semantics of performative *request* does not impose the receiver to communicate to the sender that the requested action has been actually performed. The sender might hang indefinitely while waiting for the receiver to tell it that the action has been performed.

Integrating speech-act ACLs into BDI agents is a particularly challenging and relevant issue, see e.g. [18]: using such an ACL provides an agent with a linguistic environment that attaches semantics to its utterances. By virtue of the speech act theory, utterances become actions, with their attached pre- and post-conditions. Still, an agent is situated within an environment that is not limited to its social milieu; there are actions to perform and events to perceive that are not linguistic. Moreover, even linguistic acts often refer to entities belonging to something else than the language itself. These entities belong to the *domain* of the discourse, i.e. the external environment itself, and are typically described within a *domain model* or *ontology*. This ontology not only shapes the content of exchanged messages, but can also constrain the available actions of an agent associating them with domain-specific pre-conditions. In ParADE, the domain model works as the non-linguistic counterpart of the ACL semantics, enabling uniform processing of both the interactions with other agents and with the external environment.

In order to support socially fruitful communication, the ParADE agent model provides *interaction laws*. These are rules that an agent decides to adopt to govern its interactions with other agents. The interaction laws that an agent decides to follow are part of its capabilities and they are published. As an example, consider the interaction law $I_r done(a) \leftarrow B_r I_s done(a)$ for the agent r, which means that whenever he believes that agent s intends the action a to be executed, then this becomes an intention of r as well. This law should characterize an agent always willing to cooperate with s. In particular, as shown in the example we provide in Section 6.2, if s asks r to execute action a by means of a *request* message, then r will come to believe that the rational effect of the message is intended by the sender, that is $B_r I_s done(a)$. Then, the above interaction rule may be applied that makes $done(a)$ become an intention of r as well. In general, interaction laws are an elegant and flexible way to describe interaction protocols, they can be linked to the possible roles that an agent can play in the MAS, and they may also vary over time.

The ACL semantics, the domain model, and the interaction laws work together to expose an observable model of a ParADE agent that enables semantically meaningful communication with others. However, they don't fully specify the agent behavior; an agent programmer using ParADE is able to define several rules that drive the evolution of the agent mental states, only a subset of which will be published as interaction laws. This means that there is an internal set of rules that completes the agent specification, but is visible to nobody else than the agent designer. Though in most cases the designer wants to abstract away from the agent internal evolution rules, it is still useful to notice that even this relatively low-level part of the agent specification is still described declaratively.

6   Iterated Refinement

In this section we shown an application of our technique for formalizing the behavior of an agent by successive refining an initial description, taking as a reference architecture the ParADE framework. We refer to the term *tier* when describing these different levels, each of which focuses on a different behavioral aspect and is then amenable to a separated description, thus fostering the understanding of its key features. The tiers we analyze not only correspond to the main features of ParADE, but also include most of the main aspects that an agent implementation has to take into account: orderly *(i)* the *interaction tier*, managing interactions with the environment, *(ii)* the *linguistic tier*, dealing with aspects related to the ACL semantics, *(iii)* the *domain tier*, concerning the specific ontology of the application, *(iv)* the *social tier*, where interaction laws define the role and public peculiarities of the agent, and finally *(v)* the *internal tier*, dealing with other aspects such as private laws, planning, and proactiveness. The order of these tiers reflects their impact on the external, observable behavior of the agent, from tackling interaction issues to considering internal reasoning. It worth noting that the actual implementation of a ParADE agent is not actually separated into these tiers, which are instead a modeling tool useful at design-time independently from the actual agent implementation, representing conceptual levels that isolate the different behavioral aspects of agents within MAS.

In order to keep the presentation clear and reasonably compact, locally to a tier we sometime abstract away from some policy or management that is of a too lower abstraction level – either concerning details of the ParADE architecture or of the specific agent peculiarities –, referring to some generic function, relation or set encapsulating the actual behavior.

6.1   Splitting the Agent Specification into Tiers

The Interaction Tier. From the point of view of the MAS, the most distinctive aspect of an agent is its ability of interacting with other agents and of performing actions on the environment. So, not surprisingly, the first tier we introduce is the one dealing with the interaction abilities of an agent, namely listening and performing acts. In the following, we denote by Ic and Oc the sets of input and output communicative acts, and by Ip and Op the sets of input and output physical acts, so that $I = Ic \cup Ip$ and $O = Oc \cup Op$.

The task of this tier is to decouple the actual agent interactions with respect to their internal processing, which is a common feature of almost all agent implementations – sometimes mentioned to contrast the notion of agent with respect to that of component (or object). Here, we suppose that the set X of states unobservable by the internal machinery is defined as a multiset of pending input acts waiting to be processed and pending output acts waiting to be executed, namely, $X = \overline{I} \cup \overline{O}$. The set P of places is defined as the set of agent mental states: a mental state $\Phi_M \in P$ at a given time is a set of formulae $\phi \in \Phi$, representing current beliefs and intentions of the agent. This is explicitly represented in this tier because, typically, the occurrence of interactions has an immediate representation in the knowledge of an agent.

A composition operator between such formulae is defined so that if $\Phi_M \subseteq \Phi$ is the current mental state and $\Phi_n \subset \Phi$ contains some new beliefs and intentions, then $\Phi_M \circ \Phi_n$ is the new mental state obtained from Φ_M by adding formulae in Φ_n. Clearly, this composition should be defined according to the specific update policy for mental states, which we here abstract away from, analogously e.g. to [19]. Similarly, given a mental state Φ_M, we suppose that if this is of the kind $\Phi' \circ \Phi_n$ then the agent mental state includes all the beliefs and intentions of Φ_n.

An element of the set $P \times X$ is hence a couple $\langle \Phi_M, \overline{i}||\overline{o} \rangle$, here denoted as $\Phi_M||\overline{i}||\overline{o}$ for uniformity of notation. The set of events E coincides to I, representing the input acts listened from outside. The set of updates U is $O \cup \mathcal{P}(\Phi)$, representing either output acts to perform or requests to change the mental state by adding a subset of formulae in Φ (with $\mathcal{P}(\Phi)$ being the powerset of Φ). Transition relation $\rightarrow_\mathcal{A}$, describing the behavior of the interaction tier, is then defined by the rules:

$$\Phi_M \xrightarrow{?i}_\mathcal{A} i \ || \ \Phi_M \circ \{B_r done(i)\} \qquad \Phi_M||i \xrightarrow{\triangleright i}_\mathcal{A} \Phi_M$$

$$\Phi_M||o \xrightarrow{!o}_\mathcal{A} \Phi_M \circ \{B_r done(o)\} \qquad \Phi_M \xrightarrow{\triangleleft o}_\mathcal{A} \Phi_M||o$$

$$\Phi_M \xrightarrow{\triangleleft \Phi_n}_\mathcal{A} \Phi_M \circ \Phi_n$$

The first rule simply states that when input act i is received ($?i$), the mental state is updated so as to reflect the reception ($B_r done(i)$), and then the act i is stored in the state X waiting for being notified as an event by means of the second rule ($\triangleright i$). The third and fourth rule, conversely handle output acts, which are inserted in X by updates ($\triangleleft o$), and are later sent outside by output actions ($!o$), affecting the mental state. Finally, fifth rule handles a mental state update requested by the internal machinery ($\triangleleft \Phi_n$), according to the semantics of composition operator $\circ$.

Different implementations of interactions dispatching could be specified in this tier, including the case where acts are stored into queues representing the agent mailbox instead of being immediately served as in the model above – where a precondition for receiving and sending acts is that no act is still pending.

The Linguistic Tier. A fundamental aspect of the ParADE framework is that it exploits an ACL semantics to enjoy true semantic interoperability between agents [7], as currently promoted by the FIPA ACL and KQML approaches.

So, as next tier we take into account the constraints imposed on communicative acts by the specific ACL. Then, we define a completion $\mathcal{B}$ specifying the main concepts of the ACL, namely, the syntax of messages and their impact on the agent mental state.

Syntax is defined by introducing sets $I_{ACL} \subseteq Ic$ and $O_{ACL} \subseteq Oc$ of communicative acts allowed by the ACL: when a message ic is received that does not conform to that syntax this is simply ignored. The set of visible states Y is here void, since no new information is to be added to the mental state Φ_M that should be visible to the internal machinery. Instead, set Z of local, invisible states is used to store scheduled updates $\bar{u}$ to be propagated to the interaction tier, thus $Z = \overline{U}$: in particular, such updates are requests for updating the mental state with formulae Φ_n. On the other hand, events F produced by this tier are of the kind $ic \in I_{ACL}$, while updates V coincides with U.

In order to deal with the effect of a communicative act on the agent mental state, we define $\mathit{eff}_M^I : I_{ACL} \mapsto \mathcal{P}(\Phi)$ as a function associating to a communicative act its intended effect on the mental state of the receiver – formed by beliefs and intentions to be added –, and $\mathit{cnd}_M^O : O_{ACL} \mapsto \mathcal{P}(\Phi)$ as the function associating to a communicative act the condition on the local mental state enabling its sending, expressed as facts the agent has to believe and intend. In the case of ParADE, and similarly to FIPA ACL, we have e.g. $\mathit{eff}_M^I(ic) = \{B_r FP(ic), B_r I_s RE(ic)\}$, that is, when the message is processed the receiver comes to believe that the feasibility preconditions of the act are satisfied, and that the sender intends its rational effects. Analogously, $\mathit{cnd}_M^O(oc) = \{B_s FP(oc), I_s RE(oc)\}$, that is, a message can be sent out only if the sender believes the feasibility preconditions and intends the rational effects of the act. The rules for transition relation $\rightarrow_{\mathcal{B}}$ that deal with communicative acts are as follows:

- $\xrightarrow{\Phi_M : ic \triangleright ic}_{\mathcal{B}} \mathit{eff}_M^I(ic)$ if $ic \in I_{ACL}$

- $\xrightarrow{\Phi_M : ic \triangleright \bot}_{\mathcal{B}} \bullet$ if $ic \notin I_{ACL}$

- $\xrightarrow{\Phi_M : oc \triangleleft oc}_{\mathcal{B}} \bullet$ if $oc \in O_{ACL}$ and $\Phi_M = \Phi_M' \circ \mathit{cnd}_M^O(oc)$

- $\xrightarrow{\Phi_M : \bot \triangleleft oc}_{\mathcal{B}} \bullet$ if $oc \notin O_{ACL}$ or $\Phi_M \neq \Phi_M' \circ \mathit{cnd}_M^O(oc)$

The first rule says that when the communicative act ic arrives that is correct with respect to the ACL ($ic \in I_{ACL}$), then this is redirected as event f (by an action of the kind $p : e \triangleright f$), and an update for changing the mental state is correspondingly scheduled; the second rule says that acts that do not belong to the ACL are ignored. Dually, the third rule handles the case where an output act that is correct with respect to the ACL syntax is to be sent out, which is actually performed only if the proper conditions hold on the mental state (ϕ_M includes conditions $\mathit{cnd}_M^O(oc)$). On the other hand, if the act is not correct or these conditions are not satisfied, the fourth rule makes the update be simply ignored and discarded. The remaining rules are as follows:

- $\xrightarrow{\Phi_M : ip \triangleright ip}_{\mathcal{B}} \bullet$ $\bullet \xrightarrow{\Phi_M : op \triangleleft op}_{\mathcal{B}} \bullet$ $\bullet \xrightarrow{\Phi_M : \bot \triangleleft \Phi_n}_{\mathcal{B}} \Phi_n$ $u \xrightarrow{\Phi_M : u \triangleleft \bot}_{\mathcal{B}} \bullet$

The first and second rule let input physical acts and output physical act to flow across the tier. The third rule reifies requests for changing the mental states within the tier, which by the fourth rule are redirected to the previous tier. Since this reification technique is exploited in the next tiers as well, the latter two rules are are assumed here to be included in the specification of both the ontology, social, and internal tier, even if they are not actually reported for brevity.

The Domain Tier. The domain tier is the part of the agent specification that deals with aspects related to the ontology defining the application domain where the agent lives. First of all, the syntax of communicative acts is further constrained with respect to the ACL, since e.g. the actual content of a message is limited to those terms to which the ontology gives an interpretation. We therefore denote by $Ic_{ONT} \subseteq I_{ACL}$ and $Oc_{ONT} \subseteq O_{ACL}$ the communicative acts allowed by the specific ontology. Then, the ontology also defines what are the physical acts that may be listened and executed by the agent, which are denoted by the sets $Ip_{ONT} \subseteq Ip$ and $Op_{ONT} \subseteq Op$. The sets of acts allowed by the ontology are then naturally defined as $I_{ONT} = Ip_{ONT} \cup Ic_{ONT}$ and $O_{ONT} = Op_{ONT} \cup Oc_{ONT}$. Finally, each output physical act is associated to an expected rational effect, by a function $cnd_M^P : O_{ONT} \mapsto \mathcal{P}(\Phi)$, associating output acts to sets of formulae (facts to be intended and believed) that will become satisfied. This function is here supposed to associate to communicative acts a void set, while in the case of a physical act op we have e.g. $cnd_M^P(op) = \{I_s RE(op)\}$. In the case the domain ontology binds physical input acts to predicates in the mental state, it would be sensible to introduce also the management of feasibility preconditions analogously to the linguistic tier, however, this is not considered here for it is subject of current researches.

Similarly to the case of the linguistic tier, set F is a subset of E and $V = U$. Also, sets Y and Z are the same of previous case. The rules for transition relation $\rightarrow_B$ handling input acts are as follows:

$$\bullet \xrightarrow{\Phi_M : i \rhd i}_B \bullet \quad \text{if } i \in I_{ONT} \qquad \bullet \xrightarrow{\Phi_M : i \rhd \perp}_B \bullet \quad \text{if } i \notin I_{ONT}$$

stating that when input act i arrives that is correct with respect to the ontology, then this is redirected as event f; otherwise, by the second rule the act is simply ignored. The case of output acts is handled dually:

$$\bullet \xrightarrow{\Phi_M : o \lhd o}_B \bullet \quad \text{if } o \in O_{ONT} \quad \text{and} \quad \Phi_M = \Phi'_M \circ cnd_M^P(o)$$

$$\bullet \xrightarrow{\Phi_M : \perp \lhd o}_B \bullet \quad \text{if } o \notin O_{ONT} \quad \text{or} \quad \Phi_M \neq \Phi'_M \circ cnd_M^P(o)$$

the output act is let flow toward the agent core only if it conforms to the ontology and satisfies the preconditions.

The Social Tier. This tier deals with those peculiar aspects of an agent that characterize its collaborative (or social) behavior within the MAS. In particular, interaction laws can be applied that change the mental state under some conditions, e.g. making the agent react to some input by producing some output act. Since interaction laws can be of different kinds, we here just suppose that the set of interaction laws of an agent are modeled by a relation $ilaw \subseteq \mathcal{P}(\Phi) \times \mathcal{P}(\Phi)$, associating to the current mental state the new facts (possibly none) that the agent will believe and intend after applying some enabled law.

In particular, the social tier has void set Y, while set Z – as for previous tier – may contain some pending update, namely, some change on the mental state that has to be applied. Events F and updates V coincide with E and U, respectively. The rule governing the relation transition of this tier is the following:

$$\perp \xrightarrow{\Phi_M : i \rhd i}_{\mathcal{B}} \Phi_n \qquad \text{if } ilaw(\Phi_M, \Phi_n)$$

saying that whenever a new input is received, interaction laws make a new mental state to be computed which will be propagated to the interaction tier as usual.

The Internal Tier. The internal tier is the latter tier of our specification, which includes a number of remaining implementation features of the agent. Most notably, here a further set of laws – which are not however published but forms the hidden, unobservable behavior of the agent – can be applied that may have various purposes. On the one hand, these rules can be used to drive any agent behavior that cannot be ascribed to its social role, but rather to its implementation. To the end of the formalization presented here, we model this behavior by a *private laws* function *plaw* similar to function *ilaw*. On the other hand, the internal tier is also the part of the agent responsible for proactively requesting some action to be performed. To this end, we consider a precondition function $cnd_M^E : o \mapsto \mathcal{P}(\Phi)$ associating to an output act the conditions enabling its execution. In the basic case we have $cnd_M^E(o) = \{I_s done(o), B_s FP(o)\}$, that is, the agent should intend to execute the action and should believe its feasibility preconditions.

Since no further refining is here considered, set of events F and updates U are here void. Moreover, sets Z and Y coincide with previous tier. Other than the two usual rules for dispatching updates as in the previous tier, we have the two rules:

$$\perp \xrightarrow{\Phi_M : i \rhd \perp}_{\mathcal{B}} \Phi_n \qquad \text{if } plaw(\Phi_M, \Phi_n)$$

$$\perp \xrightarrow{\Phi_M \circ cnd_M^E(o) : \tau}_{\mathcal{B}} o$$

While the former makes the mental state be updated by applying a private law, the second rule says that each time a silent action is performed by the agent core and the precondition for executing an action is satisfied, then that action is scheduled by sending the update o.

6.2   An Example

In order to grasp the flavor of this formalization, we here consider an example of simple conversation for an agent, and describe the corresponding sequence of transitions modeling its behavior. In particular, we consider the case that the agent i receives from another agent j a message a of the kind $request(j, i, b)$ where $b = inform(i, j, \phi)$, requesting i to send a message declaring that he believes ϕ. In the case where i actually believes ϕ, and by the interaction law $I_i done(a) \leftarrow B_i I_j done(a)$ – stating that i is always willing to execute the actions that j intends to be executed – we should obtain that i sends the message $inform(i, j, \phi)$. This protocol is a very simplified version of the FIPA-request protocol, and for the sake of brevity does not take into account aspects such as agreement, refusal, and so on.

The represented portion of the agent state, namely the state of the agent core, is expressed as a tuple with the state of each tier in its elements, orderly. We start by considering the agent i with a mental state of the kind $\Phi_M \circ \{B_i \phi\}$, namely, initially believing ϕ.

(1) $\langle \Phi \circ \{B_i \phi\}, \bullet, \bullet, \bullet, \bullet \rangle \xrightarrow{?a} C$

(2) $\langle a \| \Phi \circ \{B_i \phi, B_i done(a)\}, \bullet, \bullet, \bullet, \bullet \rangle \xrightarrow{\tau} C$

(3) $\langle \Phi \circ \{B_i \phi, B_i done(a)\}, \{B_i I_j done(b)\}, \bullet, \{I_i done(b)\}, \bullet \rangle \xrightarrow{\tau} C$

(4) $\langle \Phi \circ \{B_i \phi, B_i done(a), B_i I_j done(b)\}, \bullet, \bullet, \{I_i done(b)\}, \bullet \rangle \xrightarrow{\tau} C$

(5) $\langle \Phi \circ \{B_i \phi, B_i done(a), B_i I_j done(b), I_i done(b)\}, \bullet, \bullet, \bullet, \bullet \rangle \xrightarrow{\tau} C$

(6) $\langle \Phi \circ \{B_i \phi, B_i done(a), B_i I_j done(b), I_i done(b)\}, \bullet, \bullet, \bullet, b \rangle \xrightarrow{\tau} C$

(7) $\langle b \| \Phi \circ \{B_i \phi, B_i done(a), B_i I_j done(b), I_i done(b)\}, \bullet, \bullet, \bullet, \bullet \rangle \xrightarrow{!b} C$
      $\langle \Phi \circ \{B_i \phi, B_i done(a), B_i I_j done(b), I_i done(b), B_i done(b)\}, \bullet, \bullet, \bullet, \bullet \rangle$

The first transition models the reception of communicative act a: the interaction tier enqueues the request and adds to its mental state $B_i done(a)$. In the second transition, a is processed by flowing across each tier: in the linguistic tier it makes the agent believing the sender's intentions $B_i I_j done(b)$ (feasibility preconditions are here avoided for simplicity), while in the social tier the interaction law $I_i done(b) \leftarrow B_i I_j done(b)$ is applied leading to the new intention $I_i done(b)$. In the third and fourth rule both these facts are propagated back to the interaction tier affecting the mental state. In the fifth rule, the internal tier recognizes the intention $I_i done(b)$, and by means of function cnd_M^E fires the action b, which the sixth rule moves to the interaction tier. Finally, since the feasibility precondition $B_i \phi$ to b is satisfied the communicative act b is sent outside. Notice that another precondition for sendind would be $I_i B_j \phi$ (the agent i must intend the rational effect of b), which is not considered here for in most agent architectures – such as FIPA – it is generally entailed by $I_i done(b)$. Then, the spurious formulae $\{B_i I_j done(b), I_i done(b)\}$ are meant to be subsequently dropped from the mental state by means of private laws in the internal tier.

7   Conclusions

In this paper we tackle the problem of formalizing the behavior of complex agents by a technique underlying the notion of grey-box modeling. An existing description, focusing on the agent behavior at a given abstraction level, can be refined by adding the specification of a new aspect. This formal approach is here described and put to test on the ParADE framework, describing a number of relevant agent aspects such as the ACL and its semantics, ontology, and social role, providing a means by which different system levels and views of a MAS can be represented in isolation. A crucial role in this methodology is played by the framework of LTS, which allows us to describe in an operational way the behavior of an agent implementation, and facilitates the task of composing specifications.

Related Works. LTS have been applied to agent systems in other works as well. The grey-box modeling approach has been first studied in the context of the so-called observation framework [4,2], where agents are modeled as sources of information. In [3], a grey-box formal approach similar to the one described in this paper has been applied to represent the semantics of ACLs. In [19], specifications based on operational semantics are evaluated for ACLs, using a process algebra to describe how interaction may affect the mental state. In [20], agent internal aspects such as planning are modeled through the ψ-calculus, a language whose operational semantics is meant to capture the allowed internal dynamics of the agent. Another significant formalism from concurrency theory that is being successfully applied to MAS interaction specification are Colored Petri Nets [21], as described e.g. in Ferber's book [22]. Most of these previous works applying LTS and CPN to MAS interaction modeling focused on agent conversations and interaction protocols, while we claim that the approach presented in this paper can be fruitfully applied to the whole design of agent-based systems, enjoying the fact that separating specifications may allow to study their properties separately. A deeper investigation will reveal further relationship with the work in [20], which is closer to our spirit.

It worth also noting that our refining approach, based on the idea of conceptually separating the many different aspects of an agent design, contrasts to other agent languages approaches such as [23], where these heterogeneity is meant to be addressed by relying on multi-paradigm languages, featuring logic, object-oriented, functional, and even coordination styles.

Future Works. A main advantage of an operational specification is that it should allow properties of interest to be formally proved. In our case, where one such specification is applied at design-time to model an agent collaborative behavior, we may expect them to state the soundness – in the broad meaning of the term – of an agent design, especially as far as its interactions with other agents of the MAS are concerned. Notice that the specification we provided is parametric in a number of mathematical structures (I_{ACL}, O_{ACL}, eff_M^I, cnd_M^O, I_{ONT}, O_{ONT}, cnd_M^P, ilaw, plaw, cnd_M^E), describing both peculiar aspects of the agent model (e.g. ACL semantics) as well as peculiar aspects of the individual agent (e.g. its private laws).

Some of the properties of interest may be independent of these parameters, mostly concerning the internal structure of the specification. For instance, by-hand proofs should emphasize that any reception of an input act a is reified as a believe $B_i done(a)$, and that requests for mental state updates raised by the internal tier are eventually applied (flowing towards the interaction tier) preserving their order.

Other properties, that instead depend on the parameters of the specification, can be more concerned with the correctness of the resulting agent behavior, that is, concerning its rationality and social attitude. As an example, our specification may provide a suitable framework for proving that under a given ACL semantics (eff_M^I, cnd_M^O, I_{ACL}, O_{ACL}) and a given ontology (cnd_M^P, I_{ONT}, O_{ONT}), a specific set of interact laws ($ilaw$) and private laws ($plaw$) are sufficient for the agent correctly participating in a given conversation protocol, e.g. the simple request conversation showed in Section 6.2.

An expected feature of our framework is that properties concerning only one aspect of the MAS design could be studied considering agent specifications only up to the corresponding tier, by virtue of the refinement notion of transition systems. For instance, stating that a conversation protocol is consistent with respect to the ACL semantics should require us to consider agents as made of the interaction and linguistic tiers only: as mentioned in Section 4 such a specification refines the actual agent behavior, but consider all the aspects of interest. On the other hand, evaluating the evolutions of conversations depending on the agents social attitude requires to consider the domain and social tiers as well.

In general, deepening all these issues, that concern the applicability of formal verification tools to the validation of MAS design, is the main future work of this research.

References

1. Glabbeek, R.v.: The linear time – branching time spectrum I. The semantics of concrete, sequential processes. [12] chapter 1 3–100
2. Viroli, M., Omicini, A.: Specifying agent observable behaviour. In Castelfranchi, C., Johnson, W.L., eds.: 1st International Joint Conference on Autonomous Agents and Multiagent Systems (AAMAS 2002). Volume 2., Bologna, Italy, ACM (2002) 712–720
3. Rimassa, G., Viroli, M.: An operational framework for the semantics of agent communication languages. In: Engineering Societies in the Agents World (ESAW 2002). Lecture Notes in Artificial Intelligence, Vol. 2577. Springer-Verlag (2003) 111–125
4. Viroli, M., Omicini, A.: Modelling agents as observable sources. Journal of Universal Computer Science **8** (2002)
5. Newell, A.: The knowledge level. Artificial Intelligence **18** (1982) 87–127
6. Jennings, N.R.: On agent-based software engineering. Artificial Intelligence **117** (2000) 277–296
7. Bergenti, F.: A discussion of two major benefits of using agents in software development. In: Engineering Societies in the Agents World (ESAW 2002). Lecture Notes in Artificial Intelligence, Vol. 2577. Springer-Verlag (2003) 1–12
8. Bergenti, F., Poggi, A.: A development toolkit to realize autonomous and interoperable agents. In: Conference on Autonomous Agents. (2001) 632–639

9. Hindriks, K.V., de Boer, F.S., van der Hoek, W., Meyer, J.J.C.: Agent programming in 3APL. Autonomous Agents and Multi-Agent Systems **2** (1999)

10. Norling, E., Ritter, F.E.: Embodying the jack agent architecture. In: 14th Australian Joint Conference on Artificial Intelligence. Lecture Notes in Artificial Intelligence, Vol. 2256. Springer (2001) 368–377

11. Plotkin, G.: A structural approach to operational semantics. Technical Report DAIMI FN-19, Department of Computer Science, AArhus University (1991)

12. Bergstra, J.A., Ponse, A., Smolka, S.A., eds.: Handbook of Process Algebra. North-Holland (2001)

13. Milner, R.: Communication and Concurrency. Prentice Hall (1989)

14. Cohen, P.R., Levesque, H.: Intention is choice with commitment. Artificial Intelligence **42(2-3)** (1990) 213–361

15. Trân, B., Harland, J., Hamilton, M.: A combined logic of expectation and observation (a generalization of BDI logics). In this volume.

16. Ancona, D., Mascardi, V.: BCDI: Extending the BDI model with collaborations. In this volume.

17. FIPA: FIPA communicative act library specification. http://www.fipa.org (2000) Doc. XC00037H.

18. Moreira, Á.F., Vieira, R., Bordini, R.H.: Extending the operational semantics of a bdi agent-oriented programming language for introducing speech-act based communication. In this volume.

19. van Eijk, R.M., de Boer, F.S., van der Hoek, W., Meyer, J.J.C.: Operational semantics for agent communication languages. In: Issues in Agent Communication. Lecture Notes in Artificial Intelligence, Vol. 1916. Springer (2000) 80–95

20. Kinny, D.: Vip: a visual programming language for plan execution systems. In Castelfranchi, C., Johnson, W.L., eds.: 1st International Joint Conference on Autonomous Agents and Multiagent Systems (AAMAS 2002). Volume 2., Bologna, Italy, ACM (2002) 721–728

21. Jensen, K.: Coloured Petri Nets - Basic Concepts, Analysis Methods and Practical Use. Springer-Verlag, Berlin (1992)

22. Ferber, J.: Multi-Agent Systems: An Introduction to Distributed Artifical Intelligence. Addison-Wesley, London (1999)

23. Clark, K.L., McCabe, F.G.: Go! for multi-threaded deliberative agents. In this volume.

Go! for Multi-threaded Deliberative Agents

Keith L. Clark[1] and Frank G. McCabe[2]

[1] Dept. of Computing, Imperial College, London
[2] Fujitsu Labs of America, Sunnuvale, CA

Abstract. Go! is a multi-paradigm programming language that is oriented to the needs of programming secure, production quality, agent based applications. It is multi-threaded, strongly typed and higher order (in the functional programming sense). It has relation, function and action procedure definitions. Threads execute action procedures, calling functions and querying relations as need be. Threads in different agents communicate and coordinate using asynchronous messages. Threads within the same agent can also use shared dynamic relations acting as memory stores.

In this paper we introduce the essential features of Go! illustrating them by programming a simple multi-agent application comprising hybrid reactive/deliberative agents interacting in a simulated ballroom. The dancer agents negotiate to enter into joint commitments to dance a particular dance (e.g. polka) they both desire. When the dance is announced, they dance together. An agent's reactive and deliberative components are concurrently executing threads which communicate and coordinate using belief, desire and intention memory stores. We believe such a multi-threaded agent architecture represents a powerful and natural style of agent implementation, for which Go! is well suited.

1 Introduction

Go! is a logic programming descendant of the multi-threaded symbolic programming language April [1][1], with influences from IC-Prolog II [2] and L&O [3]. April was initially developed as the implementation language for the much higher level MAI²L [4] agent programming of the EU Imagine project. It has more recently been used to implement one of the FIPA compliant agent platforms of the EU AgentCities project [5], and the agent services running on that platform at Imperial College and Fujitsu. We are currently investigating the use of Go! as an ontology server within that agent platform.

A significant theme in the design of Go! is software engineering in the service of high-integrity intelligent systems. To bring the benefits of logic programming to applications developers requires fitting the language into current best-practice; and, especially since applications are increasingly operating in the public Internet, security, transparency and integrity are critical to the adoption of logic programming technology.

---

[1] Go is the sound of a Japanese word for 5. April is the 4th month.

J. Leite et al. (Eds.): DALT 2003, LNAI 2990, pp. 54–75, 2004.

Although Go! has many features in common with Prolog, particularly multi-threaded Prolog's, there are significant differences related to transparency of code and security. Features of Prolog that mitigate against transparency, such as the infamous *cut* (!) primitive, are absent from Go!. Instead, its main uses are supported by higher level programming constructs, such as single solution calls, *iff* rules, and the ability to define 'functional' relations as functions.

In Prolog, the same clause syntax is used both for defining relations, with a declarative semantics, and for defining procedures, say that read and write to files, which really only have an operational semantics. In Go!, behaviours are described using action rules, which have a different syntax. While Prolog is a *meta-order* language, Go! is higher-order (in the functional programming sense) and strongly typed, using a modified Hindley/Milner style type inference technique [6].

A key feature of Go! is the ability to group a set of definitions into a lexical unit by surrounding them with {} braces. We call such a unit a *theta environment*. Theta environments are Go!'s program structuring mechanism. Two key uses of theta environments are *where* expressions, analogous to the *let ... in ...* construct of some functional programming languages, and labeled theories, which are labeled theta environments.

Labeled theories are based on McCabe's *L&O* [3] extension of Prolog. A labeled theory is a theta environment labeled by a term where variables of the label term are global variables of the theory. Instances of the theory are created by given values to these label variables. Labeled theories are analogous to class definitions, and their instances are Go!'s objects. Objects can have state, recorded by *cell* and *dynamic relation* objects. New labeled theories can be defined in terms of one or more existing theories using inheritance rules. Labeled theories provide a rich knowledge representation notation akin to that of frame systems [7].

Go! does not directly support any specific agent architecture or agent programming methodology, although this could be done using library modules. It is a language is which different architectures and methodologies can be quickly prototyped and explored. We illustrate this by developing a simple multi-agent application comprising hybrid reactive/deliberative agents interacting at a simulated ball. Although an artificial example we believe it is representative of many multi-agent applications.

In section 2 we give a brief overview of Go! and its facilities for programming task orientated agents. In the limited space available we cannot give a comprehensive description of Go!. For a more complete description of the language see [8].

In section 3 we explore Go! in the context of the simulated ballroom. Each dancer agent is programmed using multiple concurrently executing threads that implement different aspects of its behaviour – coordinated by shared **belief**, **desire** and **intention** dynamic relation memory stores. This internal run-time architecture has *implicit* interleaving of the various activities of the agent. This contrasts with the *explicit* interleaving of observation, short deliberation and partial execution of the classic single threaded BDI (*Beliefs,Desires,Intentions*) architecture [9].

The `belief`, `desire` and `intention` memory stores are used in a manner similar to Linda tuple stores [10]. For example, memory store updates are atomic, and a thread can suspend waiting for a belief to be added or deleted. Linda tuple stores have been used for inter-agent coordination [11]. For scalability and other reasons, we prefer to use asynchronous point-to-point messages between agents, as in KQML [12]. However, we strongly advocate concurrency and Linda style shared memory co-ordination for internal agent design.

In section 4 we briefly discuss related work before giving our concluding remarks.

2 Key Features of Go!

`Go!` is a multi-paradigm language with a declarative subset of function and relation definitions and an imperative subset comprising action procedure definitions.

2.1 Function, Relation and Action Rules

Functions are defined using sequences of rewrite rules of the form:

$$f(A_1,..,A_k)::Test \Rightarrow Exp$$

where the guard *Test* is omitted if not required.

As in most functional programming languages, the testing of whether a function rule can be used to evaluate a function call uses *matching* not unification. Once a function rule has been selected there is no backtracking to select an alternative rule.

Relation definitions comprise sequences of Prolog-style :- clauses ; with some modifications – such as permitting expressions as well as data terms, and no cut. We can also define relations using *iff* rules.

The locus of action in `Go!` is a *thread*; each `Go!` thread executes a procedure. Procedures are defined using non-declarative *action* rules of the form:

$$a(A_1,..,A_k)::Test \rightarrow Action_1;...;Action_n$$

As with equations, the first action rule that matches some call, and whose test is satisfied, is used; once an action rule has been selected there is no backtracking on the choice of rule.

The permissible actions of an action rule include: message dispatch and receipt, I/O, updating of dynamic relations, the calling of a procedure, and the spawning of any action, or sequence of actions, to create a new action thread.

Threads in a single `Go!` invocation can communicate either by thread-to-thread message communication or by synchronisable access and update of shared data, such as dynamic relations. Threads in different `Go!` invocations can only communicate using messages. To support thread-to-thread communication, each thread has its own buffer of messages it has not yet read, which are ordered in the buffer by time of arrival. To place a message in a thread's buffer the sender has to have the threads unique handle identity.

The message send action:

Msg >> *To*

sends the message *Msg* to the thread identified by the handle *To*. It is a non-blocking asynchronous communication. Handles are terms of the form hdl(Id,Group) where Id and Group are symbols that together uniquely identify the thread. Typically, threads within the same agent share the same Group name, which can be the unique agent's name.

To look for and remove from the message buffer a message matching *Ptn* sent by a thread *From* the receive action:

Ptn << *From*

can be used.

To look for any one of several messages, and to act appropriately when one is found, the conditional receive:

```
( Ptn₁ << From₁ -> Actions₁
| ...
| Ptnₙ << Fromₙ -> Actionsₙ
)
```

can be used. When executed, the message buffer of the thread is searched to find the first message that will *fire* one of these alternate message receive rules. The matched message is removed from the message buffer and corresponding actions are executed. Messages that don't match are left in the message buffer for a later message receive to pick up.

Both forms of message receive suspend if no matching message is found, causing the thread to suspend. The thread resumes only when a matching message is received. This is the message receive semantics of Erlang [13] and April [1].

Communication daemons and a special external communications system module allow threads in different invocations of Go! to communicate using the same message send and receive actions as are used between threads of a single invocation, see [8]. This allows an application comprising several modules, developed and tested as one multi-threaded Go! invocation, to be converted into a distributed application with minimal re-programming.

2.2 Programming Behaviour with Action Rules

As an example of the use of action rules let us consider programming the top level of an agent with a mission: this is to achieve some fixed goal by the repeated execution of an appropriate action. The two action rule procedure:

```
performMission()::Goal -> {}.
performMission() -> doNextStep; performMission().
```

captures the essence of this goal directed activity. ({} is the empty action.) This procedure would be executed by one thread within an agent whilst another concurrently executing thread is monitoring its environment, constantly updating the agent's beliefs about the environment; these beliefs being queried by *Goal*, and by *doNextStep*. performMission is a tail recursive procedure and will be executed as an iteration by the Go! engine.

Some missions – such as survival – do not have a termination goal but rather one or more continuation actions:

```
survive()::detectDanger(D) -> hideFrom(D);survive().
survive()::detectFood(F) -> eat(F); survive().
survive() -> wanderFor(safeTime()); survive().
```

The order of the rules prioritises avoiding danger. safeTime is a function that queries the belief store to determine a 'safe' period to wander, given current knowledge about the environment, before re-checking for danger. Again we assume the belief store is being concurrently manipulated by an environment monitoring thread within the agent. hideFrom(D) would typically cause the survival thread to suspend until the monitoring thread deletes those beliefs that made detectDanger(D) true.

Invoking Queries from Actions. The declarative part of a Go! program can be accessed from action rules in a number of ways:

- Any expression can invoke functions.
- An action rule guard – $(A_1,..,A_k)::Q$ – can augment the argument matching test with a query Q.
- If Q is a query, $\{Q\}$, indicating a single solution to Q, can appear as an 'action' in an action rule body.
- We can use a set expression $\{Trm \mid\mid Q\}$ to find all solutions to some query. This is Go!'s findall. Since Trm can involve defined functions, it can also be used to map a function over the set of solutions to Q.
- We can use Go!'s *forall* action. $(Q \mathbin{*>} A)$ iterates the action A over all solutions to query Q.
- We can use a conditional action. $(Q\ ?\ A_1\ \mid\ A_2)$ executes A_1 if Q succeeds, else A_2.

As an example of the use of *>:

```
(is_a_task(Task), \+ Icando(Task), cando(Ag,Task)
  *> request(Task) >> Ag)
```

might be used to send a 'request' message, for each task that the agent cannot itself do, to some agent it believes can do the task. \+ is Go!'s negation-as-failure operator.

2.3 Type Definitions and Type Inference

Go! is a strongly typed language; using a form of Hindley/Milner's type inference system [6]. For the most part it is not necessary for programers to associate types with variables or other expressions. However, all constructors and *unquoted* symbols are required to be introduced using type definitions. If an identifier is used as a function symbol in an expression it is assumed to refer to an 'evaluable' function unless it has been previously introduced in a type definition.

The pair of type definitions:

```
dance::= polka | jive | waltz | tango | quickstep | samba.
Desire::= toDance(dance,number) | barWhen(dance).
```

introduce two new types – an enumerated type dance, which has 6 literal values:

```
polka, jive, waltz, tango, quickstep, samba
```

and a Desire type that has a constructor functions toDance mapping a dance and a number into a Desire and barWhen mapping a dance.

Go! has primitives types such as symbol, string and number and the polymorphic recursive type list[T] - a list of elements of of type T of unbounded length. So:

```
[1,4,-8]
[('harry',23),('paul',12)]
```

are respectively of type list[number], list[(symbol,number)]. Notice that 'harry' and 'paul' are quoted. This is because Go! does not have a variable name convention like Prolog. Variable names can begin with upper or lower case letters. So, unless a symbol has been declared as a term of an enumerated type, such as dance, it must be quoted.

2.4 Dynamic Relations

In Prolog we can use assert and retract to change the definition of a dynamic relation whilst a program is executing. The most frequent use of this feature is to modify a definition comprising a sequence of unconditonal clauses. In Go!, such a dynamic relation is an object with updateable state. It is an instance of a polymorphic system class dynamic[T], T being the type of the argument of the dynamic relation. All Go! dynamic relations are unary, but the unary argument can be a tuple of terms.

The dynamic relations class has methods: add, for adding an argument term to the end of the current extension of the relation, del for removing the first argument term that unifies with a given term, delall for removing all argument terms unifying with a given term, mem, for accessing the instantiation of each current argument term that unifies with a given term, and finally ext for retrieving the current extension as a list of terms.

Creating a New Dynamic Relation. A dynamic relation object can be created and initialised using:

```
desire = $dynamic[Desire]([toDance(jive,2), toDance(waltz,1),
                    ...,barWhen(polka)])
```

`dynamic` takes two kinds of argument. The type of the argument terms to be stored, in this case `Desire`, and any initial extension given as a list of terms. This list could be empty. The above initialisation is equivalent to giving the following sequence of clauses for a Prolog dynamic relation:

```
desire(toDance(jive,2)).
desire(toDance(waltz,1)).
...
desire(barWhen(polka)).
```

Querying a Dynamic Relation. If we want to query such a dynamic relation we use the `mem` method as in:

```
desire.mem(todance(D,N)),N>2
```

Modifying a Dynamic Relation. To modify a dynamic relation we can use the `add`, and `del` action methods. For example:

```
desire.add(barWhen(quickstep))
```

and:

```
desire.del(toDance(jive,N));desire.add(toDance(jive,N-1))
```

The second is analogous to the following sequence of `Prolog` calls:

```
retract(desire(toDance(jive,N))),NewN is N-1,
assert(toDance(jive,NewN))
```

One difference is that we cannot backtrack on a `del` call to delete further matching facts. This is because it is an action, and all `Go!` actions are deterministic. A `del` call always succeeds, even if there is no matching term. The `delall` method deletes all unifying facts as a single action:

```
desire.delall(barWhen(_))
```

will delete all current `barWhen` desires. `delall` is the similar to `prolog`'s `retractall`.

2.5　Multi-threaded Applications and Data Sharing

It is often the case, in a multi-threaded `Go!` application, that we want the different threads to be able to share information. For example, in a multi-threaded agent we often want all the threads to be able to access the beliefs of the agent, and we want to allow some or all these threads to be able to update these beliefs.

We can represent the relations for which we will have changing information as dynamic relations. A *linda* a polymorphic subclass of the dynamic relations class has extra methods to facilitate the sharing of dynamic relations across threads. Instances if this subclass are created using initializations such as:

```
LinRel = $linda[type]([...])
```

For example, it has a **replace** method allowing the deleting and adding of a shared linda relation term to be executed atomically, and it has a **memw** relation method. A call:

```
LinRel.memw(Trm)
```

will suspend if no term unifying with **Trm** is currently contained in **LinRel** until such a term is added by *another thread*.

There is also a dual, **notw** such that:

```
LinRel.notw(Trm)
```

will suspend if a term unifying with **Trm** is currently contained in **LinRel** until all such terms are deleted by *other threads*. It also has a suspending delete method, **delw**.

memw and **delw** and the analogues of the Linda [10] **readw** and **inw** methods for manipulating a shared tuple store. There is no analogue of **notw** in Linda.

2.6   Theta Environments

In many ways, theta environments form the 'heart' of **Go!** programs: they are where most programs are actually defined; they are also the only place where new types may be defined. The scope of the type definition is the theta environment in which it appears.

A theta environment is of a set of definitions, each of which is either a

- A *Var=Expression* assignment definition
- A *Type::=TypeEpression* new type definition
- A *Type:>TypeEpression* renaming type definition
- A relation definition
- A function definition
- An action procedure definition
- A DCG grammar [14]
- A labeled theta environment - a class definition (see 2.7)
- A class rule - defining an inheritance relation (see 2.7)

grouped inside {} brackets. The rules and definitions are separated by the '.␣' operator[2].

---

[2] Where '.␣' means a period followed at least one whitespace character.

where *Expressions.* A common use of a theta environment is a *where* expression, which is an expression of the form:

Exp..ThetaEnvironment

The .. is read as *where*. *Exp* is evaluated relative to the definitions inside *ThetaEnvironment* which otherwise are local the environment.

where *Calls.* As well as expressions, calls can be evaluated relative to a theta environment. The call, whether relation or action call, is written:

Call..ThetaEnvironment

2.7   Classes and Objects

Classes in `Go!` are labeled theta environments, which we can view as labeled theories as in L&O [3][3]. The labels can contain variables, which are global to all the definitions of the theory. The label variables *must* be explicitly typed, by attaching a type annotation.

Class definitions also double as type definitions - the functor of the class label is implicilty defined as a new type name that can be used to characterise the type of the object instances of the class.

We can create an instance of a labeled theory by giving values to the global variables of the theory label. The instance is an object characterised by these global variable values - they define its *static state*. Different object instances of the theory will generally have different values for these global variables.

Two system classes, the dynamic relations class and the cell class, have instances with mutable state. A new labeled theory can contain variables bound to instances of these mutable state classes. If so, instances of the theory will be objects with *mutable state.*

Finally, inheritance can be used to define a new labeled theory. This is done using inheritance rules using the class labels.

The following set of definitions constitute a mini-theory of a person:

```
dateOfB :> (number,number,number).    -- type renaming def
sex::= male | female.                 -- new type def.
person(Nm:symbol,BrthDate:dateOfB,Sx:sex,Home:symbol){
    age()= _yearsBetween(time2date(now()),BrthDate).
    sex=Sx.
    name=Nm.
    lives(Home).
    _yearsBetween(....) => .....
}.
```

The label arguments Nm, Brthdate, Sx, Home are parameters to the theory which, when known, make it the theory of a specific person.

---

[3] We shall use the terms *labeled theory* and *class* interchangeably.

A person's age is computed by converting the difference between the current time returned by the primitive function **now**, converted to a date, and the person's date of birth. The conversion is done using a function __yearsBetween that is private to the theory. It is private since its name begins with __.

We can create two instances of the theory, i.e. two **person** objects, and query them as follows:

```
P1=$person('Bill',(1978,3,22),male,'London,England').
P2=$person('Jane',(1986,11,1),female,'Cardiff,Wales').

P1.name            -- returns name 'Bill' of P1
P2.age()            -- returns current age of P2
P2.lives(Place)   -- gives solution: Place='Cardiff,Wales'
```

Inheritance. The following is a labeled theory for a student. It inherits from the person theory.

```
student(Nm, BrthDate,Sx, Hm, _,_)<=person(Nm, BrthDate,Sx,Hm).
student(_, _,_,_,Cge,Sbj){
  lives(Pl):-location_of(Cge,Pl).
  lives(Pl):-super.person.lives(Pl).
  studies_at(Sbj,Cge).
}.
```

The separate **<=** rule says that this theory inherits from the **person** theory with overriding inheritance. This means that any attribute defined in student with the same name as a person attribute automatically replaces the inherited definition. In this case, there is only one relation, **lives**, which is so redefined but its new definition explicitly extends the definition of the **parent** super class by virtue of its second clause.

location_of is defined outside the **student** theory. It has a normal definition such as:

```
location_of('Imperial','London,England').
location_of('Caltec','Pasadena,CA').
...
```

We can create the *theory* of a specific student and query it as follows:

```
S=$student( 'mary',19,female,'Bath,England' ,'Imperial',
                                        'computing')
S.lives(Place)   -- has two answers:
                 -- Place='Bath,England', Place='London,England'
S.age()          -- returns 19
```

Te above two labeled theories can be viewed as a small ontology about the **person** and **student** concepts. The use of **Go!**'s for ontology construction and querying is further explored in [15].

2.8   Modules

A module is a *where* expression that evaluates to a single higher order value, or to a tuple of values, some of which are higher order. A module that contains the class definitions for person and student given earlier, which exports both definitions, has the form:

```
(person,student)..{
person(Nm,Age,Sx,Hm){...}.
student(...)<=person(...).
student(_,_,_,_,Cge,Sbj){...}
}
```

The following is a module that exports the relation ordered and the function reverse. The definition of the auxiliary relation ord and the auxiliary function rev are local to the theta environment and not visible outside. ordered and reverse iare themselves defined using *where* expressions.

```
(ordered,reverse) .. {
   ordered(list,less) :- ord(list) .. {
     ord([]).
     ord([_]).
     ord([E1,E2,..L]):- less(E1,E2),ord([E2,..L]).
   }.
   reverse(L) => rev(L,[])..{
     rev([],R) => R.
     rev([E,..L],R) => rev(L,[E,..R]).
   }
}.
```

Incidentally, ordered is a higher order polymorphic relation of type:

```
[T]-(list[T], (T,T){}){}
```

which says that for any T ([T]- inidicates the quantification), it is a binary relation (signaled by the postfix {}), taking as first argument a list of elements of type T (the type expression list(T)) , and as second argument a binary relation over elements of type T (the type expression (T,T){}).

2.9   Higher Order Values

The ordered relation is *parameterized* with respect to the ordering relation used to compare elements of the list. ordered is further defined in terms of the auxilliary relation ord, itself defined in a subsiduary *where* expression. This illustrates how *where* expressions may be used at many levels – not just the top-level of a program. Note that the less variable – which holds the ordering relation – is only mentioned where it is important: where it is introduced as a parameter of ordered and where it is used in ord. This is an example of variables having a somewhat extended scope compared to Prolog. In Prolog, to achieve the same effect, we would have had to 'pass down' the less relation through all the intermediate programs from the top-level to where it is needed; this is a significant source of irritation in Prolog programming.

A call to ordered must supply the list to be checked and an ordering relation. In many cases the ordering relation is given as the value of a variable with a higher order value[4]; however, it is also possible to use a lambda rule, or a disjunction of such rules, to give an on-the-fly definition of the relation. For example, the call:

```
ordered([(3,5),(3,8),(10,12),...],
       ( ((X1,_),(X2,_)):-X1=<X2  | ((X,Y1), (X,Y2)) :-Y1=<Y2 ) )
```

The relation argument is given as a disjunction of lambda relation rules that uses the standard =< relation to define an ordering on pairs of numbers.

Go! has lambda forms of all of its rule types: relation rules, function rules, action rules and grammar rules.

3   Multi-threaded Dancer Agents at a Ball

In our agents' ball, we have male and female dancer agents that are attempting to dance with each other and a band that 'plays' music for different kinds of dances. The two kinds of dancer agent are required to discover like-minded agents and to negotiate over possible dance engagements. In addition to dancing, dancer agents may have additional goals – such as getting refreshed at the bar. This scenario is a compact use case that demonstrates many of the aspects of building intelligent agents and of coordinating their activities.

Following a BDI model [9,16], each agent has a belief, a desire and an intention relation. The belief relation contains beliefs about what other dancers there currently are and what dances they like to do. The desire relation contains the goals each dancer would like to achieve, for example, which dances it would like to dance. The intention relation holds its current intentions – these normally represent the agent's commitments to perform some particular dance with some partner agent; however, it can also be an intention to go to the bar when a dance is announced.

The dancers use a directory server to discover one another. As each dancer agent 'arrives' at the dance in some random and phased order, it registers with the directory server. The dancers also subscribe in order to be informed about other dancers that are already 'at the dance', and those that will arrive later.

The internal execution architecture of each dancer agent comprises three threads – corresponding to the three key activities of the agent: a directory

---

[4] Note the contrast with Prolog. In Prolog a relation is passed as argument by passing in its name - which is an atom. Prolog's metal level call is then used to map the name to the value at run-time by accessing a run-time dictionary linking atom names with code values. In Go! the code value is passed, not the name. Moreover, its type is checked at compile time to make sure it is consistent with its intended use. In Prolog, a type inconsistency will generally result in a runtime error or failure.

server interface thread, a negotiations thread and an intention execution thread. The directory server interface interacts with the directory server to publish its own description and to subscribe for the descriptions of other dancer agents. The negotiations thread communicates with other dancer agents in order to agree joint intentions to dance the next dance of a particular kind. The intentions execution thread coordinates the actual dance activities and any 'drinking' activities. The architecture is depicted in figure below.

These threads communicate using the shared linda dynamic relations: belief, desire and intention. Note that while all the dancers could be executed in a single invocation of the Go! engine, they will *not* have direct access to each others' beliefs, desires and intentions. Furthermore, it is a simple task to distribute the progam across multiple invocations and machines, making each dancer a separate Go! process. The internal architecture of each agent is depicted in the figure above. The fat arrows indicate the internal agent communication through the shared dynamic relations, and the thin arrows indicate the external message communciation.

Agent architecture

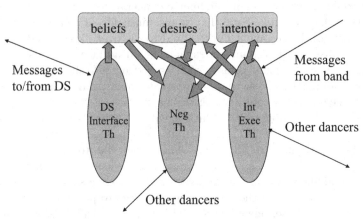

3.1   A Dancer's Intention Execution Thread

A dancer's intention execution thread handles the execution of intentions when they are triggered by dance announcements. We assume a band agent which sends an announcement message to every currently registered dancer when it starts, and when it later stops playing each dance 'number'.

The procedures for the intention execution threads of the male and female dancers are very similar with respect to how they 'listen' for announcements from the band. They differ in what happens when a dance is starting and there is an intention to do that dance. We present here only the male case – as the male dancer is expected to take the initiative during the dance[5].

---

[5] This symmetry is an aspect of the ballroom scenario; one that we would not expect for general agent systems.

```
maleIntention..{
... -- type defs
maleIntention(belief,desire,intention,band) ->
   ( starting(D) << band ->
     belief.replace(bandNotPlaying,bandPlaying(D));
     check_intents(D);
      maleIntention(belief,desire,intention,band)
   | stopping(D) << band ->
     belief.replace(bandPlaying(D),bandNotPlaying);
      maleIntention(belief,desire,intention,band)
   | ball_over << band -> belief.add(ballOver)
   ).
  check_intents(D)::intention.mem(toDanceWith(D,FNm)) ->
      intention.del(toDanceWith(D,FNm));
      maleDance(D,FNm)).
... }
```

The above is a module that exports the maleIntention action procedure. The procedure iterates 'listening' for messages; in this case messages from the band. It terminates when it receives a ball_over message.

When it receives a starting(D) message, and there is an intention to do that dance, the maleDance procedure is executed. The intended partner should similarly have called its corresponding femaleDance procedure and the interaction between the dance procedures of the two dancers is the joint dancing activity.

Notice that the maleIntention procedure reflects its environment by maintaining an appropriate belief regarding what the band is currently doing and when the ball is over. replace is an atomic update action on a linda dynamic relation.

3.2   A Dancer's Negotiation Thread

The procedures executed by the negotiation threads of our dancers are the most complex. They represent the rational and pro-active activity of the agent for they convert desires into new intentions using current beliefs and intentions. In contrast, the intentions execution and directory interface threads are essentially reactive activities.

A male dancer's negotiation thread must decide which uncommitted desire to try to convert into an intention, and, if this is to do some dance the next time it is announced, which female dancer to invite to do the dance. This may result in negotiation over which dance they will do together, for the female who is invited may have a higher priority desire. Remember that each dancer has a partial model of the other dancer in that it has beliefs that tell it the desires the other dancer registered with the directory server on arrival. But it does not know the priorities, or which have already been fully or partially satisfied.

The overall negotiation procedure is satisfyDesires:

```
satisfyDesires()::belief.mem(ballOver) -> {}.
satisfyDesires() ->
  {belief.memw(bandNotPlaying)}; -- wait until band not playing
  (chooseDesire(Des,FNm),\+ intention.mem(toDanceWith(D,_)),
     still_ok_to_negotiate()) *>
               negotiateOver(Des,FNm)); -- negotiation loop
  {belief.memw(bandPlaying(_))};
     -- wait, if need be, until band playing
  satisfyDesires().
still_ok_to_negotiate():-
  belief.mem(bandNotPlaying),\+ belief.mem(ballOver).
```

The `satisfyDesires` procedure terminates when there is a belief[6] that the band
has finished – a belief that will be added by the intentions execution thread when
it receives the message `ball_over`. If not, the first action of `satisfyDesires` is
the `memw` call. This is a query action to the `belief` relation that will suspend,
if need be, until `bandNotPlaying` is believed. For our dancers we only allow
negotiations when the band is not playing. This is not a mandatory aspect of all
scenarios – other situations may permit uninterrupted negotiations over desires.

There is then an attempt to convert into commitments to dance as many
unsatisfied desires as possible, before the band restarts or announces that the
ball is over. This is done by negotiating over each such desire with a female `FNm`
whom the male dancer believes shares the desire. When the negotiation *forall*
loop terminates, either because there are no more solutions to `chooseDesire`, or
the dancer no longer believes it is appropriate to continue negotiating, the action
procedure waits, if need be, until the dancer believes the band has restarted[7].
The possible wait is to ensure there is only one round of negotiation in each
dance interval. The next time the band stops playing, the answers returned by
`chooseDesire` will almost certainly be different because the beliefs, desires and
intentions of the dancer will have changed. (Other female dancers may have
arrived, and the dancer may have executed an intention during the last dance.)
Even if one of the answers is the same, a re-negotiation with the same female
may now have a different outcome because of changes in her mental state.

```
chooseDesire(toDance(D,N),FNm) :-
   uncmtdFeasibleDesire(toDance(D,N),FNm),
   (desire.mem(toDance(OthrD,OthrN)),OthrD\=D *> OthrN < N).
chooseDesire(toDance(D,N),FNm) :-
   uncmtdFeasibleDesire(toDance(D,N),FNm),
   \+ belief.mem(haveDanced(D,_)).
...
```

---

[6] All the procedures for this thread access the linda dynamic relations as global variables since the procedures will be defined in the environment where these relations
are introduced.

[7] The `bandPlaying` belief will be added by its intention execution thread. If the band
does not restart, the negotiation thread never resumes.

```
uncmtdDesire(toDance(D,N)):-
   desire.mem(toDance(D,N)), N>0,
   \+ intention.mem(toDanceWith(D,_)).
...
```

The above clauses are a partial definition of a `chooseDesire` that might be
used by one of the male dancers. The two given clauses both return a dance
desire only if it is currently uncommitted and feasible. It is an uncommitted
desire if it is still desired to perform the dance at least once, and there is not
a current intention to do that dance. (We allow a dancer to enter into at most
one joint commitment to do a particular type of dance since this is understood
as a commitment to do the dance with the identified partner the *next* time *that*
dance is announced.) It is feasible if the male believes some female still desires
to do that dance. The first rule selects a dance if, additionally, it is desired more
times than any other dance. The second selects a dance if it has not so far been
danced with *any* partner. Each male dancer can have a different `chooseDesire`
definition.

Below is a `negotiateOver` procedure for a simple male dancer negotiation
strategy that starts with a dance proposal:

```
negotiateOver(Dance(D,N),FNm) ->
  ngtOverDance(D,N,FNm,hdl('neg',FNm),[]).
ngtOverDance(D,N,FNm,FNgtTh,PrevDs) ->
  willYouDance(D) >> FNgtTh; -- invite female to dance D
  ( okDance(D) << FNgtTh ->   -- female has accepted
      desire.replace(toDance(D,N),toDance(D,N-1));
      intention.add(toDanceWith(D,FNm))
  | sorry << FNgtTh -> {}  -- female has declined
  | willYouDance(D2)::uncmtdDesire(toDance(D2,N2))) << FNgtTh ->
      -- a counter-proposal to dance D2 accepted since uncom. des.
      intention.add(toDanceWith(D2,FNm));
      desire.replace(toDance(D2,N2),toDance(D2,N2-1));
      okDance(D2) >> FNgtTh
  | willYouDance(D2) << FNgtTh ->
      -- to dance D2 not an uncom. des., must counter-propose
      counterP(FNm,FNgtTh,[D,D2,..PrevDs])
  | barWhen(D2)::uncmtdDesire(BarWhen(D2)) << FNgtTh ->
      -- a counter-proposal to go to the bar D2 accepted
      intention.add(toBarWhen(D2,FNm));
      desire.del(BarWhen(D2));
      okBar(D2) >> FNgtTh
  | barWhen(D2) << FNgtTh ->
      -- to go to the bar when D2 not an uncom. des., counter-propose
      counterP(FNm,FNgtTh,[D,D2,..PrevDs])
  ).
counterP(FNm,FNgtTh,PrevDs)::
  (chooseDesire(toDance(D,N),FNm),\+(D in PrevDs))->
    -- continue with a proposal to do a new dance
  ngtOverDance(D,N,FNm,FNgtTh,PrevDs).
```

```
counterP(_,FNgtTh,_) -> -- terminate the negotiation
    sorry >> FNgtTh)).
```

The negotiation is with the negotiation thread, hdl('neg',FNm), in the female dancer with name FNm.

The negotiation to fulfill a dance desire with a named female starts with the male sending a willYouDance(D) message to her negotiation thread. There are four possible responses: an okDance(D) accepting the invitation, a sorry message declining, or a counter proposal to do another dance, or to go to the bar when some dance is played. A counter proposal is accepted if it is currently an uncommitted desire. Otherwise, the counterP procedure is called to suggest an alternative dance. This calls chooseDesire to try find another feasible dance D for female FNm, different from all previous dances already mentioned in this negotiation (the PrevDs argument). If this succeeds, the dance negotiation procedure is re-called with D as the new dance to propose. If not, a sorry message is sent and the negotiation with this female ends. Each negotiation could be spawned as a new thread providing we use another dynamic relation to keep track of the current desire being considered in each negotiation to ensure they do not result in conflicting commitments.

3.3   The Male Dancer Agent

Below we give the overall structure of the male dancer class definition. It uses modules defining the maleIntention and DSinterface procedures and it spawns them as separate threads.

```
maleDancer(MyNm,MyDesires,DS,band){
  .. -- type defs
  belief=$linda[Belief]([]).
  desire=$linda[Desire]([]).
  intention=$linda[Intention]([]).
  init() ->
    (Des on MyDesires *> desire.add(Des));
    spawn DSinterface(MyNm,male,belief,MyDesires,DS);
    spawn maleIntention(belief,desire,intention,band)
                        as hdl('exec',MyNm);
    spawn satisfyDesires() as hdl('neg',MyNm);
    waitfor(hdl('exec',MyNm)).
  .. -- defs of satisfyDesires etc
}
```

The init method of this class is the one called to activate an instance of the class: $maleDancer(MyNm,MyDesires,DS,band).init(). If we launch several dancers inside one Go! process this call would be spawned as a new thread.

An instance is specified by four parameters: a unique symbol name MyNm of the dancer agent, such as 'bill l. smith', a list MyDsires of its initial desires such as [toDance(jive,2),barWhen(polka),..], and the handles DS, band of the directory server and band agent of the ball it is to attend. Each instance will have its own three linda dynamic relations encoding the dynamic state of the dancer.

The `init` action method adds each desire of `MyDesires` parameter to the dancer's `desire` linda relation. It then `spawns` the directory server interface, the intention execution and the negotiation threads for the dancer. The latter are assigned standard handle identities based on the agents symbol name. The `init` procedure then waits for the intention execution thread to terminate (when the ball is over). Termination of `init` terminates the other two spawned threads.

The negotiation thread executes concurrently with the other two threads. The directory interface thread will be adding beliefs about other agents to the shared `belief` relation as it receives `inform` messages from the directory server, and the execute intentions thread will be concurrently accessing and updating all three shared relations.

The female dancer is similar to the male dancer; we assume that the female never takes the initiative. The female negotiation thread must wait for an initial proposal from a male but thereafter it can make counter proposals. It might immediately counter propose a different dance or to go to the bar, depending on its current desires and commitments.

4   Related Work

4.1   Other Logic Based Programming Languages

Qu-Prolog [17], BinProlog [18], CIAO Prolog [19], SICStus-MT Prolog [20], IC-Prolog II [2] are all multi-threaded Prolog systems. The closest to Go! are Qu-Prolog and IC-Prolog II.

Threads in Qu-Prolog communicate using messages or via the dynamic data base. As in Go!, threads can suspend waiting for another thread to update some dynamic relation. Threads in IC-Prolog II communicate either using unidirectional pipes, shared data base, or mailboxes. Mailboxes must be used for communication between threads in different invocations of IC-Prolog II. IC-Prolog also supports the L&O class notation [3]. Neither language has higher order features or type checking support, and all threads in the same invocation share the same global dynamic data base. In Go!, a dynamic relation is the value of a variable. Only threads whose procedures access the variable as a global variable, or which are explicitly given access to the dynamic relation as a call argument or in a message, can access it.

SICStus-MT [20] Prolog threads also each have a single message buffer, and threads can scan the buffer looking for a message of a certain form. But this buffered communication only applies to communication between threads in the same Prolog invocation. Threads running on different hosts must use lower level TCP/IP communication primitives.

Mozart/Oz [21] is a higher order, untyped, concurrent constraint language with logic, functional and object oriented programming components. Threads are explicitly forked and can communicate either via shared variable bindings in the constraint store, which acts as a shared memory, or ports which are multiple writer/single reader communication channels similar to Go! message queues. Threads in different hosts can communicate using public names for ports, which ascii strings called tickets. Tickets can be used to share any data value across a network.

In BinProlog [18], threads in the same invocation communicate through the use of Linda tuple spaces [10] acting as shared information managers. BinProlog also supports the migration of threads, with the state of execution remembered and moved with the thread[8]. The CIAO Prolog system [19] uses just the global dynamic Prolog database for communicating between thread's in the same process. Through front end compilers, the system also supports functional syntax and modules.

Mercury [22] is a pure logic programming language with polymorphic types and modes. The modes are used to aid efficient compilation. It is not multi-threaded.

Escher [23], and Curry [24] are both hybrid logic/functional programming languages with types, the latter with type inference similar to Go!. They differ from Go! in using lazy evaluation of functions and Curry uses narrowing - function evaluations can instantiate variables in the calls. Escher has a proposed [25] explicit fork primitive ensemble that forks a set of threads. The threads communicate via a shared global blackboard that contains mutable variables has well as I/O channels and files. Curry also has concurrent execution and its threads can communicate as in concurrent logic programming via incremental binding of shared variables, or via Oz style ports.

Concurrent MetateM [26] is based on temporal logic. Each agent executes a program comprising a set rules with preconditions that refer to past or current events. The rules specify future events that may or must occur, that are in the control of the agent. A broadcast communication to all other agents is one such event. Receipt of a message of a certain form is a possible current or past event. The agent uses the rules to determine its behaviour by endeavoring to make the description of the future implied by the rules and events come true.

Dali [27] is an extension of Prolog which has reactive rules as well as normal clauses. It is untyped and not explicitly multi-threaded. The reactive rules define how a Dali agent reacts to external and internal events. The arrival of a message sent by another agent is an external event, as is a signal, such as alarm_clock_ring, sent by the environment. An internal event is a goal G that can be inferred from the history of past events. Internal events are generated as a result of the agent automatically attempting to prove certain goals at a frequency that can be specified by *try G* ... statements. The periodic retrying of these goals gives the agent implicit multi-threading. In that a Dali program determines future actions based on the history of past events it is similar to Concurrent MetateM [26].

---

[8] A Go! thread executing a recursive procedure can also be migrated by sending a closure containing a 'continuation' call to this procedure in a message. The recipient then spawns the closure allowing the threads computation to continue in a new location. The original thread can even continue executing, allowing cloning.

4.2   Logic and Action Agent Languages

Vip [28], AgentSpeak(L) [29], 3APL [30], Minerva [31] and ConGolog [32] are all proposals for higher level agent programming languages with declarative and action components. We are currently investigating whether the implied architectures of some of these languages can be readily realised in Go!. Vip and 3APL have internal agent concurrency.

These languages typically have plan libraries indexed by desire or event descriptors with belief pre-conditions of applicability. Such a plan library can be encoded in Go! as a set of `planFor` and `reactTo` action rules of the form:

```
planFor(Desire)::beliefCond -> Actions
reactTo(Event)::beliefCond -> Actions
```

The actions can include updates of the belief store, or the generation of new desires whose fulfillment will complete the plan. Calls to `planFor` or `reactTo` can be spawned as new threads, allowing concurrent execution of plans.

5   Conclusions

Go! is a multi-paradigm programming language – with a strong logic programming aspect – that has been designed to make it easier to build intelligent agents while still meeting strict software engineering best practice. There are many important software engineering features of the language that we have not had the space to explore – for example the I/O model, permission and resource constrained execution and the techniques for linking modules together in a safe and scalable fashion. We have also omitted any discussion of how Go! applications are distributed and of how Go! programs interoperate with standard technologies such as DAML, SOAP and so on. Some of these topics are covered in [8].

The ballroom scenario is an interesting use case for multi-agent programming. Although the agents are quite simple, it encompasses key *behavioural* features of agents: autonomy, adaptability and responsibility. Our implementation features inter-agent communication and co-ordination via messages, multi-threaded agents, intra-agent communication and co-ordination via shared memory stores. We believe these features, which are so easily implemented in Go!, are firm foundations on which to explore the development of much more sophisticated deliberative multi-threaded agents.

Acknowledgments

The first named author wishes to thank Fujitsu Labs of America for a research contract that supported the collaboration between the authors on the design of Go! and the writing of this paper.

References

1. McCabe, F., Clark, K.: April - Agent PRocess Interaction Language. In Jennings, N., Wooldridge, M., eds.: Intelligent Agents, LNAI, 890. Springer-Verlag (1995) 324–340

2. Chu, D., Clark, K.L.: IC-Prolog II: a multi-threaded Prolog system. In Succi, G., Colla, G., eds.: Proceedings of the ICLP'93 Workshop on Concurrent & Parallel Implementations of Logic Programming Systems. (1993) 115–141

3. McCabe, F.: L&O: Logic and Objects. Prentice-Hall International (1992)

4. Haugeneder, H., Steiner, D.: Co-operative agents: Concepts and applications. In Jennings, N.R., Wooldridge, M.J., eds.: Agent Technology, Springer-Verlag (1998) 175–202

5. Willmott, S.N., Dale, J., Burg, B., Charlton, C., O'Brien, P.: Agentcities: A World-wide Open Agent Network. Agentlink News (2001) 13–15

6. Milner, R.: A theory of type polymorphism in programming. Computer and System Sciences **17** (1978) 348–375

7. Minsky, M.: A framework for representing knowledge. In Winston, P., ed.: Psychology of Computer Vision. MIT Press (1975) 211–277

8. Clark, K., McCabe, F.: Go! – a multi-paradigm programming language for implementing multi-threaded agents. Annals of Mathematics and Artificial Intelligence (2004, to appear)

9. Bratman, M.E., Israel, D.J., Pollack, M.E.: Plans and resource bounded practical reasoning. Computational Intelligence **4** (1988) 349–355

10. Carriero, N., Gelernter, D.: Linda in context. Communications of the ACM **32** (1989) 444–458

11. Omicini, A., Zambonelli, F.: Coordination for internet application development. Autonomous Agents and Multi-agent systems **2** (1999) 251–269

12. Finin, T., Fritzson, R., McKay, D., McEntire, R.: KQML as an agent communication language. In: Proceedings 3rd International Conference on Information and Knowledge Management. (1994)

13. Armstrong, J., Virding, R., Williams, M.: Concurrent Programming in Erlang. Prentice-Hall International (1993)

14. Pereira, F., Warren, D.H.: Definite clause grammars compared with augmented transition network. Artificial Intelligence **13** (1980) 231–278

15. Clark, K., McCabe, F.: Ontology representation and inference in Go! Technical report, Dept. of Computing, Imperial College, London (2003)

16. Roa, A.S., Georgeff, M.P.: An abstract architecture for rational agents. In: Proceedings of Knowledge Representation and Reasoning (KR&R92). (1992) 349–349

17. Clark, K.L., Robinson, P.J., Hagen, R.: Multi-threading and message communication in Qu-Prolog. Theory and Practice of Logic Programming **1** (2001) 283–301

18. Tarau, P., Dahl, V.: Mobile Threads through First Order Continuations. In: Proceedings of APPAI-GULP-PRODE'98, Coruna, Spain (1998)

19. Carro, M., Hermenegildo, M.: Concurrency in Prolog using Threads and a Shared Database. In Schreye, D.D., ed.: Proceedings of ICLP99, MIT Press (1999) 320–334

20. Eskilson, J., Carlsson, M.: Sicstus MT - a multithreaded execution environment for SICStus Prolog. In Catuscia Palamidessi, Hugh Glaser, K.M., ed.: Principles of Declarative Programming. LNCS 1490. Springer-Verlag (1998) 36–53

21. Van Roy, P., Haridi, S.: Mozart: A programming system for agent applications. In: International Workshop on Distributed and Internet Programming with Logic and Constraint Languages, `http://www.mozart-oz.org/papers/abstracts/diplcl99.html` (1999) Part of International Conference on Logic Programming (ICLP 99).

22. Zoltan Somogyi, F.H., Conway, T.: Mercury: an efficient purely declarative logic programming language. In: Proceedings of the Australian Computer Science Conference. (1995) 499–512

23. LLoyd, J.W.: Programming in an integrated functional and logic programming language. Journal of Functional and Logic Programming (1999) 1–49
24. Hanus, M.: A unified computation model for functional and logic programming. In: Proc. 24st ACM Symposium on Principles of Programming Languages (POPL'97). (1997) 80–93
25. Lloyd, J.: Interaction and concurrency in a declarative programming language. Unpublished report, Dept. of Computer Science, Bristol University, London (1988)
26. Fisher, M.: A survey of concurrent MetateM- the language and its applications. In Gabbay, D., Ohlbach, H., eds.: Temporal Logic, Springer-Verlag, LNAI, Vol 827 (1994) 480–505
27. Constantini, S., Tocchio, A.: A logic programming language for multi-agent systems. In: Proc. JELIA02 - 8th European Conf. on Logics in AI, Springer-Verlag, LNAI, Vol 2424 (2002) 1–13
28. Kinny, D.: VIP:A visual programming language for plan execution systems. In: 1st International Joint Conf. Autonomous Agents and Multi-agent Systems, ACM Press (2002) 721–728
29. Roa, A.S.: AgentSpeak(L): BDI agents speak out in a logical computable language. In: Agents Breaking Away. LNAI 1038, Springer-Verlag (1996) 42–55
30. Hindriks, K.V., de Boer, F.S., van der Hoek, W., Meyer, J.J.C.: Formal semantics for an abstract agent programming language. In Singh, Rao, Wooldridge, eds.: Intelligent Agents IV. LNAI. Springer-Verlag (1997) 215–230
31. Leite, J.A., Alferes, J.J., Pereira, L.M.: Minerva-A dynamic logic prorgamming agent architecture. In: Intelligent Agents VIII, LNAI 2333. (2001) 141–157
32. De Giacomo, G., Lesperance, Y., Levesque, H.: Congolog, a concurrent programming language based on the situation calculus. Artificial Intelligence $1–2$ (2000) 109–169

An Agent-Based Domain Specific Framework for Rapid Prototyping of Applications in Evolutionary Biology

Tran Cao Son[1], Enrico Pontelli[1], Desh Ranjan[1],
Brook Milligan[2], and Gopal Gupta[3]

[1] Department of Computer Science
New Mexico State University
{tson,epontell,dranjan}@cs.nmsu.edu
[2] Department of Biology
New Mexico State University
brook@biology.nmsu.edu
[3] Department of Computer Science
University of Texas at Dallas
gupta@utdallas.edu

Abstract. In this paper we present a brief overview of the ΦLOG project, aimed at the development of a domain specific framework for the rapid prototyping of applications in evolutionary biology. This includes the development of a domain specific language, called ΦLOG, and an agent-based implementation for the monitoring and execution of ΦLOG's programs. A ΦLOG program – representing an intended application from an evolutionary biologist – is a specification of *what to do* to achieve her/his goal. The execution and monitoring component of our system will automatically figure out *how to do* it. We achieve that by viewing the available bioinformatic tools and data repositories as *web services* and casting the problem of execution of a sequence of bioinformatic services (possibly with loops, branches, and conditionals, specified by biologists) as the web services composition problem.

1 Introduction and Motivation

In many fields of science, data is accumulating much faster than our ability to convert it into meaningful knowledge. This is perhaps nowhere more true than in the *biological sciences* where the Human Genome Project and related activities have flooded our databases with molecular data. The size of the DNA sequence database (e.g., at NCBI), for example, has surpassed 15 million sequences and 17 billion nucleotides, and is growing rapidly. Our modeling tools are woefully inadequate for the task of integrating all that information into the rest of biology, preventing scientists to effectively take advantage of these data in drawing meaningful biological inferences. Thus, one of the major challenges faced by computer scientists and biologists *together* is the enhancement of information

J. Leite et al. (Eds.): DALT 2003, LNAI 2990, pp. 76–96, 2004.

technology suitable for modeling a diversity of biological relationships and processes, leading to a greater *understanding* from the influx of data. Instead of allowing the direct expression of high-level concepts natural to a scientific discipline, current software development techniques require mastery of computer science and access to very low level aspects of software development in order to construct significantly complex applications. Even in places where attempts to introduce domain-specific concepts have been made – e.g., design of database formats – scientists are hampered in their efforts by complex issues of interoperation. As a result, currently only biologists with strong quantitative skills and high computer literacy can realistically be expected to undertake the task of transforming the massive amounts of available data into real knowledge. Very few scientists (domain experts) have such computing skills; even if they do, their skills are better utilized in dealing with high-level scientific models than low-level programming issues. To enable scientists to effectively use computers, we need a well-developed methodology, that allows a domain expert (e.g., a biologist) to solve a problem on a computer by developing and programming solutions at the same level of abstraction they are used to think and reason, thus moving the task of programming from software professionals to the domain experts, the end-users of information technology. This approach to software engineering is commonly referred to as *Domain Specific Languages* and it has been advocated by many researchers over the years [1]. The relevance of domain-specific approaches to bioinformatics has been underlined by many recent proposals (both in computer science as well as in biology) [2,3,4,5,6]. Domain-specific languages like ΦLOG offer biologists with work-benches for the rapid exploration of ideas and experiments, without the burden of low-level coding of data and processes and interoperation between existing software tools.

In this project we investigate the *design*, *development*, and *application* of a *Domain Specific Language (DSL)*, called ΦLOG, for rapid prototyping of bioinformatic applications in the area of phylogenetic inference and evolutionary biology. Phylogenetic inference involves study of evolutionary change of traits (genomic sequences, morphology, physiology, behavior, etc.) in the context of biological entities (genes, individuals, species, higher taxa, etc.) related to each other by a phylogenetic tree or genealogy depicting the set of common ancestors. It finds important applications in areas such as study of ecology and dynamics of viruses. To be attractive to biologists, an effective DSL should provide:

(1) descriptions of the concepts and operations naturally associated with biology (e.g., data sources, types of data, transformations of the data),
(2) mechanisms allowing users to manipulate those concepts in a compact, intuitive manner at a high level of abstraction,
(3) models specialized enough to reflect the real biological processes of interest, and
(4) efficient execution mechanisms that do not require extensive intervention and programming by the end user.

Furthermore, a large class of biological models integrates information on relationships among organisms, homology of traits, and specifications of evolutionary change in traits; this commonality can be used to advantage in designing the structure of domain-specific representations and transformations of biological data. Information technology based on the major commonality evident in problems explicitly involving relationships, homology, and trait evolution can readily be expanded to incorporate a much broader range of biological models. To date no software development environment or methodology available to biologists has identified all of these elements and explicitly designed uniform solutions incorporating them. Instead, there exist a large array of mostly ad hoc technologies. Existing tools provide monolithic interfaces (rather than libraries encapsulating the basic computational elements from which larger constructions can be built) and a black box structure, that does not provide access to the underline mechanisms and heuristics [7] used to solve biological problems.

ΦLOG is part of a comprehensive computational framework, based on agent technology, capable of harnessing local, national, and international data repositories and computational resources to make the required modeling activities feasible. Solving a typical problem in phylogenetic inference requires the use of a number of different bioinformatic tools, the execution of a number of manual steps (e.g., judging which sequence alignment for two genes is the "best"), and extra low-level coding to glue everything together (e.g., low-level scripting). An important characteristic of the ΦLOG framework is its ability to *interoperate* with the existing biological databases and bioinformatic tools commonly used in phylogenetic processing, e.g., CLUSTAL W, BLAST, PHYLIP, PAUP. These existing tools and data repositories are treated as *semantic Web services*, automatically accessed by ΦLOG to develop the solution requested by the domain expert. From a semantic point of view, these existing components are regarded as semantic algebras [8], used for defining the valuation predicates in the denotational specification of the DSL. Thus, ΦLOG provides a uniform language through which biologists can perform complex computations (involving one or more of these software systems) without much effort. In absence of such a DSL, biologists are required to perform significant manual efforts (e.g., locating and accessing tools, determine adequate input/output data formats) and to write considerable amount of glue code.

The execution model of ΦLOG is built on an agent infrastructure, capable of transparently determining the bioinformatic services needed to solve the problem and the data transformations that are required to seamlessly stream the data between such components during the execution of a ΦLOG program. Bioinformatic services are viewed as actions in situation calculus, and the problem of deriving a correct sequence of service invocations is reduced to the problem of deriving a successful plan. The agent infrastructure relies on a *service broker* for the discovery of bioinformatic services, and each agent makes use of logic-based planner for composition and monitoring of services. The framework implements typical agents' behaviors, including planning, interaction, and interoperation.

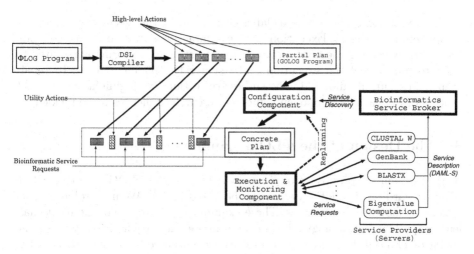

Fig. 1. System Organization

2   The ΦLOG System

ΦLOG is based on a comprehensive agent-based platform, illustrated in Figure 1.

The higher level is represented by the ΦLOG language, a DSL specifically designed for evolutionary biologists – described in Section 3.

The execution of each ΦLOG program is supported by a *DSL compiler* – described in Section 4 – and an *Execution Agent* – described in Section 5. The execution agent is, in turn, composed of a *configuration component* and an *execution/monitoring component*. In this framework, bioinformatic services are viewed as *actions*, and execution of ΦLOG programs as an instance of the planning problem. The compiler translates each ΦLOG program into a *partial plan* – specifically a GOLOG program [9]; this describes the steps required to execute the ΦLOG program in terms of high-level actions and their sequencing. The plan is considered partial for various reasons:

(i) each high-level action has to be resolved into invocation of actual bioinformatic software tools and data sources;
(ii) interaction between successive steps in the plan may require the introduction of intermediate low-level actions (e.g., interoperation between existing tools).

The actual execution requires transformation of the partial plan into a *concrete plan* – whose (low-level) actions are actual accesses to the data repositories and execution of bioinformatic tools. This transformation is accomplished by the configuration component of the agent, via a planning process. This planning process is performed in cooperation with a *service broker*, which supplies description and location of the existing data sources and software tools. The configuration agent makes use of these services descriptions to develop the action theory needed to generate the concrete plan.

The execution of the concrete plan is carried out by the execution/monitoring component of the agent. Execution involves contacting data sources and software tools and requesting the appropriate execution steps. Monitoring is required to validate progress of the execution and re-enter the planning phase to repair eventual execution failures. In the successive sections we highlight the relevant aspects of the various components and the research challenges to be tackled.

3   The Design of the *Φ*LOG Language

In this section we propose a preliminary design of the *Φ*LOG language. More details regarding this initial design can be found in [10]. We use problems from biology as motivating examples. These examples relate to one of the most challenging problems in biology: that of determining the evolution of species. The evolution of a set of species can naturally be represented by an *evolutionary tree* with leaf nodes representing sampled species, interior nodes representing ancestors, and edges representing the ancestor-descendant relationship in the usual fashion. Given a set of related species there is a multitude of possibilities as to how they evolved. The goal is to use the biological data to determine the most likely evolutionary history. One way to determine how a set of related species evolved is based on modeling DNA sequence data using a stochastic model of evolutionary change [7]. The evolutionary tree that "best" fits this model and data is adopted as the most likely evolutionary history. The starting point of this process is represented by the collection of similar DNA sequences for the set of species of interest from the huge set of DNA sequence data that is stored in databases like GSDB and GenBank. In its simplest form, both the set of taxa and the set of genes are completely specified, and the task is simply to determine occurrences (i.e., sequences) of the genes in the taxa. Matching sequences are determined by comparing the given genes with the sequences belonging to each taxon, and applying a set of filtering criteria. This result is typically constructed by iterating (manually or using ad-hoc scripts) the application of *similarity* search programs – e.g., the *Basic Local Alignment Search Tool (BLAST)* – using the provided genes as input and (manually) filtering the output with respect to the taxa of interest. During each iteration one of the genes is used to detect reasonable matches against a sequence database. The resulting matches have to be filtered to extract only matches relative to the taxa of interest and to remove false matches.

The successive step is to find the most likely evolutionary tree for a given set of species from the given DNA sequence data and a model of evolution [7]. The current methodology to solve this problem is to:

(i) align the input sequences – sequence alignment can be performed using a standard tool for multiple sequence alignment, such as CLUSTAL W – and

(ii) use the aligned sequences and the given model(s) to generate and rank possible phylogenetic trees for the sequences, using tools such as PHYLIP and PAUP.

In this approach, users are responsible for proper pipelined execution of all the components (including data format translation, if needed). Furthermore, most tree building software uses a very limited set of evolutionary models, and existing software considers only limited parameter optimizations for parametric models [7].

3.1 Preliminary DSL

In this section we provide a brief overview of the ΦLOG language. Rather than providing a comprehensive definition of the language, we will introduce the concepts and elements of the language through examples. We appeal to the users for the intuitive meaning of the keywords used in this section. For a more complete description, the interested reader is referred to [10]. In what follows, sample codes of ΦLOG are written in verbatim font.

Overall Program Structure. ΦLOG programs consist of modules. Each module contains a collection of global declarations and a collection of procedures. In turn, each procedure contains a sequence of declarations and a sequence of instructions. The declaration part of each procedure is used to

- (i) describe the data items used by the procedure,
- (ii) allow user selection of the computational components to be used during execution; and
- (iii) provide parameters affecting the behavior of the different components.

Data items used in the program must be declared. Declarations are used to explicitly describe data items, by providing a name (<item name>), a description of the nature of the values that are going to be stored in it (<item type>) and eventual properties of the item. Formally, a declaration is written as

<item name> : <item type>

For example, the expression

gene1 : Gene (gi | 557882)

declares an entity called gene1, of type Gene, and identifies the initial value for this object – the gene which has GI number 557882 in the GenBank database.

Declarations are also used to identify computational components to be used during the execution – which allows the user to customize some of the operations performed. For example, the declaration

```
similar: operation (BLASTX -- alignment=ungapped
                    database=drosophila matrix=BLOSUM45)
```

allows the user to explicitly configure the behavior of the language operation similar – by associating this operation with the BLAST similarity search program.

Data Types. The design of the collection of data types of ΦLOG has been driven by observing the commonalities present between various languages for biological data description proposed in the literature (e.g., BSML and NEXUS [2]). ΦLOG provides two classes of data types that can be used to create data items. The first class includes generic (non-domain specific) data types, while the second class provides a number of *Domain Specific Data Types*, which are relevant for the specific domain. E.g.,

- `Sequence, Gene, and Taxon`: These data types are used to describe molecular sequence data (e.g., DNA, RNA), Genes, and Taxons (e.g., species along with their traits). The sequence data type allows users to describe the sequence in different ways, e.g., by providing its description in the standard formats. Using the FASTA format one could describe a sequence as follows:

  > g : Sequence (protein)
  > g is FOSB_HUMAN P53539 homo sapiens (HUMAN).
  >   MFQAFPGDYDSGSRCSSSSPSAESQYLSSVDSFGPPT...

  Transformation between the different formats is transparent. Each object of type `Gene` and `Taxon` is characterized by a number of (optional and mandatory) attributes, including name, accession number, GI number, and sequence data [2]. The actual set of attributes depends on the detail of the description provided by the user and/or on the existing attributes present in the gene database used. For example:

  > g1 : Gene is (gi | 557882)
  > se is sequence(g1)

  assigns to the item `g1` the gene having GI number `gi|557882` and extracts its sequence data, which is stored in the item `se`. The `Taxon` data type is polymorphic in the sense that items of type `Taxon` can be used to represent higher-order taxa as well, which are interpreted in the language as (hierarchically organized) sets of taxa.

- `Model`: A model data type is used to describe models of evolution, used to perform inference of phylogenies [7]. In the simple case, a model is a matrix containing the individual evolutionary rates:

  > t : Model is ({A → (0.1)C, A → (0.04)T, ···}).

  ΦLOG allows symbolic description of models [10] and access to standard models [7], e.g., `t1 is K80(kappa)`.

ΦLOG also provides a number of polymorphic data types which are used to aggregate in different ways collection of entities. ΦLOG allows operations on `Trees` (described using Newick format) and `Sets`. In particular, various externally accessible sources of information are mapped in the DSL as sets of elements. For example, external databases, e.g., GenBank, can be accessed in the language using traditional set operations, e.g.,

> {name(x) | x: Gene, x in GenBank}

In ΦLOG a `Map` represents a function which maps elements of a domain into elements of another domain. The mapping can be specified either as an enumeration of pairs or using an intensional definition – i.e., the mapping is described via properties. For example,

```
match ( tax : Taxon, x : Gene ) : Map
    ( S is { y : Sequence | y in genes(tax),
                            score(similar(x,y)) > threshold }
      if S is empty
        then match is undefined
        else match is (any y in S) )
```

defines a `Map`, named `match`, which is a function. In this example, we have a function which maps a taxon and a gene to a sequence. More precisely, given a taxon `tax` and a gene `x`, `match` returns a sequence of a gene which is sufficiently similar to `x`. In the above code, the first line declares that `match` is a function (i.e., of the type `Map`) with two input parameters; the rest specifies how the function is computed. First, a set `S` of sequences which are sufficiently similar to `x` is computed. If this set is empty then `match` is undefined (the 'then' clause); otherwise, it is defined as an arbitrary sequence in `S` (the 'else' clause). In computing `S`, the `similar` operation is expected to return a data item measuring the similarity of the two sequences; in this example we expect an attribute called `score` to be present.

Maps can be used in various ways – in the previous example, if `Ta` is a set of taxa, then `match(Ta,seq)` is a set of sequences (constructed according to the map definition), while an expression such as `select X (seq1 is match(X,seq2))` searches for a taxon `X` containing the sequence `seq1` which is similar to sequence `seq2`. Other polymorphic types include the ability to describe probability distributions and homologies [10].

Control Structures. The language provides two levels of control constructs. At the higher level, control of the execution is expressed using declarative constructs, such as function applications and quantifications. Existential quantification (`select`) is used to express search tasks, while universal quantification (`forall`) can be used to express iterations and global properties. In this respect, the structure of the language closely resembles the structure of many functional languages. For example, the code

```
select a in Trees
    forall b in Trees
    likelihood(a,model) ≥ likelihood(b,model)
```

selects a tree `a` from the collection of trees `Trees` that has the maximum likelihood.

At the lower level, the language provides control constructs which are closer to those in traditional programming languages, such as `if-then-else` conditional statements and `repeat` iterative constructs. These are mostly used by users who want to customize the basic operations of the language (as described in the

following example). The previous example can be rewritten as (best, t are of
type Tree)

```
best in Trees
repeat  (t in Trees)
        if    (likelihood(t,model)>likelihood(best,model))
              then best is t
```

The first statement selects as initial value for best an arbitrary element of Trees,
and the loop performs an iteration for each element in Trees. The language
provides also the capability of asserting constraints on the computation. These
constraints are assertions that have to be satisfied at any point during the computation. Constraints are asserted using the constraint statement. E.g., if we
want the computation to generate a tree t whose root has only two children,
with branch lengths 10 and 20, then we can use the statement

```
constraint : t is (X : label1 , Y : label2)Z and
             label1 is 10 and label2 is 20
```

The execution model adopted by the language provides the user with both batch
and interactive execution. Under batch mode, programs are compiled and completely executed. Under interactive mode, programs are executed incrementally
under user supervision. The user is allowed to select breakpoints in the execution, run the program statement by statement, and modify *both the data and the
program* on the fly. For example, the user is allowed to introduce new constraints
during the execution, thus modifying on the fly the behavior of the computation.
Another feature that ΦLOG provides is the ability to make data items *persistent*,
allowing users to create with no extra effort databases containing the results of
the computations, and to share partial results.

3.2   Some Examples Coded in ΦLOG

Let us start by looking at how we can express the problem of, given a collection
of taxa and a collection of genes, determining in which taxa those genes occur.
Both the set of taxa and the set of genes can be either explicitly provided by the
user or the result of some computation. Regarding the selection of taxa, we need
to determine a set of taxa of interest, eventually involving higher-order taxa.
This set could be the result of some computation, e.g., to select 40 taxa out of
a given higher-order taxon:

```
Tax is {y : Taxon | y in murinae} and |Tax|=40
```
or, given a collection of higher-order taxa (InputSet), select a taxon from each
of them:

```
Tax is union ( x in InputSet , t is (any in x) ).
```
Regarding the selection of the genes of interest, this can be either a user defined
collection of genes or it could be itself the result of some computation. E.g., to
select all genes from a given set of taxa (T) which contain a certain name:

```
Gen is {x : Gene | taxa in T, x in genes(taxa),
                   name(x) contains "Adh" }
```

Once a set of taxa (Tax) and a set of genes (Gen) have been identified, then we would like to determine occurrences of the identified genes in the taxa of interest – this can be accomplished using the match map defined earlier. The selection of the components of the map requires a filtering of the result of the similarity search. E.g., if we are interested in defining the map in order to produce the sequence with the longest aligned region, then we simply replace the any statement with

```
w in S and forall z in S
   length_alignment(similar(y,w)) ≥
                      length_alignment(similar(y,z))
```

As part of the definition of the Sequence data type, the language provides an operation, align, which provides the sequence alignment capabilities. The align operation accepts a single argument which represents the set of sequences to be aligned. The result of the operation is a set of sequences, containing the original sequences properly expanded to represent the desired alignment. The behavior of align can be customized by the user similarly to what is described in the case of similar. E.g., the declaration:

```
align : operation (CLUSTAL W -- model=PAM)
```

asserts that the align operation should be performed by accessing the CLUSTAL W software with the appropriate parameters. We envision generalizing the behavior of align to produce as result not just a set of aligned sequences but a more general object – a data item of type Homology. The next step requires the definition of the model which is going to be used to describe evolutionary rates – i.e., a data item of the type Model. At the highest level, we can assume the presence of a build_tree operation which directly interfaces to dedicated tools for inference of phylogenies:

```
build_tree : Operation ( DNAML -- )
t            : Tree is build_tree(Seqs,model1)
```

This reflects the current standard approach, based on the development of a tree using a single model across the entire sequence and the entire tree [7]. The operation build_tree can be redesigned by the user whenever a different behavior is required. A simple declarative way of achieving this is as follows: given a list list

```
constraint : forall [X,Y] in list
             (likelihood(X,model) ≥likelihood(Y,model))
list is      [ t : Tree | t in Tree(Seqs) ]
```

which expresses the fact that list contains all the trees over the sequences in the set Seqs, sorted according to the likelihood of each tree under the model model. The best tree is the first in the list. A finer degree of control can be obtained by switching to the imperative constructs of the language and writing explicit code for the search. E.g., the following ΦLOG code picks the best of the first 1000 trees generated:

```
t    is      initialTree(Seqs)
best is      t
    repeat (i from 1 to 1000)
        t is nextTree(t,Seqs,model)
        if likelihood(t,model)>likelihood(best,model)
            then best is t
```

By providing different definitions of the operations initialTree and nextTree it is possible to customize the search for the desired tree. The same mechanisms can be used to select a set of trees instead of just one.

Given a set of trees Trees computed from a set of sequences and given a model model, we can construct a relative likelihood for the given set of trees:

```
prob :   Probability(Trees)
total is summation(x in Trees,likelihood(x,model))
     forall x in dom(prob)
```
$$\text{prob}(x) \text{ is } \frac{\text{likelihood}(x,\text{model})}{\text{total}}$$

This model can be easily extended to accommodate a distribution of models instead of an individual model. This allows us to use expected likelihood for the evaluation and selection of the trees. Assuming a finite collection of models Models and an associated probability distribution prob, we can replace the likelihood function by the fit function defined below:

```
fit (t : Tree) : map
    (fit is sum(m in Models,prob(m)*likelihood(t,m)))
```

4   Compilation of ΦLOG Programs

The goal of the ΦLOG compiler is to translate ΦLOG programs – manually developed by a biologist or developed via high-level graphical interfaces [10] – into partial plans. The components of the partial plan are high-level actions, extracted from an ontology of bioinformatic operations; each high-level operation will be successively concretized into one or more invocations of bioinformatic services (by the execution agent).

4.1   Bioinformatic Services

Data sources and software tools employed to accomplish phylogenetic inference tasks are uniformly viewed by ΦLOG as *bioinformatic services*. Each service provides a uniform interface to the data repository or software tool along with a description of the functionalities of the service (e.g., inputs, outputs, capabilities). Service descriptions are represented using a standard notation for service description in the semantic web (specifically DAML-S [11]). Service providers register their services with the *services broker*. The task of the broker is to maintain a directory of active services (including the location of the service and its description) and to provide matchmaking services between service descriptions and service requests.

The creation and management of service descriptions require the presence of a very refined *ontology*, describing all entities involved in service executions. Ontologies provide an objective specification of domain information, representing a community-wide consensus on entities and relations characterizing knowledge within a domain. The broker employs the ontology to instantiate high-level requests incoming from configuration agents into actual service requests. Considerable work has been done in the development of formal ontologies for biological concepts and entities [12,13]. Our project will build on these efforts, taking advantage of the integrated description of biological entities provided in these existing proposals. Nevertheless, this project aims at covering aspects that most of these ontologies currently do not provide:

(i) Description of an actual hierarchy of *bioinformatic operations*, their relationships, and their links to biological entities; each operation is described in terms of input and output types as well as its effect.

(ii) Description of an actual hierarchy for *bioinformatic types* and *bioinformatic data representation formats*, their relationships, and the links to biological entities and to the bioinformatic applications.

Thus, our objective is to concretize biological ontologies by introducing an ontology level describing the data formats and transformations that are commonly employed in phylogenetic inference, and linking them to the existing biology ontologies. This additional level (i.e., an ontology for bioinformatic tools) is fundamental to effectively accomplish the instantiation of a partial plan into a concrete plan – e.g., automatically selecting appropriate data format conversion services for interoperation.

Standard semantic web services description languages – i.e., DAML-S – have been employed for the development of these ontologies.

Service descriptions as well as the bioinformatic ontologies are maintained and managed by a service broker. In this project, the service broker is developed using the *Open Agent Architecture (OAA)* [14]. This will allow us to apply previously developed techniques in web services composition and GOLOG programs's execution and monitoring in [15] in our application. The advantages of this approach have been discussed in [16]. Currently, we have developed a minimal set of service descriptions that will allow us to develop simple ΦLOG programs that will be used as testbeds for the development of other components of the systems. We use OAA in this initial phase as it provides us the basic features that we need for the development of other components. In the later phases of the project, we will evaluate alternative architectures with similar capabilities (e.g. InfoSleuth [17]) or multi-agent architectures (e.g. RETSINA [18] or MINERVA [19]).

4.2   ΦLOG Compiler

The derivation of the ΦLOG compiler has been obtained using a semantic-based framework called *Horn-Logic Denotations (HLD)* [20]. In this framework, the syntax and semantics of the DSL is expressed using a form of denotational semantics and encoded using an expressive and tractable subset of first-order logic (Horn clauses). Following traditional denotational semantic specifications, in HLD a DSL $\mathcal{L}$ is described by three components: *(i)* syntax specification – realized by encoding a context free grammars as Horn clauses (using the Declarative Clause Grammars commonly used in logic programming); *(ii)* interpretation domains – described as logic theories; *(iii)* valuation functions – mappings from syntax structures to interpretation domains (encoded as first-order relations). In our specific application, the interpretation domains are composed of formulae in an action theory [21], describing properties and relationships between bioinformatic services. The action theories are encoded using situation calculus [21] – see also Section 5 – and they are extracted by the compiler from the services ontologies described in the previous section. The semantic specification also allows for rapid and correct implementations of the DSL. This is possible thanks to the use of an encoding in formal logic and the employment of logic-based inference systems – i.e., the specifications are *executable*, automatically yielding an interpreter for the DSL. Moreover, the Second Futamura Projection [22] proves that compiled code can be obtained by *partially evaluating* an interpreter w.r.t. a source program. Thus, our DSL interpreter can be partially evaluated (using a partial evaluator for logic programming [23]) w.r.t. a program expressed in the DSL to obtain compiled code [20]. In our context, the final outcome of the process is the automatic transformation of specifications written in ΦLOG to programs written in GOLOG.

The semantic specification can also be extended to support verification and debugging: the denotational specifications provide explicit representation of the state [8,20], and manipulation of such information can be expressed as an alternative semantics of the DSL – i.e., as an *abstract semantics* of the DSL [20]. This verification process is also possible thanks to the existence of *sound and complete* inference systems for meaningful fragments of Horn clause logic [24]. Given that the interpreter, compiler, and verifiers are obtained directly from the DSL specification, the process of developing and maintaining the development infrastructure for the DSL is very rapid. Furthermore, syntax and semantic specifications are expressed in a *uniform* notation, backed by effective inference models.

5 Execution Agent

5.1 ΦLOG's Program Execution as Planning and Plan Execution Monitoring

A ΦLOG program specifies the general steps that need to be performed in a phylogenetic inference application. Some steps can be achieved using built-in operations – this is the case for the primitive operations associated to the various data types provided by ΦLOG– e.g., compose two sets using a union operation or selecting the members of a set that satisfy a certain condition. Other steps might involve the use of a bioinformatic service, e.g., CLUSTAL W for sequence alignment, BLAST for similarity search, PAUP for phylogeny construction, etc. In several cases, intermediate steps, not specified by the compiler, are required; this may occur whenever the ΦLOG program does not explicitly lay out all the high-level steps required, or whenever additional steps are required to accomplish interoperability between the bioinformatic services. For example, the sequence alignment formats provided by CLUSTAL W cannot be used directly as inputs to the phylogenetic tree inference tool PAUP (which expects a Nexus file as input). As such, a ΦLOG program could be viewed as a skeleton of an application rather than its detailed step-by-step execution. Under this view, *execution of ΦLOG programs could be viewed as an instance of the planning and plan execution monitoring problem.* This will allow us to apply the techniques which have been developed in that area to implement the ΦLOG engine. We employ the approach introduced in [15] in developing the ΦLOG system. In this approach, each bioinformatic service is viewed as an *action* and a phylogenetic inference application as a GOLOG program [9].

We will now review the basics of GOLOG and the agent architecture that will be used in the development of the ΦLOG system. Since GOLOG is built on top of the situation calculus (e.g.,[21]), we begin with a short review of situation calculus.

Situation Calculus. The basic components of the situation calculus language, following the notation of [21], include a special constant S_0, denoting the initial situation, a binary function symbol *do* where $do(a, s)$ denotes the successor situation to s resulting from executing the action a, fluent relations of the form $f(s)$, denoting the fact that the fluent f is true in the situation s, and a special predicate $Poss(a, s)$ denoting the fact that the action a is executable in the situation s.

A dynamic domain can be represented by a theory containing: (i) axioms describing the initial situation S_0; (ii) action precondition axioms (one for each action a, characterizing $Poss(a, s)$); (iii) successor state axioms (one for each fluent F, stating under what condition $F(\boldsymbol{x}, do(a, s))$ holds, as a function of what holds in s); (iv) unique name axioms for the primitive actions; and some foundational, domain independent axioms.

GOLOG. The constructs of GOLOG [9] are:

α	*primitive action*
$\phi?$	*wait for a condition*
$(\sigma_1; \sigma_2)$	*sequence*
$(\sigma_1 \mid \sigma_2)$	*choice between actions*
$\pi x.\sigma$	*choice of arguments*
σ^*	*nondeterministic iteration*
if ϕ **then** σ_1 **else** σ_2	*synchronized conditional*
while ϕ **do** σ	*synchronized loop*
proc $\beta(\boldsymbol{x})\sigma$	*procedure definition*

The semantics of GOLOG is described by a formula $Do(\delta, s, s')$, where δ is a program, and s and s' are situations. Intuitively, $Do(\delta, s, s')$ holds whenever the situation s' is a terminating situation of an execution of δ starting from the situation s. For example, if $\delta = a; b \mid c; f?$, and $f(do(b, do(a, s)))$ holds, then the GOLOG interpreter will determine that $a; b$ is a successful execution of δ in the situation s.

The language GOLOG has been extended with various concurrency constructs, leading to the language *ConGolog* [25]. The precise semantic definitions of GOLOG and ConGolog can be found in [9,25]. Various extensions and implementations of GOLOG and ConGolog can be found at http://www.cs.toronto .edu/~cogrobo web site. An *answer set programming* interpreter for GOLOG has been implemented [26].

Bioinformatic Services as Actions and ΦLOG's Programs as GOLOG Programs. A bioinformatic service is a web service – i.e., a computational service accessible via the Web. Adopting the view of considering web services as actions for Web service composition application [15], we view each bioinformatic service as an action in situation calculus. Roughly speaking, an action description of a web service consists of the service name, its invocation's description, and its input and output parameters with their respective formats. Let $\mathcal{D}$ be the set of actions representing the bioinformatic services. Under this framework, the problem of combining bioinformatic services to develop a phylogenetic inference application is a planning problem in $\mathcal{D}$. Since $\mathcal{D}$ contains all the external operations that a user of ΦLOG can use, each ΦLOG program P can be compiled into a GOLOG program in the $\mathcal{D}$ language by:

- Introducing variables and fluents representing the variables of the ΦLOG program.
- Replacing each instruction V is operation(x) in the ΦLOG program with the action τ(operation)(x, V), where τ is a mapping that associates ΦLOG operations to invocations of bioinformatic services. The ΦLOG compiler implements the τ operation through the following steps:
  - terms in the ΦLOG program are used to identify the set of *high-level actions* requested by the ΦLOG programmer. The process is accomplished by identifying relevant entries in the hierarchy of bioinformatic operations (see Section 4.1).
  - high-level operations are used to query the services broker and retrieve the description of relevant registered services that implement the required operations.
- Replacing the control constructs such as **if-then, for-all**, etc. in the ΦLOG program with their corresponding constructs in GOLOG.

In turn, the description of the various services retrieved from the services broker (DAML-S descriptions) are converted [15] into action precondition axioms and successor state axioms. This translation will be achieved by the compiler of the ΦLOG system. The GOLOG program obtained through this translation may contain the *order* construct (denoted by $\sigma_1 : \sigma_2$), an extended feature of GOLOG suggested in [15], and used to describe a partial order between parts of the program. This feature is essential in our context; the ΦLOG program determines the ordering between the main steps of the computation (expressed using the order construct), while the configuration agent may need to insert additional intermediate steps to ensure interoperation between services and executability of the plan. E.g., if a ΦLOG program indicates the need to perform a sequence alignment (mapped to the `clustalw` service) followed by a tree construction (mapped to the `paup` service), then the GOLOG program will contain `clustalw : paup`; the agent may transform this into the plan `clustalw; parse_nexus; paup`, by inserting a data format conversion action (`parse_nexus`). Using a GOLOG interpreter we can find different sequences of services which can be executed to achieve the goal of the ΦLOG program, provided that $\mathcal{D}$ is given. Precise details in the translation and execution monitoring under development.

5.2   Configuration Component

The configuration component is in charge of transforming a partial plan (expressed as a GOLOG program with extended features, as described in [15]) into a concrete plan (*instantiation*). This process is a *planning problem* [26], where the goal is to develop a concrete plan which meets the following requirements:

(i) each high-level action in the partial plan is instantiated into one or more low-level actions in the concrete plan, whose global effect correspond to the effect of the high-level action (i.e., the τ operation mentioned earlier);

(ii) successive steps in the concrete plan correctly interoperate.

This process is intuitively illustrated in Example 1. The configuration component makes use of the high-level actions in the partial plan to query the services broker and obtain lists of concrete bioinformatic services that can satisfy the requested actions. The querying is realized through the use of the bioinformatic tools ontology mentioned earlier.

The configuration component attempts to combine these services into an effective concrete plan – i.e., an executable GOLOG program. The process requires fairly complex planning methodologies, since:

- the agent may need to repeatedly backtrack and choose alternative services and/or add intermediate additional services (e.g., filtering and data format transformation services) to create a coherent concrete plan;

- planning may fail if some of the requested actions do not correspond to any service or services cannot be properly assembled (e.g., lack of proper interoperation between data formats); sensing actions may be employed to repair the failure, e.g., by cooperating with the user in locating the missing service;

- planning requires the management of *resources* – e.g., management of a budget when using bioinformatic services with access charges;

- planning requires *user preferences* – e.g., choice of preferred final data formats.

Most of these features are either readily available in GOLOG or they have been added by the investigators [15,26,27] to fit the needs of similar planning domains.

Example 1. Consider the original simple *Φ*Log program (*g* is of type *Genes*, *s* of type *Alignment(dna)* and *t* of type *Tree(dna)*):

```
g is { x : Gene | name(x)  contains  ''martensii''}
s is align(g)
t is phylogenetic_tree(s)
```

The high-level plan detected by the compiler:

```
database_search(gene,[(GeneName,''martensii'')], o1) ;
              sequence_alignment(dna, o1, o2) ;
                phylogenetic_tree(dna, o2, o3) ;
                          display_output(o3)
```

The action theory derived from the agent broker will include:

$genebank("GeneName = martensii", o1)$ **causes** $genes(o1, G)$ **if** ...
$clustalw(o1, o2)$ **causes** $alignment(dna, o2, A)$ **if** $sequences(dna, o1, S),...$
$dnaml(o2, o3)$ **causes** $tree(dna, o3, T)$ **if** $alignment(dna, o2, A),...$

Additional actions are automatically derived from the type system of the language; for example, Gene is seen as a subclass of DNA_Sequence, which provides an operation of the type:

$gene\_to\_dnasequence(o)$ **causes** $sequence(dna, o)$ **if** $gene(o)$

The operation will be associated to built-in type conversion actions. Finally, the high level plan will have to be replaced by a GOLOG program, where each high-level action should be replaced by a choice of actions construct (a choice from the set of the services implementing such high-level action), e.g.,

```
genebank(''Gene Name = martensii'',o1) | ··· :
                   clustalw(o1, o2) | ··· :
                      dnaml(o2,o3) | ··· :
                      display_output(o3) ;
                          ? tree(dna,o3).
```

5.3   Execution and Monitoring Agent

Once a concrete plan has been developed, the execution/monitoring component of the agent proceeds with its execution. Executing the concrete plan corresponds to the creation and execution of the proper service invocations corresponding to each low-level action. Each service request involves contacting the appropriate service provider – which can be either local or remote – and supply the provider with the appropriate parameters to execute the desired service. The monitoring element supervises the successful completion of each service request. In case of failure (e.g., a timeout or a loss of connection to the remote provider), the monitor takes appropriate repair actions. Repair may involve either repeating the execution of the service or re-entering the configuration component. The latter case may lead to exploring alternative ways of instantiating the partial plan, to avoid the failing service. The replanning process is developed in such a way to attempt to reuse as much as possible of the part of the concrete plan executed before the failure.

6   Discussion and Conclusions

6.1   Technology

The development of this framework employs a combination of novel and existing software technology. DAML-S is used as representation format for the description of services. In the preliminary prototype, the ontologies for bioinformatic services and for bioinformatic data formats have been encoded using logic-based descriptions – specifically, using the OO extensions provided by SICStus Prolog.

The reasoning part of the agent (configuration, execution, and monitoring) is based on *situation calculus*. This is in agreement with the view adopted by the semantic web community – Web Services, encoded in DAML-S, can be viewed as actions. GOLOG is employed as language for expressing the partial plans derived from ΦLOG programs, as well as describing the complete plans to be executed. In this work we make use of a GOLOG interpreter encoded in answer set programming [28]. The advantage of this approach is that it allows us to easily extend GOLOG to encompass the advanced reasoning features required by the problem at hand – i.e., user preferences [27] and planning with domain specific knowledge [26].

6.2   Related Work

An extensive literature exists in the field of DSL [1]. Design, implementation, and maintenance of DSLs have been identified as key issues in DSL-based software development and various methodologies have been proposed (e.g., [29,1]. HLD is the first approach based on logic programming and denotational semantics, and capable of completely specifying a DSL in a uniform executable language.

Various languages have been proposed to deal with the issue of describing biological data for bioinformatic applications. Existing languages tend to be application-specific and limited in scope, they offer limited modeling options, are mostly static, and are poorly interconnected. Various efforts are undergoing to unify different languages, through markup languages (e.g., GEML and BSML) and/or ontologies [12]. Some proposals have recently emerged to address the issues of interoperability, e.g., [4,6].

The work that comes closest to ΦLOG includes programming environments which allows scientists to *write programs* to perform computational biology tasks. Examples of these include TAMBIS [4], Darwin [3] and Mesquite [5]. They combine a standard language (imperative in Darwin, visual in Mesquite) with a collection of modules to perform computational biological tasks (e.g., sequence alignments). Both Darwin and Mesquite provide only a small number of models that a biologist can use to create bioinformatic applications, and they both rely on a "closed-box" approach. The modules which perform the basic operations have been explicitly developed as part of the language and there is little scope for integration of popular bioinformatic tools. TAMBIS provides a knowledge base for mapping graphically expressed queries to accesses of a set of bioinformatic data sources.

6.3   Conclusions and Future Work

In this paper we presented a brief overview of the ΦLOG project, aimed at the development of a domain specific framework for the rapid prototyping of applications in evolutionary biology. The framework is based on a DSL, that allows evolutionary biologists to express complex phylogenetic analysis processes at a very high level of abstraction. The execution model of ΦLOG relies on an agent infrastructure, capable of automatically composing and monitoring the execution of bioinformatic services, to accomplish the goals expressed in the original ΦLOG program. The framework is currently under development as a collaboration between researchers in Computer Science, Biology, and Biochemistry at NMSU.

Acknowledgments

The authors wish to thank the anonymous referees for their helpful comments. Research has been supported by NSF grants EIA-0130887, CCR-9875279, HRD-9906130, EIA-0220590, and EIA-9810732.

References

1. van Deursen, A., Klint, P., Visser, J.: Domain-Specific Languages: an Annotated Bibliography. www.cwi.nl/~arie/papers/dslbib (2000)
2. Maddison, D.R., Swofford, D., Maddison, W.: NEXUS: An Extensible File Format for Systematic Information. Syst. Biol. **464** (1997) 590–621
3. Gonner, G., Hallet, M.: Darwin 2.0. Technical report, ETH-Zurich (2000)
4. Baker, P., Brass, A., Bechoofer, S., Goble, C., Paton, N., Stevens, R.: TAMBIS – Transparent Access to Multiple Bioinformatics Information Sources. In: Proceedings of the International Conference on Intelligent Systems for Molecular Biology. (1998)
5. Maddison, D.R., Maddison, W.: Mesquite: A Modular System for Evolutionary Analysi. Technical report, U. of Arizona (2001)

6. Standardizing Biological Data Interchange Through Web Services
   `omnigene.sourceforge.net` (2001)
7. Swofford, D.L., Olsen, G.J., Waddell, P.J., Hillis, D.M.: Phylogenetic inference.
   In: Molecular Systematics. Sinauer Associates, Sunderland, Massachusetts (1996)
   407–514
8. Schmidt, D.: Denotational Semantics: a Methodology for Language Development.
   W.C. Brown Publishers (1986)
9. Levesque, H., Reiter, R., Lesperance, Y., Lin, F., Scherl, R.: GOLOG: A logic
   programming language for dynamic domains. Journal of Logic Programming **31**
   (1997) 59–84
10. Pontelli, E., Ranjan, D., Milligan, B., Gupta, G.: Design and Implementation of
    a Domain Specific Language for Phylogenetic Inference. Journal of Bioinformatics
    and Computational Biology **1** (2003) 1–29
11. DAML-S Coalition: A. Ankolekar, Burstein, M., Hobbs, J., Lassila, O., Martin,
    D., McIlraith, S., Narayanan, S., Paolucci, M., Payne, T., Sycara, K., Zeng, H.:
    DAML-S: Semantic markup for Web services. In: Proc. International Semantic
    Web Working Symposium (SWWS). (2001) 411–430
12. Stevens, R.: Bio-Ontology Reference Collection
    `cs.man.ac.uk/~stevens/onto-publications.html`
13. Bio-Ontologies Consortium `www.bioontology.org`
14. Cheyer, A., Martin, D.: The Open Agent Architecture. Journal of Autonomous
    Agents and Multi-Agent Systems **4** (2001) 143–148
15. McIlraith, S., Son, T.: Adapting golog for composition of semantic web services.
    In: Proceedings of the Eighth International Conference on Principles of Knowledge
    Representation and Reasoning (KR'2002), Morgan Kaufmann Publisher (2002)
    482–493
16. McIlraith, S., Son, T., Zeng, H.: Semantic Web services. IEEE Intelligent Systems
    (Special Issue on the Semantic Web) **16** (2001) 46–53
17. Fowler, J., Perry, B., Nodine, M., Bargmeyer, B.: Agent-Based Semantic Interop-
    erability in InfoSleuth. In: SIGMOD Record 28:1. (1999) 60–67
18. Sycara, K., Paolucci, M., van Velsen, M., Giampapa, J.: The retsina mas infras-
    tructure. In: Autonomous Agents and MAS. (2003) to appear.
19. Leite, J., Alferes, J., Pereira, L.: MINERVA: a Dynamic Logic Programeing Agent
    Architecture. In: Intelligent Agents VIII, Springer Verlag (2002)
20. Gupta, G., Pontelli, E.: Specification, Implementation, and Verification of Domain
    Specific Languages: a Logic Programming-based Approach. In: Computational
    Logic: from Logic Programming into the Future. Springer Verlag (2001)
21. Reiter, R.: KNOWLEDGE IN ACTION: Logical Foundations for Describing and
    Implementing Dynamical Systems. MIT Press (2001)
22. Jones, N.: Introduction to Partial Evaluation. ACM Computing Survey **28** (1996)
    480–503
23. Sahlin, D.: The mixtus approach to the automatic evaluation of full prolog. In:
    Proceedings of the North American Conference on Logic Programming, MIT Press
    (1990) 377–398
24. Niemela, I., Simons, P.: Smodels - An Implementation of the Stable Model
    and Well-Founded Semantics for Normal LP. In: Logic Programming and Non-
    monotonic Reasoning, Springer Verlag (1997) 421–430
25. De Giacomo, G., Lespérance, Y., Levesque, H.: *ConGolog*, a concurrent program-
    ming language based on the situation calculus. Artificial Intelligence **121** (2000)
    109–169

26. Son, T., Baral, C., McIlraith, S.: Domain dependent knowledge in planning - an answer set planning approach. In: Proceedings of the 6th International Conference on Logic Programming and NonMonotonic Reasoning, Vienna (2001) 226–239
27. Son, T., Pontelli, E.: Reasoning about actions in prioritized default theory. In Flesca, S., Greco, S., Leone, N., Ianni, G., eds.: Proceedings of the Eighth European Conference on Logics in Artificial Intelligence, JELIA'02, Springer Verlag, LNAI 2424 (2002) 369–381
28. Lifschitz, V.: Answer set planning. In: International Conference on Logic Programming. (1999) 23–37
29. Bentley, J.: Programming pearls: Little languages. Communications of the ACM **29** (1986) 711–721

A Logic for Ignorance

Wiebe van der Hoek[1] and Alessio Lomuscio[2],[*]

[1] Department of Computer Science, University of Liverpool
Liverpool L69 7ZF, UK
wiebe@csc.liv.ac.uk
[2] Department of Computer Science, King's College London
London WC2R 2LS, UK
alessio@dcs.kcl.ac.uk

Abstract. We introduce and motivate a non-standard multi-modal logic to represent and reason about ignorance in Multi-Agent Systems. We argue that in Multi-agent systems being able to reason about what agents *ignore* is just as important as being able to reason about what agents know. We show a sound and complete axiomatisation for the logic. We investigate its applicability by restating the feasibility condition for the FIPA communication primitive of inform.

As we know, there are known knowns; there are things we know that we know. We also know there are known unknowns; that is to say we know there are some things we do not know. But there are also unknown unknowns – the ones we don't know we don't know.
Donald Rumsfeld (US Secretary of State for Defence)

1 Introduction

Following Dennet's influential work [1] MAS are traditionally modelled by taking an *intentional stance*. This amounts to ascribing notions such as knowledge, beliefs, desires, intentions etc. to agents in order to model, and specify their behaviour. Concepts such as knowledge, beliefs, are not easy to model by means of first order logic. On the one hand they are referentially opaque, on the other they require a formalism in which operators can be arbitrarily nested one into another. It has long been argued that modal logic provides a possible solution for these problems. Indeed, many of the most important and widely used approaches to model Multi-Agent Systems (MAS) are now based on various modal logics [2].

A considerable amount of research has gone in the past 20 years into exploring the formalisations of concepts such as knowledge and beliefs in MAS. Many of the most successful theories we now have (such as the area of epistemic logic, variations of the BDI model, etc.) are based on earlier work in AI, or philosophical logic. For example, the foundations of the modern use of epistemic logic (such

---

[*] Alessio Lomuscio acknowledges support from the Nuffield Foundation (grant NAL/00690/G).

J. Leite et al. (Eds.): DALT 2003, LNAI 2990, pp. 97–108, 2004.

as the one proposed in [3]) can be found in the work of Hintikka and Aumann of the 1950s. The basis for the BDI work ([4,5]) take inspiration from the work of Bratman, and Cohen [6], [7]. This is not to say that work in MAS theories consists simply in a rediscovery exercise of previously explored ideas. The theories as they are used now are considerably more refined than they were at the time, and they are now integrated with specification and verification techniques from software engineering (witness recent progress in verification of MAS theories [8,9].

Still, while it is encouraging that the field of MAS has taken inspiration from successful theories first appeared elsewhere, it would be interesting to see whether MAS call for the use of previously unexplored concepts. One way this may happen in MAS theories is for a logic arising directly from MAS studies, and applications. In this paper we argue that this may be the case for the concept of ignorance.

Consider the typical scenario in Agent Communication Languages in which one agent queries another for information, perhaps by using the FIPA construct of *query-if*. Assuming honesty, the agent will reply it is unable to answer the query if it is *ignorant* about the value of the information it is being asked. Indeed, in a model where full cooperation is assumed, the fact that it is actually ignorant about the value of what it is being asked may be a precondition for a negative answer of an agent. Consider a similar example in which agents are exchanging data over a channel on which an intruder may be listening. A desirable property of the interaction is that the state of *ignorance* of the intruder with respect to the content of the messages is preserved. We argue that in these and other examples a key property that we want to reason about is *states of ignorance*. Note that by ignorance we do not mean the mere lack of knowledge, but something stronger. When an agent does not know a fact p, it may be that it does not know p, because in fact it knows that $\neg p$. For instance, by using the usual properties of knowledge in MAS in a particular example it is true to say that an agent does not know that the printer is connected, because in fact it knows that printer is *not* connected. We would not call ignorance this simple lack of knowledge. By state of ignorance about φ in the following we shall refer to a mental state in which the agent is unsure about the truth value of φ. So, not only the agent does not know the truth value of φ but also that of $\neg\varphi$.

The reader acquainted with the epistemic logic literature will note that it is possible to express this concept in epistemic logic by stipulating that one agent is ignorant about φ if it does not know φ and it does not know $\neg\varphi$. We argue that this is cumbersome to express in many interesting examples. For instance, the reader may try and express the concept of one agent being ignorant about the ignorance of another agent:

$$\neg K_i(\neg K_j\varphi \wedge \neg K_j\neg\varphi) \wedge \neg K_i\neg(\neg K_j\varphi \wedge K_j\neg\varphi)$$

This constitutes a typical notion in use in security when the recipient of a message is reasoning about whether or not the intruder has been able to decode the content of the message. The above looks unnecessarily complicated. Further, this complexity makes it difficult to investigate what properties ignorance should have. For example, if an agent is ignorant about φ should it be ignorant about its ignorance? Still, ignorance must be related to epistemic states – when an agent is ignorant about φ, intuitively it is because it contemplates some alternatives in which φ is true, and others in which it is false.

What we do in this paper is to build upon these very simple observations. We aim at defining ignorance as a first class citizen, investigate its properties and explore a logic that is able to represent this concept formally. Technically this will be done by means of modal logic. We shall be using a syntax that allows for a modal operator to express the notion of ignorance of an agent with respect to a formula. Semantically we shall be using the standard possible worlds epistemic interpretation – the satisfaction definition for the operator of ignorance will obviously need to be introduced. We try and provide an in-depth analysis of the logic by giving a completeness result, and we apply this analysis to a concrete example from the literature.

The rest of this paper is organised as follows. In Sections 2 and 3 we give a formal account of ignorance, establishing some of its properties. In Section 4, we investigate a richer framework where ignorance is paired with the classical operator for knowledge. In Section 5 we show how the operator of ignorance can be used to simplify the semantic definition of the communication act of inform as defined in FIPA semantics. We conclude in Section 6.

2   Ignorance: Language and Semantics

We assume familiarity with basic concepts of modal logic. We refer the reader to [2] for details. We base our discussion on the monomodal case.

2.1   Syntax

We use a very simple mono-modal language $\mathcal{L}_I$ defined as follows in BNF:

$$\varphi ::= p \mid \neg\varphi \mid \varphi \wedge \varphi \mid I\varphi$$

Other propositional operators can be defined as standard, and are to be read as usual. A formula $I\varphi$ is to be read as 'the agent is ignorant about φ', i.e., he is not aware of whether or not φ is true. As an example the formula $I\varphi \rightarrow \neg II\varphi$ is to be read as "If the agent is ignorant about φ, then it is not ignorant about it being ignorant about φ".

We ground our discussion on classically minded agents, so we assume that statements cannot both be true or false at the same time. So, to anticipate semantical considerations made clear below, the agent in order to be ignorant about φ will have to conceive at least two epistemic alternatives, one in which φ is true, and one in which φ is false.

In our concept of ignorance we do not intend to capture degrees of ignorance with respect to a formula. There is a whole spectrum of concepts that seem worth exploring. On the one side we have agents which have absolutely no information about a fact, so are in a way "truly ignorant" about it. On the other side of the spectrum we have agents which may regard a fact to be a lot more likely to be true (or false) but still contemplate the possibility of the fact being false. In our formalism we shall not be able to differentiate between these. This, and various variants of probabilistic reasoning seem worth exploring, but are left for future work.

2.2   Semantics

We use standard possible worlds semantics to give an interpretation to the language above. A model will be built on a set of epistemic alternatives (or worlds), and a relation built on these. Intuitively, like in standard modal epistemic logic, we consider two epistemic alternatives to be related if up to the agent's information they may both be models of the real situation.

Definition 1 (Frames, Models, and Satisfaction). *A Kripke Frame $F = (W, R)$ is a tuple where W is a set of epistemic alternatives for the agent, and $R \subseteq W \times W$ is an accessibility relation. A Kripke Model $M = (F, \pi)$, is a tuple where F is a Kripke frame and $\pi : P \to 2^W$ is an interpretation for a set of propositional variables P.*

Given a model M and a formula φ, we say that φ is true in M at world w, written $M, w \models \varphi$ if:

- $M, w \models p$ *if* $w \in \pi(P)$,
- $M, w \models \neg\varphi$ *if it is not the case that* $M, w \models \varphi$,
- $M, w \models \varphi \wedge \psi$ *if* $M, w \models \varphi$ *and* $M, w \models \psi$,
- $M, w \models I\varphi$ *if there exist* w', w'' *such that*
  $Rww', Rww'', M, w' \models \varphi$, *and* $M, w'' \models \neg\varphi$.

A formula φ is *valid*, written $\models \varphi$, if it is true in every world in every model. We write $F, w \models \varphi$ to represent $M, w \models \varphi$ where M is an arbitrary model whose underlaying frame is F.

We assume the standard definitions for metalogical properties such as axiomatisation, completeness, etc. We refer to [2] for details.

Lemma 1. *The following formulas are valid on the class of arbitrary Kripke models.*

A1 $I\varphi \leftrightarrow I\neg\varphi$
A2 $I(\varphi \wedge \psi) \to (I\varphi \vee I\psi)$

The properties above seem rather reasonable for ignorance. Axiom $A1$ says that being ignorant about φ is logically equivalent to being ignorant about $\neg\varphi$. Since by ignorance we mean no definite information about the truth of the object of ignorance, intuitively this is correct.

Property $A2$ is maybe best understood in its contrapositive form ($\neg I\varphi \wedge \neg I\psi) \to \neg I(\varphi \wedge \psi)$. If an agent is neither ignorant about φ, nor about ψ it is surely not ignorant about the conjunction $\varphi \wedge \psi$. This also seems reasonable.

3   A Logic for Ignorance

In this section we aim at presenting a completeness result (Theorem 1) for a logic of ignorance. In order to do this we need some preliminary results.

3.1   Preliminary Remarks

Axiom $A2$ regulates how to distribute I over a boolean connective. Similarly, note that the following is also valid.

$$I(\varphi \to \psi) \to I\varphi \vee I\psi \tag{1}$$

As a proof, note that $I(\varphi \to \psi) \equiv I\neg(\varphi \to \psi) \equiv I(\varphi \wedge \neg\psi)$. Also, $I(\varphi \wedge \neg\psi) \to (I\varphi \vee I\neg q)$, the latter being equivalent to $I\varphi \vee I\psi$.

$$I(\varphi \vee \psi) \to (I\varphi \vee I\psi) \tag{2}$$

Since negation and implication (or, for that matter, negation and disjunction) are functionally complete, we can generalise (1) and (2) into the following lemma:

Lemma 2. *Let $A \subseteq P$ be a set of propositional atoms, and $b(A)$ be a Boolean function on A. Then there exist literals $\ell_1 \ldots \ell_k$ over A, such that $I(b(A)) \to \bigvee_{i \leq k} I(\ell_i)$ is valid.*

Corollary 1. *Let $A \subseteq P$ be a set of propositional atoms, and $b(A)$ be Boolean function on A. Then*

$$\models I(b(A)) \to \bigvee_{a \in A} I(a)$$

Corollary 1 states that, in order to be ignorant about a complex formula, one must be ignorant about one of its atoms. Again, this corresponds to our intuition.

Let us now turn our attention to possible inference rules for a system of ignorance. We begin by observing that the following is sound.

$$\text{from } \vdash \varphi, \text{ infer } \vdash \neg I\varphi \tag{3}$$

Indeed, this corresponds to the intuition that an agent cannot be ignorant about propositional tautologies, and formulas following from them. Note the rule above is related to the commonly accepted rule of necessitation in epistemic logic that states that the agent knows all propositional tautologies.

A more complex inference rule that can also be shown to be sound is the following.

$$\vdash (\psi_1 \to \chi) \wedge (\chi \to \psi_2) \Rightarrow \vdash \neg I\chi \to (\neg I\psi_1 \vee \neg I\psi_2) \tag{4}$$

In fact, note that rule (3) follows from rule (4) when $\neg I\top$ is a validity (like it is in our case) by taking $\psi_1 = \psi_2 = \varphi$ and $\chi = \top$. It is easy to see that Equation 4 provides for a sound inference rule for the semantics described above. It says that if an agent is not ignorant about an interpolant χ for a stronger ψ_1 and a weaker ψ_2, that it cannot be ignorant about both the ψ_i's. If the agent is not ignorant about χ, it either thinks χ is true (in which case it also should consider ψ_2 as being true), or that χ is false (in which case it should be convinced of ψ_1's falsity as well).

3.2   A Complete System for Ignorance

We now present a system that we can show to be complete with respect to the semantics above.

Definition 2. *The modal system* **Ig** *for ignorance is defined as follows:*
$I0$ *All instances of propositional tautologies*
$I1$ $I\varphi \leftrightarrow I\neg\varphi$
$I2$ $I(\varphi \wedge \psi) \to (I\varphi \vee I\psi)$
$I3$ $(\neg I\varphi \wedge I(\alpha_1 \wedge \varphi)) \wedge \neg I(\varphi \to \psi) \wedge I(\alpha_2 \wedge (\varphi \to \psi))$
$\quad\quad \to (\neg I\psi \wedge I(\alpha_1 \wedge \psi))$
$I4$ $(\neg I\psi \wedge I\alpha) \to (I(\alpha \wedge \psi) \vee I(\alpha \wedge \neg\psi))$
RI $\vdash_{\mathbf{Ig}} \varphi \Rightarrow \vdash_{\mathbf{Ig}} \neg I\varphi \wedge (I\alpha \to I(\alpha \wedge \varphi))$
MP *Modus Ponens*
Sub *Substitution of equivalences*

Observation 1 *Before we prove soundness of* **Ig**, *we make the following remark about occurrences in axiom $I3$ of the form $\neg I\varphi \wedge I(\alpha \wedge \varphi)$. If such a formula is true, either the agent is sure about the truth value of φ, or of $\neg\varphi$. Moreover, the truth of $I(\alpha \wedge \varphi)$ implies that the agent regards as possible an $\alpha \wedge \varphi$-world[1], which is both a φ- and an α-world. But this then implies that all the agents' conceivable worlds verify φ. Therefore the agent is sure about the value of φ. But $I(\alpha \wedge \varphi)$ also implies that the agent considers a $\neg(\alpha \wedge \varphi)$-world possible, which is also a $(\neg\alpha \vee \neg\varphi)$-world. But since all the conceivable worlds verified φ, this implies that the agent considers one world possible in which $\neg\alpha$ is true. This, together with the fact that an α-world was an alternative to the agent, gives us that the agent is ignorant about α, but knows that φ.*

Lemma 3 (Soundness). *The system* **Ig** *is sound with respect to the class of arbitrary Kripke models.*

We begin by noting that the following is a theorem of **Ig**.

Lemma 4. *We have that* $\vdash_{\mathbf{Ig}} Cb$, *where* Cb *is defined as:*
Cb $(\neg I\gamma_1 \wedge I(\delta_1 \wedge \gamma_1)) \wedge (\neg I\gamma_2 \wedge I(\delta_2 \wedge \gamma_2))$
$\quad\quad \to I(\delta_2 \wedge (\gamma_1 \wedge \gamma_2))$

Note that it can be proven that the disjunctive conclusion in $I4$ is in fact exclusive.

---

[1] A world w is an α-world if α is true at w in the model under consideration.

In order to show completeness we build maximal consistent sets of formulas and show that the canonical model for the logic **Ig** can be built on these. Although the canonical model construction will be non-standard, much of the background definitions that we use are standard. In particular we assume the usual definitions for logical consistency, and maximal consistent sets. We refer to [2] for details. Since we only refer to system **Ig** in this section we shall refer to consistency to mean **Ig**-consistency.

Lemma 5. *Let Γ be a maximal consistent set, containing some formula $I\alpha$. Then the set $K^\alpha(\Gamma) = \{\psi \mid \neg I\psi, I(\alpha \wedge \psi) \in \Gamma\}$ has the following properties:*

1. *If $\neg I\psi \in \Gamma$, then either $\psi \in K^\alpha(\Gamma)$ or $\neg \psi \in K^\alpha(\Gamma)$;*
2. *$K^\alpha(\Gamma) \cup \{\beta\}$ is consistent, for every $I\beta \in \Gamma$.*

Lemma 6. *The set $K^\alpha(\Gamma) = \{\psi \mid \neg I\psi, I(\alpha \wedge \psi) \in \Gamma\}$ is independent of the choice of α: if $I\alpha_1, I\alpha_2 \in \Gamma$, then $K^{\alpha_1}(\Gamma) = K^{\alpha_2}(\Gamma)$.*

Observe now that since system **Ig** is consistent (this follows immediately from the soundness theorem), the existence of maximal consistent sets is guaranteed by Lindembaum's Lemma. So, for any **Ig**-consistent set of formulas there exists at least a maximal extension that properly includes the elements of the set. To prove completeness we now define a rather ad-hoc canonical model, as follows.

Definition 3 (Canonical Model). *The canonical model $M^C = (W^C, R^C, \pi^C)$ for the logic **Ig** is defined as follows:*

- *W^C is the set of all maximal **Ig**-consistent sets of formulas (denoted as $\Sigma, \Delta, \Gamma \ldots$).*
- *$R^C \subseteq W^C \times W^C$ is defined by $R^c \Gamma \Sigma$ if $\Sigma \supseteq K^\alpha(\Gamma)$ for some $I\alpha \in \Gamma$.*
- *$p \in \pi(\Gamma)$ if $p \in \Gamma$.*

Note that in the canonical model, every world Γ has either no successors (if there is no $I\alpha \in \Gamma$), or at least two successors (if $I\alpha \in \Gamma$, then also $I\neg\alpha \in \Gamma$, and, according to Lemma 5 part b) together with Lindembaum's Lemma, there are at least two successors $\Sigma_1 \supseteq K^\alpha(\Gamma) \cup \{\alpha\}$ and $\Sigma_2 \supseteq K^\alpha(\Gamma) \cup \{\neg\alpha\}$).

Lemma 7 (Truth-Lemma). *For all formulas φ, and all **Ig**-maximal consistent sets Γ, we have:*

$$M^c, \Gamma \models \varphi \Leftrightarrow \varphi \in \Gamma$$

Theorem 1 (Completeness). *Given system **Ig**, for any formula φ we have the following: $\vdash_{\mathbf{Ig}} \varphi$ if and only if $\models \varphi$.*

Note that the completeness result above applies to the general class of Kripke frames. This contrasts with system K being the standard system to axiomatise arbitrary frames for a standard modality.

4   Ignorance and Knowledge

Now that we have a result for a basic system for ignorance we can ask the question of how this relates to what is known already in epistemic logic [3]. After all the semantics that we have used is based on the one for epistemic logic: we regard two points as related if the agent considers the two as epistemically indistinguishable. What we have done so far amounts to using this semantic concept to express ignorance as opposed to knowledge. But since intuitively it must be possible to build a correspondence between the two concepts, the curious reader must then be left wondering whether ignorance can in fact be precisely expressed in terms of knowledge. Crucially, one must consider the question of whether one could have ultimately proven Theorem 1 by a careful translation of epistemic operators from the usual modal systems used for epistemic logic such as S5. We explore this and other questions in the rest of this section.

Let us first ask the question of whether our ignorance operator can in fact be expressed in terms of knowledge, not just by using the semantics as we have done but also syntactically. We have taken being ignorant about φ to mean that the agent conceives two opposite alternatives for φ. In the usual epistemic language this not just implies, but is semantically equivalent to saying that the agent does not know φ, and does not know $\neg\varphi$ (an alternative definition would come from exploiting $K\varphi \equiv \neg I\varphi \wedge \varphi$, but this would assume reflexivity of the epistemic relations as will become clearer later on):

$$I\varphi \equiv (\neg K\varphi \wedge \neg K\neg\varphi).$$

We have been unable to prove a completeness result simply by using this equivalence. Indeed, surprisingly little is known about logics for modalities that are defined from others, the only constructions available resulting from work in algebraic modal logic. One may try coding epistemic axioms for K in view of the definition above to deduce properties for I but this attempt is hindered with technical difficulties. Even if this exercise were to be successful, we would be left with a logic for I that assumes S5 as the underlaying model for K. S5 is often a good model for knowledge, but at other times it is useful to consider weaker models. In the way we proceeded we have made no assumption on the properties of the underlaying relations between points, and the resulting framework is a rather weak one. Indeed, we believe this to be a good feature of the logic – we have a rather weak system to begin with and we can add more properties to it if required. Given this one can define a logic for both K and I by taking the standard satisfaction definition for both operators.

We also point out that K cannot be defined in terms of I. Consider the frames of Figure 1; note that, by induction, for all formulas φ in the language for ignorance $\mathcal{L}_I$, we have

$$F_1, w_1 \models \varphi \text{ iff } F_2, w_2 \models \varphi \text{ iff } F_3, w_3 \models \varphi$$

Indeed, note that for every w_i ($i \leq 3$), no $I\varphi$ can be true: the agent considers too few alternatives possible to have any doubt whatsoever. From this, it immediately follows that K cannot be defined in terms of I, since we have for instance $F_3, w_3 \models K\bot$, but $F_1, w_1 \not\models K\bot$. In other words: K can distinguish between frames that I cannot.

4.1   Nested Ignorance

We now analyse the consequences of considering additional properties for the accessibility relations, thereby producing stronger systems then **Ig**. Let us start with transitive relations; these define positively introspective agents (in the sense of the knowledge they have, i.e., agents whose knowledge satisfies axiom 4: $K\varphi \rightarrow KK\varphi$ holds). By definition a positively introspective agent cannot be ignorant about what it knows. In fact we would have the axiom:

$I4 \; \neg I\psi \rightarrow \neg I \neg I\psi$.

Note that axiom $I4$ is, in the context of **Ig** equivalent to $II\psi \rightarrow I\psi$.

Can an agent be ignorant about one's ignorance? Clearly, a negatively introspective agent cannot be. This would suggest the validity of the axiom:

$I5 \; I\psi \rightarrow \neg II\psi$.

In line with epistemic logic we would expect properties $I4$ and $I5$ to impose transitivity and Euclidicity, respectively, on the canonical model. Let us first note that $I4$ is indeed true on transitive models.

Lemma 8. $\mathcal{F}_4 \models I4$, where $\mathcal{F}_4$ is the class of transitive frames.

However, it is illustrative to see that the converse does not hold: validity of $I4$ on a frame does not guarantee transitivity. Consider the frame with three worlds w, u, v, such that Rwu and Ruv. In w, for no formula ψ, $I\psi$ is true (since w has only one successor). Hence, $I4$ is valid in w, a point in a non-transitive frame. As for $I5$ and Euclidicity, one can do a similar analysis: $I5$ is valid on all Euclidean frames, but validity of $I5$ does not force the underlying frame to be Euclidean.

One way to proceed to achieve completeness results for stronger systems then **Ig** is to start from the semantic properties and see whether there are formulas that correspond to transitivity and Euclidicity. Here, we can use the insight of Section 3.2, i.e., that we can interpret $\neg I\varphi \wedge I\alpha \wedge I(\alpha \wedge \varphi)$ as $\neg K\alpha \wedge \neg K\neg\alpha \wedge K\varphi$. To give an indication of the kind of axiomatisations that one would have by doing so, we show the result for transitivity.

Lemma 9. *Consider the following axiom scheme:*
$G4 \; I\alpha \rightarrow [(\neg I\varphi \wedge I(\varphi \wedge \alpha)) \rightarrow$
$\qquad \neg I(\neg I\varphi \wedge I(\alpha \wedge \varphi)) \wedge I(\neg I\varphi \wedge I(\varphi \wedge \alpha) \wedge \alpha)]$

Then, **Ig** $\cup\{G4\}$ *is sound and complete with respect to transitive models.*

We leave axiomatisations of other classes of frames for further work.

We conclude by stressing that we are using a modal logic quite dissimilar to the one that the reader may be familiar with. For example we have that reflexivity is not definable by means of operator I only. This can be checked by using Figure 1 again: were reflexivity definable with the $\mathcal{L}_I$-formula ψ, then we would have $F_2, w_2 \models \psi$. However, we already observed that then also $F_1, w_1 \models \psi$, which would imply that F_1 is reflexive as well, at w_1, which it obviously is not.

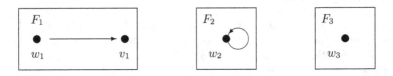

Fig. 1. Three worlds without any ignorance

5   Another Look at FIPA's Feasibility Precondition

Logic is used in MAS and AI in a variety of topics ranging from negotiation to specification of behaviour. Of particular interest is the role that theories of beliefs and intention play in the area of communication languages. It has been argued long ago that one possible way to give a semantics to the speech act **inform** in agent communication languages is by means of pre-conditions and post-conditions. In particular, let us consider FIPA's pre-condition (called "feasibility condition" in [10]) for an inform speech act $< i, inform(j, \varphi) >$, i.e., an act in which agent i informs agent j of the formula φ. The feasibility condition is given as:

$$B_i\varphi \wedge \neg B_i(Bif_j\varphi \vee Uif_j\varphi)$$

There are three different operators at play here. B stands for "belief". Bif stands for "believe whether". Uif stands for "uncertain whether". All these are indexed with the agent for which they are referred to. So the formula above is read as: "agent i believes that φ, and it is not the case that agent i believes that either agent j believes whether or not φ is the case, or that agent j is uncertain about φ". The last term in the original formulation is meant to have a fuzzy interpretation of the kind "j suspects φ may be true but he is not sure about it.".

FIPA's specification does not define formally the way these operators are to be interpreted. In the following we try to do this by using the formal machinery of this paper. Roughly speaking, the above makes two requirements.

1. Agent i believes φ.
2. Agent i believes that agent j is not aware of the truth value of φ.

1) is a sincerity condition - the agent would not send false information without violating its specification. 2) requires that agents are not sending information that they believe is redundant. Given the difficulties of expressing formally the notion of being biased towards φ we do not incorporate it into our reading. This model is best suited for cooperative systems where benevolent agents aim

at distributing correct information. We do recognise our translation above may be simply an approximation of what is intended in the specification; but given that the semantics of the operators of Bif and Uif is not given, this could still prove beneficial. In this interpretation, the feasibility precondition above can be formally expressed in the logical language of this paper as:

$$B_i\varphi \wedge B_i I_j \varphi$$

In the above B is a KD45 operator defined like knowledge, but for which the relation does not enjoy reflexivity, and I is the operator built on the same relation, and discussed in this paper. While this attempt does not incorporate the operator of uncertainty, the above does seem to capture the intuition of FIPA's specifiers, and its semantics can be given formally by using the machinery of this paper – something that is currently not possible to do for any precondition of FIPA's speech acts. Completeness results for logics in which interaction between the two operators occur can now be investigated.

6 Conclusions

We have argued that the concept of an agent being ignorant is worth investigating further, and suggested examples from MAS as to why this is the case. We showed that this analysis can be carried out independently from the commonly adopted logics for knowledge. Semantic definitions for a non-standard modal operator, and completeness results have been presented. We would contend that the technical results of the paper offer some insights into the possibility of expressing other operators that are not defined on the set of accessible points as it is traditionally done in mainstream modal logic.

Some technical questions are still left open at this stage. As we have seen in Figure 1 there may be frames that satisfy the same formulas but are not bisimilar. It would be interesting to study what technical concept is relevant here for this notion. Since our language is in many respects similar to that of *graded modalities* (cf. [11]), the notion of generalised n-bisimulation introduced there might provide a hint to find such a similarity. From a purely epistemic logic point of view, the connection with logics for *only knowing* ([12]) seems promising. The idea of saying that an agent only knows φ is that he knows φ and all of its consequences ($K_i\psi_1$, if $\vdash \varphi \rightarrow \psi_1$), but he is ignorant about any stronger formula $I\psi_2$, if $\vdash \psi_2 \rightarrow \varphi$.

More broadly we feel there is much scope for further work with respect to connections to specific MAS areas. One avenue we like to investigate is the application of this work to MAS security. The formalisms resulting from the refinements of BAN logic [13] are concerned with proving that particular protocols are secure, i.e., that any intruder would not be able to decrypt the messages being exchanged. In the language of this paper this means that its state of *ignorance* is an *invariant* in the execution. BAN logic in its standard form suffer from the lack of semantics and is purely an axiomatic system. Maybe the machinery of this paper can be used to solve this problem.

The semantics of the speech act **inform** presented above seems also a promising area for further development. Irrespective of whether the particular translation given here captures the actual intuition of FIPA's specifiers, the operator of ignorance seems to be a useful ingredient for a definition that can actually be interpreted on a formal semantics. The interest here is not purely theoretical – having a clear semantics is an essential ingredient to move to compliance testing and verification [14]. This is something that is lacking in all FIPA's implementations at present.

References

1. Dennet, D.: The Intentional Stance. MIT Press (1987)
2. Blackburn, P., de Rijke, M., Venema, Y.: Modal logic. Cambridge University Press (2001)
3. Fagin, R., Halpern, J.Y., Moses, Y., Vardi, M.Y.: The Intentional Stance. Reasoning About Knowledge (1995)
4. Rao, A.S., Georgeff, M.P.: Modeling rational agents within a BDI-architecture, Morgan Kaufmann Publishers (1991) 473–484
5. Rao, A.S., Georgeff, M.P.: Decision procedures for BDI logics. Journal of Logic and Computation **8** (1998) 293–343
6. Bratman, M.E.: What is intention? In Cohen, P.R., Morgan, J.L., Pollack, M.E., eds.: Intentions in Communication, The MIT Press: Cambridge, MA (1990) 15–32
7. Cohen, P.R., Levesque, H.J.: Intention is choice with commitment. Artificial Intelligence **42** (1990) 213–261
8. van der Hoek, W., Wooldridge, M.: Model checking knowledge and time. In: SPIN 2002 – Proceedings of the Ninth International SPIN Workshop on Model Checking of Software, Grenoble, France. (2002)
9. Penczek, W., Lomuscio, A.: Verifying epistemic properties of multi-agent systems via model checking. Fundamenta Informaticae **55** (2002)
10. FIPA: Foundation for Intelligent Physical Agents. http://www.fipa.org.
11. van der Hoek, W.: On the semantics of graded modalities. Journal of Applied Non Classical Logics **2** (1992) 81–123
12. Halpern, J.: Theory of knowledge and ignorance for many agents. Journal of Logic and Computation **7** (1997) 79–108
13. Burrows, M., Abadi, M., Needham, R.: A logic of authentication. ACM Transactions on Computer Systems **8** (1990) 18–36
14. Wooldridge, M.: Semantic issues in the verification of agent communication languages. Journal of Autonomous Agents and Multi-Agent Systems **3** (2000) 9–31

Coo-BDI: Extending the BDI Model
with Cooperativity

Davide Ancona and Viviana Mascardi

DISI - Università di Genova
Via Dodecaneso 35, 16146, Genova, Italy
{davide,mascardi}@disi.unige.it

Abstract. We define Coo-BDI, an extension of the BDI architecture with the notion of cooperativity. Agents can cooperate by exchanging and sharing plans in a quite flexible way. As a main result Coo-BDI promotes adaptivity and sharing of resources; as a by-product, it provides a better support for dealing with agents which do not possess their own procedural knowledge for processing a given event.

1 Introduction

Intelligent agents [1,2] are a powerful abstraction for conceptualizing and modeling complex systems in a clear and intuitive way. For this reason many declarative agent models have been proposed in the last years. One of the most successful is the Belief, Desire and Intention (BDI) one [3], whose wide appreciation is witnessed by the development of a BDI logic [4], the definition of BDI-based languages (AgentTalk [5], 3APL [6], AgentSpeak(L) [7]) and the creation of BDI-based development tools such as JACK [8], PRS [9] and dMARS [10].

Despite this large consensus, some BDI concepts and mechanisms are not represented and implemented in a uniform way. To make an example, let us consider the notion of "goals", namely, consistent sets of desires. For many authors, they should be explicitly represented in order to reason about their properties and ensure their consistence. This explicit representation is not available in current BDI systems and languages such as dMARS, AgentSpeak(L) and JACK where goals, if represented at all, have only a transient representation as a type of event. A similar situation occurs when events (or subgoals, since they are considered the same entity in implemented systems) cannot be managed because of the lack of suitable plans. In the original specification of the BDI architecture and in many high level BDI languages this case is not considered at all, and implemented systems solve it in very different ways: in most of them, the event or subgoal is simply ignored; in others the definition of a default "catch-all" plan is required. This heterogeneity is partly due to the little attention received by the notion of *agent cooperativity* which, instead, should deserve a major role in the BDI architecture.

Cooperativity is the ability of an agent to help other agents to achieve their desires. While this feature needs to be implemented in a rather ad hoc way each

J. Leite et al. (Eds.): DALT 2003, LNAI 2990, pp. 109–134, 2004.

time it must be exhibited by a BDI agent, Coo-BDI overcomes this problem by providing a rather powerful mechanism for promoting agent cooperativity, by allowing agents to exchange their plans. This feature turns out to be useful in many application fields such as:

Personal Digital Assistants (PDAs). The physical resources of a PDA are usually limited and for the PDA technology to be really effective, dynamic loading and linking of code is a fundamental aspect. If the traditional BDI approach is adopted, implementing this feature is not easy: BDI agents are expected neither to possess the capability of looking for external plans nor to dynamically extend their plan library with the plans retrieved from other agents. Coo-BDI can cope with both issues and allows an agent to discard the external plans after their usage: this may prove useful when the space resources of the PDA have strict bounds.

Self-repairing Agents. By self-repairing agent we mean an agent situated in a dynamically changing software environment and able to identify the portions of its code that should be updated to ensure its correct functioning in the evolving environment. When the agent finds out pieces of code that have become obsolete, it replaces them with new code, provided by a server agent, without needing to stop its own activity or the whole system. Coo-BDI allows to dynamically replace local plans with external ones and thus can be used for modeling such a self-repairing agent.

Digital Butlers. A "digital butler" is an agent that assists the user in some task such as managing her/his agenda, filtering incoming mail, retrieving interesting information from the web. A typical feature of a digital butler is its ability to dynamically adapt its behavior to the user needs. This ability is achieved by cooperating both with more experienced digital butlers and with the assisted user. In our setting we may think that, through a user friendly interface, the user may train the agent by showing the right sequence of actions to perform in particular situations. The agent may treat this sequence as an externally retrieved plan which enriches its plan library, as well as plans retrieved from peer agents.

More in general, Coo-BDI is suitable for modeling all kinds of "learning agents" which learn from the interaction with other agents. This is made possible by the main novel feature of Coo-BDI consisting of a built-in mechanism for exchanging plans between agents when there are no local applicable plans for achieving a certain desire[1]. As a consequence, the notions of *desire* and *event* must be kept clearly distinct; an agent has an event queue containing events generated by the environment or by other agents. Managing an event means removing it from the queue and generating the set of desires associated with it; note that such a process is inherently local, in the sense that each agent decides which are its own desires associated with a certain event without any interference from the outside (that is, there is no cooperativity at this stage).

---

[1] We prefer to use the term "desire" rather than "goal" for coherence with the Belief, Desires, Intentions acronym.

For example, the event *"reception of an e-mail asking to join the party at Liza's place at 7 p.m."* may generate the desires *"cancel all the appointments for this evening"* and *"reach Liza's place at 7 p.m."* in a given agent, and the desire *"phone Liza for thanking and declining"* in another agent. Therefore, desires must be kept distinct from events and maintained as explicit information in an ad hoc structure.

In Coo-BDI cooperativity can be exploited only after desires generation, when the appropriate plans for achieving the generated desires must be selected. Let us go on with the previous example, by supposing that the agent which desires to reach Liza's place at 7 p.m. has no procedural knowledge (namely, no plans) for achieving that desire. In the existing BDI languages and systems, the agent would give up or would apply a default plan. In the extension we propose, the agent asks to other agents if they have a good plan for reaching Liza's home. Some of the agents contacted for advice could cooperate by suggesting plans for achieving this desire, allowing the requiring agent to join the party.

The structure of the paper is the following: in Section 2 we recall the main BDI concepts and survey the common approaches to the "no applicable plans" problem; in Section 3 we introduce Coo-BDI. In Section 4 we provide the structural specification of Coo-BDI and in Section 5 we provide its behavioral specification. The usefulness of our extension is shown by means of an example in Section 6. Section 7 outlines related and future work.

2   The BDI Model

The BDI model is characterized by the following concepts:

- *Beliefs*: the agent's knowledge about the world.
- *Desires*: objectives to be accomplished; are similar to goals, but they do not need to be consistent.
- *Intentions*: plans currently under execution.
- *Plans*: "recipes" representing the procedural knowledge of the agent. They are usually characterized by a trigger which fires the adoption of the plan, a precondition that the current state must satisfy for the plan to be applicable, a body of actions to perform, an invariant condition that must hold during all the plan execution, a set of actions to be executed if the plan execution terminates successfully and a set of actions to be executed in case of plan failure. Plans are static: they can not change neither can be exchanged during the agent's life cycle.

All BDI systems also include an *event queue* where external events (perceived from the environment) and internal subgoals (generated by the agent itself while trying to achieve a main goal) are stored.

The typical BDI execution cycle is characterized by the following steps:

1. observe the world and the agent's internal state, and update the *event queue* consequently;

2. generate possible new plan instances whose trigger event matches an event in the event queue (*relevant* plan instances) and whose precondition is satisfied (*applicable* plan instances);

3. select for execution one instance from the set of applicable plan instances;

4. push the selected instance onto an existing or new *intention stack*, according to whether or not the event is a (sub)goal;

5. select an intention stack, take the topmost plan instance and execute the next step of this current instance: if the step is an action, perform it, otherwise, if it is a subgoal, insert it on the event queue.

This description is not detailed enough to answer to the question: *what should the agent do if the set of applicable plans is empty?* This issue is usually not considered by the BDI high level specifications. In [3], Rao and Georgeff write that after the plan instance generator reads the event queue and returns a list of applicable instances, the deliberator selects from this list a subset of instances which are added to the intention structure. We can guess that if no instances can be adopted the interpreter simply jumps to the next step but this is not explicitly established by the specification. In [10], d'Inverno, Kinny, Luck and Wooldridge provide a more detailed specification, however, the case "no applicable plans found" is not considered. In the original specification of AgentSpeak(L) [7], it is not clear what the interpreter does if the set of applicable plan instances is empty. According to the more operational-oriented specification of AgentSpeak(L) given in [11,12], whose brief description can be found in [13], an event should be discarded if it has no relevant plan instances.

When we move from specification to implementation, the problem above cannot be ignored any more. There are different implementation solutions BDI systems adopt. When the implemented BDI systems AgentTalk, JACK, dMARS select an event from the event queue for which there are no applicable instances, they simply ignore the event and remove it from the queue. Such an "ignore and discard" behavior can be modified in JACK and dMARS only by exploiting the ad hoc meta-programming features offered by the languages. The implementation of 3APL (`http://www.cs.uu.nl/3apl/`) adopts a default instance if no other instances can be applied to deal with the selected event. In the implementation of AgentSpeak(L) developed by Bordini et al. [14] (`http://www.inf.ufrgs.br/~massoc`) the user has two possible options if there are no applicable instances for a given event: she/he can ask the interpreter either to discard the event or to keep it in the set of events. In the latter case, the event can be eventually managed if at a certain time it has an applicable plan instance.

This short overview shows that 1) BDI does not provide a built-in mechanism allowing plan exchange between agents and 2) in BDI systems the "no applicable instances" problem is either neglected or solved in rather naive ways. On the contrary, Coo-BDI promotes cooperation by allowing agents to exchange their plans and exploits such a feature for partly solving the "no applicable instances" problem in a rather natural and general way.

3   Coo-BDI: A Gentle Introduction

Coo-BDI (Cooperative BDI) is based on the dMARS specification [10] and extends the traditional BDI architecture described in Section 2 in many respects.

The first Coo-BDI extension is that external events and main desires are kept separate. In Coo-BDI there are two structures which maintain events and desires: the "event queue" which only contains external events, and the "desire set", which only contains *achieve* desires generated by events. We distinguish between *main desires*, which are kept in the desire set, and *subaltern desires*, which are generated while trying to achieve a main desire and remain implicit in the intention stack structure. When a main desires fails backtracking is applied and a "fresh" (not already attempted) plan instance is selected for it. The main desire is removed by the set if there are no more fresh plan instances for it. Subaltern desires are not backtracked, both to keep the Coo-BDI interpreter and data structures simpler and to maintain the same strategy implemented by dMARS.

The main extension of Coo-BDI, however, involves the introduction of *co-operations* among agents to retrieve external plans for achieving desires (both main and subaltern), the extension of plans with *access specifiers*, the introduction of *default* plans, the extension of *intentions* to take into account the external plan instances retrieval mechanism and the modification of the Coo-BDI *engine* (interpreter) to cope with all these issues.

Cooperation Strategy. The cooperation strategy (or, simply, the cooperation) of an agent A includes the set of agents with which is expected to cooperate, the plan retrieval policy and the plan acquisition policy. The cooperation strategy may evolve during time allowing the maximum flexibility and autonomy of the agents.

Plans. Coo-BDI plans are classified in *specific* and *default* ones; like BDI plans, both kinds of plans consist of a trigger, a precondition, a body, an invariant and two sets of success and failure actions. Besides these components, they also have an *access specifier* which determines the set of agents the plan can be shared with. It may assume three values: *private* (the plan cannot be shared), *public* (the plan can be shared with any agent) and *only(TrustedAgents)* (the plan can be shared only with the agents contained in the *TrustedAgents* set). A default plan is a plan where the access specifier is *private*, the trigger is a variable and the precondition is the *true* constant; therefore, by definition, a default plan can always be applicable and can never be exchanged. Each agent must always provide at least one default plan, so that every desire can be managed. A specific plan is simply a non default plan.

Intentions. Coo-BDI intentions are in a one-to-one relation with main desires: each intention is created when a new main desire enters the desires set, and it is deleted when the main desire fails or is achieved. Intentions are characterized by "standard" components plus components introduced to manage the external plan retrieval mechanism. External plans are retrieved, according to the retrieval policy, both for main and for subaltern desires.

Coo-BDI Engine. The engine of Coo-BDI departs from the classical one to take into account both desires generation and cooperations. It is characterized by three macro-steps:

1. process the event queue;
2. process suspended intentions;
3. process active intentions.

Before describing these three steps, we need to explain the mechanism for retrieving relevant plans, which is essential for understanding how steps 1 and 3 work. Such a mechanism consists of four sequential steps. a) The intention is suspended. b) The local relevant plan instances for the desire are generated and associated with the intention. c) According to the cooperation, the set S of the agents expected to cooperate is defined. d) A plan request for the desire is created and sent to all the agents in S.

Events in the queue may be either *cooperation* or *ordinary* events. Cooperation events include requests of relevant plan instances for a desire and answers to a plan request. Ordinary events include at least message reception and notification of updates performed on the agent's beliefs set. When an agent receives a request for a desire from another agent A, it sends to A the (possibly empty) set of all its local plan instances which are both relevant for that desire and visible to A (recall that, by definition, default plans cannot be visible). On the other hand, when an agent receives an answer to a plan request for a desire, it checks if the answer is still valid and if so it updates the intention associated with the desire to include the just obtained plan instances and to remember that answer. Finally, if the event is an ordinary one, the set of corresponding desires is generated and added to the desire set. For each new desire an empty intention is created and the mechanism for retrieving relevant plans is started.

The management of suspended intentions consists in looking for all suspended intentions which can be resumed. When an intention is resumed the set of applicable plan instances is generated from the set of relevant plan instances except for the already failed instances, one applicable plan instance is selected and the corresponding plan instance execution is created. If the applicable plan instances set is empty, the desire fails and is deleted from the desire set, and the intention is destroyed. Otherwise, the selected plan instance is pushed onto the intention stack. If the selected plan is an externally retrieved one, it may be used and discarded, or added to the plan library or used to replace plans with a unifying trigger according to the acquisition policy.

Finally, active intentions are managed like in the BDI architecture except for the mechanism for retrieving external relevant plans triggered by desire achievement.

The reader may find the structural specification of Coo-BDI in Section 4 and its behavioral specification in Section 5. Both Coo-BDI data structures and behavior are specified using Prolog.

4   Structural Specification of Coo-BDI

The structural specification of Coo-BDI is given by means of a BNF. We will use the following informally defined non-terminals:

- **Variable**: a variable symbol
- **Pred**: a predicate symbol
- **Term**: a term
- **GroundTerm**: a ground term
- **AgentId**: a string representing the identity of an agent
- **RequestId**: a string identifying a request
- **IntentionId**: a string identifying an intention
- **Message**: any kind of term eventually containing free variables
- **Substitution**: a mapping from variables to terms
- Every non terminal NT followed by Set (eg: **AgentIdSet**) represents a set of elements in NT.
- Every non terminal NT followed by Sequence (eg: **InternalActionSequence**) represents a sequence of elements in NT.
- Every non terminal NT followed by Queue (eg: **EventQueue**) represents a queue of elements in NT.
- Every non terminal NT followed by Stack (eg: **PlanInstanceExecutionStack**) represents a stack of elements in NT.

Clearly, the only difference for the last four items consists in the primitives that will be used.

Beliefs, Desires, Queries and Actions. A belief formula is either an atom or the negation of an atom. Beliefs are ground belief formulas. Desires have the form `achieve(BeliefFormula)`. Queries are denoted by `query(SituationFormula)` where a situation formula is either a belief formula, or the constant `true` or `false`, or conjunctions and disjunctions of situation formulas.

Actions may be internal or external. Internal actions are updates of the data base of an agent's beliefs: `add(BeliefFormula)` and `remove(BeliefFormula)`. These actions can only be executed if their argument is ground. External actions include at least the ability of sending messages to agents: `send(AgentId, Message)`.

```
BeliefFormula ::= Pred(Term, ...., Term) | not(Pred(Term, ...., Term))
Belief ::= Pred(GroundTerm, ...., GroundTerm) |
  not(Pred(GroundTerm, ...., GroundTerm))
SituationFormula ::= true | false | BeliefFormula |
  SituationFormula and SituationFormula |
  SituationFormula or SituationFormula
Desire ::= achieve(BeliefFormula)
Query   ::= query(SituationFormula)
InternalAction ::= add(BeliefFormula) | remove(BeliefFormula)
ExternalAction ::= send(AgentId, Message)
Action ::= InternalAction | ExternalAction
```

Plans. There are no syntactic differences between specific and default plans: both are defined by an access specifier, a trigger, a precondition, a body, an invariant, and two sets of internal actions to be used respectively when the plan succeeds or fails.

The access specifier may assume the following values:

- private, meaning that the plan cannot be provided;
- public, meaning that the plan can be provided to any agent;
- only(TrustedAgents) where TrustedAgents is a set of agent identifiers specifying the only trusted agents which can receive instances of the plan.

The trigger of a specific plan is the desire the plan is designed to achieve.
Preconditions and invariants are situation formulas.

Plan bodies are non empty trees where nodes are execution states and edges
are labelled by either desires, or queries, or (both external and internal) actions.
Success and failure actions are sequences of internal actions.

```
AccessSpecifier ::= private | public | only(AgentIdSet)
EdgeLabel ::= Desire | Query | Action
Body ::= state(EdgeBodySequence)
EdgeBody ::= (EdgeLabel, Body)
Plan ::= plan(AccessSpecifier, Desire, SituationFormula, Body,
SituationFormula, InternalActionSequence, InternalActionSequence)
```

Plan Instances. A plan instance is a pair (Plan, Substitution) formed by a plan
and a substitution.

A plan instance (Plan, Substitution) is called *relevant* w.r.t. a desire if Substitution is a most general unifier for that desire and the trigger of Plan. Note
that plan instances formed by a default plan are always relevant.

A plan instance (Plan, Substitution) is called *applicable* if the formula obtained by applying Substitution to the precondition of Plan is a logical consequence of the beliefs of the agent's data base. Note that plan instances formed
by a default plan are always applicable.

The execution of a plan instance is defined by its plan instance together with
the computed substitution, the current state of the body of the plan and the set
of the remaining siblings of the current state which have not been executed yet.

```
PlanInstance ::= (Plan, Substitution)
PlanInstanceExecution ::=
planInstanceExecution(PlanInstance, Substitution, State, StateSet).
```

Intentions and Requests. An intention is composed by a unique identifier, a stack
of executions of plan instances, a status, a set of relevant plan instances, a set
of agent identifiers and a set of failed plan instances.

The intention identifier is used for modeling in a convenient way the two
relations DesireIntention and IntentionRequest, represented by the two predicates relationDesireIntention(Desire, IntentionId) and relationIntentionRe-
quest(IntentionId, Request), which associate with each main desire exactly one
corresponding intention and with each suspended intention the corresponding (if
any) request of relevant plan instances, respectively.

The stack of executions of plan instances is similar in spirit to the execution
stack of logic programs.

The status may be either suspended or active. An intention is suspended if
the execution of the plan instance on top of the stack needs to achieve a desire for

which no plan instance has been selected yet; in this case the relevant instances set contains the relevant plan instances which have been already collected for the desire, and the set of agent identifiers contains all the identifiers of those agents which are still expected to cooperate for achieving the desire.

A cooperation request is specified by a unique identifier, the identifier of the requesting agent and the desire to achieve.

A relation `relationIntentionRequest` associates with any intention identity of suspended intentions its current (if any) request for cooperation, and with any request the suspended intention it originates from, if the request is still valid.

```
Intention ::= intention(IntentionId, PlanInstanceExecutionStack, Status,
  PlanInstanceSet, AgentIdSet, PlanInstanceSet)
Status ::= suspended | active
Request ::= request(RequestId, AgentId, Desire)
```

Events. There are two kinds of events: cooperation and ordinary events. A cooperation event is either `requested(request(RequestId, ReqAgentId, Desire))` with the meaning "agent identified by `ReqAgentId` is requesting relevant plan instances for `Desire`", or `provided(AgentId, request(RequestId, ReqAgentId, Desire), Instances)` with the meaning "agent identified by `AgentId` has cooperated in response of the request `request(RequestId, ReqAgentId, Desire)` by providing a set `Instances` of relevant plan instances for `Desire`".

Ordinary events include at least the following ones:

- `received(AgentId, Message)` with the meaning "message `Message` has been received from the agent identified by `AgentId`";
- `added(Belief)` with the meaning "the new belief `Belief` has been added to the agent's data base";
- `removed(Belief)` with the meaning "the belief `Belief` has been removed from the agent's data base".

Events perceived from the agent are stored in a priority queue `eventQueue(EventQueue)`.

```
Event ::= CooperationEvent | OrdinaryEvent
CooperationEvent ::= requested(request(RequestId, AgentId, Desire)) |
  provided(AgentId, request(RequestId, AgentId, Desire), PlanInstanceSet)
OrdinaryEvent ::= received(AgentId, Message) | added(Belief) |
  removed(Belief)
```

Agent Definition. An agent is defined by the following predicates (defined in the agent's knowledge base):

- `agentId(AgentId)` specifying the unique agent's identifier;
- `eventQueue(EventQueue)` specifying the current agent's event queue;
- `isDesire(Desire)` specifying the current set of agent's main desires;
- `isPlan(Plan)` specifying the current set of (both specific and default) agent's plans;
- `isIntention(Intention)` specifying the current set of agent's intentions;

- the current agent's beliefs;
- three predicates specifying the current agent's *cooperation*:
  - `trustedAgents(TrustedAgents)` specifying the current set of identifiers of the agents trusted by the agent;
  - `retrievalPolicy(Retrieval)` specifying the current retrieval policy, where `Retrieval ::= always | noLocal`;
  - `acquisitionPolicy(Acquisition)` specifying the current plan acquisition policy, where `Acquisition ::= discard | add | replace`.
- `relationDesireIntention(Desire,IntentionId)` specifying a one-to-one relation between all the current main desires of the agent and the identifiers of all its current intentions;
- `relationIntentionRequest(IntentionId,Request)` specifying a one-to-one relation between the identifiers of some of the currently suspended intentions of the agent and some requests issued by the agent;
- `canResume(Request, AgentIdentifiers, PlanInstances)` specifying whether a certain suspended intention, waiting on the cooperation request `Request`, can be resumed, provided that the set of agents which still have to reply to the request is `AgentIdentifiers`, and the set of relevant plan instances collected so far is `PlanInstances`;
- `getDesires(OrdinaryEvent, Desires)` specifying a total function mapping every ordinary event into the (possibly empty) set of main desires that must be generated from that event;
- `selectInstance(PlanInstances, SelectedPlanInstance)` specifying a total function returning a specific member `SelectedPlanInstance` of each non empty sets of plan instances `PlanInstances`, s.t. if `SelectedPlanInstance` is an instance of a default plan, then `PlanInstances` does not contain instances of specific plans;
- `selectIntention(Intentions, SelectedIntention)` specifying a total function returning a specific member `SelectedIntention` of each non empty set of active intentions;
- `selectState(States, SelectedState)` specifying a total function returning a member `SelectedState` of each non empty set of states `States`.

Among the predicates listed above, `agentId`, `canResume`, `getDesires`, `selectInstance`, `selectIntention` and `selectState` are *static* in the sense that they cannot be modified during the agent's lifetime, whereas all the others can be dynamically modified.

5   Behavioral Specification of Coo-BDI

The behavioral specification of Coo-BDI is given using Prolog.

Besides obtaining a working prototype for free, using a logic programming language for specifying a multi-agent system has other advantages:

- *MAS execution*: the evolution of a MAS consists of a nondeterministic succession of events; from an abstract point of view a logic programming language is a nondeterministic language in which computation occurs via a search process.

- *Meta-reasoning capabilities*: agents may need to dynamically modify their behavior so as to adapt it to changes in the environment. Thus, the possibility given by logic programming of viewing programs as data is very useful in this setting.
- *Rationality and reactiveness of agents*: the *declarative* and the *operational* interpretation of logic programs are strictly related to the main characteristics of agents, i.e., *rationality* and *reactiveness*. In fact, we can think of a *pure* logic program as the specification of the rational component of an agent and we can use the operational view of logic programs (e.g. left-to-right execution, use of non-logical predicates) to model the reactive behavior of an agent. The adoption of logic programming for combining reactivity and rationality is described in [15].

These advantages motivate our choice to use Prolog to specify Coo-BDI. Finally, note that the set of clauses specified in the sequel should be considered as part of a formal (executable) specification, rather than a Prolog program implementing an interpreter for Coo-BDI agents. Therefore, we have preferred to sacrifice implementation issues and efficiency in favor of a better clarity.

Notations and Assumptions. Variables begin with an uppercase letter or with _ (we use the last notation for unnamed variables which appear only once in a clause).

We exploit meta-logical, extra-logical and second-order predicates of the language, as well as red cuts to implement negation.

- *Meta-logical predicates.* We use `var(Term)` to test whether `Term` is a variable or not; `Term1\=Term2` to test not unificability of terms `Term1` and `Term2`; `Term1==Term2` to unify terms `Term1` and `Term2`; `call(Goal)` to call `Goal`; `(Goal1; Goal2)` to denote the logical disjunction of `Goal1` and `Goal2`.
- *Extra-logical predicates.* To specify updates to the agent state, we use the standard predicates `assert(Fact)`, `retract(Fact)` and the non standard `retractall(Fact)` which always succeeds and retracts all clauses of a dynamic predicate whose head unifies with `Fact`. The use of update primitives can introduce incoherence in the knowledge base if they appear within a failing goal. To avoid this undesirable effect and keep the semantics of our specification clear, we always leave update primitives at the end of the goal; furthermore, `retract(Fact)` is always called after checking that `Fact` is present in the knowledge base, in order to avoid undesired failures.
- *Second-order predicates.* To specify the retrieval of a set of elements satisfying a given condition (goal), we use the `setof` standard predicate, s.t. `setof(Template, Goal, Set)` succeeds if `Set` is the set of all instances of `Template` such that `Goal` is satisfied, where that set is non empty. For our convenience, we assume that an empty set constant `emptySet` is returned by `setof` when no instances satisfying `Goal` are found.
- *Negation.* We use a `not(Fact)` predicate to express negation. Its implementation can be given using `cut` and `fail`.

We assume that a set of standard primitives on commonly used data structures is defined. We avoid discussing their meaning when it is clear or well-known.

- *Primitives on queues.* emptyQueue (constant empty queue), get(EventQueue, Element, ResultingEventQueue), put(Element, EventQueue, ResultingEventQueue).
- *Primitives on sets and relations.* emptySet (constant empty set), setUnion(Set1, Set2, Set1UnionSet2), singleton(Element, SetContainingOnlyElement), setDifference(Set1, Set2, Set1MinusSet2), belongs(Element, Set).
- *Primitives on stacks.* emptyStack (constant empty stack), push(Element, Stack, ResultingStack), pop(Stack, ResultingStack), top(Stack, TopElement).
- *Primitives on trees.* root(Tree, Node), children(Tree, Node, Set), leaf(Tree, Node), label(Tree, NodeOrigin, NodeDestination, LabelOfArcFromOriginToDestination).
- *Primitives on sequences.* emptySeq (constant empty sequence), head(Sequence, Head, RemainingSequence), tail(Sequence, RemainingSequence).

We assume that a set of Coo-BDI-specific primitives for plan exchange and for sociality is provided:

- multicastRequestOp(AgentIdSet, Request): takes a set of agent identifiers AgentIdSet and a request Request and puts requested(Request) into the event queue of each agent in AgentIdSet;
- provideOp(ProviderId, request(RequestId, AgentId, Desire), Instances): takes an agent identifier ProviderId, a request request(RequestId, AgentId, Desire) and a set of instances Instances and puts provided(ProviderId, request(RequestId, AgentId, Desire), Instances) into the event queue of AgentId;
- sendOp(SenderId, ReceiverId, Message): takes two agent identifiers, SenderId and ReceiverId, and a message Message, and puts received(SenderId, Message) into the event queue of ReceiverId. Currently we do not conform to any specific agent communication language: Message may be any kind of term eventually containing free variables implementing information passing.

Finally, we assume that a primitive newId(Identity) for generating new fresh identities is available as well as a set of logical primitives. We refer to [16] for the notion of substitution, composition of substitutions and most general unifier.

- ground(Literal): true if Literal (Atom or not(Atom)) is ground.
- apply(Theta, Term, TermTheta): takes a substitution Theta and a term Term and returns the term obtained from Term by replacing each variable X by Theta(X).
- compose(Sigma, Theta, SigmaTheta): takes two substitutions Sigma and Theta and returns their composition.
- mgu(Expr1, Expr2, Mgu): takes two expressions and returns their most general unifier.

Coo-BDI Engine. As already said in Section 3, the engine of Coo-BDI departs from the classical one to take into account both desires generation and cooperations, and is characterized by processing the event queue, processing suspended intentions and processing active intentions.

```
cooBDIengine :- processEventQueue, processSuspendedIntentions,
  processActiveIntentions.
```

Processing Events. If the event queue is empty, nothing is done (first clause). Otherwise, an event Event is taken from the event queue. The event is managed and the agent's event queue is updated.

```
processEventQueue :- eventQueue(EventQueue), empty(EventQueue).

processEventQueue :- eventQueue(EventQueue), not(empty(EventQueue)),
  get(Event, EventQueue, RemainingEventQueue), manageEvent(Event),
  retract(eventQueue(EventQueue)),
  assert(eventQueue(RemainingEventQueue)).
```

When managing an event, three situations may occur: 1) If Event is of kind requested(request(RequestId, RequestingAgentId, Desire)), then getRel-Instances(Request) retrieves all the instances of specific plans relevant for Desire and whose specifier is either public or only(TrustedAgents), and TrustedAgents includes RequestingAgentId. The retrieved Instances set is posted into the RequestingAgentId event queue by calling ProvideOp(AgentId, Request, Instances), where AgentId is the identifier of the agent performing the provideOp action.

```
manageEvent(requested(request(ReqId, ReqAgentId, Desire))) :-
  agentId(AgentId),
  getRelInstances(Instances, request(ReqId, ReqAgentId, Desire)),
  provideOp(AgentId, request(ReqId, ReqAgentId, Desire), Instances).

getRelInstances(Instances, request(_ReqId, ReqAgentId, Desire)) :-
  setof((plan(AccessSpecifier, Trigger, Precondition, Body, Invariant,
              SuccessActions, FailureActions), Substitution),
        (isPlan(plan(AccessSpecifier, Trigger, Precondition, Body,
                    Invariant, SuccessActions, FailureActions)),
        (AccessSpecifier == public;
          (AccessSpecifier == only(TrustedAgents),
            belongs(ReqAgentId, TrustedAgents))),
          mgu(Trigger, Desire, Substitution)), Instances).
```

2) Event is of kind provided(ProvidingAgentId, request(RequestId, AgentId, Desire), RetrievedInstances). If there exists an intention Intention s.t. the intention identifier and the request request(RequestId, AgentId, Desire) belong to the relationIntentionRequest then the retrieval of relevant plan instances for Desire is still ongoing. Intention is updated by adding the retrieved Instances to the relevant instances and by removing the identifier of the answering agent (ProvidingAgentId) from the set WaitingOnAgents. The updated intention replaces Intention (first clause). Otherwise, if there is no Intention s.t. the intention identifier and the request belong to the relationIntentionRequest, the event is ignored (not shown).

```
manageEvent(provided(ProvidingAgentId, request(ReqId, AgentId,
        Desire), Instances)) :-
relationIntentionRequest(IntentionId, request(ReqId, AgentId, Desire),
isIntention(intention(IntentionId, Stack, Status, RelevantInstances,
  WaitingOnAgents, FailedInstances)),
singleton(ProvidingAgentId, SingletonProvidingAgentId),
setDifference(WaitingOnAgents, SingletonProvidingAgentId,
  UpdatedWaitingOnAgents),
setUnion(Instances, RelevantInstances, UpdatedRelevantInstances),
retract(isIntention(intention(IntentionId, Stack, Status,
  RelevantInstances, WaitingOnAgents, FailedInstances))),
assert(isIntention(intention(IntentionId, Stack, Status,
  UpdatedRelevantInstances, UpdatedWaitingOnAgents, FailedInstances))).
```

3) If `Event` is an ordinary event, the set of corresponding desires is retrieved
by means of `getDesires(OrdinaryEvent, Desires)` and the main desire set is updated to contain them. For each generated desire not already present in the main
desire set, a new intention stack is created and initialized (`createIntention`), the
intention set and the `DesireIntention` relation are updated to take into account
the newly created intention and the retrieval of relevant plan instances for the
intention and the desire is started (`retrieveRelevantInstances(Intention, De-
sire)`).

```
manageEvent(Event) :- Event \= provided(_,_,_), Event \= requested(_),
  getDesires(Event, DesireSet), createIntentionsForDesires(DesireSet).

createIntentionsForDesires(DesireSet) :- belongs(Desire, DesireSet),
  not(isDesire(Desire)), assert(isDesire(Desire)),
  setDifference(DesireSet, Desire, RemainingDesireSet),
  createOneIntentionForOneDesire(Desire),
  createIntentionsForDesires(RemainingDesireSet).

createIntentionsForDesires(DesireSet) :- belongs(Desire, DesireSet),
 isDesire(Desire), setDifference(DesireSet, Desire, RemainingDesireSet),
 createIntentionsForDesires(RemainingDesireSet).
createIntentionsForDesires(emptySet).

createOneIntentionForOneDesire(Desire) :- newId(NewIntentionId),
  createIntention(NewIntentionId),
  retrieveRelevantInstances(NewIntentionId, Desire).
```

When a new intention is created its `RelevantInstances`, `WaitingOnAgents` and
`FailedInstances` components are set to the empty set and its status is set to
suspended.

```
createIntention(IntentionId) :-
  assert(isIntention(intention(IntentionId, emptyStack, suspended,
  emptySet, emptySet, emptySet))).
```

Updating an intention by retrieving the relevant plan instances for the desire
that the intention is currently achieving (either main or subaltern) means setting
the intention status to suspended, getting the instances of local plans relevant for

the desire (getLocalRelevantInstances(Desire, LocalRelevantInstances)), setting the RelevantInstances component to the returned set and updating the WaitingOnAgents component according to the plan retrieval policy. If the retrieval policy is always or no local relevant instances of specific plans are found, the WaitingOnAgents component is set to the trusted agents set, a plan request for the desire is issued to each trusted agent (multicastRequestOp(TrustedAgents, Request)) and the relationIntentionRequest relation is updated (first clause). Otherwise, WaitingOnAgents is set to the empty set and no plan requests are sent (second clause).

```
retrieveRelevantInstances(IntentionId, Desire) :- agentId(AgentId),
  getLocalRelevantInstances(Desire, LocalRelInst),
  (retrievalPolicy(always); specificPlans(LocalRelInst, emptySet)),
  trustedAgents(TrustedAgents), newId(RequestId),
  multicastRequestOp(AgentId, TrustedAgents,
    request(RequestId, AgentId, Desire)),
  retract(isIntention(intention(IntentionId, Stack, _Status,
    _RelevantInstances, _WaitingOnAgents, FailedInstances))),
  assert(isIntention(intention(IntentionId, Stack, suspended,
    LocalRelInst, TrustedAgents, FailedInstances))),
  assert(relationIntentionRequest(IntentionId,
    request(RequestId, AgentId, Desire))).

retrieveRelevantInstances(IntentionId, Desire) :-
  getLocalRelevantInstances(Desire, LocalRelevantInstances),
  retrievalPolicy(noLocal),
  not(specificPlans(LocalRelevantInstances, emptySet)),
  retract(isIntention(intention(IntentionId, Stack, _Status,
    _RelevantInstances, _WaitingOnAgents, FailedInstances))),
  assert(isIntention(intention(IntentionId, Stack, suspended,
    LocalRelevantInstances, emptySet, FailedInstances))).

getLocalRelevantInstances(Desire, LocalRelInst):-
  setof((plan(AccessSpec, Trigger, Precondition, Body,
    Inv, SuccActions, FailActions), Subst),
    (isPlan(plan(AccessSpec, Trigger, Precondition, Body,
    Inv, SuccActions, FailActions)), mgu(Trigger, Desire, Subst)),
    LocalRelInst).

specificPlans(PlanInstancesSet, Plans) :-
  setof(plan(AccessSpec, Trigger, Precondition, Body,
    Inv, SuccActions, FailActions),
    (belongs((plan(AccessSpec, Trigger, Precondition, Body, Inv,
    SuccActions, FailActions), _Substitution), PlanInstancesSet),
    specific(plan(AccessSpec, Trigger, Precondition, Body, Inv,
    SuccActions, FailActions))), Plans).

specific(plan(AccessSpecifier, Trigger, Precondition, _Body,
  _Invariant, _SuccessActions, _FailureActions)) :-
  not((Precondition == true, var(Trigger), AccessSpecifier == private)).
```

Processing Suspended Intentions. During this step the engine checks if there are suspended intentions which can be resumed since the associated `Request`, the `WaitingOnAgents` component and the `RelevantInstances` component satisfy the `canResume` condition (first clause). If no resumable intention is found, `process-SuspendedIntentions` succeeds without doing nothing (not shown).

```
processSuspendedIntentions :-
   isIntention(intention(IntentionId, _Stack, _Status, RelevantInstances,
   WaitingOnAgents, _FailedInstances)),
   relationIntentionRequest(IntentionId, Request),
   canResume(Request, WaitingOnAgents, RelevantInstances),
   resume(IntentionId, Request).
```

If one resumable intention is found, two cases must be considered: 1) The intention stack is empty: the desire for which the relevant plan instances have been collected is a main desire. To implement backtracking on the plan instances which can be used to achieve the main desire, the already failed plan instances (the `FailedInst` component of the intention) are not re-attempted. The applicable plan instances are thus evaluated starting from the collected relevant instances `RelevantInst` minus the failed instances.

```
resume(IntentionId, Request) :-
   isIntention(intention(IntentionId, emptyStack, _Status,
   RelevantInst, _WaitingOnAgents, FailedInst)),
   setDifference(RelevantInst, FailedInst, NotAttemptedInst),
   getApplInstances(ApplicableInstSet, NotAttemptedInst),
   manageApplicableInstances(ApplicableInstSet, IntentionId, Request).
```

2) The intention stack is not empty: the desire for which the relevant plan instances have been collected is a subaltern desire, and no backtracking is implemented for it. The applicable plan instances are thus evaluated starting from `RelevantInst`.

```
resume(IntentionId, Request) :-
   isIntention(intention(IntentionId, Stack, _Status, RelevantInst,
   _WaitingOnAgents, _FailedInst)), not(empty(Stack)),
   getApplInstances(ApplicableInstSet, RelevantInst),
   manageApplicableInstances(ApplicableInstSet, IntentionId, Request).
```

The atom `getApplInstances(ApplicableInstSet, RelevantInst)` unifies `ApplicableInstancesSet` with the set of couples (`Plan`, `Substitution`) obtained from `RelevantInst` such that the plan precondition instantiated with `Substitution` is a ground logical consequence of the agent's beliefs. By definition, for any desire there is at least one relevant plan instance (the one originated by one default plan), and this instance is also applicable (the precondition is always true): when `getApplInstances` is applied to a non empty set of relevant plan instances it always returns at least one plan instance; it returns the empty set if and only if its argument is the empty set. In the specification given so far, `ApplicableInstancesSet` may be empty only if the intention relevant instances minus the intention failed instances is the empty set, namely, all the relevant instances for the main desire have failed.

```
getApplInstances(ApplicableInstancesSet, RelevantInstances) :-
  setof((plan(AccessSpecifier, Trigger, Precondition, Body, Invariant,
  SuccessActions, FailureActions), Substitution),
  (belongs((plan(AccessSpecifier, Trigger, Precondition, Body,
  Invariant, SuccessActions, FailureActions), Substitution),
  RelevantInstances),
  apply(Substitution, Precondition, InstantiatedPrecondition),
  call(InstantiatedPrecondition)), ApplicableInstancesSet).
```

In the applicable instances set is empty the desire fails: both the desire and
the intention must be removed by the corresponding sets and the relations involving them must be updated.

```
manageApplicableInstances(emptySet, IntId, request(ReqId, AgId, Des)) :-
  isDesire(Des), isIntention(intention(IntId, _Stack, _Status,
  _RelevantInstances, _WaitingOnAgents, _FailedInstances)),
  relationDesireIntention(Des, IntId),
  relationIntentionRequest(IntId, request(ReqId, AgId, Des)),
  retract(isDesire(Des)),
  retract(isIntention(intention(IntId, _Stack, _Status,
  _RelevantInstances, _WaitingOnAgents, _FailedInstances))),
  retract(relationDesireIntention(Des, IntId)),
  retract(relationIntentionRequest(IntId, request(ReqId, AgId, Des))).
```

If the applicable instances set is not empty, a plan instance is selected from
it and its execution is created by setting the instance field to the selected plan
instance, the substitution field to Substitution, the current state to the root
of the plan body and the next states to the children of the current state. The
intention execution is pushed onto the intention stack and the intention's status
specifier is set to active. If the plan was already present in the plan library (first
clause of acquire plan), nothing is done. Otherwise, according to the agent's plan
acquisition policy, the selected plan is discarded (second clause), added to the
plan library (third clause) or used to replace all the existing plans whose trigger
unifies with the plan's trigger to which Substitution is applied (fourth clause).

```
manageApplicableInstances(ApplicableInstancesSet, IntentionId,
  _Request) :- ApplicableInstancesSet \= emptySet,
  selectInstance(ApplicableInstancesSet, (Plan, Substitution)),
  createExecution((Plan, Substitution), Execution),
  isIntention(intention(IntentionId, Stack, Status, RelevantInstances,
  WaitingOnAgents, FailedInstances)),
  push(Execution, Stack, UpdatedStack), acquirePlan(Plan),
  retract(isIntention(intention(IntentionId, Stack, Status,
  RelevantInstances, WaitingOnAgents, FailedInstances))),
  assert(isIntention(intention(IntentionId, UpdatedStack, active,
  RelevantInstances, WaitingOnAgents, FailedInstances))).
```

```
createExecution((plan(AccessSpecifier, Trigger, Precondition, Body,
  Invariant, SuccActions, FailActions), Substitution), Execution) :-
  root(Body, CurrentState), children(Body, CurrentState, NextStates),
  Execution == planInstanceExecution(
```

```
    (plan(AccessSpecifier, Trigger, Precondition, Body,
     Invariant, SuccActions, FailActions), Substitution),
     Substitution, CurrentState, NextStates).

acquirePlan(Plan) :- isPlan(Plan).

acquirePlan(Plan) :- not(isPlan(Plan)), acquisitionPolicy(discard).

acquirePlan(Plan) :- not(isPlan(Plan)), acquisitionPolicy(add),
  assert(isPlan(Plan)).

acquirePlan(plan(AccessSpecifier, Trigger, Precondition, Body,
  Invariant, SuccessActions, FailureActions)) :-
  not(isPlan(plan(AccessSpecifier, Trigger, Precondition, Body,
  Invariant, SuccessActions, FailureActions))),
  acquisitionPolicy(replace),
  retractall(isPlan(plan(_AccessSpecifier, Trigger, _Precondition,
  _Body, _Invariant, _SuccessActions, _FailureActions))),
  assert(plan(AccessSpecifier, Trigger, Precondition, Body, Invariant,
  SuccessActions, FailureActions)).
```

Processing Active Intentions. Active intentions are processed like in dMARS. For space constraints, we just provide an informal description, however the interested reader may find the complete formal specification at ftp://ftp.disi.unige.it /pub/person/AnconaD/Coo-BDIspec.pl.

If there are no active intentions, there is nothing to do, otherwise one is selected and the topmost plan instance execution is taken. Three cases may arise.

1. The current state of the topmost plan instance execution is a leaf: the plan instance succeeds and its execution is removed from the intention stack. The substitution associated with the execution is applied to the success internal actions sequence which can be executed thereafter. If there are no more elements in the stack, then the intention has succeeded and can be removed, as well as the main desire which generated it (the relation relationDesireIntention needs to be updated). Otherwise, the substitution of the removed execution is composed with the substitution of the instance execution currently on top of the stack.

2. The topmost plan instance execution does not verify its invariant or its current state is not a leaf, and there are no more states reachable from it: the plan instance fails. The substitution of the execution is applied to the plan failure actions which can be executed thereafter; finally, the set of failed instances is updated with the instance at the stack base and all the elements of the stack are removed. New alternatives for the main desire which the intention tried to achieve are then attempted.

3. The topmost plan instance execution neither fails nor succeeds: the action to perform, which labels the edge between the current state and the selected successive state, is retrieved. The action may be:

(a) `add(BeliefFormula)` or `remove(BeliefFormula)`: `BeliefFormula` (which, at the time of the operation call, must be ground) is added (removed) to (from) the agent's belief set. The agent sends a message to itself notifying that the belief set changed.

(b) `send(ReceiverAgentId, Message)`: `agentId(AgentId)` is used to find the sender's identity and `sendOp(ReceiverAgentId, AgentId, Message)` is used to send the message.

(c) `query(SituationFormula)`: if `SituationFormula` instantiated with the current execution substitution can be grounded, and the ground instance is a logical consequence of the agent's beliefs, then the execution substitution is updated by composing it with the grounding substitution. Otherwise, the selected successive state is removed from the set of states reachable from the current state.

(d) `achieve(Desire)`: if `Desire` instantiated with the current execution substitution can be grounded, and the ground instance is a logical consequence of the agent's beliefs, then the execution substitution is updated by composing it with the grounding substitution. Otherwise, the relevant instances retrieval mechanism is started with the desire instantiated with the current execution substitution.

After the action has been executed, the current plan instance execution is updated.

6   Coo-BDI at Work

To show the advantages of our Coo-BDI extension, we discuss the simple example introduced in Section 1. We want to model the following situation:

1. Mary and Thomas receive an e-mail from John asking to reach him at Liza's home for a party at 7 p.m.
2. Mary would like to join the party: she desires to cancel all previous appointments for this evening and to reach Liza's place at 7 p.m. Instead, Thomas doesn't like parties: he desires to phone Liza at home and decline her invitation.
3. Mary knows how to cancel previous appointments.
4. Mary does not know how to reach Liza's place. Thomas does not how to phone Liza at home.

For each of the four assertions above, we will show how it can be modeled in both BDI and Coo-BDI. We will then discuss the behavior of BDI and Coo-BDI interpreters on the given agent model.

Mary and Thomas Receive an E-mail from John. Both in BDI and Coo-BDI, the reception of an e-mail from John can be modeled by the presence of an event

```
received(john,
    message(by(e-mail), content(join_party, liza_home, today, 7pm)))
```

in the event queues of Mary and Thomas.

Mary Desires to Cancel Previous Appointments and Reach Liza's Place. Thomas Desires to Phone Liza and Decline. In BDI there are no clear means to model a mapping between external events and related desires. This mapping can be modeled in an implicit way by defining a plan whose trigger is the external event and whose body contains the desires to achieve. BDI plans are represented by plan(Trigger, Precondition, Body, Invariant, SuccessActionSequence, FailureActionSequence). For sake of readability, throughout the example we will represent plan bodies as drawn trees. In our example, the BDI plan for Mary could be:

```
plan(received(Sender, message(by(CommunicationMeans),
     content(join_party, Where, Day, Hour))),    ⇐ Trigger
   true,                                           ⇐ Precondition
   s0 •
     ↓ achieve(del_appointments(Day, Hour))
   s1 •                                            ⇐ Body
     ↓ achieve(go_to(Where, Day, Hour))
   s2 •,
   true, emptySeq, emptySeq)                       ⇐ Inv., Succ. and Fail.
```

A similar plan, with a different body, could be used to simulate Thomas' generation of desires.

In Coo-BDI mapping between external events and desires is explicitly represented by the getDesire(OrdinaryEvent, DesireSet) predicate which every agent must define. The specification of agent Mary includes:

```
getDesires(received(Sender,message(by(CommunicationMeans),
   content(join_party, Where, Day, Hour))),
   {achieve(del_appointments(Day, Hour),
   achieve(go_to(Where, Day, Hour))})
```

while the specification of agent Thomas includes

```
getDesires(received(Sender,message(by(CommunicationMeans),
   content(join_party, Where, Day, Hour))),
   {achieve(phone(Where, content(decline))})
```

Once the main desires related to John's email reception have been found, one intention is created for each of them. We identify the intention for the achieve(go_to(liza_home, today, 7pm)) desire by go_to_liza_intention.

Mary Knows How to Cancel Previous Appointments. Both in BDI and Coo-BDI, the fact that Mary knows how to cancel previous appointments means that at least one plan triggered by achieve(del_appointments(today, 7pm)) belongs to Mary's plan library. For example, the BDI plan shown below models the fact that deleting appointments with a list of persons requires that the list of persons is retrieved and a message is sent to each person in the list. A plan for managing achieve(get_appointment_list(Day, Hour, List)) should belong to Mary's plan library, and the external action multicast(List, content(delete_appointment)) should be defined in terms of send.

The Coo-BDI plan could look exactly as the BDI plan plus the access specifier.

```
plan(achieve(del_appointments(Day, Hour)),        ⇐ Trigger
    true,                                          ⇐ Precondition
    s0 •
      ↓ achieve(get_appointment_list(Day, Hour, List))
    s1 •                                           ⇐ Body
      ↓ multicast(List, content(delete_appointment))
    s2 •,
    true, emptySeq, emptySeq)                      ⇐ Inv., Succ. and Fail.
```

Mary Does Not Know How to Reach Liza's Place. Thomas Does Not Know How to Phone Liza at Home. Both in BDI and Coo-BDI this situation is modeled by the absence, in Mary's plan library, of plans triggered by the `achieve(go_to(liza_home, today, 7pm))` desire and by the absence, in Thomas plan library, of plans triggered by the `achieve(phone(Where, content(decline)))` desire.

The difference between BDI and Coo-BDI lies in the way the lack of relevant plans for achieving these desires are managed.

Let us consider Mary's case first. In most BDI systems, Mary can drop this desire or she can adopt a default plan. Dropping the desire does not correctly model the usual human behavior: none gives up joining a party just because she/he does not know how to reach the party's place! Using a default plan may be a better solution, but default plans should be carefully designed to be useful in all the situations where no specific plans are available. This requires some intuition to guess all these situations in advance. For example, a default plan saying "search through a white/yellow pages server" may be useful in many situations, including the one of our running example, but it is completely useless to achieve a "prepare a cake" or "pass an exam" desire.

Extending the BDI model with cooperation helps overcoming the lack of relevant plans in an intuitive and human-like way. Let us suppose that Mary's cooperation strategy is characterized by:

```
trustedAgents({john, pattie, michelle})
retrievalPolicy(noLocal)
acquisitionPolicy(add)
```

Since Mary has no local relevant plans for `achieve(go_to(liza_home, today, 7pm))` desire, the retrieval of external plans starts:

- A request `request(go_to_liza_request, mary, achieve(go_to(liza_home, today, 7pm)))` to provide relevant plans for the desire is created.
- The request is issued to each agent in {`john, pattie, michelle`} by means of the `multicastRequestOp` primitive.
- The `WaitingOnAgent` component of the intention `go_to_liza_intention` is set to {`john, pattie, michelle`}.
- The intention `go_to_liza_intention` is suspended.

The cooperative plan retrieval process goes on according to the content of John's, Pattie's and Michelle's plan library.

John has the only relevant public plan shown below. When he receives Mary's request, he delivers the corresponding plan instance to Mary.

```
plan(public,                                    ⇐ Access specifier
    achieve(go_to(liza_home, Day, Hour)),       ⇐ Trigger
    true,                                        ⇐ Precondition
    s0 •
       ↓ achieve(drive_to(collins_street, Day, (Hour-30min)))
    s1 •                                                        ⇐ Body
       ↓ achieve(park_near(main_church))
    s2 •,
    true, emptySeq, emptySeq)                   ⇐ Inv., Succ. and Fail.
```

Pattie has only a private plan for reaching Liza's place, therefore she sends to Mary an empty set of instances.

Finally, Michelle has the unique relevant plan shown below. Since Mary is included among the allowed recipients of the plan, Michelle sends the corresponding instance to Mary.

```
plan(only({mary, paul}),                        ⇐ Access specifier
    achieve(go_to(liza_home, Day, Hour)),       ⇐ Trigger
    true,                                        ⇐ Precondition
    s0 •
       ↓ achieve(take_a_bus(number(168), Day, (Hour-40min)))
    s1 •                                                        ⇐ Body
       ↓ achieve(get_off(collins))
    s2 •,
    true, emptySeq, emptySeq)                   ⇐ Inv., Succ. and Fail.
```

When Mary receives all the three answers, she does the following:

– She realizes that the intention go_to_liza_int can be resumed.
– She generates all the applicable plans from the set of relevant ones (the two plans received from John and Michelle plus all default plan instances). In this simple example, all relevant plans are applicable as well.
– She selects one of the specific applicable plans associated with the intention.
– Since the chosen plan is an external one (the only specific applicable plans are the ones received from John and Michelle), she records it.

Probably, a human being would behave in a similar way: she/he would contact some friends asking for advice, she/he would select the more convenient instructions and she/he would record the instructions for future reuse.

Thomas will behave like Mary to retrieve the phone number of Liza's home and decline. If we did not decouple events from desires, the completely different attitudes of Mary and Thomas towards parties could not be easily captured. Let us suppose that the reception of the event received(john, message(by(e-mail), content(join_party, liza_home, today, 7pm))) triggers a plan like in the BDI setting, and that neither Mary nor Thomas posses a relevant plan for it. The cooperative strategy we implement in Coo-BDI would result into asking plans for managing such an event to all trusted agents. But this makes little sense, since the retrieved relevant plans would represent really heterogeneous suggestions including declining, reaching the party, asking to postpone the party, or quickly inventing an excuse. How could an agent select the right plan among these, if it does not even know which state it desires to achieve? Associating external events with internally generated desires, and cooperating for achieving desires rather than for managing external events overcome this problem.

7   Related and Future Work

Starting from the BDI model, many extensions have been proposed in literature. Most of them add some attitude or ability to the basic BDI theory or provide a better formalization of the relationships between existing ones. Just to make some examples, [17] extends the theoretical BDI framework with the notion of *capability* and investigates how capabilities affect the agent's reasoning about intentions. The BOID (Beliefs, *Obligations*, Intentions, Desires) architecture [18] contains feedback loops to consider all effects of actions before committing to them, and mechanisms to resolve the conflicts between the outputs of the B, O, I, D components. In [19], classical BDI agents are extended with *conditional mental attitudes* represented by interconnected components. The paper [20] investigates the impact that *sociality* has on mental states and how it can be formalized within a BDI model, while [21] focuses on actions and their formalization by adding three more operators to the basic BDI ones: *capabilities, opportunities* and *results*. An approach to social reasoning that integrates prior work on *norms* and *obligations* with the BDI approach is discussed in [22]. A generalization of the BDI logic which combines *observation* (formally defined as a bisimulation between the real world and an agent's mental model) and *expectation* (the images of the world in the agent's mind that are associated with observations as about to happen) is proposed in [23].

All these works are more concerned with the logical formalization of the theory behind the extended BDI model than with the complete specification of an implementable system, as our work is.

More similar in spirit to our pragmatic approach are the attempts to extend BDI systems with *mobility*. In [24] the TOMAS (Transaction Oriented Multi Agent System) architecture is described: it combines the distributed nested transaction paradigm with the BDI model. An algorithm is presented which enables agents in TOMAS to become mobile. A re-implementation of TOMAS within a Java 2 Enterprise Edition application server is outlined in [25]. It can be used to develop session beans and demonstrates how the distributed transaction model nicely fits into a state-of-the-art environment for mission critical systems in domains such as e-business and Web services. The JAM BDI-theoretic mobile agent architecture [26] provides plan and procedural representations, meta-level and utility-based reasoning over simultaneous goals and goal-driven and event-driven behavior. Mobility is realized by an *agentGo* primitive for agent migration that may appear in the body of plans.

The paper [13] extends the operational semantics of AgentSpeak(L) by giving semantics to speech-act based messages received by an AgentSpeak(L) agent. AgentSpeak(L) is extended to include a mailbox where messages, of the form ⟨IllocutionaryForce, SenderId, Content⟩, are kept. Three kind of messages are considered: ⟨tell, SenderId, Atom⟩, meaning that Atom is in the knowledge base of SenderId; ⟨achieve, SenderId, Atom⟩ meaning that SenderId requests that the recipient of the message achieves a state where Atom is true; and ⟨tellHow, SenderId, Plan⟩ meaning that SenderId uses the plan Plan to deal with the event given by Plan's triggering event.

The illocutionary forces (or performatives) of each of them have a dual form (untell, unachieve, untellHow) whose informal meaning is "revert the effect of the previously sent message". While tell, untell, achieve and unachieve are standard KQML [27] performatives, tellHow and untellHow are new ones.

The definition of an agent *Ag* is also extended to keep track of the sources of the beliefs of *Ag*, with the set of the agents that *Ag* trusts and with the set of agents that have some power on *Ag*.

With respect to other works we have considered in this section, [13] is the work closest to ours. In fact, the extension to AgentSpeak(L) is detailed enough to be implemented. The same holds for our extension. Also, the extension to AgentSpeak(L) allows agents to cooperate by exchanging information (tell, untell) and by delegating some tasks to other agents (achieve, unachieve). Our extension has the same aim of enforcing cooperation among agents.

The most significant similarity between the extended AgentSpeak(L) and Coo-BDI, however, lies in the fact that both of them allow agents to exchange plans. In the extension to AgentSpeak(L), plan exchange is realized by means of the ⟨tellHow, SenderId, Plan⟩ message. In Coo-BDI it is realized by means of the provided(SenderId, Request, RelevantInstances) message. The semantics of ⟨tellHow, SenderId, Plan⟩ is that, if the source is trusted, the plan is added to the plan library. The semantics of provided(SenderId, Request, RelevantInstances) is that if Request is still under management, and one of the applicable RelevantInstances is selected to manage the desire inside Request, the plan associated to the selected instance is added, discarded or used to replace existing plans according to the agent's acquisition policy.

In both cases, a "basic" BDI agent can be easily modeled. In the extension to AgentSpeak(L), when the set of trusted and powered agents are empty, the agent may simply discard information and requests. A classic BDI agent can be modeled in Coo-BDI by setting the access specifier of all its plans to *private* and by setting the trusted agents set to the empty set. In this way, the agent will never look for external relevant plans, and will never share its own plans, exactly as it happens in the original BDI model.

The extensions proposed in [13] and the ones proposed in our paper are so close that it is natural to think they should converge into a unified architecture for highly cooperative BDI agents. Messages should adhere to the form proposed in [13], so that they have a clear semantics. Plans should be extended with access specifiers, so that the agents can decide when a plan should be shared with other agents by means of a `tellHow` message. The interpreter should take both extensions into account. It should be implemented to get feedbacks on the formalization, (possibly) confirming the adequacy of the approach presented in both papers. We are currently working with the authors of [13] to realize this extension.

Acknowledgments

The authors thank Rafael Bordini, Paolo Busetta, Mehdi Dastani, Mark D'Inverno and Michael Winikoff for the useful discussions on the "no applicable plans" problem and the anonymous referees for their thoughtful and constructive comments.

References

1. Wooldridge, M., Jennings, N.R.: Intelligent agents: Theory and practice. The Knowledge Engineering Review **10** (1995) 115–152
2. Jennings, N.R., Sycara, K., Wooldridge, M.: A roadmap of agent research and development. Autonomous Agents and Multi-Agent Systems **1** (1998) 7–38
3. Rao, A.S., Georgeff, M.: BDI agents: from theory to practice. In Lesser, V., Gasser, L., eds.: Proc. of the 1st International ICMAS Conference). (1995) 312–319
4. Rao, A.S., Georgeff, M.: Decision procedures for BDI logics. Journal of Logic and Computation **8** (1998) 293 – 342
5. Winikoff, M.: AgentTalk Home Page. `http://goanna.cs.rmit.edu.au/~winikoff/agenttalk` (2001)
6. d'Inverno, M., Hindriks, K.V., Luck, M.: A formal architecture for the 3APL agent programming language. In Bowen, J.P., Dunne, S., Galloway, A., King, S., eds.: Proc. of the 1st International ZB Conference, Springer Verlag (2000) 168–187 LNCS 1878.
7. Rao, A.S.: AgentSpeak(L): BDI agents speak out in a logical computable language. In de Velde, W.V., Perram, J.W., eds.: Agents Breaking Away. Springer Verlag (1996) 42–55 LNAI 1038.
8. Busetta, P., Ronnquist, R., Hodgson, A., Lucas, A.: JACK intelligent agents – components for intelligent agents in Java. AgentLink News Letter **2** (1999)
9. Myers, K.L.: User guide for the procedural reasoning system. Technical report, Artificial Intelligence Center, Menlo Park, CA (1997)
10. d'Inverno, M., Kinny, D., Luck, M., Wooldridge, M.: A formal specification of dMARS. In Singh, M.P., Rao, A., Wooldridge, M., eds.: Proc. of the 4th International ATAL Workshop, Springer Verlag (1997) 155–176 LNAI 1365.
11. Bordini, R.H., Moreira, Á.F.: Proving the asymmetry thesis principles for a BDI agent-oriented programming language. In Dix, J., Leite, J.A., Satoh, K., eds.: Proc. of the 3rd International CLIMA Workshop. Electronic Notes in Theoretical Computer Science 70(5), Elsevier (2002)
12. Moreira, Á.F., Bordini, R.H.: An operational semantics for a BDI agent-oriented programming language. In: Proc. of the LABS Workshop, held in conjunction with KR'02. (2002) 45–59

13. Moreira, Á.F., Vieira, R., Bordini, R.H.: Extending the operational semantics of a BDI agent-oriented programming language for introducing speech-act based communication. In this volume.
14. Bordini, R.H., Bazzan, A.L.C., de O. Jannone, R., Basso, D.M., Vicari, R.M., Lesser, V.R.: AgentSpeak(XL): efficient intention selection in BDI agents via decision-theoretic task scheduling. In Castelfranchi, C., Johnson, W.L., eds.: Proc. of the 1st International AAMAS Joint Conference, ACM Press (2002) 1294–1302
15. Kowalski, R., Sadri, F.: Towards a unified agent architecture that combines rationality with reactivity. In Pedreschi, D., Zaniolo, C., eds.: Proc. of the LID International Workshop, Springer Verlag (1996) 137–149
16. Robinson, J.A.: Computational logic: The unification computation. Machine intelligence 6 (1971) 63–72
17. Padgham, L., Lambrix, P.: Agent capabilities: Extending BDI theory. In: Proc. of the 7th AAAI National Conference, AAAI Press–The MIT Press (2000) 68–73
18. Broersen, J., Dastani, M., Hulstijn, J., Huang, Z., van der Torre, L.: The BOID architecture: conflicts between beliefs, obligations, intentions and desires. In: Proc. of the 5th International Agents Conference, ACM Press (2001) 9–16
19. Dastani, M., van der Torre, L.: An extension of BDI_{CTL} with functional dependencies and components. In Baaz, M., Voronkov, A., eds.: Proc. of the 9th International LPAR Conference, Springer Verlag (2002) 115–129
20. Panzarasa, P., Norman, T., Jennings, N.R.: Modeling sociality in the BDI framework. In Liu, J., Zhong, N., eds.: Proc. of the 1st Asia-Pacific Conference on Intelligent Agent Technology, World Scientific Publishing (1999) 202–206
21. Padmanabhan, V., Governatori, G., Sattar, A.: Actions made explicit in BDI. In Stumptner, M., Corbett, D., Brooks, M.J., eds.: Proc. of the 14th Australian Joint Conference on AI, Springer Verlag (2001) 390–401
22. Dignum, F., Morley, D., Sonenberg, E., Cavendon, L.: Towards socially sophisticated BDI agents. In: Proc. of the 4th International ICMAS Conference, IEEE Computer Society (2000) 111–118
23. Trân, B.V., Harland, J., Hamilton, M.: A combined logic of expectation and observation (a generalization of BDI logics). In this volume.
24. Busetta, P., Ramamohanarao, K.: An architecture for mobile BDI agents. In: Proc. of the 1998 ACM SAC Symposium. (1998)
25. Busetta, P., Bailey, J., Kotagiri, R.: A reliable computational model for BDI agents. In: Proc. of the Workshop on Safe Agents. Held in conjuction with AAMAS'03. (2003)
26. Huber, M.J.: JAM: A BDI-theoretic mobile agent architecture. AgentLink News Letter 5 (2000)
27. Mayfield, J., Labrou, Y., Finin, T.: Evaluation of KQML as an agent communication language. In Wooldridge, M., Müller, J.P., Tambe, M., eds.: Proc. of the 2nd International ATAL Workshop. Springer Verlag (1995) 347–360

Extending the Operational Semantics of a BDI Agent-Oriented Programming Language for Introducing Speech-Act Based Communication

Álvaro F. Moreira[1], Renata Vieira[2], and Rafael H. Bordini[3]

[1] Departamento de Informática Teórica
Instituto de Informática
Universidade Federal do Rio Grande do Sul
Porto Alegre RS, 91501-970, Brazil
afmoreira@inf.ufrgs.br
[2] Centro de Ciências Exatas
Universidade do Vale do Rio dos Sinos
CP 275, CEP 93022-000, São Leopoldo, RS, Brazil
renata@exatas.unisinos.br
[3] Department of Computer Science
University of Liverpool
Liverpool L69 7ZF, UK
R.Bordini@csc.liv.ac.uk

Abstract. Work on agent communication languages has since long striven to achieve adequate speech act semantics; partly, the problem is that references to an agent's architecture (in particular a BDI-like architecture) would be required in giving such semantics more rigorously. On the other hand, BDI agent-oriented programming languages have had their semantics formalised for abstract versions only, neglecting practical aspects such as communication primitives; this means that, at least in what concerns communication, implementations of BDI programming languages have been *ad hoc*. This paper tackles, however preliminarily, both these problems by giving semantics to speech-act based messages received by an AgentSpeak(L) agent. AgentSpeak(L) is a BDI, agent-oriented, logic programming language for which interpreters have been developed, and its theoretical foundations are of great interest. Our work here builds upon a structural operational semantics to AgentSpeak(L) that we have given in previous work. The contribution of this paper is two-fold: we here extend our earlier work on providing a solid theoretical background on which to base existing implementations of AgentSpeak(L) interpreters, as well as we shed light on a more computationally grounded approach to giving semantics for some key illocutionary forces used in speech-act based agent communication languages.

1 Introduction

The AgentSpeak(L) programming language was introduced by Rao in [1]. The language was quite influential in the definition of other agent-oriented pro-

J. Leite et al. (Eds.): DALT 2003, LNAI 2990, pp. 135–154, 2004.

gramming languages. After a period of apparent disinterest, work related to AgentSpeak(L) has been done in many fronts recently, from developing interpreters [2] and applications to formal semantics and model-checking [3,4]. AgentSpeak(L) is particularly interesting, in comparison to other agent-oriented languages, in that it retains the most important aspects of the BDI-based reactive planning systems on which it was based, it has a working interpreter, and at the same time its formal semantics and relation to BDI logics [5] is being thoroughly studied [6,7,8].

In our previous work on giving operational semantics to AgentSpeak(L) [6], we considered only the main constructs of the language, as originally defined by Rao. However, Rao's definition considered an abstract programming language; for AgentSpeak(L) to be useful in practice, various extensions to it have been proposed [2]. Still, the interpreter described in that paper does not yet support communication, which is essential when it comes to engineering *multi-agent systems*. Speech act theory (see Section 3) is particularly adequate as a foundation for communication among intentional agents. Through communication, an agent can share its internal state (beliefs, desires, intentions) with other agents, as well as it can influence other agents' states. Speech-act based communication for AgentSpeak(L) agents has already been used, in a very simple way (so as to allow model checking), in [4].

This paper deals exactly with this aspect of AgentSpeak(L), by extending its operational semantics to account for the main illocutionary forces related to communicating AgentSpeak(L) agents. Our semantics tells exactly how to implement the processing of messages received by an AgentSpeak(L) agent (how its computational representation of Beliefs-Desires-Intentions are changed when a message is received). Note that in implementations of the BDI architecture, the concept of *plan* is used to simplify aspects of deliberation and knowing what course of action to take in order to achieve desired states of the world. Therefore, an AgentSpeak(L) agent *sends* a message whenever a special action for sending messages to other agents appears in the body of an intended plan that is being executed. The important issue is then how to interpret a message that has been *received*. This is precisely the aspect of agent communication that we consider in this paper.

In extending the operational semantics of AgentSpeak(L) to account for inter-agent communication, we also touch upon another long-standing problem in the area of multi-agent systems, namely the semantics of speech acts. As Singh pointed out [9], semantics of agent communication languages such as KQML and FIPA have incurred in the mistake (for those concerned with general interoperability and legacy systems) of emphasising *mental agency*. The problem is that if the semantics makes reference to an agent believing (or intending a state satisfying) a certain proposition, there is no way to ensure that any software using that communication language complies with the expected underlying semantics of belief (or intention, or mental attitudes in general). This problem is avoided here as the AgentSpeak(L) agents for which such speech-act based communication language is being used, are indeed agents for which a precise notion of Belief-Desire-Intention has been given [7,8]. Another way of putting this, is that we give a more "computationally grounded" [10] semantics of speech-act based agent communication.

Previous attempts to give semantics to agent communication languages, e.g. [11], were based on the "pre-conditions – action – post-conditions" approach, referring to agent mental states in modal languages based on Cohen and Levesque's work on intention [12]. Our semantics for communication, besides being more instrumental in implementations (as it serves as the specification for an interpreter), can also be used in the proof of communication properties [13]. More recently, the work reported in [14,15] also provides an operational semantics for an agent communication language. However, again they do not consider the effects of communication in terms of BDI agents. To the best of our knowledge, our work is the first to give operational semantics incorporating the core illocutionary forces in a BDI programming language.

The paper is organised as follows. Section 2 gives a very brief (informal) overview of AgentSpeak(L), and Section 3 provides the general background on speech-act based agent communication. We then present formally the syntax and semantics of AgentSpeak(L) in Section 4; this is the syntax and semantics of AgentSpeak(L) first presented in [6], and reproduced here so that the paper is self-contained. Section 5 provides the main contribution in this paper, i.e., the semantics of speech-act based communication for AgentSpeak(L) agents. Brief conclusions and plans for future work are given in the last section.

2   An Overview of AgentSpeak(L)

The AgentSpeak(L) programming language was introduced in [1]. It is a natural extension of logic programming for the BDI agent architecture, and provides an elegant abstract framework for programming BDI agents. The BDI architecture is, in turn, the predominant approach to the implementation of "intelligent" or "rational" agents [16]. An AgentSpeak(L) agent is created by the specification of a set of beliefs forming the initial *belief base*, and a set of plans forming the *plan library*. The agent's belief base is a set of ground first-order predicates.

AgentSpeak(L) distinguishes two types of goals: *achievement goals* and *test goals*. Achievement and test goals are predicates (as for beliefs) prefixed with operators '!' and '?' respectively. Achievement goals state that the agent wants to achieve a state of the world where the associated predicate is true. (In practice, these initiate the execution of *subplans*.) A *test goal* returns a unification for the associated predicate with one of the agent's beliefs; they fail otherwise. A *triggering event* defines which events may initiate the execution of a plan. An *event* can be internal, when a subgoal needs to be achieved, or external, when generated from belief updates as a result of perceiving the environment. There are two types of triggering events: those related to the *addition* ('+') and *deletion* ('−') of mental attitudes (beliefs or goals).

Plans refer to the *basic actions* that an agent is able to perform on its environment. Such actions are also defined as first-order predicates, but with special

predicate symbols (called action symbols) used to distinguish them from other
predicates. A plan is formed by a *triggering event* (denoting the purpose for
that plan), followed by a conjunction of belief literals representing a *context*.
The context must be a logical consequence of that agent's current beliefs for the
plan to be *applicable*. The remainder of the plan is a sequence of basic actions or
(sub)goals that the agent has to achieve (or test) when the plan, if applicable,
is chosen for execution.

```
+concert(A,V) : likes(A)
    ← !book_tickets(A,V).

+!book_tickets(A,V) : ¬busy(phone)
    ← call(V);
      ...;
      !choose_seats(A,V).
```

Fig. 1. Examples of AgentSpeak(L) Plans

Figure 1 shows some examples of AgentSpeak(L) plans. They tell us that,
when a concert is announced for artist A at venue V (so that, from perception of
the environment, a belief concert(A,V) is *added*), then if this agent in fact likes
artist A, then it will have the new goal of booking tickets for that concert. The
second plan tells us that whenever this agent adopts the goal of booking tickets
for A's performance at V, if it is the case that the telephone is not busy, then it can
execute a plan consisting of performing the basic action call(V) (assuming that
making a phone call is an atomic action that the agent can perform) followed
by a certain protocol for booking tickets (indicated by '...'), which in this case
ends with the execution of a plan for choosing the seats for such performance at
that particular venue.

3   Background on Speech-Act Based Agent Communication Languages

As BDI theory is based on the philosophical literature on practical reasoning
[17], agent communication in multi-agent systems is inspired by philosophical
studies on the speech act theory, in particular the work of Austin [18] and Searle
[19].

Speech act theory is based on the conception of language as action, and
different types of speech actions are explained according to their illocutionary
force, which represents the speaker's intention for a certain semantic content. In
natural language, one has an illocutionary force associated to a utterance (or
locutionary act) such as "the door is open" and another to "open the door".
The former aims at belief revision, whereas the latter aims at a change in the

plans (intentions) of the hearer. As seen in the utterances above, in natural language the illocutionary force is implicit. When the theory is adapted to agent communication, the illocutionary force is made explicit in agent messages in order to facilitate the computational processing of the communication act.

Other pragmatical factors related to communication such as social roles and conventions have been discussed in the literature [20,21,22]. Illocutionary forces may require the existence of certain relationships between speaker and hearer for them to be felicitous. A *command*, for instance, requires a subordination relation between the individuals involved in the communication, whereas such subordination is not required in a *request*. To some extent, this has been made explicit in the semantics of communicating AgentSpeak(L) agents that we give in Section 5. We require that an agent specification provides "trust" and "power" relations to other agents, as the semantics of illocutionary forces in messages being processed by that agent depends on them. This is a simple mechanism, which should incorporate more elaborate conceptions of trust and power from the literature on the subject (see, e.g., [23]).

Apart from illocutionary forces and social roles, other classifications regarding relations among the speech acts have been proposed [20]; e.g., a reply follows a question, a threatening is stronger than a warning. Such categories conceive messages in a dialogue context. In multi-agent systems, communicative interactions can be seen as communication protocols, which can be related to a specific cooperation method. The well-known Contract Net Protocol [24], for example, focus on task allocation activities.

The "Agent Communication Language" developed in the context of the "Knowledge Sharing Effort" project [25], was the first attempt to define a practical agent communication language that included high level (speech-act based) communication as proposed in the distributed artificial intelligence literature. The Knowledge Query and Manipulation Language (KQML) is a language that adds intentional context to communication messages [11,26]. KQML "performatives" refer to illocutionary forces and they make explicit the agent intentions with a message being sent: `tell` is used to change the beliefs of the receiver, whereas `achieve` is used to change the receiver's goals. Besides a format for messages, KQML proposes an architecture that includes *facilitators*, which are agents that intermediate message exchanges.

In this paper, as a first attempt to give semantics to communication aspects of BDI programming languages, we focus on four illocutionary forces (which are particularly relevant for AgentSpeak(L) agents), named exactly as the associated KQML performatives; we also consider two new illocutionary forces, which we introduce in Section 5. The four KQML performatives which we consider in the semantics given in this paper are listed below, where S denotes the agent that *sends* the message, and R denotes the agent that *receives* the message.

`tell`: S informs R that the sentence in the message (i.e., the message content) is true of S — that is, the sentence is in the knowledge base of S (or S believes that the content of the message is true, for BDI-like agents);

`untell`: the message content is *not* in the knowledge base of S;

achieve: S requests that R try to achieve a state of the world where the message content is true;

unachieve: S wants to revert the effect of an **achieve** previously sent.

A complete semantic representation for speech acts needs to consider action and planning theories, and to conceive communication as a special kind of action which has direct effect over the mental states of agents. Most formalisms used for the representation of actions use the "pre-conditions – action – post-conditions" approach. For the description of mental states, most of the work in the area is based on the Cohen and Levesque's work on intention [12,27].

In [11], an initial attempt to introduce semantic principles to KQML was made. The communication process is defined according to the influence that messages have on the agents' beliefs and intentions. The semantics is given through the description of agent states before and after sending or receiving a message, in terms of pre- and post-conditions. Pre-conditions describe the required state for an agent to send a message and for the receiver to accept and process it. Post-conditions describe the interlocutors' states after an utterance or after receiving and processing a message.

Agent states are described in [11] by means of mental attitudes such as the ones below (where P is a proposition and W is a state of the world):

$bel(A, P)$
  Agent A believes proposition P; i.e., P is in A's belief base or can be proved from it.

$know(A, W)$
  An agent may know about its own state $know(A, bel(A, P))$, but this modality cannot be established directly to a proposition. A description like $know(A, P)$ is not allowed.

$want(A, W)$
  Agents may desire an action to happen or an state to be achieved; for instance, an agent may wish to know about another agent's state.

$intend(A, W)$
  An agent may intend to perform an action or to know about an agent state.

In the style introduced in [11], the semantics for a performative **tell**, for example, is given as follows. Consider a message $\text{tell}(S, R, P)$; that is, S tells R that S believes P to be true.

– Pre-conditions on the states of S and R:
  • $Pre(S)$: $bel(S, P) \land know(S, want(R, know(R, bel(S, P))))$
  • $Pre(R)$: $intend(R, know(R, bel(S, P)))$
– Post-conditions on S and R:
  • $Pos(S)$: $know(S, know(R, bel(S, P)))$
  • $Pos(R)$: $know(R, bel(S, P))$
– Action completion:
  • $know(R, bel(S, P))$

Post-condition and *completion* hold unless `sorry` or `error` messages are returned (i.e., when R was unable to process the `tell` message).

As we mentioned in the introduction, the problem with the usual approach to giving semantics to an agent communication language is that it makes reference to an agent's mental attitudes, and there is no way to ensure that any software in general, using that communication language, complies with the expected underlying semantics of the mental attitudes. This is true of the semantic approaches to both KQML and FIPA (see [9] for a discussion). As an example, consider a legacy software wrapped in an agent that uses KQML or FIPA to interoperate with other agents. One could not prove communication properties of the system, as there is not such a thing as a precise definition of when that legacy system believes or intends a formula P, as appears in the semantics of the communication language. In our approach, it is possible to prove such properties given that in [7,8] we gave a precise definition of what it means for an AgentSpeak(L) agent to believe, desire, or intend a certain formula.

4   Syntax and Semantics of AgentSpeak(L)

This section presents the syntax and semantics of AgentSpeak(L), as originally given in [6] and then used in [7,8]. The semantics is given in the style of Plotkin's structural operational semantics, a widely used method for giving semantics to programming languages and studying their properties.

4.1   Abstract Syntax

An AgentSpeak(L) agent specification ag is given by the following grammar:

$$
\begin{array}{lll}
ag & ::= & bs \quad ps \\
bs & ::= & b_1 \ldots b_n & (n \geq 0) \\
at & ::= & \mathsf{P}(t_1, \ldots, t_n) & (n \geq 0) \\
ps & ::= & p_1 \ldots p_n & (n \geq 1) \\
p & ::= & te : ct \leftarrow h \\
te & ::= & +at \quad | \quad -at \quad | \quad +g \quad | \quad -g \\
ct & ::= & at \quad | \quad \neg at \quad | \quad ct \wedge ct \quad | \quad \top \\
h & ::= & a \quad | \quad g \quad | \quad u \quad | \quad h;h \\
a & ::= & \mathsf{A}(t_1, \ldots, t_n) & (n \geq 0) \\
g & ::= & !at \quad | \quad ?at \\
u & ::= & +at \quad | \quad -at
\end{array}
$$

In AgentSpeak(L), an agent is simply specified by a set bs of beliefs (the agent's initial belief base) and a set ps of plans (the agent's plan library). The atomic formulæ at of the language are predicates where P is a predicate symbol and $t_1, \ldots, t_n$ are standard terms of first order logic. We call a *belief* an atomic formula at with no variables and we use b as a metavariable for beliefs. The set of initial beliefs of an AgentSpeak(L) program is a sequence of beliefs bs.

A plan in AgentSpeak(L) is given by p above, where te is the *triggering event*, ct is the plan's context, and h is sequence of actions, goals, or belief updates; $te : ct$ is referred as the *head* of the plan, and h is its *body*. Then the set of plans of an agent is given by ps as a list of plans. Each plan has in its head a formula ct that specifies the conditions under which the plan can be executed. The formula ct must be a logical consequence of the agent's beliefs if the plan is to be considered applicable.

A triggering event te can then be the addition or the deletion of a belief from an agent's belief base ($+at$ and $-at$, respectively), or the addition or the deletion of a goal ($+g$ and $-g$, respectively). A sequence h of actions, goals, and belief updates defines the body of a plan. We assume the agent has at its disposal a set of *actions* and we use a as a metavariable ranging over them. They are given as normal predicates except that an action symbol A is used instead of a predicate symbol. Goals g can be either *achievement goals* (!at) or *test goals* (?at). Finally, $+at$ and $-at$ (in the body of a plan) represent operations for updating (u) the belief base by, respectively, adding and removing at.

4.2   Semantics

An agent and its circumstance form a configuration of the transition system giving operational semantics to AgentSpeak(L). The transition relation:

$$\langle ag, C \rangle \longrightarrow \langle ag', C' \rangle$$

is defined by the semantic rules given in the next section.

An agent's circumstance C is a tuple $\langle I, E, A, R, Ap, \iota, \rho, \varepsilon \rangle$ where:

- I is a set of *intentions* $\{i, i', \ldots\}$. Each intention i is a stack of partially instantiated plans.
- E is a set of *events* $\{(te, i), (te', i'), \ldots\}$. Each event is a pair (te, i), where te is a triggering event and the plan on top of intention i is the one that generated te.
  When the belief revision function, which is not part of the AgentSpeak(L) interpreter but rather of the general architecture of the agent, updates the belief base, the associated events (i.e., additions and deletions of beliefs) are included in this set.
- A is a set of *actions* to be performed in the environment.
  An action expression included in this set tells other architecture components to actually perform the respective action on the environment, thus changing it.
- R is a set of *relevant plans*. In Definition 1 (in the appendix) we state precisely how the set of relevant plans is obtained.
- Ap is a set of *applicable plans*. The way this set is obtained is given in Definition 2 (in the appendix).
- Each circumstance C also has three components called ι, ε, and ρ. They keep record of a particular intention, event and applicable plan (respectively) being considered along the execution of an agent.

In order to keep the semantic rules neat, we adopt the following notations:

- If C is an AgentSpeak(L) agent circumstance, we write C_E to make reference to the component E of C. Similarly for all the other components of C.
- We write $C_\iota = \_$ (the underline symbol) to indicate that there is no intention being considered in the agent's execution. Similarly for C_ρ and C_ε.
- We use $i, i', \ldots$ to denote intentions, and we write $i[p]$ to denote an intention that has plan p on its top, i being the remaining plans in that intention.

The semantic rules are given in Appendix A. They appeared in [6,7], but we include them here so that the paper is self-contained.

5 Semantics of Communicating AgentSpeak(L) Agents

In order to endow AgentSpeak(L) agents with the capability of processing communication messages, we first change the syntax of atomic propositions so that we can annotate, for each belief, what is its source. This annotation mechanism provides a very neat notation for making explicit the sources of an agent's belief. It has advantages in terms of expressive power and readability, besides allowing the use of such explicit information in an agent's reasoning (i.e., in selecting plans for achieving goals).

By using this information source annotation mechanism, we also clear up some practical issue in the implementation of AgentSpeak(L) interpreters concerning, e.g., the problem of keeping track of which beliefs are internal (i.e., the ones that originate from the execution of plans) in contrast to those that result from perception of the environment. It is important to keep track of these different types of beliefs, otherwise belief revision from perception of the environment could delete internal beliefs that are required for the agent's internal reasoning. In the interpreter reported in [2], we temporarily dealt with that problem by creating a separate belief base where the internal beliefs are included or removed; this extra belief base, together with the current list of percepts, is then used in the belief revision process.

The following new grammar rule is used instead of the one given in Section 4, so that we can annotate each *atomic formula* with its *source*: either a term identifying the agent in the society (id) that previously sent the information in a message, self to denote internal beliefs, or percept to indicate that the belief was acquired through perception of the environment.

$$at \quad ::= \quad \mathrm{P}(t_1, \ldots, t_n)[s_1, \ldots, s_m] \qquad (n \geq 0, m > 0)$$

where $s_i \in \{\texttt{percept}, \texttt{self}, id\}$, $1 \leq i \leq m$.

Note that with this new language construct, it is possible to make sure, in a plan context, what was the source of a belief before using that plan as an intended means. All of these details that are consequence of the new syntax that we introduce here are in fact hidden in the mgu function used in the auxiliary functions of the semantics in Section 4, as well as in the logical consequence relation that is also referred to in the semantics. We intend to make such details more clear in future work.

Next, we need to change the definition of an agent's circumstance, as we now need a set M which represents an agent's mail box. As usual in practice (and used, e.g., in [4]), we assume that the implementation of the AgentSpeak(L) interpreter provides, as part of the overall agent architecture, a mechanism for receiving and sending messages asynchronously; messages are stored in a mail box and one of them is processed by the agent at the beginning of a reasoning cycle. The format of the messages stored in the mail box is $\langle Ilf, id, content \rangle$, where $Ilf \in \{Tell, Untell, Achieve, Unachieve, TellHow, UntellHow\}$ is the illocutionary force associated with the message, id identifies the agent that sent the message (as mentioned above), and $content$ is the message content, which can be either an atomic proposition (at) or a plan (p).

An agent's circumstance C is now defined as a tuple $\langle I, E, M, A, R, Ap, \iota, \rho, \varepsilon \rangle$ where M is the set of messages that the agent has received and has not processed yet (the "mail box"), and everything else is as in Section 4. For processing messages, a new selection function is necessary, which operates in the same way as the three selection functions described in the previous section as well. The new selection function is called S_M, and selects one particular message from M.

Further, in processing messages we now need two more "given" functions, in the same way that the selection functions are assumed as given in an agent's specification. First, $\mathsf{Trust}(id, at)$ is true if id identifies a trusted information source on the subject denoted by the atomic formula at. It is only used to decide whether received messages will be processed, without any reference to more complex notions of trust. When the source is "trusted" (in the sense used here), the information source for a belief acquired from communication is annotated alongside the atomic formula in the belief base, so further consideration on degrees of trust may still take place during the agent's reasoning, or the agent may chose to ignore the source annotations and use that formula as if it were a belief of its own. The agent simply discards messages arriving from untrusted agents. Information on beliefs of completely untrusted sources are not worth even keeping in the belif base. Second, $\mathsf{Power}(id, at)$ is true if the agent has a subordination relation towards agent id in regards to the denotation of the atomic formula at. Again "power" should not be interpreted with particular social or psychological nuances: the user defines this function so as to account for all possible reasons for an agent to do something for another agent (from actual subordination to true altruism). In that case, messages of type $Achieve$ (requesting that the agent achieve a certain state of affairs), should be considered by the agent. The idea of having user-defined "trust" and "power" functions has already been used in practice in [4].

We now extend the semantics to cope with the processing of speech-act based messages received by an AgentSpeak(L) agent. We use a new metavariable $sources$ ranging over $\mathcal{P}(\{\texttt{percept}, \texttt{self}, id\})$ (the possible sources of a belief, as described earlier). The new semantic rules are as follows.

Receiving a Tell Message

$$\text{TellRec} \frac{S_M(C_M) = \langle Tell, id, at \rangle \quad \text{Trust}(id, at)}{\langle ag, C \rangle \longrightarrow \langle ag', C' \rangle}$$

where: $C'_M = C_M - \{\langle Tell, id, at \rangle\}$
$$bs' \models \begin{cases} at[sources \cup \{id\}], & \text{if } bs \models at[sources] \\ at[id], & \text{otherwise} \end{cases}$$
$$C'_E = C_E \cup \{\langle +at[id], \top \rangle\}$$

The content of the message is added to the belief base in case it was not there previously. If the information is already there, the sender of the message is included in the set of sources giving accreditation to that belief.

Receiving an Untell Message

$$\text{UnTellRec} \frac{S_M(C_M) = \langle Untell, id, at \rangle \quad \text{Trust}(id, at)}{\langle ag, C \rangle \longrightarrow \langle ag', C' \rangle}$$

where: $C'_M = C_M - \{\langle Untell, id, at \rangle\}$
$$bs' \not\models at[id], \qquad \text{if } bs \models at[id]$$
$$bs' \models at[sources - \{id\}], \qquad \text{if } bs \models at[sources]$$
$$C'_E = C_E \cup \{\langle -at[id], \top \rangle\}$$

Only the sender of the message is removed from the set of sources giving accreditation to the belief. In cases where the sender was the only source for that information, the belief is removed from the receiver's belief base.

Receiving an Achieve Message

$$\text{AchieveRec} \frac{S_M(C_M) = \langle Achieve, id, at \rangle \quad \text{Power}(id, at)}{\langle ag, C \rangle \longrightarrow \langle ag, C' \rangle}$$

where: $C'_M = C_M - \{\langle Achieve, id, at \rangle\}$
$$C'_E = C_E \cup \{\langle +!at, \top \rangle\}$$

If the sender has power over the AgentSpeak(L) agent, the agent will try to execute a plan whose triggering event is $+!at$; that is, it will try to achieve the goal associated with the propositional content of the message. All that needs to be done is to include an external event in the set of events (recall that external events have the triggering event associated with the true intention $\top$).

Note that, interestingly, now it is possible to have a new focus of attention (each of the stacks of plans in the set of intentions I) being started by an addition (or deletion, see below) of an achievement goal. Originally, only a change of belief from perception of the environment started a new focus of attention; the plan chosen for that event could, in turn, have achievement goals in its body, thus pushing new plans onto the stack.

Receiving an Unachieve Message

$$\mathbf{UnAchieveRec} \;\; \frac{S_M(C_M) = \langle Unachieve, id, at \rangle \quad \mathsf{Power}(id, at)}{\langle ag, C \rangle \longrightarrow \langle ag, C' \rangle}$$

$$where: \; C'_M = C_M - \{\langle Unachieve, id, at \rangle\}$$
$$C'_E = C_E \cup \{\langle -!at, \top \rangle\}$$

Similarly to the previous rule, except that now a deletion (rather than addition) of achievement goal is included in the set of events. If the agent has a plan with such triggering event, that plan should handle all aspects of dropping an intention. However, doing so in practice may require the alteration of the set of intentions, thus requiring special mechanisms which are not available in AgentSpeak(L) as yet (neither formally, nor in implemented AgentSpeak(L) interpreters, to the best of our knowledge).

Receiving a Tell-How Message

$$\mathbf{TellHowRec} \;\; \frac{S_M(C_M) = \langle TellHow, id, p \rangle \quad \mathsf{Trust}(id, at)}{\langle ag, C \rangle \longrightarrow \langle ag', C' \rangle}$$

$$where: \; C'_M = C_M - \{\langle TellHow, id, p \rangle\}$$
$$ps' = ps \cup \{p\}$$

The concept of plans in reactive planning systems such as those defined by AgentSpeak(L) agents is associated with Singh's notion of know-how [22]. Accordingly, we use the *TellHow* performative when an external source wants to inform an AgentSpeak(L) agent of a plan it uses for handling certain types of events (given by the plan's triggering event). If the source is trusted, the plan (which is in the message content) is simply added to the agent's plan library.

Receiving an Untell-How Message

$$\mathbf{UntellHowRec} \;\; \frac{S_M(C_M) = \langle UntellHow, id, p \rangle \quad \mathsf{Trust}(id, at)}{\langle ag, C \rangle \longrightarrow \langle ag', C' \rangle}$$

$$where: \; C'_M = C_M - \{\langle UntellHow, id, p \rangle\}$$
$$ps' = ps - \{p\}$$

Similarly to the rule above. An external source may find that a plan is no longer valid, or efficient, for handling the events it was supposed to handle. It may then want to inform an AgentSpeak(L) agent of that fact. Thus, when receiving and *UntellHow*, the agent drops the associated plan (in the message content) from its plan library.

All of the rules above require either the Trust or the Power function to be true. If the receiver does not trust the sender, or if the sender does not have enough power over the receiver, the message is simply removed from the set of messages. Below we present the rule for receiving a *Tell* message from a untrusted source.

$$\textbf{TellRec2}\ \frac{S_M(C_M) = \langle\,Tell,\,id,\,at\,\rangle \quad \neg\mathsf{Trust}(id,\,at)}{\langle\,ag,\,C\,\rangle \longrightarrow \langle\,ag,\,C'\,\rangle}$$

$$where:\ C'_M = C_M - \{\langle\,Tell,\,id,\,at\,\rangle\}$$

Similar rules apply to all other illocutionary forces (using Trust or Power accordingly).

6   Conclusion

We have given formal semantics to the processing of speech-acted based messages received by an AgentSpeak(L) agent. The operational semantics we have used in previous work proved quite handy: in this extension, all we had to do (apart from minor changes in the syntax of the language and in the configuration of the transition system) was to provide new semantic rules, one for each illocutionary force used in the communication language. In giving semantics to communicating AgentSpeak(L) agents, we have provided the means for precise implementation of AgentSpeak(L) interpreters with such functionality, as well as given a more computationally grounded semantics of speech-act based agent communication. If on one hand Singh's [9] proposal for a social-agency based semantics may be the best way towards giving semantics to general purpose agent communication languages such as FIPA or KQML, on the other hand, within the context of a BDI agent programming language, a mental agency approach to semantics of communication can be used without any of the drawbacks pointed out by Singh.

A number of papers in this volume present work that is relevant to ours in one way or another. Interestingly, Ancona and Mascardi show very clearly in [28] the need for agents to communicate plans (besides, information, requests, etc.). This emphasises the importance of the clear semantics that we have given to agent communication. In that paper, one of the contributions that we find particularly interesting is the idea of access specifiers associated with plans to determine the agents that are allowed to share a certain plan. Work is under way in trying to integrate our approach with that reported in [28]. Another work that is similar to ours in motivation is the one presented in [29], which introduces the notion of "social integrity constraints", a mechanism that allows for the verification of interaction protocols, aimed at ensuring sound social interaction. So far, our approach to verification of AgentSpeak agents has concentrated on proving properties of individual agents in a multi-agent environment (see [8], and also the recent work on model checking for AgentSpeak [3,4]). Given the clear semantics for communicating AgentSpeak agents given here, existing approaches to proving properties of AgentSpeak agents can be extended to deal with properties of social interactions, as discussed in [29]. Two other papers in this volume present agent-oriented programming languages [30,31]. They emphasise practical aspects of the languages which make them suitable for production environments, while we concentrate on formally defining agent communication.

We expect that this work can be valuable when speech-act based communication is implemented in existing interpreters for BDI languages. In fact, work is underway to extend an AgentSpeak interpreter implemented in Java to account for the semantics of communication as defined in this paper. The communication infra-structure being used is provided by J. Hübner's SACI[1] [32].

Future work should consider other performatives, in particular: *AskIf*, *AskAll*, *Reply*, and for plans *AskHow*, *AskAllHow* and *ReplyHow*. Also, we need to give a better formal treatment for the annotations of information source within atomic propositions; unification and logical consequence of annotated atomic propositions was not formalised in this paper. Further, we plan to tackle other communication issues, such as ontological agreement among AgentSpeak(L) agents. As we mentioned earlier, an aspect of this work that needs further consideration in future work is the agent's reasoning about information sources (e.g., while the agent is executing test goals, or choosing plans based on those annotations). The work presented here has augmented the belief base with annotations of information sources, but mechanisms for efficient use of such annotations to improve the agent's action and interaction must also be devised.

References

1. Rao, A.S.: AgentSpeak(L): BDI agents speak out in a logical computable language. In Van de Velde, W., Perram, J., eds.: Proceedings of the Seventh Workshop on Modelling Autonomous Agents in a Multi-Agent World (MAAMAW'96), 22–25 January, Eindhoven, The Netherlands. Lecture Notes in Artificial Intelligence, Vol. 1038. Springer-Verlag (1996) 42–55
2. Bordini, R.H., Bazzan, A.L.C., Jannone, R.O., Basso, D.M., Vicari, R.M., Lesser, V.R.: AgentSpeak(XL): Efficient intention selection in BDI agents via decision-theoretic task scheduling. In Castelfranchi, C., Lewis Johnson, W., eds.: Proceedings of the First International Joint Conference on Autonomous Agents and Multi-Agent Systems (AAMAS-2002), 15–19 July, Bologna, Italy, New York, NY, ACM Press (2002) 1294–1302
3. Bordini, R.H., Visser, W., Fisher, M., Pardavila, C., Wooldridge, M.: Model checking multi-agent programs with CASP. In Hunt Jr., W.A., Somenzi, F., eds.: Proceedgins of the Fifteenth Conference on Computer-Aided Verification (CAV-2003), Boulder, CO, 8–12 July. Lecture Notes in Computer Science, Berlin. Springer-Verlag (2003) 110–113 Tool description.
4. Bordini, R.H., Fisher, M., Pardavila, C., Wooldridge, M.:   Model checking AgentSpeak. In Rosenschein, J.S., Sandholm, T., Michael, W., Yokoo, M., eds.: Proceedings of the Second International Joint Conference on Autonomous Agents and Multi-Agent Systems (AAMAS-2003), Melbourne, Australia, 14–18 July, New York, NY, ACM Press (2003) 409–416
5. Rao, A.S., Georgeff, M.P.: Decision procedures for BDI logics. Journal of Logic and Computation **8** (1998) 293–343
6. Moreira, Á.F., Bordini, R.H.: An operational semantics for a BDI agent-oriented programming language. In Meyer, J.J.C., Wooldridge, M.J., eds.: Proceedings of the Workshop on Logics for Agent-Based Systems (LABS-02), held in conjunction with the Eighth International Conference on Principles of Knowledge Representation and Reasoning (KR2002), April 22–25, Toulouse, France. (2002) 45–59

---

[1] URL: http://www.lti.pcs.usp.br/saci

7. Bordini, R.H., Moreira, Á.F.: Proving the asymmetry thesis principles for a BDI agent-oriented programming language. In Dix, J., Leite, J.A., Satoh, K., eds.: Proceedings of the Third International Workshop on Computational Logic in Multi-Agent Systems (CLIMA-02), 1st August, Copenhagen, Denmark. Electronic Notes in Theoretical Computer Science 70(5), Elsevier (2002)

8. Bordini, R.H., Moreira, Á.F.: Proving BDI properties of agent-oriented programming languages: The asymmetry thesis principles in AgentSpeak(L). Annals of Mathematics and Artificial Intelligence (2003) Accepted for publication in a Special Issue on Computational Logic in Multi-Agent Systems.

9. Singh, M.P.: Agent communication languages: Rethinking the principles. IEEE Computer 31 (1998) 40–47

10. Wooldridge, M.: Computationally grounded theories of agency. In Durfee, E., ed.: Proceedings of the Fourth International Conference on Multi-Agent Systems (ICMAS-2000), 10–12 July, Boston, Los Alamitos, CA, IEEE Computer Society (2000) 13–20 Paper for an Invited Talk.

11. Labrou, Y., Finin, T.: A semantics approach for KQML—a general purpose communication language for software agents. In: Proceedings of the Third International Conference on Information and Knowledge Management (CIKM'94), ACM Press (1994)

12. Cohen, P.R., Levesque, H.J.: Intention is choice with commitment. Artificial Intelligence 42 (1990) 213–261

13. Wooldridge, M.: Semantic issues in the verification of agent communication languages. Autonomous Agents and Multi-Agent Systems 3 (2000) 9–31

14. de Boer, F.S., van Eijk, R.M., Van Der Hoek, W., Meyer, J.J.C.: Failure semantics for the exchange of information in multi-agent systems. In Palamidessi, C., ed.: Eleventh International Conference on Concurrency Theory (CONCUR 2000), University Park, PA, 22–25 August. Lecture Notes in Computer Science, Vol. 1877. Springer-Verlag (2000) 214–228

15. van Eijk, R.M., de Boer, F.S., Van Der Hoek, W., Meyer, J.J.C.: A verification framework for agent communication. Autonomous Agents and Multi-Agent Systems 6 (2003) 185–219

16. Wooldridge, M.: Reasoning about Rational Agents. The MIT Press, Cambridge, MA (2000)

17. Bratman, M.E.: Intentions, Plans and Practical Reason. Harvard University Press, Cambridge, MA (1987)

18. Austin, J.L.: How to Do Things with Words. Oxford University Press, London (1962)

19. Searle, J.R.: Speech Acts: An Essay in the Philosophy of Language. Cambridge University Press, Cambridge (1969)

20. Levinson, S.C.: The essential inadequacies of speech act models of dialogue. In Parret, H., Sbisa, M., Verschuren, J., eds.: Possibilities and limitations of pragmatics: Proceedings of the Conference on Pragmatics at Urbino, July, 1979. Benjamins, Amsterdam (1981) 473–492

21. Ballmer, T.T., Brennenstuhl, W.: Speech Act Classification: A Study in the Lexical Analysis of English Speech Activity Verbs. Springer-Verlag, Berlin (1981)

22. Singh, M.P.: Multiagent Systems—A Theoretic Framework for Intentions, Know-How, and Communications. Lecture Notes in Artificial Intelligence, Vol. 799. Springer-Verlag, Berlin (1994)

23. Castelfranchi, C., Falcone, R.: Principles of trust for MAS: Cognitive anatomy, social importance, and quantification. In Demazeau, Y., ed.: Proceedings of the Third International Conference on Multi-Agent Systems (ICMAS'98), Agents' World, 4–7 July, Paris, Washington, IEEE Computer Society Press (1998) 72–79
24. Smith, R.G.: The contract net protocol: High-level communication and control in a distributed problem solver. IEEE Transactions on Computers **c-29** (1980) 1104–1113
25. Genesereth, M.R., Ketchpel, S.P.: Software agents. Communications of the ACM **37** (1994) 48–53
26. Mayfield, J., Labrou, Y., Finin, T.: Evaluation of KQML as an agent communication language. In Wooldridge, M., Müller, J.P., Tambe, M., eds.: Intelligent Agents II—Proceedings of the Second International Workshop on Agent Theories, Architectures, and Languages (ATAL'95), held as part of IJCAI'95, Montréal, Canada, August 1995. Lecture Notes in Artificial Intelligence, Vol. 1037. Springer-Verlag (1996) 347–360
27. Cohen, P.R., Levesque, H.J.: Rational interaction as the basis for communication. In Cohen, P.R., Morgan, J., Pollack, M.E., eds.: Intentions in Communication. MIT Press, Cambridge, MA (1990) 221–255
28. Ancona, D., Mascardi, V.: Coo-BDI: Extending the BDI model with cooperativity. In this volume.
29. Alberti, M., Gavanelli, M., Lamma, E., Mello, P., Torroni, P.: Modeling interactions using social integrity constraints: a resource sharing case study. In this volume.
30. Clark, K.L., McCabe, F.G.: Go! for multi-threaded deliberative agents. In this volume.
31. Castaldi, M., Constantini, S., Gentile, S., Tocchio, A.: A logic-based infrastructure for reconfiguring applications. In this volume.
32. Hübner, J.F.: Um Modelo de Reorganização de Sistemas Multiagentes. PhD thesis, Universidade de São Paulo, Escola Politécnica (2003)

A   Operational Semantics

A.1   Preliminaries

We define some auxiliary syntactic functions to be used in the semantics. If p is a plan of the form $te : ct \leftarrow h$, we define $\mathsf{TrEv}(p) = te$ and $\mathsf{Ctxt}(p) = ct$, which retrieve the triggering event and the context of the plan, respectively. We use these to define the auxiliary functions below, which will be needed in the semantic rules.

A plan is considered relevant in relation to a triggering event if it has been written to deal with that event. In practice, that is verified by trying to unify the triggering event part of the plan with the triggering event that has been selected from E for treatment. In the definition below, we write mgu for the procedure that computes the most general unifying substitution of two triggering events.

Definition 1. *Given the plans ps of an agent and a triggering event te, the set RelPlans(ps, te) of relevant plans is given as follows:*

$$RelPlans(ps, te) = \{p\theta \mid p \in ps \ \wedge \ \theta = mgu(te, TrEv(p))\}.$$

A plan is applicable if it is both relevant and its context is a logical consequence of the agent's beliefs.

Definition 2. *Given a set of relevant plans R and the beliefs bs of an agent, the set of applicable plans AppPlans(bs, R) is defined as follows:*

$$\text{AppPlans}(bs, R) = \{p\theta \mid p \in R \ \wedge \ \theta \text{ is s.t. } bs \models \text{Ctxt}(p)\theta\}.$$

An agent can also perform a test goal. The evaluation of a test goal $?at$ consists in testing if the formula at is a logical consequence of the agent's beliefs. One of the effects of this test is the production of a set of substitutions:

Definition 3. *Given the beliefs bs of an agent and a formula at, the set of substitutions Test(bs, at) produced by testing at against bs is defined as follows:*

$$\text{Test}(bs, at) = \{\theta \mid bs \models at\theta\}.$$

We use the following notation for AgentSpeak(L) selection functions: S_E for the event selection function, S_{Ap} for the applicable plan selection function, and S_I for the intention selection function.

A.2   Semantic Rules

Event Selection: The rule below assumes the existence of a selection function S_E that selects events from a set of events E. The selected event is removed from E and it is assigned to the ε component of the circumstance.

$$\textbf{SelEv} \ \frac{S_E(C_E) = \langle te, i \rangle}{\langle ag, C \rangle \longrightarrow \langle ag, C' \rangle} \quad \sharp \ C_\varepsilon = \_ , \ \ C_{Ap} = C_R = \{\}$$

$$where: C'_E = C_E - \langle te, i \rangle$$
$$C'_\varepsilon = \langle te, i \rangle$$

Relevant Plans: The rule **Rel₁** initialises the R component with the set of relevant plans. If no plan is relevant, the event is discarded from ε by **Rel₂**.

$$\textbf{Rel}_1 \ \frac{\text{RelPlans}(ps, te) \neq \{\}}{\langle ag, C \rangle \longrightarrow \langle ag, C' \rangle} \qquad \textbf{Rel}_2 \ \frac{\text{RelPlans}(ps, te) = \{\}}{\langle ag, C \rangle \longrightarrow \langle ag, C' \rangle}$$

$$\sharp \ C_\varepsilon = \langle te, i \rangle \ \ C_{Ap}, C_R = \{\} \qquad \qquad \sharp \ C_\varepsilon = \langle te, i \rangle \ \ C_{Ap}, C_R = \{\}$$
$$where: C'_R = \text{RelPlans}(ps, te) \qquad \qquad where: C'_\varepsilon = \_$$

Applicable Plans: The rule **Appl₁** initialises the Ap component with the set of applicable plans. If no plan is applicable, the event is discarded from ε by **Appl₂**. In either case the relevant plans are also discarded.

$$\textbf{Appl}_1 \quad \frac{\textsf{AppPlans}(bs, C_R) \neq \{\}}{\langle ag, C \rangle \longrightarrow \langle ag, C' \rangle}$$

$$\sharp\, C_\varepsilon \neq \_ \,, C_{Ap} = \{\}, C_R \neq \{\}$$
$$where: \; C'_R \;\; = \{\}$$
$$C'_{Ap} = \textsf{AppPlans}(bs, C_R)$$

$$\textbf{Appl}_2 \quad \frac{\textsf{AppPlans}(bs, C_R) = \{\}}{\langle ag, C \rangle \longrightarrow \langle ag, C' \rangle}$$

$$\sharp\, C_\varepsilon \neq \_ \,, C_{Ap} = \{\}, C_R \neq \{\}$$
$$where: \; C'_R = \{\}$$
$$C'_\varepsilon = \_$$
$$C'_E = C_E \cup \langle te, i \rangle$$

Selection of Applicable Plan: This rule assumes the existence of a selection function S_{Ap} that selects a plan from a set of applicable plans Ap. The plan selected is then assigned to the ρ component of the circumstance and the set of applicable plans is discarded.

$$\textbf{SelAppl} \quad \frac{S_{Ap}(C_{Ap}) = p}{\langle ag, C \rangle \longrightarrow \langle ag, C' \rangle} \quad \sharp\, C_\varepsilon \neq \_ \,, C_{Ap} \neq \{\}$$

$$where: \; C'_\rho \;\; = p$$
$$C'_{Ap} = \{\}$$

Preparing the Set of Intentions: Events can be classified as external or internal (depending one whether they were generated from the agent's perception, or whether they were generated by the previous execution of other plans, respectively). Rule **ExtEv** says that if the event ε is external (which is indicated by T in the intention associated to ε) a new intention is created and its single plan is the plan p annotated in the ρ component. If the event is internal, rule **IntEv** says that the plan in ρ should be put on top of the intention associated with the event. Either way, both the event and the plan can be discarded from the ε and ι components, respectively.

$$\textbf{ExtEv} \quad \frac{}{\langle ag, C \rangle \longrightarrow \langle ag, C' \rangle}$$

$$\sharp\, C_\varepsilon = \langle te, \textsf{T} \rangle, \;\; C_\rho = p$$
$$where: \; C'_I = C_I \cup \{\, [p] \,\}$$
$$C'_\varepsilon = C'_\rho = \_$$

$$\textbf{IntEv} \quad \frac{}{\langle ag, C \rangle \longrightarrow \langle ag, C' \rangle}$$

$$\sharp\, C_\varepsilon = \langle te, i \rangle, \;\; C_\rho = p$$
$$where: \; C'_I = C_I \cup \{\, i[p] \,\}$$
$$C'_\varepsilon = C'_\rho = \_$$

Note that, in rule **IntEv**, the whole intention i that generated the internal event needs to be inserted back in C_I, with p on its top. This is related to suspended intentions, in rule **Achieve**.

Intention Selection: This rule uses a function that selects an intention (i.e., a stack of plans) for processing.

$$\textbf{IntSel} \quad \frac{S_I(C_I) = i}{\langle ag, C \rangle \longrightarrow \langle ag, C' \rangle} \quad \sharp\, C_\iota = \_$$

$$where: \; C'_\iota = i$$

Executing the Body of Plans: This group of rules expresses the effects of executing the body of plans. The plan being executed is always the one on the top of the intention that has been previously selected. Observe that all the rules in this group discard the intention ι. After that, another intention can be eventually selected.

– *Basic Actions:* the action a on the body of the plan is added to the set of actions A. The action is removed from the body of the plan and the intention is updated to reflect this removal.

$$\textbf{Action}\ \frac{}{\langle ag, C\rangle \longrightarrow \langle ag, C'\rangle}\quad \sharp\ C_\iota = i[head \leftarrow a;h]$$

$$where: C'_\iota = \_$$
$$C'_A = C_A \cup \{a\}$$
$$C'_I = (C_I - \{C_\iota\}) \cup \{i[head \leftarrow h]\}$$

– *Achievement Goals:* this rule registers a new internal event in the set of events E. This event can then be eventually selected (see rule **SelEv**).

$$\textbf{Achieve}\ \frac{}{\langle ag, C\rangle \longrightarrow \langle ag, C'\rangle}\quad \sharp\ C_\iota = i[head \leftarrow !at;h]$$

$$where: C'_\iota = \_$$
$$C'_E = C_E \cup \{\langle +!at, C_\iota\rangle\}$$
$$C'_I = C_I - \{C_\iota\}$$

Note how the intention that generated the internal event is removed from the set of intentions C_I. This denotes the idea of *suspended intentions* (see [7] for details).

– *Test Goals:* these rules are used when a test goal $?at$ should be executed. Both rules try to produce a set of substitutions that can make at a logical consequence of the agent's beliefs. The rule **Test₁** says basically that nothing is done if no substitution is found, and the rule **Test₂** says that one of the substitutions is applied to the plan.

$$\textbf{Test}_1\ \frac{\text{Test}(bs, at) = \{\}}{\langle ag, C\rangle \longrightarrow \langle ag, C'\rangle}\qquad \textbf{Test}_2\ \frac{\text{Test}(bs, at) \neq \{\}}{\langle ag, C\rangle \longrightarrow \langle ag, C'\rangle}$$

$$\sharp\ C_\iota = i[head \leftarrow ?at;h]\qquad\qquad \sharp\ C_\iota = i[head \leftarrow ?at;h]$$
$$where: C'_\iota = \_\qquad\qquad\qquad where: C'_\iota = \_$$
$$C'_I = (C_I - \{C_\iota\})\cup\qquad\qquad C'_I = (C_I - \{C_\iota\}) \cup \{i[(head \leftarrow h)\theta]\}$$
$$\{i[head \leftarrow h]\}\qquad\qquad\qquad \theta \in \text{Test}(bs, at)$$

– *Updating Beliefs:* rule **AddBel** simply adds a new event to the set of events E. The formula $+b$ is removed from the body of the plan and the set of intentions is updated properly. Rule **DelBel** works similarly. In both rules, the set of beliefs of the agent should be modified in a way that either the predicate b follows from the new set of beliefs (rule **AddBel**) or it does not (rule **DelBel**).

$$\textbf{AddBel}\ \frac{}{\langle ag, C\rangle \longrightarrow \langle ag', C'\rangle}\qquad \textbf{DelBel}\ \frac{}{\langle ag, C\rangle \longrightarrow \langle ag', C'\rangle}$$

$$\sharp\ C_\iota = i[head \leftarrow +b;h]\qquad\qquad \sharp\ C_\iota = i[head \leftarrow -b;h]$$
$$where: C'_\iota = \_\qquad\qquad\qquad where: C'_\iota = \_$$
$$bs' \models b\qquad\qquad\qquad\qquad bs' \not\models b$$
$$C'_E = C_E \cup \{\langle +b, C_\iota\rangle\}\qquad\qquad C'_E = C_E \cup \{\langle -b, C_\iota\rangle\}$$
$$C'_I = (C_I - \{C_\iota\})\cup\qquad\qquad C'_I = (C_I - \{C_\iota\})\cup$$
$$\{i[head \leftarrow h]\}\qquad\qquad\qquad \{i[head \leftarrow h]\}$$

Removing Intentions: The two rules below can be seen as "clearing house" rules. The rule **ClearInt₁** simply removes an intention from the set of intentions of an agent when there is nothing left (goal or action) in that intention. The rule **ClearInt₂** removes from the intention what is left from the plan that had been put on the top of the intention on behalf of the achievement goal $!at$ (which is also removed as it has been accomplished).

$$\text{ClrInt}_1 \; \dfrac{}{\langle ag, C \rangle \longrightarrow \langle ag, C' \rangle}$$
$$\sharp \, C_\iota = [head \leftarrow]$$
$$where: C'_\iota = \_$$
$$C'_I = C_I - \{C_\iota\}$$

$$\text{ClrInt}_2 \; \dfrac{}{\langle ag, C \rangle \longrightarrow \langle ag, C' \rangle}$$
$$\sharp \, C_\iota = i'[head' \leftarrow !at; h'][head \leftarrow]$$
$$where: C'_\iota = \_$$
$$C'_I = (C_I - \{C_\iota\}) \cup \{i'[head' \leftarrow h']\}$$

A Combined Logic of Expectation and Observation
A Generalisation of BDI Logics

Bình Vũ Trân, James Harland, and Margaret Hamilton

School of Computer Science and Information Technology
RMIT University, Australia
{tvubinh,jah,mh}@cs.rmit.edu.au

Abstract. Although BDI logics have shown many advantages in modelling agent systems, the crucial problem of having computationally ungrounded semantics poses big challenges when extending the theories to multi-agent systems in an interactive, dynamic environment. The root cause lies at the *inability of modal languages to refer* to the world states which hampers agent reasoning about the connection of its mental attitudes and its world. In this paper, following ideas in hybrid logics, we attempt to readdress the computational grounding problem. Then, we provide a formalism for observations – the only connection between mind and worlds – and expectations – the mental states associated with observations. Finally, we compare our framework with BDI logics.

1 Introduction

The most widely held view for practical reasoning agents is that they are *intentional systems* whose behaviour can be explained and predicted through the attribution of mental attitudes such as beliefs, desires, hopes, fears... Since the seminal work of Hintikka [1], formal analyses of mental attitudes are mainly carried out using *modal logics*. Among these models, Belief-Desire-Intention (BDI) model [2] and BDI logics [3] have been one of the most successful. Unfortunately, BDI logics are usually claimed as having *ungrounded semantics* [4], that is, there have been no work showing a **one-to-one correspondence** between a mental model and any concrete computational interpretation. This results in a large gap between theory and practice [5]. The problem, however in our view, should be stated more precisely that since the relationship between mental and computational models realizing the same modal language is a **many-to-many relation**, it is unclear which computational model is the most suitable for simulating an agent's mental model in a dynamic interactive environment.

In this paper, we will demonstrate that the inability to find a concrete and useful computational model is due to the lack of expressive power in the heart of modal languages which are used as agent specifications. This limitation results in a situation where many models with completely different structures look indistinguishable to an agent. Look at this example, imagine an eagle is chasing a

J. Leite et al. (Eds.): DALT 2003, LNAI 2990, pp. 155–172, 2004.
© Springer-Verlag Berlin Heidelberg 2004

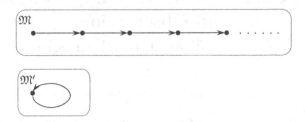

Fig. 1. Invariance and modal languages

sparrow in a cave system where every cave appears identical. At any cave, there is only one identical unidirectional passageway to another cave. Modal language would express this by saying "All caves accessible from this cave are identical to it." But the eagle cannot tell whether it has flown through a cave before. So either the cave system has an infinite number of caves connected with each other, so that the eagle cannot visit a cave twice, or it has only one cave looping back on itself, the eagle would not be able to distinguish using orthodox modal language (*see* **Fig. 1.**). If a distinction could be recognised, the eagle would be able to justify its expectation where the sparrow could be. Hence it would speed up to catch the sparrow in the former case, but it would stay still in the current cave waiting for the sparrow in the latter.

It may become apparent that a mechanism to mark the visited worlds will be a significant advantage for the exploring agent allowing it to redraw a map of the real world in its mind. It would not only help the agent to differentiate between two different models, but also provide a tool to base its future predictions. Hybrid languages by Blackburn and Tzakova [6,7] provide such a naming mechanism for modal languages by introducing a unique label of each world and an operator to jump and evaluate formulae in any world. We believe that such mechanism is strongly related to the concept of observation – the only connection between mind and world. Hence, a formalism that describes observation and its associated mental states, expectations will bridge the mental models and the computational models.

In this paper, following Blackburn and Tzakova we develop a formalism for expectation and observation in hybrid logics and compare this with the BDI model. The paper commences by elaborating in detail the computational grounding problem, and giving an overview of hybrid logics. We then describe the observation-expectation system's details in section §3 and its comparison with BDI logics in section §4. Finally, we briefly outline our approach towards the application of our framework in multi-agent systems.

2   Computational Grounding Problem

2.1   What Is the Computational Grounding Problem?

The computational grounding problem has been recognised by many researchers. Wooldridge's thesis [8] was the first attempt to put the recognitions together.

The problem description however was vague "The problem seems to be with the ontological status of possible worlds". This view was extended as "there is no relationship between a (logical) model $mod(\mathcal{L})$ for $\mathcal{L}$ and computations $\mathcal{C}$" in a more recent paper [4]. Hence, he adopted the approach in [9] "giving *possible-worlds* a precise meaning in the real world" [8]. In other words, computational model can be used directly for possible-worlds model.

Having a more precise view than Wooldridge, Rao identified the problem as the gap between theory and practice for BDI model and stated in [5] as "the inability to show a **one-to-one correspondence** between the model theory, proof theory, and the abstract interpreter." Rao's approach towards this problem is to show such a one-to-one correspondence with a reasonably useful and expressive language. This resulted in an operational semantics AgentSpeak(L).

In this paper, we are with Rao. However, our starting point is from modal languages. Since bisimulation, the relationship between invariant models to an orthodox modal language, is **a many-to-many relation**, we are unable to show a one-to-one correspondence between theoretical and practical models. Hybrid languages [10], being modal languages with a naming mechanism, however, overcome this problem. We are going to show the appropriateness of hybrid languages in this section to resolve the computational grounding problem.

2.2   Why Modal Languages Are Not Expressive Enough to Specify Agent?

Blackburn *et al.* in their definitive book about modal logic [11] insist the importance of modal languages as a way to look at world structures from a local and internal perspective. The truth value of any formula is evaluated inside the structure, at a particular (current) state. Even though modal operators also provide access to information at other states, only states that are *directly accessible* from the current are allowed. This property has attracted many scholars in various disciplines such as cognitive science, psychology, and artificial intelligence to use modal logic as a formal analytical tool for mental models.

The relationship between models in modal logic has been well studied under the notion of *bisimulation* [11]. (cf. *p*-relations [12, Definition 3.7]). It is revealed that with only restrictions on identical atomic information and matching accessibility relations to make modal languages invariant, bisimulations are *many-to-many* relations.

Definition 1 (Bisimulation) *Let $\Phi = \{p, q, \ldots\}$ be a set of atomic propositions. Given two models $\mathfrak{M} = (W, \sim, \pi)$ and $\mathfrak{M}' = (W', \sim', \pi')$, where W, W' are non-empty sets of possible worlds, $\sim \subseteq W \times W, \sim' \subseteq W' \times W'$ are two accessibility relations on W and W', and $\pi : \Phi \to \wp(W), \pi' : \Phi \to \wp(W')$ are two interpretation functions which respectively tell the sets of worlds of W and W' where each proposition holds.*

A bisimulation between two models $\mathfrak{M}$ and $\mathfrak{M}'$ is a non-empty binary relation $Z \subseteq W \times W'$ ($\mathfrak{M}$ and $\mathfrak{M}'$ are called bisimilar*) if the following conditions are satisfied:*

- **(prop)** if wZw' and $w \in \pi(p)$, then $w' \in \pi'(p)$ for all $p \in \Phi$
- **(forth)** if wZw' and $w \sim v$, then there exists $v' \in W'$ such that vZv' and $w' \sim' v'$
- **(back)** if wZw' and $w' \sim' v'$, then there exists $v \in W$ such that vZv' and $w \sim v$

Therefore, many models with completely different structures can be modally equivalent. Given an arbitrary model, there can be many other models bisimilar to it. For example, let's describe the two cave systems above using a modal framework. The first cave system can be modelled by a model $\mathfrak{M}$, which has the natural numbers in their usual order as its frame ($W = \mathbb{N}$) and every propositional symbol is **true** at every world, and the second cave system by model $\mathfrak{M}'$ which has a single reflexive world as its frame and all propositional symbols are **true** at this world (*see* **Fig. 1**). Apparently, one is infinite and irreflexive whilst the other is finite and reflexive. However, they both recognise the same modal language.

One may argue that this would be an advantage of modal languages. So, for example, if the model $\mathfrak{M}$ above is a mental model of the real world (the cave system), its identical isomorphic structure would not be implementable on a computer due to the infinite set of mental states. However, the modally equivalent model $\mathfrak{M}'$ has a finite set of states, and hence would certainly be implementable. The main problem arisen is that in many modally equivalent models, which computational model would be the best. What is the process of selecting such best model? Conversely, given a particular computational model, how can one determine it is the best model simulating the mental model?

In fact, the process of selecting and verifying the best computational model is essentially a process of using additional information to enable a one-to-one mapping. In certain domains, a process that maps the above model $\mathfrak{M}$ to $\mathfrak{M}'$ could be useful. However, we strongly believe that in an unpredictable, dynamic, changing environment, where an agent has to continuously update its mental state, the isomorphic model to the mental model is the best.

Lemma 1 *Two modally equivalent $\mathfrak{N}$ and $\mathfrak{N}'$ are isomorphic if and only if any changes in $\mathfrak{N}$ requires the same number of changes in $\mathfrak{N}'$ to keep them isomorphic and vice versa.*

Proof. – *Necessity* Easy and left for readers.
- *Sufficiency* From $\mathfrak{N} \rightarrow \mathfrak{N}'$: Since $\mathfrak{M}$ and $\mathfrak{N}'$ are bisimilar, for any n changes to $w \in W$, it requires n changes for any $w' \in W'$ such that $w \leftrightarrow w'$. If w has k bisimilar worlds in W' it will require $k.n$ changes. Hence, to keep the same number of changes k must be 1. In other words, every world $w \in W$ has only one image $w' \in W'$. Similarly, from $\mathfrak{N}' \rightarrow \mathfrak{N}$. We do not need to consider the number of edges since this can easily be proven from the definition of bisimulation.

A direct contrapositive conclusion from **Lemma. 1** is that the possibility of substantial changes to synchronise does exist, if one of the two non-isomorphic structures change. In a dynamic unpredictable environment, the agent is continuously updating its mental models. The properties of the models may very well be changed under such updates. Hence, if the computational model is not isomorphic to the mental model, it may subject to expensive changes. For example, if we add one more world v related to a particular world w in the above model $\mathfrak{M}$, where only some propositional symbols are true, it may require a total reconstruction of $\mathfrak{M}'$ to reflect the change.

Condition 1 *The specification language of agent in dynamic, changing, unpredictable environment must allow only isomorphic models to be modally equivalent.*

Secondly, whilst *axiomatic* verification is as hard as the complexity of a proof problem, *semantic* verification (model checking) is more efficient [13, p 296]. This is done through a two-step process to show a program π implements a specification φ as follows [13, p 296]:

1. take π and from it generate a model $\mathfrak{M}_\pi$ that corresponds to π, in the sense that $\mathfrak{M}_\pi$ encodes all the possible computations of π;
2. determines whether or not $\mathfrak{M}_\pi \models \varphi$, i.e. whether the specification formula φ is valid in $\mathfrak{M}_\pi$; the program π satisfies the specification φ just in case the answer is 'yes'.

The second step has been showed to be done efficiently in polynomial time for BDI logics [14,15]. However, unfortunately, it is unclear how to derive appropriate accessibility relations and hence construct the logical model $\mathfrak{M}_\pi$ from a given **arbitrary** concrete program π. It is apparently easy to use the relation between computational states of the computational model to construct the only accessibility relation in a unimodal logic. However, for multi-modal logics such as BDI logics where we have belief-, desire-, intention-accessibility relations, the construction is usually ad hoc. There are two reasons for this difficulty.

1. *Partitioning problem*: It is unclear how to partition the only relational structure between computational states of **one** particular computational model, and use these partitions for their corresponding accessibility relations' constructions. It is as hard as an exhaustive search for all possible combinations.
2. *Modality interaction problem*: Assuming the first problem were solved, for any sub-model of the original computational model $\mathfrak{M}'$, since bisimulation is a many-to-many relation, there can be many mental models with very different structures corresponding to it. This results in the difficulty of verifying the constraints between modalities.

The partitioning problem could be reduced if the relational structure can be classified using an abstract classification scheme. One of the possible approach is to classify formulae derived from the single relational structure into different sorts. Each sort corresponds to a mental attitude. The partition that realises that sort can then be used to derive the corresponding accessibility relation of the mental modality. This ultimately provides a two-tier approach. The first tier is totally based on a single accessibility relation with an additional sorting mechanism. The second tier with various accessibility relations is then constructed on the first tier. Unfortunately, such sorting mechanism is not provided in orthodox modal languages.

Condition 2 *The construction of accessibility relations must be based on only one relational structure with a syntactical classification scheme for the specification language.*

The above issues lead us to a definite conclusion: modal languages are not expressive enough for specifying agents in a dynamic, changing, unpredictable environment. We are unable to update our computational model reliably and cheaply for changes in theory. More seriously, it is also expensive to verify correctness of a computational model. We call this problem *the computational grounding problem of modal languages* (cf. [4]). An appropriate agent specification language must satisfy the two above conditions.

2.3   Hybrid Languages – Modal Languages with Markers

Hybrid languages [6,7], overcome the problem by two simple additions to modal languages: a new sort of formulae, called *nominals*, and *satisfaction operators* @. Basically, nominals are just atomic propositions disjoint from the set of normal propositions. The crucial difference is that, each nominal is **true** only at a unique world in the possible worlds structure. Therefore, nominals can be considered as the name, or label for worlds. Satisfaction operators @ are used to assert satisfaction of a formula at a certain world. They allow us to jump to the world where the formula is evaluated.

The additions are relatively simple, but they have significant contributions. Though *hybrid bisimulation* could be altered slightly by adding nominals to the set of proposition Φ in the **(prop)** rule, the addition of the (@) rule insists that nominals must be true at a unique world in each model.

- (@) for all nominals s, if $\pi(s) = \{w\}$ and $\pi'(s) = \{w'\}$, then wZw' where $w \in W, w' \in W'$.

The (@) rule guarantees every world $w \in W$ has a unique corresponding world $w' \in W'$. Therefore, though bisimulation Z is a relation, under this condition, it becomes a one-to-one function. In other words, a hybrid bisimulation now becomes an isomorphism [10]. With these results, two necessary conditions to solve the grounding problem are satisfied.

The path of hybrid logics represented in this paper is led by Blackburn [16]. Computational complexity and characterisation of hybrid logics were studied in [10]. The web site *http://www.hylo.net* provides further resources and development in hybrid logics.

3   Observation-Expectation System

Based on the recognition in previous section, we start to find appropriate concepts corresponding to the added features in modal languages. In this section, we discuss the use of two notions: *observation* and *expectation*, and introduce a formalism to represent these notions using a hybrid language.

3.1   Agents, Observations and Expectations

The real world has its own structure and properties. An agent's mental model is only a reflected part of that structure in the agent's mind. The only means that the agent has to discover its environment is through its *observation*. Therefore, in order to formalise the connection between an agent's mind and its real world, we make observation our essential concept.

According to the *Merriam-Webster Unabridged* dictionary [17], an observation is "an act of recognising and noting a fact or occurrence..." or "an act of seeing or of fixing the mind upon anything." In our framework, observation is a bisimulation between the real world and an agent's mental model. A single object in the real world, e.g. the planet *Venus*, can have multiple images in an agent's mind, '*the morning star*' and '*the evening star*' through two different observations. Conversely, a single mental state can refer to various real world objects, e.g. a tiger refers to any individual which is a large carnivorous feline mammal having a tawny coat with transverse black stripes. This ability of rational agents is usually known as *abstraction*.

Definition 2 *An observation relation* $\mathbf{O} \subseteq \mathbb{G} \times \mathcal{E}_i$ *is a relation between the real world* $\mathbb{G}$ *and a subset of mental states called expectation set* $\mathcal{E}_i \subseteq L_i$, *where* $i \in \mathcal{I}$ *is an identity of an agent* a_i.

Unfortunately, this only connection to the real world is not always available due to various reasons, e.g. limitations of sensors, noises or disruptions from the environment. In such conditions, a rational agent is still able to continually construct the world model in its mind using its inferential mechanisms and act upon this model accordingly. Thus in the above example, when chasing the sparrow, if the sparrow disappears into a passageway, the eagle would predict the sparrow's movement and keep flying to the other end of the passageway to catch the sparrow there, instead of stopping the chase. The images of the world in the agent's mind that are associated with observations as about to happen are called *expectations*.

In this section, firstly we describe how observations are linked in an observation system and the association of observation with expectation. Secondly, we introduce the formalism for expectation logic based on the observation system.

3.2   Observation System

In any observation system, sensors and effectors are the primary sources that generate observations. Each sensor or effector is associated with a set of observations. Given a sensor set ($\mathbb{S} = \bigcup_{i \in \mathcal{I}} \mathbb{S}_i$) and an effector set ($\mathbb{E} = \bigcup_{i \in \mathcal{I}} \mathbb{E}_i$), where $\mathbb{S}_i$ and $\mathbb{E}_i$ are respectively the sets of sensors and effectors of an individual agent a_i. Let's look at the eagle and the cave system in the above example as an agent in an observation system. The eagle's sensors $\mathbb{S}_i$ (eyes, ears, skin, ...) and effectors $\mathbb{E}_i$ (wings, neck, ...) and any combination of them bring different observations (Obs_i) about the environment to the eagle. The eyes ($\varsigma \in \mathbb{S}_i$) bring visual images of the caves ($e_1 \in \varsigma$), and sparrow ($e_2 \in \varsigma$) to the eagle's brain $\mathcal{E}_i \subseteq L_i$. The wings ($\epsilon \in \mathbb{E}_i$) when flapping may bring an observation that its position would be closer to the sparrow e_3. However, this can be verified by the eagle's eyes if $e_3 \in \varsigma$.

Observing the world by obtaining observations directly from sensors and effectors is called *primitive observation method* $\mathbb{M}_0$ (e.g. $\epsilon, \varsigma \in \mathbb{M}_0$). Consequently, each primitive observation method returns a set of expectations extracted from the set of observations associated with the corresponding sensor or effector. A more complicated set of observation methods $\mathbb{M}_k$ would arrange the k expectations of other observation methods in a sequence to generate new expectations about the world. These expectations are also associated with global states to form more complex observations.

An important note is that the observations from an effector are only *hypothetical*. That is, an agent is always *uncertain* about the consequences of its actions until it uses its sensors to verify the results. Thus, an observation of an effector is justified if and only if it is also associated with a sensor. Observation methods are formally defined as follows:

Definition 3 *(Observation methods)* *An observation method family is a set of observation method sets* $\mathcal{M} = \{\mathbb{M}_k\}_{k \in \mathbb{N}}$ *where* $\mathbb{M}_k$ *is a set of observation methods of arity k for every $k \in \mathbb{N}^+$. $\mathbb{M}_0 = \mathbb{S} \cup \mathbb{E}$ is called primitive observation method set. $\mathbb{M}_k$ is inductively defined as follows:*

- $e \in \mathcal{E}$ *for all* $e \in \mu_0, \forall \mu_0 \in \mathbb{M}_0$
- $\mu_k(e_1, \ldots, e_k) \subseteq \wp(\mathcal{E})$ *for all* $\mu_k \in \mathbb{M}_k$ *and* $e_1, \ldots, e_k \in \mathcal{E}$

Thus, if the eagle expects the sparrow would reach the end of the passageway, and it also expects with a flap it would get to the same place at the same time, a combination of the two expectations $\mu_2(e_2, e_3) \in \mathbb{M}_2$ provides a way of chasing the sparrow which generates an expectation that two birds would be at the same place (e_4). However, if the eagle executed the "chasing the sparrow" method $\mu_2(e_2, e_3)$, and it got the expectation e_5 that the sparrow was not at the same place, it would not be able to distinguish the two resulting expectations e_4 and e_5.

We can now formally define an observation system with its corresponding real-world global states:

Definition 4 *(Observation system)* *Let $\mathcal{I}$ be a set of agent identities, L_i be a set of local states for any agent a_i, where $i \in \mathcal{I}$. An observation system is a quadruple* $OS = \langle \mathbb{G}, \tau, \mathcal{M}, g_0 \rangle$ *where*

- $\mathbb{G} \subseteq \prod_{i \in \mathcal{I}} L_i$ *is the set of global states with each $g \in \mathbb{G}$ being an instantaneous global state.*

- $g_0 \in \mathbb{G}$ is the initial state of the system.
- The environment of an agent a_i is $Env_i \subseteq \prod_{j \in \mathcal{I} \setminus i} L_j$
- An agent a_i's collection of observations is a relation $Obs^i \subseteq \mathbb{G} \times \mathcal{E}_i$, where $\mathcal{E}_i \subseteq L_i$ is the set of expectations and each pair (g, e) is called an observation taken by the agent a_i. e is the agent's expectation about g through the observation.
- Let $\mathfrak{G} \subseteq \mathcal{I}$. A group $\mathfrak{G}$'s collection of observations is a relation $Obs^{\mathfrak{G}} \subseteq \mathbb{G} \times \mathcal{E}_{\mathfrak{G}}$ where $\mathcal{E}_{\mathfrak{G}} = \bigcup_{i \in \mathfrak{G}} \mathcal{E}_i$. The pair $(g, e) \in Obs^{\mathfrak{G}}$ is called a group observation.
- $\tau : \mathbb{G} \times \mathcal{M} \to \mathbb{G}$ is a system state transformer function that depicts how a global state transits to another when a set of observation methods from the observation method family $\mathcal{M}$ defined below are carried out by some or all agents in the system.

3.3   Expectation Logic

We can now study how an agent generates its expectations from its observations about its environment by introducing an expectation logic $\mathcal{L}$ based on an observation system. Consider the set of agents identified by the identity set $\mathcal{I}$. To view an observation system as a hybrid Kripke structure, we introduce the observation interpretation function $\pi : (\Phi \cup \Xi) \to \wp(\mathbb{G})$ which based on available set of observations to tell which expectation is associated with which global state. $\Phi = \{p, q, r, \ldots\}$ is called the primitive expectation proposition set and $\Xi = \{s, t, \ldots\}$ is called the observation naming set. The crucial difference from orthodox modal logic is that for every observation name s, π returns a singleton. In other words, s is **true** at a unique global state, and therefore tags this state. Yet, it is possible that a global state can have different observation names. We refer the couple $\mathfrak{M} = \langle OS, \pi \rangle$ as a model of expectation in an observation system.

Definition 5 The semantics of expectation logic $\mathcal{L}$ are defined via the satisfaction relation $\models$ as follows

1. $\langle \mathfrak{M}, g \rangle \models p$ iff $g \in \pi(p)$ (for all $p \in \Phi$)
2. $\langle \mathfrak{M}, g \rangle \models \neg \varphi$ iff $\langle \mathfrak{M}, g \rangle \not\models \varphi$
3. $\langle \mathfrak{M}, g \rangle \models \varphi \vee \psi$ iff $\langle \mathfrak{M}, g \rangle \models \varphi$ or $\langle \mathfrak{M}, g \rangle \models \psi$
4. $\langle \mathfrak{M}, g \rangle \models \varphi \wedge \psi$ iff $\langle \mathfrak{M}, g \rangle \models \varphi$ and $\langle \mathfrak{M}, g \rangle \models \psi$
5. $\langle \mathfrak{M}, g \rangle \models \varphi \Rightarrow \psi$ iff $\langle \mathfrak{M}, g \rangle \not\models \varphi$ or $\langle \mathfrak{M}, g \rangle \models \psi$
6. $\langle \mathfrak{M}, g \rangle \models \langle \mathcal{E}_i \rangle \varphi$ iff $\langle \mathfrak{M}, g' \rangle \models \varphi$ for some g' such that $g \sim_e^i g'$
7. $\langle \mathfrak{M}, g \rangle \models [\mathcal{E}_i] \varphi$ iff $\langle \mathfrak{M}, g' \rangle \models \varphi$ for all g' such that $g \sim_e^i g'$
8. $\langle \mathfrak{M}, g \rangle \models s$ iff $\pi(s) = \{g\}$ (for all $s \in \Xi$), g is called the denotation of s
9. $\langle \mathfrak{M}, g \rangle \models @_s \varphi$ iff $\langle \mathfrak{M}, g_s \rangle \models \varphi$ where g_s is the denotation of s.

where $1 - 7$ are standard in modal logics with two additions of hybrid logics in 8 and 9.

We have introduced the modality $\mathcal{E}_i$ which allows us to represent the information of the environment resident in the agent a_i's mind about the output of its observation methods. The semantics of the $\mathcal{E}_i$ modality are given through the *expectation accessibility relation* defined as follows

Definition 6 *Given a binary expectation accessibility relation* $\sim_e^i \subseteq \mathbb{G} \times \mathbb{G}$ *then* $g \sim_e^i g'$ *iff* $\exists \mathcal{E} \subseteq g, \exists \mathcal{E}' \subseteq g'$, *such that* $\mathcal{E}, \mathcal{E}'$ *are indistinguishable to the agent* a_i *through an arbitrary existing observation method* $o_k(e_1, \ldots, e_k)$, *where* $e_1, \ldots, e_k \in g$ *and* $e_1, \ldots, e_k \in g'$.

Thus, if $[\mathcal{E}_i]\varphi$ is true in some state $g \in \mathbb{G}$, then by adopting observation method o_k, the local states of the agent a_i about the environment (its expectations) remains the same. An eagle expects to catch a sparrow in a cave, if and only if *wherever* it adopts the observation method "chasing the sparrow" above, the sparrow will appear close to it.

The last two lines in the **Definition 5.** hybridise expectation language $\mathcal{L}$. Satisfaction operator $@_s$ is considered as an observation operator. Thus, a formula such as $@_s\varphi$ says there is an observation about the world state labelled as s which makes φ **true** in the agent's mind. For example, by assigning the current cave to s, and "seeing the sparrow" to $p \ (= e_2)$, $@_s p$ tells us the sentence "I am seeing a sparrow in cave s." This formula remains valid even though the eagle's current cave is no longer s.

Observation operators are in fact *normal modal operators* (i.e. $@_s(\varphi \Rightarrow \psi) \Rightarrow (@_s\varphi \Rightarrow @_s\psi)$). However, specially it is a *self-dual operator* ($@_s\varphi \Leftrightarrow \neg@_s\neg\varphi$). This can be read as *for all* observations about s, φ holds in the agent's mind if and only if *there exists* no observation about s that brings $\neg\varphi$ to its mind. We can use '*for all*' and '*there exists*' in this sentence interchangeably. It also allows the expression of state equality "In cave s, it is also named Happy Cave", by $@_s u$ if u represents 'Happy Cave'.

A formula with both observation operator and expectation modality is more interesting. $@_s\langle\mathcal{E}_i\rangle t$ will tell us that the eagle expects one of the next caves from s will be t. In other words, there is an observation about the connection from the cave s to the cave t. $@_s[\mathcal{E}_i]t$ strongly asserts that t is the only subsequent cave the eagle expects (since t is true at a unique world).

3.4   Expectation Reasoning – Observation Logic

The construction of expectation logic is strongly dependent on two crucial factors: the set of observations, which provides a basis to observation interpretation function π for assigning truth values to formulae, and the set of observation methods which is the skeleton for constructing accessibility relation between expectations. Unfortunately, due to limitations of primitive sensors and effectors, an agent will not always be able to obtain all observations about the real world.

Therefore, in such conditions a rational agent should carefully select its observations in order to maximise the synchronisation between its mental models and the real world. Thus, when the sparrow flies into a dark passageway, the eagle can no longer take an observation of its prey. Yet, based on its existing expectations (mental images) and available observation methods at the current world, the eagle can still deliberate and determine the next observation to take. Such deliberation is possible since the eagle's reasoning now relies on another model – the *attention model*.

Definition 7 (Attention model) *A model of the mental states at world s is called an* attention model $\mathcal{A}_i(s) = \langle W_e, \sim^i_{@_s}, \rho_s \rangle$ *where W_e is the set of expectation worlds which are uniquely named by primitive propositions $p \in \Phi$, the function $\rho_s : \Xi \to \wp(W_e)$ interprets what are possible expectations for an observation at s, and $\sim^i_{@_s} \subseteq W_e \times W_e$ is an* observability accessibility relation.

The semantics of observation logic are defined via the satisfaction relation $\models_s$ as follows

- $\langle \mathcal{A}_i(s), w \rangle \models_s t$ *iff* $w \in \rho_s(t)$ *(for all $t \in \Xi$)*
- $\langle \mathcal{A}_i(s), w \rangle \models_s p$ *iff* $\rho_s(p) = \{w\}$ *(for all $p \in W_e$)*
- $\langle \mathcal{A}_i(s), w \rangle \models_s \neg\varphi$ *iff* $\langle \mathcal{A}_i(s), w \rangle \not\models \varphi$
- $\langle \mathcal{A}_i(s), w \rangle \models_s \varphi \vee \psi$ *iff* $\langle \mathcal{A}_i(s), w \rangle \models_s \varphi$ *or* $\langle \mathcal{A}_i(s), w \rangle \models_s \psi$
- $\langle \mathcal{A}_i(s), w \rangle \models_s \varphi \wedge \psi$ *iff* $\langle \mathcal{A}_i(s), w \rangle \models_s \varphi$ *and* $\langle \mathcal{A}_i(s), w \rangle \models_s \psi$
- $\langle \mathcal{A}_i(s), w \rangle \models_s \varphi \Rightarrow \psi$ *iff* $\langle \mathcal{A}_i(s), w \rangle \not\models_s \varphi$ *or* $\langle \mathcal{A}_i(s), w \rangle \models_s \psi$
- $\langle \mathcal{A}_i(s), w \rangle \models_s \langle \mathcal{O}_i \rangle\varphi$ *iff* $\langle \mathcal{A}_i(s), w' \rangle \models_s \varphi$ *for some w' such that $w \sim^i_{@_s} w'$*
- $\langle \mathcal{A}_i(s), w \rangle \models_s [\mathcal{O}_i]\varphi$ *iff* $\langle \mathcal{A}_i(s), w' \rangle \models_s \varphi$ *for all w' such that $w \sim^i_{@_s} w'$*
- $\langle \mathcal{A}_i(s), w \rangle \models_s \text{\textcircled{e}}_p\varphi$ *iff* $\langle \mathcal{A}_i(s), w_p \rangle \models_s \varphi$ *where w_p is the denotation of p.*

Definition 8 (Observation accessibility relation) *An expectation q is observable (reachable) from an expectation p, $p \sim^i_{@_s} q$ iff there exists an observation method $o_k(e_1, \ldots, e_k)$ where*

- $e_1, \ldots, e_k$ *are valid at g_s*
- $p \in \{e_1, \ldots, e_k\}$
- $\exists \mathcal{E} \in o_k(e_1, \ldots, e_k)$, *such that $q \in \mathcal{E}$.*

Hence $[\mathcal{O}_i]\varphi$ says from the current expectation, φ will hold after *any* available observation method is carried out. So if the eagle is currently expecting that it will see the sparrow, it will expect the proposition q $(= e_4)-$ "the sparrow is caught" holds (i.e. observable) regardless of what observation methods "chasing the sparrow" or "staying in the cave" is taken. $\langle \mathcal{O}_i \rangle\varphi$ however says from the current expectation, there are only *some* observation methods that would bring φ into the agent's mind.

The expectation operator $\text{\textcircled{e}}$ is defined similarly to the observation operator @. $\text{\textcircled{e}}_p\varphi$ hence asserts that there is an expectation p where φ holds. Hence, if p is the expectation "seeing a sparrow", and r is "there is some light", $\text{\textcircled{e}}_p r$ is read "There is some light whenever I expect to see a sparrow".

The eagle's deliberation can now be formalised using the rules in **Table 1**. Consider the case when the cave system consists of only one cave looping back on itself. The passageway is dark, but there is some light in the cave. The eagle can only see the sparrow if there is some light $\text{\textcircled{e}}_p r$. When the sparrow flies into

Table 1. Some modality inference rules for observation system

$$\frac{@_p\langle\mathcal{O}_i\rangle\varphi}{@_p\langle\mathcal{O}_i\rangle a}\ (\Diamond);\quad \frac{\neg@_p\langle\mathcal{O}_i\rangle\varphi;@_p\langle\mathcal{O}_i\rangle q}{\neg@_q\varphi}(\neg\Diamond);\quad \frac{@_p[\mathcal{O}_i]\varphi\quad@_p\langle\mathcal{O}_i\rangle q}{@_q\varphi}(\Box);\quad \frac{\neg@_p[\mathcal{O}_i]\varphi}{@_p\langle\mathcal{O}_i\rangle a}\ (\neg\Box)$$

the dark passageway, the eagle would say I expect whatever I do, I can only see the sparrow in this cave s, $@_p[\mathcal{O}_i]s$. Whenever I see the sparrow, I know a way to catch it $@_p\langle\mathcal{O}_i\rangle q$. Using the ($\Box$) rule the eagle will decide to stay in s to catch the sparrow $@_q s$.

However, if the cave system consists of an infinite number of caves linking by unidirectional passageways, the deliberation will be slightly changed. After some observations, the eagle would discover the next cave cannot be s ($\neg@_s\langle\mathcal{E}_i\rangle s$), but another cave t ($@_s\langle\mathcal{E}_i\rangle t$). Hence, when the sparrow disappears, the eagle would say, I expect whatever I do, I can only observe the sparrow in the next cave $@_p[\mathcal{O}_i]\langle\mathcal{E}_i\rangle t$. Whenever I see the sparrow, I know a way to catch it $@_p\langle\mathcal{O}_i\rangle q$. Using the ($\Box$) rule, we will be able to derive $@_q\langle\mathcal{E}_i\rangle t$, which suggests to capture the sparrow, the eagle should follow the sparrow into the passageway linking to the next cave t.

4   Labelled BDI Logics

Rao and Georgeff's *Belief-Desire-Intention* (BDI) logics are one of the most successful theories for agent specification or verification languages in agent research community. Following the philosopher Bratman [2], a formalisation of the three mental attitudes *belief, desire, intention* and their interactions has been investigated as characterisations of an agent. Most work on BDI logics focused on possible relationships between these three mental attitudes by adding different constraints on their interactions. According to Bratman [2], assuming an eagle is a rational agent, the eagle will not intend to catch the sparrow if it believes the sparrow is uncatchable. But it still tries its best (intends) to catch the sparrow for hunger though it does not believe it can catch it (*asymmetry thesis*). Also, the eagle may believe it can catch the sparrow, but it is not necessary that it intends to catch a sparrow now (*non-transference principle*). Additionally, if the eagle intends to catch a sparrow for hunger, though it believes catching the sparrow is certainly energy burning, it will not intend to burn out its energy (*side-effect free principle*). Rao and Georgeff [18] formally put these constraints in the following proposition:

Proposition 2 *A rational agent a_i must satisfy the following principles:*

- *Asymmetry thesis: An agent cannot have beliefs inconsistent with intentions, but can have incomplete beliefs about its intentions.*
  - *(BI-ICN)* $\not\models [\mathcal{I}_i]\varphi \wedge [\mathcal{B}_i]\neg\varphi$
  - *(BI-ICM)* $\exists\mathfrak{M}, \mathfrak{M} \models [\mathcal{I}_i]\varphi \wedge \neg[\mathcal{B}_i]\varphi$

- *Non-transference principle: An agent who believes φ should not be forced to intend φ.*
  - *(BI-NT) $\exists \mathfrak{M}, \mathfrak{M} \models [\mathcal{B}_i]\varphi \wedge \neg[\mathcal{I}_i]\varphi$*
- *Side-effect free principle: if an agent intends φ and believes that $\varphi \Rightarrow \psi$, it should not be forced to intend the side-effect ψ.*
  - *(BI-SE) $\exists \mathfrak{M}, \mathfrak{M} \models [\mathcal{I}_i]\varphi \wedge [\mathcal{B}_i](\varphi \Rightarrow \psi) \wedge \neg[\mathcal{I}_i]\psi$*

These constraints also apply for belief-goal, *and* goal-intention *pairs.*

The constraints between these mental attitudes are set based on the relationships between the accessibility relations. Three well known cases of these systems were studied by Cohen and Levesque in term of *realism* ($\mathbf{B}_i \subseteq \mathbf{G}_i$) [19], by Rao and Georgeff in terms of *strong realism* ($\mathbf{G}_i \subseteq \mathbf{B}_i$) [3] and *weak realism* ($\mathbf{G}_i \cap \mathbf{B}_i \neq \varnothing$) [18]. Rao and Georgeff [18] also concluded that weak realism is the only system that satisfies all desirable properties of a rational agent above.

The real world model of BDI logics is viewed as a single past-branching time future tree [20]. Each possible world of any belief, desire (goal) or intention models consists of a subtree of the above temporal structure. In other words, they are different images of the real world in the agent's mind at different time points. However, a major drawback of BDI logics is that it is very unclear which part of the real world temporal structure should be in an agent's mental attitudes, beliefs, desires, or intentions. There is no formal correspondence from the mental models to the world structure. Consider the eagle chasing the sparrow again. BDI language is unable to tell when a particular event would happen. Thus the sentence "eventually the sparrow will be caught" ($[\mathcal{B}_i]\Diamond q$) can be interpreted to be true at two different time points t_1 and t_2. Regardless of how many observations it can take, the eagle using BDI logics is unable to tell if t_1 and t_2 is a unique time point. A BDI agent would continue to seek for a sparrow after having one caught. Expectation-observation logic however allows us to tell if these points are equal by $@_{t_1} t_2$. Hence, if it is the case, the eagle will drop all subsequent goals to catch the sparrow in the future in the cave system.

A translation from BDI languages to our expectation-observation language can be useful to attain the new expressive power. Firstly, we can construct our observation system using similar temporal structure. Our expectation modality in the system becomes the expectation about the future, equivalently to future modality.

Definition 9 (Mental translation) *A mental translation taking BDI formulae to expectation-observation formulae is defined as follows:*

Expectation model	Attention model
$- \Box\varphi \stackrel{def}{=} [\mathcal{E}_i]\varphi$	
$- \Diamond\varphi \stackrel{def}{=} \langle\mathcal{E}_i\rangle\varphi$	$- [\mathcal{B}_i]\varphi \stackrel{def}{=} [\mathcal{O}_i^{\mathcal{B}}]\varphi$
$- \varphi \mathcal{U} \psi \stackrel{def}{=} \langle\mathcal{E}_i\rangle(s \wedge \psi) \wedge [\mathcal{E}_i](\langle\mathcal{E}_i\rangle s \Rightarrow \varphi)$	$- [\mathcal{G}_i]\varphi \stackrel{def}{=} [\mathcal{O}_i^{\mathcal{G}}]\varphi \wedge \neg\varphi$
$- \mathcal{O}\varphi \stackrel{def}{=} \langle\mathcal{E}_i\rangle(s \wedge \varphi) \wedge [\mathcal{E}_i](\neg\langle\mathcal{E}_i\rangle s)$	$- [\mathcal{I}_i]\varphi \stackrel{def}{=} \langle\mathcal{O}_i^{\mathcal{I}}\rangle p \wedge @_p\varphi$

where $W_e^{\mathcal{B}} = \{p \in \Phi \mid @_s p\}, W_e^{\mathcal{G}} = W_e^{\mathcal{I}} = \{p \in \Phi \mid @_s \langle\mathcal{E}_i\rangle p\}$

The crucial difference between $\mathcal{O}_i^{\mathcal{B}}, \mathcal{O}_i^{\mathcal{G}}, \mathcal{O}_i^{\mathcal{I}}$ is only based on which primitive expectations are selected into the sets of possible worlds $W_e^{\mathcal{B}}, W_e^{\mathcal{G}}, W_e^{\mathcal{I}}$. At a particular world named as s, beliefs are its mental states, where goals and intentions are its mental states about what it expects to happen next if it takes more observation.

By this translation, *beliefs* now are an agent's expectations of what will be observable. If there is no observation linking to the expectation, a belief may well be false. *Goals* are what an agent expects to be observable (in future), but are not observable now. This definition satisfies a number of required properties for goals [21]. Observable also means 'achievable' or 'possible' – the agent only has goals that it believes achievable. However, '$\neg\varphi$' guarantees the goal is *unachieved* or at least expected to be unachieved. Consistency and persistence are just normal logical properties of goals. Although *intention* could be defined as $\langle\mathcal{O}_i^{\mathcal{I}}\rangle\varphi$, the above definition insists the agent has committed to a specific observation method o_k to achieve φ at the subsequent expectation p.

The definition also satisfies weak-realism constraint. The overlapping between beliefs and goals is the set of expectations that hold now and at some time points in the future ($@_s p$ and $@_s\langle\mathcal{E}_i\rangle p$). However, the agent does not have direct observation of the expectations at the current observation. The non-overlapped part of goals are what the agent does not expect to observe now ($@_s\neg p$), but it expects them to be observable in future ($@_s\langle\mathcal{E}_i\rangle p$). Conversely, a belief is not in the goal set if there is a direct observation now ($@_s p$) or the agent expects it will not happen at all ($\neg@_s\langle\mathcal{E}_i\rangle p$).

Similarly, the overlapping between beliefs and intentions is where the subsequent expectation p is also in the set of expectations of the current observation. An intentions will no longer be in the set of beliefs if the resultant expectation of the observation method o_k which is committed to the intention, does not hold at the current observation g_s. On the other hand, a belief is out of the intention set if there is no observation method o_k links to p. In other words, the agent believes φ is observable, but it has no way to observe φ now.

The overlapping between goals and intentions is where the expectation p is in the set of expectations of all possible observations about to occur in the whole system. An intention may not be a goal if it is already observable at the current observation. On the other hand, a goal will not be a specific intention if the agent expects φ can only be achieved by other observation methods not the one associated with the intention.

By this definition, it is clear that the following proposition holds:

Proposition 3 *The agent modelled by the above observation-expectation system is a rational agent. That is, it satisfies asymmetry thesis, side-effect free and non-transference principles.*

Proof. See **Appendix A**.

5   Conclusion and Further Work

In this paper we apply hybrid logic to address a well-known unresolved problem in the agent research community, the computational grounding problem and to introduce a formal correspondence between mental and computational models. It is certainly not yet another paper about hybrid logics. Hence, we do not show decidability, completeness results which have been deeply studied by other researchers [6,7,10,22]. Instead, our crucial argument here is that any concrete computational models are extensional whereas any mental models are intensional. Agent specifications using orthodox modal languages can only express intensional aspects and therefore fail to make connection to extensional aspects.

Apart from BDI logics discussed above, a major strand of research led by the work of Fagin et al. [9,23] has attempted to bring the external to the internal perspective using interpreted systems as the basis of epistemic logic. This approach tightly connects the internal to the external. The approach hence started from a perfectly synchronised mental model with the environment where everything is directly reflected to every agent's mind. Then, the connection is loosened to reflect the fact that agents are imperfect. A dilemma has arisen in this investigation [23, Chapter 11], simultaneity (time synchronisation) strongly affects the attainability of (common) knowledge, but true simultaneity cannot be attained in reality. Interestingly, the resolution of this paradox leads to the ability to record time points and the granularity of time – timestamped (common) knowledge. However, unlike hybrid languages, their naming mechanisms cannot be manipulated and hence reasoned as formulae. An extension for time observation in our framework to link with this work hence appears very promising.

An extension of Fagin et al.'s interpreted systems, $\mathcal{VSK}$ systems and $\mathcal{VSK}$ logic [24,25], provided another attempt to formalise the connection between the states of agents within a system and the percepts received by them. The imperfect situation is captured by using the notion of "partial observability" in POMDPs [26] through $\mathcal{V}$ and $\mathcal{S}$ modalities. Their knowledge modality $\mathcal{K}$ remains the same as modal epistemic logic [23]. There are two crucial drawbacks of this work. Firstly, *visibility* function is similar to *observation function* by van der Meyden [27] which is only capable of capturing the discrete states of an environment but not the relationships between them. Secondly, $\mathcal{VSK}$ fails to fully capture human perception which can be faulty. Our framework using the idea from hybrid logic overcomes the former problem by letting an observation about a relationship be mapped onto an expectation of named state (e.g. $@_s \langle \mathcal{E}_i \rangle t$). The second problem is resolved by adding hypothetical observations from agents' effectors into the concept of observability.

Finally, our chief further work is to show completeness and correspondence results. However it is also worth noting that our work is principally based upon fibring techniques by Gabbay [28] and analytic deduction via labelled deductive systems **LKE** by D'Agostino and Gabbay [29]. These works provide a potential approach towards a uniform way of combining logical systems, hence modelling cooperative reasoning in interactive dynamic environment.

References

1. Hintikka, J.: Knowledge and Belief: An Introduction to the Logic of The Two Notions. Cornell University Press, Ithaca, New York (1962)
2. Bratman, M.E.: Intention, Plans, and Practical Reason. Harvard University Press (1987)
3. Rao, A., Georgeff, M.: Modelling rational agents within a BDI-architecture. In Fikes, R., Sandewall, E., eds.: Proceedings of the Second International Conference on Principles of Knowledge Representation and Reasoning, Cambridge (USA) (1991) 473–484
4. Woolridge, M.: Computationally Grounded Theories of Agency. In Durfee, E.H., ed.: Proceedings of the Fourth International Conference on Multi-Agent Systems (ICMAS 2000). Volume 9., IEEE Press (2000)
5. Rao, A.: AgentSpeak(L): BDI Agents speak out in a logical computable language. In Van de Velde, W., Perram, J., eds.: Proceedings of the Seventh Workshop on Modelling Autonomous Agents in Multi-Agent World (MAAMAW'96). Volume 1038 of Lecture Notes in Artificial Intelligence., Eindhoven, The Netherlands, Springer-Verlag (1996) 42–55
6. Blackburn, P.: Internalizing labelled deduction. Journal of Logic and Computation **10** (2000) 137–168
7. Blackburn, P., Tzakova, M.: Hybrid languages and temporal logic. Logic Journal of the IGPL **7** (1999) 27–54
8. Wooldridge, M.: The Logical Modelling of Computational Multi-Agent Systems. PhD thesis, University of Manchester (1992)
9. Fagin, R., Halpern, J.Y., Vardi, M.Y.: What can machines know? on the properties of knowledge in distributed systems. Journal of the ACM **39** (1992) 328–376
10. Areces, C., Blackburn, P., Marx, M.: Hybrid logics: Characterization, interpolation and complexity. Journal of Symbolic Logic **66** (2001) 977 – 1010
11. Blackburn, P., de Rijke, M., Venema, Y.: Modal logic. Cambridge University Press (2001)
12. van Benthem, J.: Modal Logic and Classical Logic. Bibliopolis, Naples (1983)
13. Woolridge, M.: An introduction to MultiAgent System. John Wiley & Sons, Chichester, England (2002)
14. Benerecetti, M., Giunchglia, F., Serafini, L.: A model checking algorithm for multiagent systems. In Müller, J.P., Singh, M.P., Rao, A., eds.: Intelligent Agents, V. Volume 1555 of LNAI., Springer (1999)
15. Rao, A., Georgeff, M.: A model-theoretic approach to the verification of situated reasoning systems. In: Proceedings of the 13th International Joint Conference on Artificial Intelligence (IJCAI-93), Chambéry, France (1993) 318–324
16. Blackburn, P.: Nominal tense logic. Notre Dame Journal of Formal Logic **34** (1993) 56–83
17. Gove, P.B., ed.: Webster's Revised Unabridged Dictionary. 3rd edn. Merriam Webster Inc. (2002)
18. Rao, A., Georgeff, M.: Asymmetry thesis and side-effect problems in linear-time and branching-time intention logics. In Myopoulos, J., Reiter, R., eds.: Proceedings of the 12th International Joint Conference on Artificial Intelligence (IJCAI-91), Sydney, Australia, Morgan Kaufmann publishers Inc.: San Mateo, CA, USA (1991) 498–505
19. Cohen, P.R., Levesque, H.J.: Intention is choice with commitment. Artificial Intelligence **42** (1990) 213–261

20. Emerson, E.A., Halpern, J.Y.: "sometimes" and "not never" revisited: on branching time versus linear time temporal logic. Journal of the ACM **33** (1986) 151–178
21. Winikoff, M., Padgham, L., Harland, J., Thangarajah, J.: Declarative and procedural goals in intelligent agent systems. In: Eighth International Conference on Principles of Knowledge Representation and Reasoning. (2002) 470–481
22. Blackburn, P.: Representation, reasoning, and relational structures: a hybrid logic manifesto. Logic Journal of the IGPL **8** (2000) 339–625
23. Fagin, R., Halpern, J.Y., Moses, Y., Vardi, M.Y.: Reasoning about Knowledge. The MIT Press, Cambridge, Massachusetts (1995)
24. Woolridge, M., Lomuscio, A.: Multi-agent $\mathcal{VSK}$ logic. In: Proceedings of the Seventh European Workshop on Logics in Artificial Intelligence (JELIA-2000), Springer-Verlag (2000)
25. Woolridge, M., Lomuscio, A.: Reasoning about visibility, perception, and knowledge. In Jennings, N., Lespérance, Y., eds.: Intelligent Agents VI. Volume Lecture Notes in AI Volume. Springer-Verlag (2000)
26. Kaelbling, L.P., Littman, M.L., Cassandra, A.R.: Planning and acting in partially observable stochastic domains. Artificial Intelligence **101** (1998) 99–134
27. van der Meyden, R.: Common knowledge and update in finite environments. Information and Computation **140** (1998) 115–157
28. Gabbay, D.: Fibring Logics. Volume 38 of Oxford Logic Guides. Oxford University Press (1999)
29. D'Agostino, M., Gabbay, D.: A generalization of analytic deduction via labelled deductive systems. Part I: Basic substructural logics. Journal of Automated Reasoning **13** (1994) 243–281

A Proof Sketches

Table 2. BDI constraints in expectation observation language

	BDI language	Expectation-observation language
BI-ICN	$\not\models [\mathcal{I}_i]\varphi \wedge [\mathcal{B}_i]\neg\varphi$	$\not\models \langle O_i^{\mathcal{I}}\rangle p \wedge @_p\varphi \wedge [O_i^{\mathcal{B}}]\neg\varphi$
BI-ICM	$\exists\mathfrak{M}, \mathfrak{M} \models [\mathcal{I}_i]\varphi \wedge \neg[\mathcal{B}_i]\varphi$	$\exists\mathfrak{M}, \mathfrak{M} \models \langle O_i^{\mathcal{I}}\rangle p \wedge @_p\varphi \wedge \langle O_i^{\mathcal{B}}\rangle q \wedge @_q\neg\varphi$
GI-ICN	$\not\models [\mathcal{I}_i]\varphi \wedge [\mathcal{G}_i]\neg\varphi$	$\not\models \langle O_i^{\mathcal{I}}\rangle p \wedge @_p\varphi \wedge [O_i^{\mathcal{G}}]\neg\varphi \wedge \varphi$
GI-ICM	$\exists\mathfrak{M}, \mathfrak{M} \models [\mathcal{I}_i]\varphi \wedge \neg[\mathcal{G}_i]\varphi$	$\exists\mathfrak{M}, \mathfrak{M} \models \langle O_i^{\mathcal{I}}\rangle p \wedge @_p\varphi \wedge \langle O_i^{\mathcal{G}}\rangle q \wedge (@_q\neg\varphi \vee \varphi)$
BG-ICN	$\not\models [\mathcal{G}_i]\varphi \wedge [\mathcal{B}_i]\neg\varphi$	$\not\models ([O_i^{\mathcal{G}}]\varphi \wedge \neg\varphi) \wedge [O_i^{\mathcal{B}}]\neg\varphi$
BG-ICM	$\exists\mathfrak{M}, \mathfrak{M} \models [\mathcal{G}_i]\varphi \wedge \neg[\mathcal{B}_i]\varphi$	$\exists\mathfrak{M}, \mathfrak{M} \models ([O_i^{\mathcal{G}}]\varphi \wedge \neg\varphi) \wedge \neg[O_i^{\mathcal{B}}]\varphi$
BG-NT	$\exists\mathfrak{M}, \mathfrak{M} \models [\mathcal{B}_i]\varphi \wedge \neg[\mathcal{G}_i]\varphi$	$\exists\mathfrak{M}, \mathfrak{M} \models [O_i^{\mathcal{B}}]\varphi \wedge (\neg[O_i^{\mathcal{G}}]\varphi \vee \varphi)$
BI-NT	$\exists\mathfrak{M}, \mathfrak{M} \models [\mathcal{B}_i]\varphi \wedge \neg[\mathcal{I}_i]\varphi$	$\exists\mathfrak{M}, \mathfrak{M} \models [O_i^{\mathcal{B}}]\mathcal{B} \wedge ([O_i^{\mathcal{I}}]\neg p \vee \neg@_p\varphi)$
GI-NT	$\exists\mathfrak{M}, \mathfrak{M} \models [\mathcal{G}_i]\varphi \wedge \neg[\mathcal{I}_i]\varphi$	$\exists\mathfrak{M}, \mathfrak{M} \models ([O_i^{\mathcal{G}}]\varphi \wedge \neg\varphi) \wedge ([O_i^{\mathcal{I}}]\neg p \vee \neg@_p\varphi)$
BI-SE	$\exists\mathfrak{M}, \mathfrak{M} \models [\mathcal{I}_i]\varphi \wedge$ $[\mathcal{B}_i](\varphi \Rightarrow \psi) \wedge \neg[\mathcal{I}_i]\psi$	$\exists\mathfrak{M}, \mathfrak{M} \models (\langle O_i^{\mathcal{I}}\rangle p \wedge @_p\varphi \wedge \langle O_i^{\mathcal{B}}\rangle q \wedge @_q\neg\varphi \wedge @_p\neg\psi)$ $\vee (\langle O_i^{\mathcal{I}}\rangle p \wedge @_p\varphi \wedge [O_i^{\mathcal{B}}]\psi \wedge @_p\neg\psi)$
GI-SE	$\exists\mathfrak{M}, \mathfrak{M} \models [\mathcal{I}_i]\varphi \wedge$ $[\mathcal{G}_i](\varphi \Rightarrow \psi) \wedge \neg[\mathcal{I}_i]\psi$	$\exists\mathfrak{M}, \mathfrak{M} \models (\langle O_i^{\mathcal{I}}\rangle p \wedge @_p\varphi \wedge \langle O_i^{\mathcal{G}}\rangle q \wedge @_q\neg\varphi \wedge @_p\neg\psi)$ $\vee (\langle O_i^{\mathcal{I}}\rangle p \wedge @_p\varphi \wedge \varphi \wedge @_p\neg\psi)$ $\vee (\langle O_i^{\mathcal{I}}\rangle p \wedge @_p\varphi \wedge [O_i^{\mathcal{G}}]\psi \wedge @_p\neg\psi)$
BG-SE	$\exists\mathfrak{M}, \mathfrak{M} \models [\mathcal{G}_i]\varphi \wedge$ $[\mathcal{B}_i](\varphi \Rightarrow \psi) \wedge \neg[\mathcal{G}_i]\psi$	$\exists\mathfrak{M}, \mathfrak{M} \models ([O_i^{\mathcal{G}}]\varphi \wedge \neg\varphi \wedge \neg[O_i^{\mathcal{B}}]\varphi \wedge (\neg[O_i^{\mathcal{G}}]\psi \vee \psi))$ $\vee ([O_i^{\mathcal{G}}]\varphi \wedge \neg\varphi \wedge [O_i^{\mathcal{B}}]\psi \wedge (\neg[O_i^{\mathcal{G}}]\psi \vee \psi))$

From **Table 2**, it is clear that (BI-ICN), (GI-ICN) and (BI-ICN) constraints are satisfied by our framework. (BI-ICM) happens when intention is not in the belief set. From the translation, it says p, q are indistinguishable to an observation method and they reside separately in the two sets intention and belief respectively. Similarly for goal-intention pair except that the agent can intend an achieved goal (i.e. no longer goal) for example to maintain its achievement. (BG-ICM) may look counter-intuitive. However, our translation insists the difference. Beliefs are based on the current observations only, where goals can come from different sources (from other agents – e.g. your boss). Hence, this constraint seems appropriate in a multi-agent system. The asymmetry thesis principle is preserved under the new language.

(BG-NT) appears obvious, since φ is observable now, the agent can hold a belief about φ without having φ as its goal. The emphasis of the commitment to an intention can now be used for (BI-NT) and (GI-NT). Commitment ties a specific mental state p to an intention. Therefore, the agent will not intend φ but it can still believe or have φ as goal. For example, a person does not intend war in Iraq, but believes war is there. This also seems intuitive in a multi-agent environment. The non-transference principle is hence preserved under expectation observation logic.

(BI-SE) can be rewritten as $([\mathcal{I}_i]\varphi \wedge \neg[\mathcal{B}_i]\varphi \wedge \neg[\mathcal{I}_i]\psi) \vee ([\mathcal{I}_i]\varphi \wedge [\mathcal{B}_i]\psi \wedge \neg[\mathcal{I}_i]\psi)$ which appears to be a restricted version of (BI-ICM) and (BI-NT). So if the agent's belief is incomplete about the intention and at the intended expectation p, ψ does not hold, the agent would not worry about the side effect. On the other hand, assuming the agent believes ψ, according to (BI-NT) it is not forced to intend ψ. The translation clarifies the situations where side-effect free can be satisfied. We can achieve similar results for (GI-SE) and (BG-SE).

A Proposal for Reasoning in Agents: Restricted Entailment

Lee Flax

Macquarie University, Sydney NSW 2109, Australia
flax@ics.mq.edu.au

Abstract. Johnson-Laird proposes a semantic theory of human reasoning taking into account finite human capacities. We cast this into logical formalism and define a notion of restricted semantic entailment. Corresponding to any set of logical structures, R, there is a restricted entailment with parameter R. The family of restricted entailments, generated as R varies over sets of structures, is shown to be a complete lattice and to approximate ordinary entailment in the sense of domain theory. A given restricted entailment, $\vDash_R$ say, can be modelled in a modal language with an operator $\downarrow_R$. The modal language is sound and complete and there is a correspondence result: $X \vDash_R \varphi$ iff $\downarrow_R X \Vdash \downarrow_R \varphi$, where X is a set of first-order sentences and φ is first-order. This forms the basis for the proposal that $\vDash_R$ be identified with agent reasoning and that $\downarrow_R$ encapsulate an agent. The existence of the lattice structure mentioned above means that several agents can be integrated into a super-agent or else distilled into a sub-agent by taking joins or meets.

1 Introduction

When we address the question of what could constitute the basis of rationality in an agent, we quickly arrive at a difficulty. If we seek an algorithmic basis founded on first-order logic, then we come up against the problem of undecidability [1, page 159]: there is no procedure which can decide for an arbitrary sentence whether it is valid (true in every model) or not. The reason for this is that algorithms are finite in nature and so, in general, cannot deal with non-enumerable processes.

Humans face these same limitations because of their finite capacities; nevertheless we know that humans are capable of reasoning. To put the issue more sharply: it is clear that no finite machine can completely store an infinite object. Nevertheless some finite machines can reason about infinite objects. For example humans can reason about and refer to the set of all integers, even though the full set cannot be stored at one time in the brain because it has finite capacities. A proper account of how humans do this falls within the domain of cognitive science. In this paper my aim is more modest. I take the view here that the logical basis of rationality is entailment. I examine the entailment relation from a viewpoint that takes seriously the finite capacities of an agent and take the first steps towards developing a computable theory of entailment.

J. Leite et al. (Eds.): DALT 2003, LNAI 2990, pp. 173–190, 2004.

Researchers such as Cherniak [2] and cognitive psychologists such as Johnson-Laird and others [3,4] have developed theories about how agents and humans might reason which take into account the limitation of their finite capacities.

Cherniak in [2] develops the concept of *minimal rationality* and uses this to account for an agent's reasoning capabilities in the face of finite limitations. The following quotes from [2, pages 7 to 9] show that, at least in principle, minimal rationality can be expressed in *linguistic* terms using first-order logic, say. His *ideal general rationality* condition is:

If *A* has a particular belief-desire set, *A* would undertake *all* and only actions that are apparently appropriate.

where

... an action is *apparently appropriate* if and only if according to *A*'s beliefs, it would tend to satisfy *A*'s desires.

Now

... The most important unsatisfactoriness of the ideal general rationality condition arises from its denial of a fundamental feature of human existence, that human beings are in the *finitary predicament* of having fixed limits on their cognitive capacities and the time available to them.

So the *minimal general rationality* condition is posited:

If *A* has a particular belief-desire set, *A* would undertake some, but not necessarily all, of those actions that are apparently appropriate.

In contrast to this, linguistic, approach Johnson-Laird in [3] claims that human reasoning and deduction is carried out by people forming mental models of the situation being reasoned about and then manipulating the mental models in certain ways. The precise nature of these mental models is not important to our argument so we do not describe them. Johnson-Laird and Byrne say in [4, page 36]:

The theory is compatible with the way in which logicians formulate a semantics for a calculus ... But, logical accounts depend on assigning an infinite number of models to each proposition, and an infinite set is far too big to fit inside anyone's head ... people construct a minimum of models: they try to work with just a single representative sample from the set of possible models ...

So Johnson-Laird claims that humans reason by building mental models but the model checking is not exhaustive at any stage because of limited human capacities. One can map this situation into the context of an agent doing semantics of first-order logic and say that in checking the validity of a first-order sentence the agent is only able to check the truth of a subset of all models. That is the agent checks a *restricted* set of models.

We take this as our point of departure and approach first-order semantics in a manner which takes seriously this limitation of restricted model checking. An appropriate notion of satisfaction is defined for this approach as well as a notion of *restricted entailment*. A restricted entailment is like an ordinary entailment except that instead of checking all possible models for satisfaction, one restricts one's checking to a subset R, say, of models. The set R is taken to be a parameter of the entailment and the restricted entailment with parameter R is denoted $\models_R$. It has the usual properties one would expect of an entailment relation: reflexivity, cut and monotony. It also has properties that are significant to the claim that it captures features characteristic of rationality: it can approximate ordinary entailment in the sense of domain theory, and it can be modelled in a modal language whose proof theory and semantics are sound and complete with respect to each other.

The idea of restricted entailment provides the basis for the crystallisation of our proposal for the notion of a finite agent. This is explained as follows. A modal operator, called "approximately true" and denoted $\downarrow_R$, is introduced which also has a parameter R, a *finite* set of models. In our proposal the operator $\downarrow_R$ defines an agent; a different agent is defined for each different parameter.

We claim that the language with modal operator "approximately true" models restricted entailment because for finite R, X a set of first-order sentences and φ a first-order sentence, $X \models_R \varphi$ if and only if $\downarrow_R X \Vdash \downarrow_R \varphi$, where $\Vdash$ is the modal forcing relation. As mentioned above, the significance of this is that it turns out that restricted entailment is able to be modelled by a modal language which has a semantics and proof theory which are sound and complete.

The restriction parameters are sets and so they are automatically endowed with lattice operations: set union and intersection. These are carried over to the set of restricted entailments; they form a lattice. However, the relationship between lattice operations in the entailment set and in the parameter set is contravariant. As a result the meet of a set of restricted entailments is given by the entailment whose parameter is the union of the individual parameters. The join is slightly more complex, but it does involve taking an intersection of sets induced by the restriction parameters. These results mean that given a set of agents one can form a new, inclusive, canonical agent encompassing the deductive powers of the individual agents, and another having the common part of the deductive powers of the individual agents. In the conclusion we sketch how this also holds for agents when they are represented by the modal operator "approximately true". The paper ends with some remarks about the computability of restricted entailment. The conditions mentioned there, which include amongst others finite restriction sets and structures having finite domains of interpretation, are sufficient to ensure computability; more work needs to be done to discover necessary conditions.

In the next section we define restricted entailment and develop machinery to show that the family of restricted entailments has a lattice structure.

2   Restricted Entailment

In this section the set of *restricted entailments* is defined. The members of this set are generalisations of ordinary entailment. For ordinary entailment, one checks that a set of sentences X entails a set Y by examining every structure that is a model of X and checking that it is also a model of Y. If this is always the case then X entails Y. In contrast, one checks for restricted entailment by specifying a subset of structures, R say, and then checking that each model of X lying in R is also a model of Y. So instead of checking all structures, one *restricts* one's checking to a subset, R, of structures. As we have said, this approach to the approximation of entailment is motivated by Johnsohn-Laird's theory of mental models in cognitive psychology.

The main result of this section is corollary 11: any set of restricted entailments has a greatest lower bound and a least upper bound, or meet and join. At the end of this section we show how these operators can be used to give meaning to the reasoning processes of subagents and superagents. Also, the existence of the meet is used in the definition of "domain" in section 3.

We work in a standard first-order language whose *vocabulary* consists of a countable number of constant symbols, a countable number of function symbols of any finite arity and a countable number of relation symbols of any finite arity. A *structure*, S, is a function having a *domain of interpretation*, $\mathsf{dom}(S)$, which is a set. It maps constants to elements in $\mathsf{dom}(S)$, function symbols to functions defined on $\mathsf{dom}(S)$ and relation symbols to relations on $\mathsf{dom}(S)$. The language also has a countable number of *individual variables*; the *connectives* $\neg$, $\vee$, $\wedge$ and $\rightarrow$; and the *quantifiers* $\forall$ and $\exists$. The *terms* of the language are defined in the usual way, as are the *formulas*. Given any formula, an individual variable is *free* in that formula if the variable is not in the scope of any quantifier in the formula. A *sentence* is a formula with no free variables. Meaning is given to sentences by defining, in the usual way, the *satisfaction relation* between structures and sentences. If the structure S satisfies the sentence φ, it is written thus: $S \vDash \varphi$.

In order to avoid difficulties with set-theoretical foundations we work entirely in a universe of sets [5]; all collections of objects are sets, all set operations produce sets and there are no classes which are not sets.

We suppose a language is given and remains fixed. The set of all structures defined on the vocabulary is denoted STRUC. The set of all subsets of STRUC is denoted PSTRUC. The relation of *elementary equivalence* between stuctures is defined as follows: two structures S and S' are elementarily equivalent, denoted $S \equiv S'$, if and only if they satisfy the same sentences.

The following fundamental *restricted* notions are now defined: set of models and entailment. The definitions are made by analogy with the unrestricted ones, which can be obtained from the following definition by omitting the subscript R.

Definition 1 *Let X and Y be sets of sentences and let $R \subseteq$ STRUC.*

1. *The* set of models of X restricted to R, *denoted* $\mathsf{mod}_R(X)$, *is* $\mathsf{mod}_R(X) = \{S \in R : S \vDash X\}$.

2. X entails Y with restriction R *iff* $\mathrm{mod}_R X \subseteq \mathrm{mod}_R Y$; *this is written as* $X \models_R Y$.

Note that $\models_R$ generalises ordinary entailment, $\models$, because $\models_{\mathsf{STRUC}}$ equals $\models$.

It is well-known that entailment satisfies three properties called *reflexivity*, *cut* and *monotony*. A straightforward argument shows that restricted entailment also satisfies appropriate versions of these properties. As they are not central to our argument we do not give them here.

In what follows, propositions 2 and 4 are needed for the important propositions 9 and 10 on the bounds of families of restricted entailments. Proposition 2 says that if a set of structures is enlarged then the associated restricted entailment is reduced, while proposition 4 provides a converse to proposition 2 under a *fullness* condition on the restriction of the entailment.

Proposition 2 *Let $I \subseteq J \subseteq \mathsf{STRUC}$, then $\models_J \subseteq \models_I$.*

Proof. Let X and Y be sets of sentences and suppose that $X \models_J Y$; that is $\mathrm{mod}_J(X) \subseteq \mathrm{mod}_J(Y)$. We must show $\mathrm{mod}_I(X) \subseteq \mathrm{mod}_I(Y)$.

$$
\begin{aligned}
\mathrm{mod}_I(X) &= I \cap \mathrm{mod}(X) \\
&= (I \cap J) \cap \mathrm{mod}(X) \quad \text{since } I \subseteq J \\
&= I \cap (J \cap \mathrm{mod}(X)) \\
&= I \cap \mathrm{mod}_J(X) \\
&\subseteq I \cap \mathrm{mod}_J(Y) \quad \text{since } \mathrm{mod}_J(X) \subseteq \mathrm{mod}_J(Y) \\
&= I \cap (J \cap \mathrm{mod}(Y)) \\
&= (I \cap J) \cap \mathrm{mod}(Y) \\
&= I \cap \mathrm{mod}(Y) \quad \text{since } I \subseteq J \\
&= \mathrm{mod}_I(Y)
\end{aligned}
$$

∎

There is a converse to proposition 2 provided J is *full*. This is defined next.

Definition 3 *Let $I \subseteq \mathsf{STRUC}$, then I is* full *if and only if given elements S and S' of STRUC, if $S \in I$ and S is elementarily equivalent to S' then S' is in I.*

Proposition 4 *Let I and J be subsets of STRUC and suppose J is full. If $\models_J \subseteq \models_I$, then $I \subseteq J$.*

Proof. We suppose $I \not\subseteq J$ and prove that $\models_J \not\subseteq \models_I$. There are two cases to consider: either J is empty or not empty.

CASE $J = \emptyset$. Let $S \in I$ and let φ be a sentence with $S \models \varphi$. Set $X = \{\varphi\}$ and $Y = \{\neg\varphi\}$, then $S \models X$ and $S \not\models Y$. So $S \in \mathrm{mod}_I(X)$ but $S \notin \mathrm{mod}_I(Y)$. Since $J = \emptyset$, $X \models_J Y$ but as we have seen $X \not\models_I Y$.

CASE $J \neq \emptyset$. Suppose $S \in I$ and $S \notin J$, then S is not elementarily equivalent to any $S' \in J$. This is so because if S is elementarily equivalent to some $S' \in J$ then since J is full $S \in J$, which is contrary to our supposition. So for each $S' \in J$ there is a sentence $\varphi_{S'}$, say, with $S \models \varphi_{S'}$ and $S' \not\models \varphi_{S'}$. Set $X = \{\varphi_{S'} : S' \in J\}$, then $\mathcal{S} \in \mathrm{mod}_I(X)$ but $\mathrm{mod}_J(X) = \emptyset$. Also pick $\mathcal{S}'' \in J$ and set $Y = \{\neg\varphi_{\mathcal{S}''}\}$, then $\mathcal{S} \notin \mathrm{mod}_I(Y)$.

Now $\mathrm{mod}_J(X) = \emptyset \subseteq \mathrm{mod}_J(Y)$, so $X \vDash_J Y$. But $\mathcal{S} \in \mathrm{mod}_I(X)$ and $\mathcal{S} \notin \mathrm{mod}_I(Y)$ so $X \nvDash_I Y$. ∎

Next we define the *greatest lower bound* and *least upper bound* of a set of restricted entailments and then show how to calculate them. We recall that a partial order is a reflexive, transitive, antisymmetric relation.

Definition 5

1. $\mathsf{ENT} = \{\vDash_I : I \subseteq \mathsf{STRUC}\}$.
2. $(\mathsf{ENT}, \subseteq)$ *is the partially ordered set where the elements of* ENT *are partially ordered by set inclusion.*
3. *Let* $E \subseteq \mathsf{ENT}$. *An element* $\vDash_H$ *of* ENT *is a* lower bound *of* E *if* $\vDash_H \subseteq \vDash_I$ *for each* $\vDash_I \in E$.
4. *An element* $\vDash_G$ *of* ENT *is the* greatest lower bound *of* $E \subseteq \mathsf{ENT}$ *if* $\vDash_G$ *is a lower bound of* E *and it is a superset of, or equal to any other lower bound of* E. *The greatest lower bound of* E, *if it exists, is denoted* $\bigwedge E$.
5. *Let* $E \subseteq \mathsf{ENT}$. *An element* $\vDash_H$ *of* ENT *is an* upper bound *of* E *if* $\vDash_I \subseteq \vDash_H$ *for each* $\vDash_I \in E$.
6. *An element* $\vDash_L$ *of* ENT *is the* least upper bound *of* $E \subseteq \mathsf{ENT}$ *if* $\vDash_L$ *is an upper bound of* E *and it is a subset of, or equal to any other upper bound of* E. *The least upper bound of* E, *if it exists, is denoted* $\bigvee E$.

We want to show that the meet of $\vDash_I$ and $\vDash_J$ is $\vDash_{I \cup J}$. We do this with the help of an operator that takes any subset I of STRUC and turns it into a full subset containing I denoted $[I]$. The operator is called the *full expansion* operator.

We recall that PSTRUC stands for the set of all subsets of STRUC. If $E \subseteq \mathsf{PSTRUC}$ then each element of E is a subset of STRUC; $\bigcup E$ means the union of all members of E.

Definition 6

1. *Let* $I \subseteq \mathsf{STRUC}$. *The* full expansion *of* I, *denoted* $[I]$, *is* $\{\mathcal{S} \in \mathsf{STRUC} : \exists \mathcal{S}' \in I \ \& \ \mathcal{S} \equiv \mathcal{S}'\}$.
2. *Let* $E \subseteq \mathsf{PSTRUC}$, *then* $[E] = \{[I] : I \in E\}$.

Proposition 7

1. *The full expansion of a set of structures is full.*
2. *The full expansion of a set of structures is unique.*
3. *The full expansion operator satisfies inclusion, idempotence and monotony:*
   (a) $I \subseteq [I]$.
   (b) $[[I]] = [I]$.
   (c) *If* $I \subseteq J$, *then* $[I] \subseteq [J]$.

Proof. Straightforward. ∎

Proposition 8 *Let* $I \subseteq$ STRUC, *then* $\vDash_I = \vDash_{[I]}$.

Proof. Full expansion satisfies inclusion so $I \subseteq [I]$ and by proposition 2 $\vDash_{[I]} \subseteq \vDash_I$.

On the other hand suppose $X \vDash_I Y$ and let $\mathcal{S}' \in [I] \cap \mathrm{mod}(X)$. We must show that $\mathcal{S}' \in [I] \cap \mathrm{mod}(Y)$. There is $\mathcal{S} \in I$ such that $\mathcal{S}' \equiv \mathcal{S}$. Also $\mathcal{S} \in \mathrm{mod}(X)$ because, as is easily seen, $\mathrm{mod}(X)$ is full and $\mathcal{S}' \in \mathrm{mod}(X)$. So $\mathcal{S} \in \mathrm{mod}_I(X)$ and therefore by our supposition $\mathcal{S} \in \mathrm{mod}_I(Y)$. By the inclusion property of full expansion $I \subseteq [I]$, therefore $\mathcal{S} \in I \cap \mathrm{mod}(Y) \subseteq [I] \cap \mathrm{mod}(Y)$. But since, as is easily seen, $[I] \cap \mathrm{mod}(Y)$ is full, we have that $\mathcal{S}' \in [I] \cap \mathrm{mod}(Y)$.   ∎

The following results allow one to calculate meets and joins. The meet of a family of restricted entailments is generated by taking the union of the restriction sets. The join, however, is generated by taking the intersection of the full expansions of the restriction sets.

Proposition 9 *Let* $E \subseteq$ PSTRUC. *The following are true.*

1. $\vDash_{\cup E} \subseteq \vDash_I$, *for each* $I \in E$.
2. *Suppose there is* $G \subseteq$ STRUC *with* $\vDash_{\cup E} \subseteq \vDash_G \subseteq \vDash_I$ *for each* $I \in E$, *then* $\vDash_G = \vDash_{\cup E}$.

Proof.   1. This follows from proposition 2 because $I \subseteq \bigcup E$ for each $I \in E$.
2. We have supposed that
$$\vDash_{\cup E} \subseteq \vDash_G \subseteq \vDash_I \text{ so}$$
$$\vDash_{[\cup E]} \subseteq \vDash_{[G]} \subseteq \vDash_I \text{ (by 8) and}$$
$$I \subseteq [G] \subseteq [\cup E] \text{ (by 4) so}$$
$$\cup E \subseteq [G] \subseteq [\cup E] \text{ and}$$
$$[\cup E] \subseteq [G] \subseteq [\cup E] \text{ (by 7 monotony and idempotence) giving}$$
$$[G] = [\cup E] \text{ and so}$$
$$\vDash_G = \vDash_{\cup E} \text{ (using 8)}$$
         ∎

The next proposition depends on the evaluation of the expression $\cap[E]$ where $E \subseteq$ PSTRUC. It can be shown that if a Bernays-von Neumann-Gödel set theory (such as in Kelley [6]) is adopted $[E]$ can be empty even when E is not (see [7, Appendix]). If this is the case then $\cap[E]$ is not a set, it is the class of all sets. We prefer to work in an environment without such "explosions". To achieve this we could either dispense with defining the least upper bound altogether or use an approach to set theory yielding more tractable results. As mentioned earlier, we have decided to work within a universe of sets (see [5,8]) where the results of all constructions are sets. In a universe of sets $[E]$ is not empty if E is not and also $\cap[E]$ is a set.

Proposition 10 *Let* $E \subseteq$ PSTRUC. *The following are true.*

1. $\vDash_I \subseteq \vDash_{\cap[E]}$, *for each* $I \in E$.
2. *Suppose there is* $L \subseteq$ STRUC *with* $\vDash_I \subseteq \vDash_L \subseteq \vDash_{\cap[E]}$ *for each* $I \in E$, *then* $\vDash_L = \vDash_{\cap[E]}$.

Proof. 1. For each $I \in E$ we have $\cap[E] \subseteq [I]$, so by 2 $\vDash_{[I]} \subseteq \vDash_{\cap[E]}$ and by 8 $\vDash_{[I]} = \vDash_I$.

2. We have supposed that
$$\vDash_I \subseteq \vDash_L \subseteq \vDash_{\cap[E]} \text{ so}$$
$$\vDash_{[I]} \subseteq \vDash_{[L]} \subseteq \vDash_{\cap[E]} \text{ (by 8) and}$$
$$\cap[E] \subseteq [L] \subseteq [I] \text{ (by 4) so}$$
$$\cap[E] \subseteq [L] \subseteq \cap[E] \text{ giving}$$
$$[L] = \cap[E] \text{ and so}$$
$$\vDash_L = \vDash_{\cap[E]} \text{ (using 8)}$$

∎

We have shown that arbitrary infinite (and hence finite) meets and joins exist in PSTRUC.

Corollary 11 *Let $E \subseteq$ PSTRUC, then*

1. $\bigwedge_{I \in E} \vDash_I = \vDash_{\cup E}$.
2. $\bigvee_{I \in E} \vDash_I = \vDash_{\cap[E]}$.

We now show how meets and joins are able to give meaning to the reasoning processes of subagents and superagents. Let Q be an index set labelling agents and let X_q, where $q \in Q$, be the *belief set* of agent q. According to Gärdenfors [9], a belief set is a consistent set of sentences closed under the consequence operator, Cn. So $X_q = \mathsf{Cn}(X_q)$. Let us take $\bigcap_{q \in Q} X_q$ to be the belief set of the subagent incorporating the common part of all the agents $q \in Q$, and $\bigcup_{q \in Q} X_q$ to be the belief set of the superagent incorporating all the agents $q \in Q$. It can be shown that

$$\mathsf{mod}_R(\textstyle\bigcap_{q \in Q} X_q) = \bigcup_{q \in Q} \mathsf{mod}_R(X_q) \text{ and}$$
$$\mathsf{mod}_R(\textstyle\bigcup_{q \in Q} X_q) = \bigcap_{q \in Q} \mathsf{mod}_R(X_q).$$

It follows from corollary 11 part 1 that the subagent's reasoning corresponds to

$$\bigwedge_{q \in Q} \vDash_{\mathsf{mod}_R X_q} = \vDash_{\bigcup_{q \in Q} \mathsf{mod}_R(X_q)}.$$

To give an expression for the superagent's reasoning, part 2 of corollary 11 needs to be generalised in terms of *relative fullness* which is defined as follows. Let $I \subseteq R \subseteq$ STRUC. Then I is full relative to R if and only if given members S and S' of R, if $S \in I$ and S is elementarily equivalent to S' then $S' \in I$. Let $I \subseteq R$. The full expansion of I relative to R is $[I]_R = \{S \in R : \exists S' \in I \ \& \ S \equiv S'\}$. It is easy to see that for any Y, $\mathsf{mod}_R Y$ is full relative to R (that is, $\mathsf{mod}_R Y = [\mathsf{mod}_R Y]_R$). With these changes the supporting results and the proof of the following generalisation of part 2 of corollary 11 then go through.

For each $I \in E$ let $I \subseteq R$, then $\bigvee_{I \in E} \vDash_I = \vDash_{\cap[E]_R}$.

The superagent's reasoning then corresponds to

$$\bigvee_{q \in Q} \vDash_{\mathsf{mod}_R X_q} = \vDash_{\bigcap_{q \in Q} \mathsf{mod}_R(X_q)}.$$

The meet and join over any family of restricted entailments always exists, however this does not always guard against vacuity in agent reasoning. The smallest subagent's reasoning corresponds to the zero entailment: $\vDash_{\mathsf{STRUC}} = \vDash$, but the largest superagent's reasoning corresponds to the unit entailment: $\vDash_\emptyset$. A proper treatment of the combination of agents' belief sets satisfying the criteria of maintenance of consistency and minimal change of belief sets is given by the theory of belief revision, and is beyond the scope of this paper (see [9]). More work needs to be done in this direction on the pragmatics of agent belief set combination.

The next section shows that the restricted entailments approximate ordinary entailment in the sense of domain theory.

3   Restricted Entailments as a Domain

Here we show that an arbitrary restricted entailment of ENT can be approximated by *compact* ones. These are of the form $\vDash_I$ where $I \subseteq \mathsf{STRUC}$ has only a *finite* number of structures which are not elementarily equivalent to each other. That is, I has finitely many equivalence classes under the relation of elementary equivalence. As a byproduct of this approach it will be shown how ordinary entailment, $\vDash$, can be approximated in this way.

It turns out that ENT is a domain in which each element is approximated by the compact elements which are set theoretically *greater than* it. So when regarding ENT as a domain the domain partial order will be taken to be $\supseteq$. The partially ordered set $(\mathsf{ENT}, \subseteq)$ has an infinitary meet operation which is taken to be the domain least upper bound operator with respect to the partial order $\supseteq$. The least element for the domain is taken to be $\vDash_\emptyset$. The definitions for a domain and its constituents come from [10].

Definition 12 (Complete Partial Order) *Let* $D = (D, \sqsubseteq, \perp)$ *be a partially ordered set with least element* $\perp$.

1. **(Directed Set)** *Let* $A \subseteq D$, *then* A *is* directed *if whenever* w *and* x *are members of* A *there is* $y \in A$ *satisfying* $w \sqsubseteq y$ *and* $x \sqsubseteq y$.
2. **(Complete Partial Order)** D *is called a* complete partial order (CPO) *if whenever* $A \subseteq D$ *and* A *is directed then the least upper bound of* A, *denoted* $\bigsqcup A$, *exists in* D.

Proposition 9 and corollary 11 justify the use of $\bigwedge$ as $\bigsqcup$ in the definition below.

Definition 13 *The set* $\mathsf{ENT} = \{\vDash_I : I \subseteq \mathsf{STRUC}\}$ *can be regarded as a CPO* $\mathsf{ENT} = (\mathsf{ENT}, \sqsubseteq, \perp)$ *by taking*

1. $\sqsubseteq$ *to be* $\supseteq$,
2. $\perp$ *to be* $\vDash_\emptyset$,
3. $\bigsqcup$ *to be* $\bigwedge$.

The compact elements in a CPO play a major role in approximation of members of the CPO so compactness is defined next.

Definition 14 (Compact element) *Let D be a CPO.*

1. *An element $d \in D$ is compact if and only if the following condition is satisfied:*
    For all $A \subseteq D$ if A is directed and $d \sqsubseteq \bigsqcup A$, then there is $x \in A$ with $d \sqsubseteq x$.
2. *The set of compact members of D is denoted* $\mathsf{comp}(D)$.

In order to characterise the compact elements in proposition 20 some results (lemma 15 to proposition 19) are needed on the cardinality of the set of equivalence classes of expansions, and related matters. Let I be a subset of STRUC, the family of equivalence classes of I under elementary equivalence is denoted $I/_{\equiv}$. If $\mathcal{S} \in I$ the equivalence class of $\mathcal{S}$ in $I/_{\equiv}$ is denoted $\|\mathcal{S}\|_I$.

Lemma 15 *Suppose $I \subseteq [H] \subseteq$ STRUC.*

1. *There is a one-to-one function $f : I/_{\equiv} \to [H]/_{\equiv}$.*
2. *If $I = H$, then f is onto.*

Proof. Straightforward. ∎

For any set X let $\mathsf{card}(X)$ denote the cardinality of X.

Proposition 16 *Let $H \subseteq$ STRUC.*

1. *Both $[H]/_{\equiv}$ and $H/_{\equiv}$ are sets satisfying*
    (a) $\mathsf{card}([H]/_{\equiv}) = \mathsf{card}(H/_{\equiv})$.
    (b) $\mathsf{card}(H/_{\equiv}) \le \mathsf{card}(H)$.
2. *If $I \subseteq [H]$, then $\mathsf{card}(I/_{\equiv}) \le \mathsf{card}(H)$.*

Proof. Straightforward, uses lemma 15. ∎

Definition 17 (Reduction) *Let $I \subseteq$ STRUC.*

1. *$J \subseteq$ STRUC is a reduction of I, denoted $J \preceq I$, if and only if*
    (a) $J \subseteq I$.
    (b) For each element $x \in I/_{\equiv}$, there is an element $\mathcal{S} \in J$ satisfying $\mathcal{S} \in x$.
    (c) No two elements of J are elementarily equivalent.
2. *I is said to be reduced if and only if $I \preceq I$.*

The proof of the following is straightforward.

Proposition 18 *Let J and I be subsets of STRUC.*

1. *If I is reduced, then $J \preceq I$ iff $J = I$.*
2. *I has a reduction.*

Proposition 19 *Suppose $J \preceq I$, then the following are true.*

1. *J is reduced.*
2. *$[J] = [I]$.*
3. *If $I/_\equiv$ is finite, then so is J.*

Proof. Straightforward. Part 2 uses monotony of expansion (see 7). Part 3 uses 15 and 16. ∎

The next result characterises compact restricted entailments.

Proposition 20 *The restricted entailment $\vDash_I$ is compact if and only if $I/_\equiv$ is finite.*

Proof. Suppose $\vDash_I$ is compact. Let $E = \{F : F \subseteq I \ \& \ F \text{ is finite}\}$ and consider $T = \{\vDash_F : F \in E\}$. T is directed and $\bigwedge T = \vDash_{\cup E} \subseteq \vDash_I$ because $I \subseteq \bigcup E$. Since $\vDash_I$ is compact there is $\vDash_H \in T$ with $\vDash_H \subseteq \vDash_I$. By definition of T, H is finite. By propositions 4 and 8 $I \subseteq [H]$ and so $I/_\equiv$ is finite by 16. This proves one half of the proposition.

To prove the other half suppose $I/_\equiv$ is finite. We must show that $\vDash_I$ is compact. Let $T = \{\vDash_R : R \in E\}$ be directed where $E \subseteq$ PSTRUC is arbitrary. Suppose $\bigwedge T \subseteq \vDash_I$. We must show there is a member of T that is a subset of $\vDash_I$. Now $\vDash_{[\cup E]} = \vDash_{\cup E} = \bigwedge T \subseteq \vDash_I$ so $I \subseteq [\bigcup E]$ by 4.

Let $J \preceq I$, then by proposition 19 J is finite. Also $J \subseteq I$ so $J \subseteq [\bigcup E]$. It follows that for each $S \in J$ there is a member of E, denote it R_S, such that $S \in [R_S]$. But J is finite and T is directed so there is $\vDash_G \in T$ with $\vDash_G \subseteq \vDash_{R_S}$ for each $S \in J$. Because $\vDash_{[G]} = \vDash_G$ we have $R_S \subseteq [G]$ by 4 and idempotence, and by monotony of expansion and idempotence $[R_S] \subseteq [G]$. So we have $J \subseteq \bigcup \{[R_S] : S \in J\} \subseteq [G]$ and it follows that $\vDash_G = \vDash_{[G]} \subseteq \vDash_J = \vDash_{[J]}$. Since $\vDash_{[J]} = \vDash_{[I]}$ by 19, we have that $\vDash_G \subseteq \vDash_{[I]} = \vDash_I$. ∎

A CPO $(D, \sqsubseteq, \bot)$ is *algebraic* if any element of D is equal to the the least upper bound of the compact elements below it.

Definition 21 (Algebraic CPO) *Let $D = (D, \sqsubseteq, \bot)$ be a CPO. For $x \in D$, denote $\{c \in \mathsf{comp}(D) : c \sqsubseteq x\}$ by $\mathsf{approx}(x)$. D is algebraic if and only if the following condition holds.*

If $x \in D$, then $\mathsf{approx}(x)$ is directed and $x = \bigsqcup \mathsf{approx}(x)$.

The next lemma is used to show that ENT is algebraic.

Lemma 22 *Let I and J be subsets of STRUC. If both $I/_\equiv$ and $J/_\equiv$ are finite, then so is $(I \cup J)/_\equiv$.*

Proof. Straightforward. ∎

Proposition 23 *The CPO ENT $= (\mathsf{ENT}, \sqsubseteq, \bot)$ is algebraic.*

Proof. From definition 13 $\sqsubseteq$ is $\supseteq$ so the set $\mathsf{approx}(\vDash_R) = \{\vDash_I : \vDash_R \subseteq \vDash_I$ & $I/_\equiv$ is finite$\}$. It is directed because if $\vDash_I$ and $\vDash_J$ are elements of $\mathsf{approx}(\vDash_R)$, then $\vDash_R \subseteq \vDash_I \wedge \vDash_J = \vDash_{I \cup J}$, which is an element of $\mathsf{approx}(\vDash_R)$ since by lemma 22 $(I \cup J)/_\equiv$ is finite if both $I/_\equiv$ and $J/_\equiv$ are.

Finally we must show that $\bigwedge \mathsf{approx}(\vDash_R) = \vDash_R$. Any finite set $F \subseteq \mathsf{STRUC}$ has finite $F/_\equiv$. Now consider $E = \{F : F \subseteq R$ & F is finite$\}$. For each $F \in E$, $\vDash_F \in \mathsf{approx}(\vDash_R)$ and $\bigcup E = R$. So $\vDash_R \subseteq \bigwedge \mathsf{approx}(\vDash_R) \subseteq \bigwedge \{\vDash_F : F \in E$ & F is finite$\} = \vDash_{\bigcup E} = \vDash_R$. ∎

A *domain* is an algebraic CPO satisfying a certain consistency condition.

Definition 24 (Consistent Set) *Let $D = (D, \sqsubseteq)$ be partially ordered and let $A \subseteq D$, then A is* consistent *if and only if A has an upper bound in D.*

Definition 25 (Domain) *Let $D = (D, \sqsubseteq, \bot)$ be a CPO, then D is a* domain *if and only if the following two conditions are satisfied.*

1. *D is an algebraic CPO.*
2. *If d and e are compact members of D and $\{d, e\}$ is consistent, then $d \vee e$ exists and lies in D.*

We have seen in proposition 23 that $\mathsf{ENT} = (\mathsf{ENT}, \sqsubseteq, \bot)$ is algebraic. By 9 any pair of elements of ENT has a least upper bound given by meet. The following proposition summarises the situation.

Proposition 26 *The CPO $\mathsf{ENT} = (\mathsf{ENT}, \sqsubseteq, \bot)$ defined in 13 is a domain in which*

1. *Ordinary entailment $\vDash = \vDash_{\mathsf{STRUC}} \in \mathsf{ENT}$.*
2. *The compact members of ENT are the restricted entailments $\vDash_I$, where $I/_\equiv$ is finite.*
3. *For $\vDash_R \in \mathsf{ENT}$, $\mathsf{approx}(\vDash_R) = \{\vDash_I : \vDash_R \subseteq \vDash_I$ & $I/_\equiv$ is finite$\}$.*

In fact, the last sentence in the proof of proposition 23 shows that any restricted entailment is the meet of a subset of the compact ones greater than it, namely the ones with *finite restrictions*.

In the next section we show how restricted entailment can be modelled in a modal language, and discuss its semantics and proof theory.

4   The Modality "Approximately True"

In this section we sketch the properties of a first-order language augmented with a single modal operator, "approximately true" with parameter R, which is denoted $\downarrow_R$. The parameter R is a finite set of structures. With R finite, $\downarrow_R$ is taken to embody a finite agent. As was mentioned earlier this is justified by the "correspondence" result for first-order sentences: proposition 30. Also the modal language has a proof theory and a semantics which are sound and complete with respect to each other. So by using the correspondence result to translate a restricted entailment into the modal language, one can use the proof theoretic and semantic facilities of a language which is sound and complete. At the end of this section we touch on the knowledge modality *knows that* treated by Fagin and others in [11] and show how we can define the modality *restricted knowledge*. How this applies to *algorithmic knowledge*, mentioned in [11], requires further work.

The semantics and proof theory of $\downarrow_R$ are summarised as well as their soundness and completeness. The discussion is brief and no proofs are given. Full detail can be found in [7, chapters 7 to 10]. In the final section some comments are made about the logic of interaction of several different agents when they are modelled by "approximately true" with different parameters.

Modal formulas are defined in the following way so as to allow the proof of completeness to go through smoothly. The definition is in two stages.

Definition 27 (Modal Formula)

1. Let $R \subseteq \mathsf{STRUC}$. *The* approximation sentences *are defined inductively as follows.*
   (a) *Any first-order sentence is an approximation sentence.*
   (b) *If φ and ψ are approximation sentences, then so are $\downarrow_R \varphi$, $\neg \varphi$ and $\varphi \circ \psi$, where $\circ$ is a boolean connective. Note that sometimes the subscript, R, in $\downarrow_R$ will be dropped if there is no danger of confusion.*
2. *The* modal formulas *are defined inductively as follows.*
   (a) *Any approximation sentence is a modal formula, and any atomic first-order formula is a modal formula.*
   (b) *If φ and ψ are modal formulas then so are $\neg \varphi$ and $\varphi \circ \psi$, where $\circ$ is a boolean connective, as well as $(\forall x)\varphi$ and $(\exists x)\varphi$.*

Modal Semantics

The modal counterpart of *satisfaction* is *forcing*, denoted $\Vdash$. Modal *models* force modal formulas. The semantics is unusual in that it uses a single possible world. Models will now be defined.

Definition 28 (Modal Model) *A* model *is a four-tuple $\mathcal{M} = (\mathcal{G}, \mathcal{R}, \mathcal{D}, \mathcal{S})$ where:*

1. $\mathcal{G}$ *is a set with one element, G, called a* world.
2. $\mathcal{R}$ *is a binary relation defined on $\mathcal{G}$ called the* accessibility relation. *There are only two possibilities for $\mathcal{R}$ in our system: it is either empty or it equals (G, G).*
3. $\mathcal{D}$ *is a set called the* domain *of the model.*
4. $\mathcal{S}$ *is a first-order structure with domain $\mathsf{dom}(\mathcal{S}) = \mathcal{D}$.*

The following is an abbreviated definition of modal forcing.

Definition 29 (Forcing) *Let* $\mathcal{M} = (\mathcal{G}, \mathcal{R}, \mathcal{D}, \mathcal{S})$ *be a model and* $\mathcal{I} = (\mathcal{S}, u)$ *be a first-order interpretation, where u is an assignment of variables. The forcing relation,* $\Vdash$*, is defined recursively as follows. Let φ and ψ be modal formulas.*

1. *If φ is an atomic formula, then $\mathcal{M} \Vdash_u \varphi$ iff $\mathcal{I} \vDash \varphi$.*
2. *Rules for forcing of $\neg\varphi$, $\varphi \circ \psi$ (where $\circ$ is a boolean connective) and quantified formulas are analogous to first-order satisfaction rules.*
3. *$\mathcal{M} \Vdash \downarrow_R \varphi$ if and only if the following holds: if $G\mathcal{R}G$ and $\mathcal{S} \in R$ then $\mathcal{M} \Vdash \varphi$.*

If X is a set of modal sentences, then we write $\mathcal{M} \Vdash X$ if and only if $\mathcal{M} \Vdash \varphi$ for each $\varphi \in X$. Also, $\downarrow X = \{\downarrow\varphi : \varphi \in X\}$. Modal entailment is defined as follows: $X \Vdash \varphi$ if and only if for every model $\mathcal{M}$, $\mathcal{M} \Vdash X$ implies $\mathcal{M} \Vdash \varphi$.

The following "correspondence" result connects restricted entailment and forcing of "approximately true". It provides the theoretical basis for regarding forcing of "approximately true" as encapsulating the reasoning of a finite agent, and hence for regarding "approximately true" as the embodiment of a finite agent.

Proposition 30 *Let φ be a first-order sentence and X a set of first-order sentences, then $X \vDash_R \varphi$ iff $\downarrow_R X \Vdash \downarrow_R \varphi$.*

Proof Theory, Soundness and Completeness

Our proof theory is based on tableaux and we use Fitting and Mendelsohn's approach [12]. Tableau rules for first-order logic are augmented to include ones for sentences issuing from "approximately true", $\downarrow$. Our method uses signed sentences. A signed sentence is one which begins with either the character T or F. A tableau is a tree having sentences as nodes, with one root node and branches which end in leaf nodes.

Generic tableau branch extension rules are given in figure 1 and then the working of a tableau proof is outlined. The rules show what can be appended to a leaf of a branch if a certain sentence (referred to as the parent) lies on the branch.

Some explanatory comments follow for the rules involving $\downarrow$; its parameter, R, has been omitted.

First, an infinitely long *separator sentence*, σ, can be set up with the property that every member of R satisfies σ and every structure not elementarily equivalent to a member of R does not satisfy σ (see [7, page 14]). The sentence σ is used as a kind of "token" in tableau rules and it is also used in the proof of completeness. The form of σ is as follows. Let R be finite and let A consist of every structure not elementarily equivalent to a member of R, and write σ as $\sigma_{A,R}$ thus making its dependence on A and R explicit. Suppose that the first-order sentences have been enumerated and the enumeration is kept fixed. Given $(\mathcal{S}, \mathcal{S}') \in A \times R$, let $\sigma_{\mathcal{S}, \mathcal{S}'}$ be the first sententence in the enumeration which satisfies $\mathcal{S} \nvDash \sigma_{\mathcal{S}, \mathcal{S}'}$ and $\mathcal{S}' \vDash \sigma_{\mathcal{S}, \mathcal{S}'}$. Set $\sigma = \sigma_{A,R} = \bigvee_{\mathcal{S}' \in R}(\bigwedge_{\mathcal{S} \in A} \sigma_{\mathcal{S}, \mathcal{S}'})$. Because the set of sentences is countable, without loss of generality, σ can be seen to be of the form $\bigvee_{i=1}^{m} C_i$, where m is an integer and $C_i = \bigwedge_{n \in N_i} \sigma_{n,i}$ for

N_i some subset (possibly all) of the integers. Each of the $\sigma_{n,i}$ is a first-order sentence corresponding to some $\sigma_{S,S'}$. Next, the comments for the rules involving $\downarrow$ follow.

1. The parent is $\mathsf{T} \downarrow \varphi$; the node $\mathsf{T}\varphi$ is appended to the leaf if $\mathsf{T}\sigma$ already appears on the branch, otherwise nothing is appended.
2. The parent is $\mathsf{F} \downarrow \varphi$; then two nodes are appended in sequence: $\mathsf{F}\varphi$ and $\mathsf{T}\sigma$.
3. The parent is $\mathsf{T}\sigma$; then m nodes are appended in parallel: $\mathsf{T}C_1, \ldots, \mathsf{T}C_m$.
4. The parent is $\mathsf{T}C_i$; then nodes $\mathsf{T}\sigma_{n,i}$ are appended in sequence, for each $n \in N_i$. We recall that each of the $\sigma_{n,i}$ is a first order sentence.

$$
\begin{array}{cc}
\mathsf{T}\varphi & \mathsf{F}\varphi \qquad \dfrac{\mathsf{T}\neg\varphi}{\mathsf{F}\varphi} \quad \dfrac{\mathsf{F}\neg\varphi}{\mathsf{T}\varphi} \\
\text{any atomic } \varphi & \text{any atomic } \varphi
\end{array}
$$

$$
\dfrac{\mathsf{T}\varphi \vee \psi}{\mathsf{T}\varphi \mid \mathsf{T}\psi} \quad \dfrac{\mathsf{F}\varphi \vee \psi}{\begin{array}{c}\mathsf{F}\varphi \\ \mathsf{F}\psi\end{array}} \quad \dfrac{\mathsf{T}\varphi \wedge \psi}{\begin{array}{c}\mathsf{T}\varphi \\ \mathsf{T}\psi\end{array}} \quad \dfrac{\mathsf{F}\varphi \wedge \psi}{\mathsf{F}\varphi \mid \mathsf{F}\psi}
$$

$$
\dfrac{\mathsf{T}\varphi \rightarrow \psi}{\mathsf{F}\varphi \mid \mathsf{T}\psi} \quad \dfrac{\mathsf{F}\varphi \rightarrow \psi}{\begin{array}{c}\mathsf{T}\varphi \\ \mathsf{F}\psi\end{array}}
$$

$$
\dfrac{\mathsf{T}\exists x \varphi(x)}{\mathsf{T}\varphi(c)} \qquad \dfrac{\mathsf{F}\exists x \varphi(x)}{\mathsf{F}\varphi(t)} \qquad \dfrac{\mathsf{T}\forall x \varphi(x)}{\mathsf{T}\varphi(t)} \qquad \dfrac{\mathsf{F}\forall x \varphi(x)}{\mathsf{F}\varphi(c)}
$$
$$
\text{some new } c \quad \text{any closed term } t \quad \text{any closed term } t \quad \text{some new } c
$$

$$
\dfrac{\mathsf{T} \downarrow \varphi}{\mathsf{T}\varphi} \qquad \dfrac{\mathsf{F} \downarrow \varphi}{\begin{array}{c}\mathsf{F}\varphi \\ \mathsf{T}\sigma\end{array}}
$$
$$
\text{If } \mathsf{T}\sigma \text{ is on branch}
$$

$$
\dfrac{\mathsf{T}\sigma}{\mathsf{T}C_1 \mid \cdots \mid \mathsf{T}C_m} \qquad \dfrac{\mathsf{T}C_i}{\begin{array}{c}\mathsf{T}\sigma_{1,i} \\ \vdots \\ \mathsf{T}\sigma_{n,i} \\ \vdots\end{array}}
$$

Fig. 1. Tableaux Branch Extension Rules

A tableau proof for the sentence ψ consists of using tableau rules to build a tree with root node $\mathsf{F}\psi$ and then checking that every branch of the tree has a contradiction, that is, a pair of expressions in sequence which are identical except that one begins with the character T and the other with F. If a branch has a contradiction it is said to be closed; if every branch has a contradiction then the tableau is said to be closed. A closed tableau is taken to be a proof.

Taken together, the tableau proof method and modal semantics can be shown to be sound and complete (see [7]). Soundness means that if a modal sentence is provable then it is valid, that is, forced by every model. Completeness is the converse of soundness: if a sentence is forced by every model then it is provable. It is not hard to extend the argument to show that a sentence ψ can be proved from premises X (a set of sentences) if and only if X forces ψ. Denoting the provability relation by $\vdash$, this means that $X \vdash \psi$ if and only if $X \Vdash \psi$. In particular, this holds for the "correspondence" of proposition 30: $\downarrow_R X \Vdash \downarrow_R \varphi$ iff $\downarrow_R X \vdash \downarrow_R \varphi$. So if we have a restricted entailment $X \vDash_R \varphi$, we can be sure $\downarrow_R \varphi$ is modally provable from $\downarrow_R X$.

We will now touch briefly on the modality *knows that* treated by Fagin and others in [11]. Their system uses a set of worlds. An agent, K, *knows that* φ is symbolised by the modal sentence $K\varphi$, with modal operator K. For a world G and model $\mathcal{M}$ and an accesibility relation $\mathcal{K}$ for K, $\mathcal{M}, G \Vdash K\varphi$ if and only if for all worlds G' such that $G\mathcal{K}G'$ we have that $\mathcal{M}, G' \Vdash \varphi$. Now letting $R \subseteq \mathsf{STRUC}$ be a restriction parameter, we define "restricted knowledge", K_R, semantically as follows: $\mathcal{M}, G \Vdash K_R\varphi$ if and only if for all worlds G' such that $G\mathcal{K}G'$ we have that $\mathcal{M}, G' \Vdash \downarrow_R \varphi$, that is, if and only if $\mathcal{M}, G \Vdash K \downarrow_R \varphi$. When the set of worlds is just the singleton $\{G\}$, this definition reduces to $\mathcal{M}, G \Vdash K_R\varphi$ if and only if $\mathcal{M}, G \Vdash \downarrow_R \varphi$. More work needs to be done to expand the system to incorporate multiple "approximately true" operators and multiple agents and to see whether this approach can be made to work in practical systems.

Some concluding remarks and directions for future work follow.

5   Discussion and Future Work

In the previous sections we have described a basis for a reasoning mechanism, restricted entailment, which can be made finitary in character by a suitable choice of parameter. We have shown that it approximates ordinary entailment in the sense of domain theory and that it can be modelled in a modal language with a semantics and proof theory that are sound and complete. We have proposed that a restricted entailment be taken to encapsulate the deductive process of an agent. This is important because it is an approach that takes seriously the finite limitations of a reasoning agent.

We need to bear in mind that even humans cannot store infinite objects in their heads, or brains. To be able to do so would require an addressing system in the brain capable of making infinitely many links to the infinitely many tokens representing the elements of the infinite object. But there are only finitely many particles in the brain to provide the raw materials. (This, however, does not rule out the possibility of a human carrying in their brain a name for an infinite object and being able to reason about that object.) In any case even if one quibbles with this argument about humans, it is still true that an artificial reasoning agent cannot carry an infinite object, such as an infinite list, in its memory. So it seems worthwhile to make a start, as we have done, in analysing what can be accomplished in a finitary way.

This brings us to another point. If we take the logical essence of rationality to be encompassed by (ordinary) entailment, it is still not clear which of its properties would be generally accepted as being definitive of rationality. When considering restricted entailment as a candidate for finitary rational agency we suggest that perhaps the selection of defining properties can be deferred because restricted entailment already enjoys several important properties of entailment such as reflexivity, cut and monotony, and it can be modelled modally by a sound and complete system.

We now touch on the topics of computability and a calculus for multi-agent rationality. In [7, chapter 14] it is shown that a restricted entailment, $\vDash_R$, is decidable provided that R is finite; the structures in R have have finite domains and are computable; assignments of variables are computable; the interpretations of function and relation symbols under structures are computable and only finite sets of sentences are considered.

When considering a restricted entailment involving the belief set of an agent (see the end of section 2), a further assumption will provide a sufficient condition for computability. The agent's belief set should have a *finite base*, that is the belief set should be of the form $\mathsf{Cn}F$ where F is a finite set of sentences. When F and R are finite, it can be shown that $\mathsf{mod}_R F$ is computable; but $\mathsf{mod}_R F = \mathsf{mod}_R(\mathsf{Cn}F)$ which is then also computable. This means that the deductive process is decidable for those agents meeting these requirements. Also, because a finite union or intersection of finite sets is finite and each agent's $\mathsf{mod}_R(\mathsf{Cn}F)$ is computable and finite, the integration of finitely many agents into a canonical subagent or superagent produces one with a reasoning process that is decidable (under the provisos mentioned above).

The semantics for $\downarrow_R$ presented in definition 29 can be easily extended to deal with several operators with different parameters co-existing in the same modal language. The first steps in a calculus can even be taken. Semantic arguments can be used to show:

1. $\mathcal{M} \Vdash \downarrow_{I \cup J} \varphi$ iff $\mathcal{M} \Vdash (\downarrow_I \varphi \vee \downarrow_J \varphi)$.
2. $\mathcal{M} \Vdash \downarrow_{I \cap J} \varphi$ iff $\mathcal{M} \Vdash (\downarrow_I \varphi \wedge \downarrow_J \varphi)$.

Also it would not be difficult to include other modal operators such as "box" and "diamond" in the language. Further work needs to be done to examine the properties of this language.

Our formalisation of agents here is semantically based. Wooldridge in [13, page 296] comments on the advantages and difficulties of semantic approaches to agent system verification. Further steps in the use of the approach proposed here would be to integrate it into an agent architecture and to see how the specification and verification of agent systems could be handled in the resulting system.

Acknowledgements

I would like to thank the reviewers of this paper for their helpful comments.

References

1. Ebbinghaus, H.D., Flum, J., Thomas, W.: Mathematical Logic. Springer (1984)
2. Cherniak, C.: Minimal Rationality. MIT Press (1986)
3. Johnson-Laird, P.N.: Mental Models. Cambridge University Press (1983)
4. Johnson-Laird, P.N., Byrne, R.M.J.: Deduction. Lawrence Erlbaum Associates, Hove (1991)
5. Cameron, P.J.: Sets, Logic and Categories. Springer (1999)
6. Kelley, J.L.: General Topology. D. Van Nostrand Company (1955)
7. Flax, C.L.: Algebraic Aspects of Entailment: Approximation, Belief Revision and Computability. PhD thesis, Macquarie University, Sydney, NSW 2109, Australia (2002) Available from http://www.comp.mq.edu.au/~flax/.
8. Moschovakis, Y.N.: Notes on Set Theory. Springer (1994)
9. Gärdenfors, P.: Knowledge in Flux. MIT Press (1988)
10. Stoltenberg-Hansen, V., Linström, I., Griffor, E.R.: Mathematical Theory of Domains. Number 22 in Cambridge Tracts in Theoretical Computer Science. Cambridge University Press (1994)
11. Fagin, R., Halpern, J.Y., Moses, Y., Vardi, M.Y.: Reasoning About Knowledge. MIT (1995)
12. Fitting, M., Mendelsohn, R.L.: First-order Modal Logic. Kluwer Academic Publishers (1998)
13. Wooldridge, M.: An Introduction to Multiagent Systems. John Wiley (2002)

A Social Approach to Communication in Multiagent Systems*

Marco Colombetti[1,2], Nicoletta Fornara[1], and Mario Verdicchio[2]

[1] Università della Svizzera italiana, via Buffi 13, 6900 Lugano, Switzerland
{nicoletta.fornara,marco.colombetti}@lu.unisi.ch
[2] Politecnico di Milano Piazza Leonardo Da Vinci 32, 20133 Milano, Italy
{mario.verdicchio,marco.colombetti}@elet.polimi.it

Abstract. This paper aims at defining the semantics of Agent Communication Languages (ACLs) in terms of changes in the social relationships between agents, represented in terms of *social commitments*. We take commitment to be a primitive concept underlying the social dimension of multiagent systems, and define a basic artificial institution that provides agents with the means to affect the commitment network that binds them to each other. Two different approaches are adopted for the presentation of our proposal: a logical formalization and an operational specification.

1 Introduction

Since the beginning of the 1990s, the community of Multiagent Systems (MAS) researchers has carried out significant efforts to design a standard, application-independent language for agent communication. As is well known, different approaches to agent communication have been advocated. While all competing proposals share the view that an Agent Communication Language (ACL) should be based on the concept of a *communicative act*, at least four different views of ACL semantics have been put forward and defended. Such views can be briefly described as follows:

- the *mentalistic* view: the semantics of a communicative act is defined in terms of its effects on the mental states of the communicating agents [1], [2], [3];
- the *social* view: the semantics of a communicative act is defined in terms of its effects on the social states binding the communicating agents [4], [5], [6];
- the *protocol-based* view: the semantics of a communicative act is defined in terms of the conversational protocols in which it occurs [7];
- the *conventional* view: the semantics of a communicative act is defined in terms of a set of conventions, which operate under a principle of informational optimality [8];

---

* Partially supported by Swiss National Science Foundation project 200021-100260, "An Open Interaction Framework for Communicative Agents"

J. Leite et al. (Eds.): DALT 2003, LNAI 2990, pp. 191–220, 2004.

Elsewhere we have advocated a social approach to agent communication, and proposed both a logical [9] and an operational model [10] [11] of ACL semantics. In this paper we try to bring the two models together. We start from the assumption that communication is, above all, an *institutional activity*, that is, a kind of social activity regulated by a collection of institutions. By an *institution* we mean a set of concepts and rules shared and jointly accepted by a group of agents. As we shall see, institutions provide a fundamental component of the context in which communication is carried out. If we regard communicative acts as institutional actions [12] (i.e., actions that are made possible by the existence of a number of institutions), an ACL is just a set of conventions to carry out institutional actions. The treatment of language as a conventional means to perform institutional actions is of course inspired by Speech Act Theory, in particular as presented by Searle [13]. However, in view of our specific goal we do not try to base our treatment on a model of human institutions; rather, we take them as a source of inspiration to define a concept of institution that suits artificial agents.

As we said before, this paper presents a model of agent communication first in logical and then in operational terms. This choice deserves some justification. There are indeed different reasons to define a model of agent communication. A first reason is to specify the semantics of an ACL so that the act of sending a message of a given form has unambiguous preconditions and effects. A further reason is to establish a basis for proving properties of ACL-related constructions, like for example conversation protocols. Yet another reason is to provide a clear guidance to the implementation of multiagent platforms allowing agents to interact through a standard ACL. Declarative models, like the one built on logic, are best suited to give a rigorous definition of ACL semantics, and can also be very useful to prove properties of conversation protocols, for example by model-checking techniques. On the other hand, declarative models do not provide useful guidance to implementation: to this purpose, an operational specification is more suitable.

In principle, the most natural approach to this kind of multiple modeling would be to develop a logical model first, and then to use it as the basis of an operational specification. However, this is not how our research activity has developed in the last few years. In fact, for practical reasons we have developed both models in parallel; as a result the two models, as they have been presented so far in the literature ([10], [11], [9]) are not completely consistent. In this paper we try to adapt our models to achieve higher consistency; however, it should be noted that a logical model and an operational specification are not just two different views of the same thing. To clarify this point, let us consider as an example a logical and an operational specification of arithmetic. Natural numbers are logically modeled by Peano axioms; however, such axioms say nothing on the computer representation of a natural number, on how to perform arithmetical operations in a digital device, and so on. Digital number crunching is often just an approximation to Peano arithmetic, for example when it implements modular arithmetic on a finite set of numbers, due to memory limitations. Analogously, the logical model and the operational specification presented in this paper are meant to highlight aspects of agent communication that are at least in part different.

To be more specific, let us now see where the two models we propose in this paper depart from each other. In the logical model we define the preconditions and effects of communicative acts in terms of *truth conditions*; in other words, we specify the state of affairs that holds in a specific kind of model structure before and after a communicative act is successfully performed. In principle, such a declarative specification could be directly implemented in an artificial agent, provided the agent has full theorem proving capacities with respect to a first order temporal logic with branching time: an assumption that would bring us very far from the current agent technology. On the contrary, when we define our operational specification we consider a set of data structures and operations that actual agents may easily implement, without relying on theorem proving techniques. In other words, while a logical model is fit for reasoning on agent systems, an operational specification provides guidance on how to realize actual agents; nevertheless, the relationship between the logical model and its operational specification is still very tight, the latter being a realistic approximation to the former. It must be noted that a different approach may be followed. Indeed, as suggested by [14], a declarative representation may be effectively used by actual agents: this approach may provide a viable alternative to operational specifications, and allow for a more direct use of at least part of a logical model. However, to understand which of the two approaches is more productive requires further research.

The rest of this paper is structured as follows. In Section 2 we introduce the fundamental concepts underlying our treatment of agent communication. In Section 3 we present our logical model of agent communication. We then show in Section 4 how the model can be specified operationally. Finally, in Section 5 we draw some conclusions.

2   The Conceptual Framework

Communicative acts are events that conventionally take place when messages are exchanged in a given context. As all events, communicative acts have effects, some of which correspond to the perlocutionary effects of Speech Act Theory [13]; for example, by informing agent b that an auction is going to close in ten minutes, agent a may significantly affect the behavior of agent b. Perlocutionary effects are often the *reason* for performing a communicative act, but they do not *define* communicative acts; analogously, one may close a door to keep a room warm, but keeping a room warm does not define an action of closing a door.

Being conventional, communicative acts can only be defined in terms of institutional effects; more specifically, we regard communicative acts as institutional actions performed by way of exchanging messages. This fact is obvious for acts of declaration, like for example declaring war or declaring a meeting open: in such cases the effects (war is declared, a meeting is open) are clearly institutional. Commissives, like for example promises, are another example of communicative acts whose effects are easily regarded as institutional: intuitively, a commissive act brings about some kind of obligation, and obligations are part of institutional reality. Less clear is how we may regard as institutional the effects of assertives, like acts of informing, or directives, like requests. This point will be developed in due course.

Regarding communicative acts as institutional presupposes a clear definition of the concept of an *institution*. By this term we mean a set of shared concepts and rules that regulate the management of a fragment of social reality [15],[16]. Suppose for example that agent a sends an order to agent b. For the order to be felicitous, it is necessary that the two agents are part of a hierarchical organization, empowering a to issue an order to b; no such organization is presupposed, on the contrary, by an act of informing or requesting. In human society, an institution can be based on spontaneous agreement (like, for example, in the case of a promise binding two individuals) or on an explicit body of regulations (like, for example, in the case of marriage in modern societies). In the case of multiagent systems, we can assume that all institutions will have to be explicitly and formally represented. The general picture we have in mind is the following. To play a part in multiagent systems, an agent must be officially recognized as a member of the "society of agents". To achieve this, the agent will first have to undergo a suitable registration procedure; if the procedure is carried out successfully, the agent will be allowed to interact with other registered agents according to the *Basic Institution*, that is, the institution setting the general concepts and rules of agent interaction.

As we shall see in the rest of the paper, the Basic Institution provides enough rules to perform a set of fundamental communicative acts, like informing, requesting, promising, and so on. Many kinds of interaction, however, require a richer social structure; as we have already remarked, for example, orders presuppose a hierarchical organization, which is not part of the Basic Institution. To deal with such cases we assume that further institutions, which we call *special institutions*, can be invoked; to make an example, electronic commerce will only be possible on the ground of special institutions regulating ownership and money.

According to our standpoint, the fundamental function of the Basic Institution is to regulate the management of *social commitments* between agents. By doing so, the Basic Institution provides for the ontological ground that is necessary and sufficient to define all communicative acts, with the possible exception of those relying on special institutions. We view commitments as institutional states that bind two agents (the creditor and the debtor of the commitment) and can be made, accepted, refused or cancelled by agents, provided they have sufficient institutional powers to do so. Moreover, a commitment may be pending, fulfilled or violated according to the fact that its content is undefined, true or false in the world.

Once the ontology of commitment is established, and the relevant institutional powers of agents are defined, it is possible to specify the effects of communicative acts in terms of commitments; in turn, the effects of communicative acts can be used to define the semantics of a library of ACL messages. By itself, however, message semantics is not sufficient to guarantee effective communication. In an electronic auction, for example, agents exchange meaningful messages according to a rigid protocol, which is itself part of the definition of an auction. Coherently with our standpoint, we view an auction as an example of a special institution that, among other things, specifies a set of *norms* to regulate the interactions of the participants. Such norms are typically, even if not necessarily, specified as an interaction protocol.

In the next section we define a logical model of the concepts we have just described in informal terms.

3   The Logical Model

We base our logical model on a first-order temporal language (which we call the *Semantic Language*, SL), that can be regarded as a metalanguage for the definition of an ACL. Coherently with all major proposals in this area, we deal with agent communication in terms of communicative acts, which we define as changes at the level of social commitments between agents. We take *commitment* to be a primitive concept that underlies the social structure of a multiagent system, and describe communicative acts as actions performed by an agent to affect the commitments that bind it to other agents. Agents communicate by message exchanges, which *count as* communicative acts only when some particular conditions hold within the context of an *artificial institution*; in particular, we call *Basic Institution* the institution that sets the general concepts and rules of agent interaction.

We articulate the presentation of our model in a number of sections. More precisely, in Section 3.1 we give a brief description of the formalism we use to describe communicative acts. Sections 3.2 to 3.6 describe the Basic Institution, which enables agents to act as members of a common society. Section 3.7 gives a general view on how all the components of the Basic Institution affect agent communication by representing the performance of communicative acts in a general form. Finally, Section 3.8 illustrates how it is possible to execute any communicative act in the form of a declaration.

3.1   Time and Action

Actions are events brought about by agents. When agent a brings about an event (or performs an action) e of type τ, the SL formula

$Done(e,a,\tau)$

holds. We sometimes use the 'n-dash' character to express existential quantification, as in the examples below:

$Done(e,-,\tau) =_{def} \exists x\, Done(e,x,\tau);$
$Done(e,-,-) =_{def} \exists x\, \exists \tau\, Done(e,x,\tau).$

To deal with events, SL includes a temporal logic with CTL*-like operators [17]. We assume that the logical model relies on a discrete-time frame with a tree-like structure, infinite both in the future and in the past, in which every state has a unique predecessor and at least one successor, and there is at most one walk between any pair of states. A *path* is an infinite sequence $p = \langle p_0, ..., p_n, ...\rangle$ of states, such that for every element p_i in the sequence, element p_{i+1} is one of the successors of p_i in the frame. All formulae on path p are evaluated with respect to p_0, which is the *starting point* of the path. Paths allow us to formalize the concepts of being "in the past" or "in the future" of some state. More precisely, we say that state s' is in the future of s if and only if there is a path p such that $s = p_0$ and, for some n, $s' = p_n$. Symmetrically, we say that s' is in the past of s if and only if there is a path p such that $s' = p_0$ and, for some n, $s = p_n$. We assume that on every path an event can happen only once, as stated by the following axiom:

(UE) $Done(e,\text{-},\text{-}) \rightarrow \mathsf{G}^-\mathsf{X}^-\neg Done(e,\text{-},\text{-}) \wedge \mathsf{AG}^+\mathsf{X}^+\neg Done(e,\text{-},\text{-})$.

Here we use some of the following temporal operators, whose intuitive meanings are illustrated below:

A for all paths;
G^+ always on the current path, at the current state and in the future;
G^- on the current path at the current state and in every state that is in the past of the path's starting point;
X^+ at the next state on the current path;
X^- at the previous state on the current path;
F^+ at the current state on the current path, or sometime in the future;
F^- at the current state on the current path, or in some state in the past of the path's starting point.

A complete account of the temporal logic in which we embed our communication framework can be found in [9].

 Communicative acts are actions that agents bring about to communicate with other agents. We regard them as institutional actions performed by way of exchanging messages. More precisely, we rely on the concept of *commitment* ([4],[5],[6]) to specify the conventional effects of message exchanges. Commitments are part of the social reality defined and regulated by the Basic Institution. Some work in the direction of defining institutions in general has already been carried out in the field of multiagent systems (see for example [18], [19]). For our purposes, we define an institution as comprised of four fundamental components:

- *core ontology*: the ontology of the social concepts defined by the institution;
- *authorizations*: the specification of the institutional effects that each member of the institution is empowered to bring about, typically authorizations are associated with *roles* in order to abstract from specific agents;
- *norms*: the obligations and the permissions imposed by the institution to its members;
- *conventions*: the specification of the relation between concrete events and their institutional effects.

 The Basic Institution regulates the general aspects of communicative interaction, including commitments, as we explain in the sequel.

3.2 Commitment

In our approach, the core ontology of the Basic Institution defines *commitment*, *precommitment*, and a set of operations for *commitment manipulation*.

Commitment and Precommitment. Commitment is a primitive concept underlying the relations between agents. More precisely, a commitment holds in a state in which an agent (the *debtor*) is bound, relative to another agent (the *creditor*), to the fact that some proposition (the *content*) is true. The content of a commitment is a sentence of a *Content Language* (CL), represented as a first-order term of SL. The relevant formula is

$Comm(e,x,y,s)$,

which states that communicative act e has brought about a situation that binds agent x, relative to agent y, to the truth of a proposition of the content language, represented by the SL term s. When a commitment is proposed to an agent (normally, the potential debtor) for acceptance, but it has not been accepted nor refused yet, we say that a *precommitment* holds. Precommitments are represented analogously to commitments:

$Prec(e,x,y,s)$

holds when e has brought about a precommitment between two agents (the potential debtor, x, and the potential creditor, y) to the truth of a CL sentence represented by s. We regard the creation and the modification of (pre)commitments as the effects of communicative events that have to be dealt with to define an effective ACL semantics.

As we already said in Section 2, a commitment may be pending, fulfilled or violated according to the fact that its content, s, is undefined, true or false in the world. Defining the truth conditions for sentences in our model is not trivial, mainly because of the branching structure of time. This issue is explored in more detail in Section 3.3.

Commitment Manipulation. Commitments and precommitments arise from the performance of communicative acts. More precisely, agents bring about communicative events by exchanging messages; a communicative event, under given conditions, counts as a *commitment manipulation action*, which creates a new (pre)commitment or modifies an existing one.

The core ontology of the Basic Institution allows for five basic operations for commitment manipulation. More specifically, agents can: make a commitment (by performing action $mc(x,y,s)$), make a precommitment ($mp(x,y,s)$), cancel a commitment ($cc(e,x,y,s)$), cancel a precommitment ($cp(e,x,y,s)$), or accept a precommitment, that is, turn it into a commitment ($ap(e,x,y,s)$). Such action types are defined by axioms that describe their constitutive effects, that is, the state of affairs that necessarily hold after a token of the given action type is successfully performed.

We now introduce further temporal operators to express our axioms in a simpler form:

φ U$^+\psi$ (φ is true until ψ is eventually true);

φ W$^+\psi =_{def}$ G$^+\varphi \vee \varphi$ U$^+\psi$ (weak until operator);

φ Z$^+\psi =_{def} \varphi$ W$^+\psi \wedge$ G$^+(\psi \rightarrow$G$^+\neg\varphi)$ (φ Z$^+\psi$ is true if and only if in the future ψ never becomes true and φ is always true, or φ is true until ψ eventually becomes true and since then φ is no longer true).

We are now ready to present the axioms that describe the commitment manipulation actions.

(MC) $Done(e,\text{-},mc(x,y,s)) \rightarrow$ A($Comm(e,x,y,s)$Z$^+$ $Done(\text{-},\text{-},cc(e,x,y,s)))$.

Axiom MC (Make Commitment) states that:

> if an agent (not necessarily x or y) performs an action of making a commitment with x as the debtor, y as the creditor, and s as the content,
> then, on all paths, x is committed, relative to y, to the truth of s,
> until an agent possibly cancels such a commitment, after which the commitment no longer exists.

(MP) $Done(e,\text{-},mp(x,y,s)) \rightarrow$
     A($Prec(e,x,y,s)$ Z$^+(Done(\text{-},\text{-},ap(e,x,y,s)) \vee Done(\text{-},\text{-},cp(e,x,y,s)))))$.

Axiom MP (Make Precommitment) is analogous to MC.

(AP) $Done(e',\text{-},ap(e,x,y,s)) \rightarrow$A($Comm(e',x,y,s)Z^+Done(\text{-},\text{-},cc(e',x,y,s)))$.

Axiom AP (Accept Precommitment) implies that if an agent performs an action of accepting a precommitment brought about by event e with x, y, and s respectively as debtor, creditor, and content, then the acceptance action brings about, on all paths, a commitment of x, relative to y, to the truth of s, which will stand until it is possibly cancelled.

There are no specific axioms for the actions of canceling a precommitment (cp) or a commitment (cc), because the analytical effects of these commitment manipulations are already illustrated in the axioms dealing with other actions, whose performance must be presupposed in order to take into account any kind of cancellation. This issue is dealt with in more detail in the next section.

Ontological Preconditions. Some of the commitment manipulation actions rely on *ontological preconditions*, that is, they can be performed only if particular states of affairs hold. For instance, the ontological precondition to a commitment's cancellation is the existence of the commitment itself. The formula

$OntPoss(\tau)$

states that the ontological preconditions of an event of type τ hold; we also say that the event is *ontologically possible*. We assume that making a commitment or a precommitment is always ontologically possible, as specified by the following axioms:

(PMC) $OntPoss(mc(x,y,s))$,
(PMP) $OntPoss(mp(x,y,s))$.

The axioms dealing with the preconditions of the actions of cancelling and accepting are the following:

(PCC) $OntPoss(cc(e,x,y,s)) \leftrightarrow X^- Comm(e,x,y,s)$;
(PCP) $OntPoss(cp(e,x,y,s)) \leftrightarrow X^- Prec(e,x,y,s)$;
(PAP) $OntPoss(ap(e,x,y,s)) \leftrightarrow X^- Prec(e,x,y,s) \land \neg Done(\text{-},\text{-},cp(e,x,y,s))$.

The core ontology also describes the states (*fulfilled, violated, pending*) in which a commitment can be. The definition of these states relies on the *truth conditions* of the content of the commitment, which are formally described in the next subsection.

3.3   The Representation of Content

Before we define the truth conditions of CL sentences, two remarks should be made. First, the truth of a temporal sentence at a given state (the *point of reference*, [20]) can be evaluated only if we know at which state the sentence has been uttered (the *point of speech*). For example, the sentence "I shall pay you within the end of the month" implicitly refers to the end of the current month, which in turn is determined by the state at which the sentence is uttered. Second, branching time brings in a semantic difficulty known as *contingent future*, which means that at a given point of reference it may be still undetermined if a sentence is going to be true or false. Consider again to the previous example, and assume that the sentence has been uttered, on January 10th, and that no payment has been made as far as January 15th; on January 15th, the sentence is still not settled true nor settled false, and thus it is undefined. Note however that a sentence that is true (false) at a state, will go on being true (false) at all states in the future of that state.

We represent CL sentences as SL terms, which allows us to define CL semantics in SL. More precisely, we first assume that for every SL term s that denotes a CL sentence, there is exactly one SL formula $\lfloor s \rfloor$ that corresponds to s, which we call the *sentence meaning* of s; then we define the truth conditions of s in SL.

CL semantics is dealt with by means of the following predicates, whose definitions we call *truth conditions* of a sentence:

$True(e,s) \leftrightarrow \mathsf{AF}^-(Done(e,\text{-},\text{-}) \land \lfloor s \rfloor)$,
$False(e,s) \leftrightarrow \mathsf{AF}^-(Done(e,\text{-},\text{-}) \land \neg \lfloor s \rfloor)$,
$Undef(e,s) \leftrightarrow \mathsf{AF}^- Done(e,\text{-},\text{-}) \land \neg True(e,s) \land \neg False(e,s)$.

Note that the A path quantifier in front of the F^- operator is necessary, even if our model structure is not branching in the past, because formula $\lfloor s \rfloor$ may include operators like F^+ that need a path to be specified.

The truth conditions of sentence s are given with respect to an event e, which does not necessarily correspond to the event of uttering s. Event e is used to set a well-defined temporal reference by which we can evaluate the truth of s.

The truth conditions of a CL sentence determine the fulfillment or the violation of the relevant commitment. More precisely, a commitment whose content is s is said to be *fulfilled*, *violated*, or *pending* respectively when s is true, false, or undefined according to the above definitions. The event with respect to which the truth conditions of the content are checked is the one that has brought about the commitment. Here are the axioms that formalize what stated above:

$Fulf(e,x,y,s) \leftrightarrow Comm(e,x,y,s) \land True(e,s),$
$Viol(e,x,y,s) \leftrightarrow Comm(e,x,y,s) \land False(e,s),$
$Pend(e,x,y,s) \leftrightarrow Comm(e,x,y,s) \land Undef(e,s).$

Intuitively, every commitment is either fulfilled, or violated, or pending. It is actually possible to prove that

$$\models Comm(e,x,y,s) \rightarrow \mathsf{xor}(Fulf(e,x,y,s), Viol(e,x,y,s), Pend(e,x,y,s)).$$

This means that only one of $Fulf(e,x,y,s)$, $Viol(e,x,y,s)$, or $Pend(e,x,y,s)$ is true in all models in every state in which $Comm(e,x,y,s)$ holds.

The core ontology delimits the set of possible institutional actions. However, not every ontologically possible action can be actually carried out: it is part of the function of an institution to constrain the execution of the actions that are ontologically possible.

3.4   Authorizations

In order to interact with other agents within the context of the Basic Institution, an agent must be *registered*. We assume that every registered agent plays a specific role, *RegAgt*, within the Basic Institution (BI). If a is a registered agent, the SL formula

$Role(a,BI,RegAgt)$

holds.

We now introduce a predicate to state that an agent is authorized to bring about an event of a certain type. In general, to effectively perform an institutional action of type τ, agent x must be authorized to do so, that is, the formula

$Auth(x,\tau)$

must hold. A reasonable set of authorizations concerning the creation and the manipulation of commitments can be defined in the form of an axiom as follows:

(ABI) $Role(x,BI,RegAgt) \land Role(y,BI,RegAgt) \rightarrow$
$Auth(x,mc(x,y,s)) \land Auth(x,mp(y,x,s)) \land Auth(x,cp(e,x,y,s)) \land$
$Auth(x,cp(e,y,x,s)) \land Auth(x,cc(e,y,x,s)) \land Auth(x,ap(e,x,y,s)).$

This formula means that: as a *debtor*, a registered agent is authorized to make a commitment with any registered agent as the creditor, and accept or cancel an existing precommitment; as a *creditor*, a registered agent has the authorization to make precommitments with any registered agent as the debtor, and cancel an existing commitment or precommitment.

All the communicative acts that comply with the authorizations defined above are institutional actions, whose execution is authorized by the Basic Institution. Other types of communicative acts, however, may require a special institution. Consider for example the act of ordering: we view it as a request that cannot be refused, that is, we can model it as creating a commitments as the creditor. If we want to follow the example of human society, orders will not be authorized by the Basic institution, and will only be effective if some special institutional framework, involving a hierarchy, is defined.

3.5 Norms

Authorizations define the institutional powers of agents; in general, however, the exercise of such powers is further regulated by a set of norms. Consider, for example, a scientific society: the president of the society typically has the power to call the general meeting of the society's members; the president, however, is also *obliged* to call such a meeting at least once a year, and may be *allowed* to call it more often if he or she has good reasons to do so. At the present stage of our research, we still do not whether some norms should be regarded as part of the Basic Institution. Consider for example the adjacency pair made up by a request and its acceptance or refusal. At some institutional level, we might want to dictate that agents should react to all requests by producing an acceptance or a refusal. But is this rule to be regarded as a norm of the Basic Institution? Or does it belong to a special institution, like for example an "Institution of Conversations"? We feel that more work has to be done in order to clarify this issue; in particular, practical applications will have to be analyzed to get a better understanding of the systems of norms involved in the functioning of real multiagent systems. For the time being, therefore, we assume that the Basic Institution specifies no norms.

3.6 Conventions

An institutional action is performed through the execution of some lower level act that conventionally counts as a performance of the institutional action; obvious examples are offered by communicative acts, which are performed by executing lower level acts of message exchange. As a consequence, institutional actions require a set of conventions for their execution. The institutional actions of the Basic Institution are commitment-manipulations actions, conventionally realized by the exchange of ACL messages.

In Section 3.4 we have illustrated the six authorizations that registered agents are granted by the Basic Institution. Now we deal with the structure of the messages that agents actually exchange to perform authorized commitment manipulation actions. We view a message as a pair made up by a *type indicator* and a *body*. Type indicators (analogous to KQML's performatives [2]) are constant symbols taken from a finite set. The body of a message is usually a

CL sentence represented in our semantic language by a first-order term. In the case of acceptance or refusal messages, the body is comprised of a more complex structure, that is, a tuple of elements $(\langle e,x,y,s\rangle)$ that identifies an existing (pre)commitment. For every message type we introduce a functor that specifies the relevant type of the action that an agent performs when exchanging a message of such a type. This approach is best explained by an example. Suppose that agent x sends a message to agent y to inform y that σ is the case (where σ is a suitable first-order formula). The exchange of such a message is an event of type $inform(x,y,s)$, where $inform$ is a three-place functor denoting the type of the message, x and y respectively denote the sender and the receiver of the message, and s is a term corresponding to formula σ. When event e is an exchange of a message of type $inform$ and content s, sent by agent x to agent y, the formula

$$Done(e,x,inform(x,y,s))$$

holds. This event, under given conditions, implies the performance of a commitment manipulation action. In other words, the meaning of the message is defined as the effect that exchanging such a message has on the network of commitments binding the sender and the receiver. The correspondence between the type τ of the message exchange and the type τ' of the commitment manipulation action is defined by a convention of the relevant institution, and is formally stated by means of the formula

$$CountAs(\tau,\tau'),$$

which means that an action of type τ conventionally counts as an action of type τ'. Below we define the communicative acts by means of which agents carry out the commitment manipulation actions authorized by the Basic Institution.

Informing is defined as committing to the truth of the message body, which, we suppose, is comprised of an arbitrary CL sentence. More precisely, when agent x exchanges with agent y an $inform$ message with content s, agent x commits, relative to y, to the truth of s:

(CAInf) $CountAs(inform(x,y,s),mc(x,y,s))$.

We assume that the body of a *request* message is comprised of an *action expression*, which indicates the requested action's type, its actor, and possibly a temporal constraint. More precisely, in the request message we use a term that represents the abstract syntax of an action expression, which is not to be confused with its concrete form, which belongs to a specific CL. In our SL, an action expression may have the form $Done(x,\tau)\mathsf{B}^+\Gamma$, in which B^+ means intuitively "before" ($\varphi\mathsf{B}^+\psi =_{def} \neg(\neg\varphi \;\mathsf{U}^+\; \psi)$), and Γ is an SL formula referring to a particular time-point. Here we are assuming that for every time-point expression of a CL there exists an SL formula which becomes periodically true according to the time-point it is indicating. Thus, in this case the body of a request message is comprised of the term $\lceil Done(x,\tau)\mathsf{B}^+\Gamma\rceil$, in which $\lceil\rceil$ is a function which, given an SL formula φ, returns the SL term $\lceil\varphi\rceil$ such that $\lfloor\,\lceil\varphi\rceil\,\rfloor$ is φ. If we denote such term with s, and then define the type $request(x,y,s)$ to denote events by which agent x requests s from agent y, the semantics of $request$ messages is defined as below:

(CAReq) $CountAs(request(x,y,s),mp(y,x,s))$.

The above-mentioned action expression is only an example. We think that the task of defining other action expressions is to be tackled only when we deal with the application of our framework to actual cases.

The act of *accepting* is not only defined with respect to requests, but with respect to precommitments in general. We assume that the body of an acceptance message is a tuple which includes all the elements that uniquely identify the relevant precommitment. We introduce the functor $accept(e,x,y,s)$, whose arguments are the same as those characterizing the precommitment that the sender of the message is accepting, and the relevant convention is as follows:

(CAAcc) $CountAs(accept(e,x,y,s),ap(e,x,y,s))$.

The body of a *cancel* message is supposed to be the same as that of an *accept* message, that is, a tuple which includes all the elements that uniquely identify the relevant (pre)commitment. To denote the event types corresponding to such message exchange we introduce the functor $cancel(e,x,y,s)$, whose arguments are the same as those characterizing the (pre)commitment which is cancelled by the relevant message exchange. The conventions are then defined like this:

(CACancP) $CountAs(cancel(e,x,y,s),cp(e,x,y,s))$,
(CACancC) $CountAs(cancel(e,x,y,s),cc(e,x,y,s))$.

A *cancel* message exchange can count as different commitment manipulation actions (cp and cc), in accordance to what is being cancelled (a precommitment or a commitment, respectively). There is no ambiguity in an actual *cancel* message exchange, as there cannot exist both a precommitment and a commitment with the same arguments, and only an action that cancels an existing object can be successfully carried out, as stated by Axioms PCC and PCP in Section 3.2. These ontological preconditions contribute to the general definition of institutional actions, as illustrated in the next subsection.

3.7   The General Representation of Communicative Acts

We are now ready to give a general definition of communicative acts. The *conventions* of the Basic Institution establish that exchanging a message of given type *counts as* a specific institutional action, provided certain conditions hold. These conditions can be classified in two categories: *ontological preconditions*, defined by the *core ontology*, and *authorizations*. While authorizations deal with the institutionalized power of agents, ontological preconditions concern the state of affairs that must hold for a communicative act to be possible. All these points are formally expressed by the following axiom that gives a general definition of institutional actions:

(IA) $Done(e,x,\tau) \wedge CountAs(\tau,\tau') \wedge OntPoss(\tau') \wedge Auth(x,\tau') \rightarrow Done(e,x,\tau')$.

As an example, let us consider the act of informing. Suppose that the formula

$Done(e_1,a,inform(a,b,s_1))$

holds, that is, agent a informs b that s_1 is the case. From Axiom CAInf we derive $CountAs(inform(a,b,s_1),mc(a,b,s_1))$, and thus we determine the commitment manipulation action that corresponds to such a message exchange. We suppose that formulae

$Role(a,BI,RegAgt)$ and
$Role(b,BI,RegAgt)$

hold, that is, both a and b are registered agents in the Basic Institution. Given these premises and Axiom ABI, which illustrates what actions registered agents are authorized to perform, we have (among other consequences)

$Auth(a,mc(a,b,s_1))$.

Axiom PMC states that it is always ontologically possible to perform a make commitment action, thus, from the premises above and Axiom IA we can derive

$Done(e_1,a,mc(a,b,s_1))$,

which, thanks to Axiom MC, gives

$Comm(e_1,a,b,s_1)$.

3.8   Declarations and Performatives

A *declaration* is a speech act that, under appropriate conditions, makes its content true. The content of a declaration must represent an institutional fact, and the agent that makes the declaration has to be authorized to bring about such an institutional fact; besides, it must be ontologically possible to bring about the fact. Consider the act of opening a society's meeting; such an act can be performed by the president of the society by making a suitable declaration. All this presupposes a special Institution of Associations, which in particular will include a definition of meetings in its core ontology, and authorize the president to open a meeting. Additional norms to regulate the exercise of institutional powers can also be defined.

Declarations can be regarded as a universal convention for the performance of all sorts of institutional actions. The logical definition of declarations is particularly interesting, because it states that

(CADecl) $CountAs(declare(\tau),\tau)$.

This definition implies that declaring an action of type τ counts as the actual performance of an action of type τ, provided such a performance is ontologically possible and the actor is authorized to perform actions of type τ, as stated below:

$Done(e,x,declare(\tau))\wedge Auth\ (x,\tau)\wedge OntPoss(\tau)\rightarrow Done(e,x,\tau).$

It is a remarkable fact that, once declarations are defined, it becomes possible to realize all communicative acts introduced so far as declarations. Suppose for example that agent x exchanges with agent y a specific message of type *declare* whose body, expressed as a suitable content language sentence, means "I commit to the truth of 'it is raining' ". The formula

$Done(e,x,declare(mc(x,y,\text{'it is raining'})))$

represents such a message exchange. We derive

$Done(e,x,mc(x,y,\text{'it is raining'}))$

from our premises and a number of axioms, and then, by Axiom MC, we have that

$Comm(e,x,y,\text{'it is raining'})$

holds.

We conclude that the exchange of such a declaration message has the same effect as the exchange of a message of type *inform*. Thus, messages of type *inform* are not strictly necessary, because the same result can be obtained by a declaration, performed in the context of the Basic Institution. If we apply the same line of reasoning to all types of messages, it turns out that all communicative acts can be realized through the use of a single type of messages, namely declaration messages. Carrying out a communicative act by declaration corresponds to the *performative execution* of the communicative act [21]. If all communicative acts that boil down to commitment-manipulation action can be carried out in performative form, then it is possible to define a full ACL starting from one single type of messages, that is, declaration messages.

4   The Operational Specification

We now give an operational specification of the concepts we have modeled in logic in the previous section. To keep close to actual agent programming practice, we shall rely on an object-oriented paradigm to define communicative acts as institutional actions.

As we have already seen, the main components of an institution are the *core ontology*, the set of *authorizations*, the set of *conventions*, and the set of *norms*. In the Basic Institution the core ontology consists of the ontology of commitments; the authorizations specify which agents are empowered to perform actions on commitments; the conventions relate the form of messages with the institutional effects achieved by sending them. No norms are specified by the Basic Institution.

4.1   Commitment

We start from the notion of commitment, that we regard as an object, that is, as a structure with data fields and methods to access and manipulate their values.

A commitment has fields for an *identifier*, a *debtor*, a *creditor*, a *content*, a *state*, used to keep track of the temporal evolution of the commitment, and a *timeout*, which is relevant only in some cases and will therefore be treated as an optional parameter. Precommitments are not regarded as a different type of objects, but as one of the possible states in the evolution of a commitment. More precisely, a commitment can be in one of the following states: *unset* (corresponding to a precommitment), *pending* (when the truth value of the content is still undefined), *fulfilled* (when the content is true), *violated* (when the content is false), and *cancelled* (when it no longer exists).

In the logical model, the use of a very expressive temporal logic makes it possible to represent a wide range of content types, like for example *one-shot conditional commitments* (i.e., commitments that bind the debtor only once, when the antecedent of a conditional becomes true) or *standing conditional commitments* (i.e., commitments that bind the debtor whenever the antecedent of a conditional becomes true). In the operational model, it would be unrealistic to assume that actual agents have sufficient logical capacities to process such an expressive language. In some previous works [10],[11] we solved this problem by introducing an additional field for the condition of the commitment. In the model presented in this paper, on the contrary, we prefer to avoid this addition, in order to keep closer to the logical model. As we shall see, the solution proposed in this paper is also more general in that, contrary to our previous proposal, it allows for the representation of standing conditional commitments. Commitment objects will be represented with the following notation:

$$C_{id}(state, debtor, creditor, content[, timeout])$$

where the brackets indicate that the *timeout* parameter is optional.

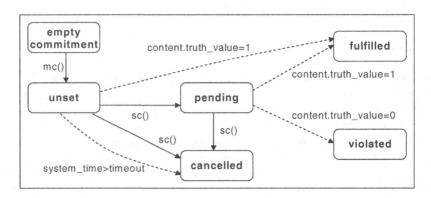

Fig. 1. The life-cycle of commitments

The content of a commitment is a *temporal proposition* (see Section 4.2). The state of a commitment undergoes a life cycle, described by the statechart diagram in Figure 1. The state of a commitment can change as an effect of the invocation of its basic methods (solid lines) or of environmental events (dotted lines). Relevant events are due to the change of the truth-value of the commitment's content or to the fact that the timeout of an unset commitment has elapsed. We assume that when a commitment object is declared, the constructor of the class creates an empty commitment object, $C_i()$. We represent the invocation of a method by the name of the object followed by a dot and by the name of the method with its parameter list. Commitments are created and manipulated through the following basic operations:

- *Make commitment.* By invoking the method $mc(a, b, P)$ with arbitrary debtor a, creditor b, and content P, a new unset commitment object is created:

$$C_i().mc(a, b, P[, to]) \rightarrow C_i(unset, a, b, P[, to])$$

- *Set commitment.* The method $sc(s)$ changes the current state of an existing commitment object to s:

$$C_i(-, a, b, P).sc(s) \rightarrow C_i(s, a, b, P)$$

There are some ontological presuppositions for the manipulation of the state of commitment objects: first of all the commitment object must exist, second the allowed state changes are only the ones reported in Figure 1.

4.2 The Representation of Content

As we have seen in Section 3, the definition of an ACL is strictly related to the specification of a content language used to express the content of messages. FIPA, the Foundation for Intelligent Physical Agents, has proposed several CLs [22] (FIPA SL, FIPA CCL, FIPA KIF, FIPA RDF), but none of these provides for a standard treatment of temporal aspects. We think that an application-independent treatment of time is crucial for any practically usable CL; this is especially true if the ACL semantics is defined in terms of commitments, because commitments often specify deadlines for the execution of actions. Therefore, even if we do not intend to define a new content language for ACLs, in this section we propose a representation of content that explicitly takes time into account.

We represent the content of ACL messages, and thus of commitments, as a type of objects that we call *temporal proposition objects*, or *temporal propositions* for short. Every temporal proposition includes a *truth value* that is continually updated by a method, that we call a *truth manager*. As remarked in the DAML Ontology of Time [23], a temporal entity may be an *instant* or an *interval*. Accordingly, our model has *instant propositions* (i.e., temporal proposition objects whose truth value depends on a single instant of time), and *interval propositions* (i.e., temporal proposition objects whose truth value depends on a whole time interval). In turn, an interval proposition can be true if a given state of affairs holds for *every instant* in the associated time interval, or for *some instant* in the associated time interval. To model this aspect, interval propositions have a *mode* attribute, whose value can be either *for all* ($\forall$) or *exists* ($\exists$). Here are a few examples of natural language statements that may be represented as temporal propositions:

- "it is the end of the month" may be represented as an instant proposition, true at all instants belonging to the last day of every month and false otherwise;
- "the service will be accessible for the whole year 2004" may be represented as an interval proposition, whose interval is year 2004 and whose mode is *for all*;
- "the product will be delivered within the current month" may be represented as an interval proposition, whose interval is the current month and whose mode is *exists*;

Besides the truth manager, in charge of updating the truth value, we assume that every temporal proposition has a method, that we call *truth notifier*, in charge notifying every change of the truth value, together with the system time at which such a change took place, to all objects which are "observing" the temporal proposition. We now give a detailed definition of temporal propositions.

Instant Propositions. An instant proposition $(p, q, ...)$ is an object with fields for:

- the *truth value* of the object, either true (1) or false (0), at the current system time;
- the *time of change*, that is, the most recent time of change of the truth value from 0 to 1 or vice versa.

To represent the semantics of instant propositions we follow an approach akin to Harnad's *symbol grounding* [24]. More specifically, the semantics of an instant proposition is embedded in its truth manager. For example, instant proposition p represents the English sentence "it is the end of the month" if, and only if, p's truth manager keeps p's truth value to 1 during the last day of every month, and to 0 during all other days. This proposition may be viewed as representing an atomic statement, in that its semantics corresponds to the English sentence "it is the end of the month".

It is also possible to build instant propositions that correspond to complex statements, and in particular to Boolean combinations of atomic statements. For example, an instant proposition representing the sentence "it is the end of January" can be built as a Boolean combination of two instant propositions, respectively representing the atomic sentences "it is the end of the month" and "it is January". We assume that for every Boolean connective we have a corresponding class, whose instances are complex instant propositions. For example, an *and* instant proposition is an object that has fields for:

- the *list of components*, which is a list of instant propositions;
- the *truth value* of the object, either 1 or 0, at the current system time;
- the *time of change*, that is, the most recent time of change of the truth value from 0 to 1 or vice-versa.

When an *and* instant proposition p is created, every instant proposition q_i belonging to p's list of components is created with its truth manager, and with a truth notifier that sends a suitable notice to p every time q_i's truth value is updated. Then, p's truth manager will update p's truth value by computing the Boolean conjunction of the truth values of all q_i's. Analogous definitions may be given for all Boolean connectives.

In our operational specification, instant propositions are the starting point for all propositional representations within the system. This assumption is coherent with the prescriptions of the logical model (see Section 3), which is based on the idea that all atomic statements are atemporal (i.e., indexical on the current time instant). In view of our general aims, it is appropriate to assume that an atomic instant proposition may represent:

- a state of affairs, for example: "the price of the product is 100 euros" or "it is the last day of the current month;"
- the execution of an action, either a communicative act defined in a suitable library (see Section 4.3) or an application-dependent action (e.g., "a payment of 100 euros has been made");
- a commitment with given attributes (see Section 4.1).

Simple Interval Propositions. A simple interval proposition is an interval proposition whose truth value depends on an instant proposition, a time interval, and a mode.

A time interval may go from a single instant to the entire life of the system, and is represented by means of its boundaries (written in brackets). In turn, the boundaries of a time interval can be:

- a fixed instant of the system time, represented by a constant numerical value;
- *now*, that is, a reference to the current time instant, typically initialized with the execution time of a communicative act;
- the time of true of an instant or interval proposition (see below);
- an arithmetic expression involving the items above.

A simple interval proposition, $(P, Q, ...)$, is an object with fields for:

- a *statement*, represented by an instant proposition (either atomic or complex);
- a *time interval*;
- a temporal *mode*, either for all ($\forall$) or exist ($\exists$), which specifies whether the statement should be true for the whole time interval or on at least one instant of the time interval;
- a *truth value*, which may be true (1), false (0) or undefined ($\perp$);
- the *time of change* of the truth value from $\perp$ to 1 or to 0.

Like instant propositions, simple interval propositions have a truth manager and a truth notifier. When it is necessary to show their components, such objects will be represented with the following notation:

$P(statement, time\ interval, mode, truth\ value, time\ of\ change)$.

A major difference between instant and interval propositions is that while the former can only be true or false, the latter can also be undefined. This important fact has to do with the branching structure of time (see Section 3). Consider for example the English sentence "the payment will be made within three days". This sentence can be represented by the simple interval proposition

$$P(p, [now, now + 3days], \exists, truth\ value, time\ of\ change),$$

where in turn statement p is an instant proposition whose truth manager monitors the execution of the relevant payment and sets p's truth value to true as soon as this is the case. The truth value of P is initialized to $\bot$, and then set to either 1 or 0 according to the rules described below. In particular, P's truth manager will be notified by p as soon as p's truth value is set to true.

In our operational model we assume that when a simple interval proposition is created, its truth value is initialized to $\bot$ and then updated by the truth manager according to the following specifications:

- if the mode is '$\forall$', the truth value is set to 0 if the statement is false at any point of the time interval, otherwise it is set to 1 when the time interval expires;
- if the mode is '$\exists$', the truth value is set to 1 if the statement is true at any point of the time interval, otherwise it is set to 0 when the time interval expires.

These rules specify the operational semantics of simple interval propositions coherently with the truth conditions of sentences as defined in Section 3.3. In particular, the specification implies that the truth value of such an object is monotonic in time, that is, it can switch from $\bot$ to 1 or to 0, and then cannot change any more.

Interval Propositions in General. Interval propositions are used to represent the content of commitments. Like with simple interval propositions, the truth value of an interval proposition is initialized to $\bot$, can switch from $\bot$ to 1 or to 0, but then cannot switch back to $\bot$. This property is important to guarantee that pending commitments will eventually become fulfilled or violated, and that fulfilled and violated commitments will not change state: indeed, coherently with the logical model (see Section 3.3) a commitment is pending, fulfilled, or violated exactly when its content is respectively undefined, true, or false.

The simplest example of an interval proposition is a simple interval proposition. However, agents need to make commitments also to complex logical combinations of interval propositions. Boolean combinations do not raise difficulties, provided we extend the truth tables to deal with $\bot$. On the basis of the definitions given in the Appendix, it can easily be shown that the truth value of a Boolean combination of interval propositions is monotonic in time. Therefore, if we apply to interval propositions the same construction we have introduced for complex instant proposition, we obtain a class of temporal proposition that behaves monotonically in time, as required for interval propositions.

Boolean combinations, however, are not always sufficient: for example, the Boolean conditional connective is not suitable for an effective operational representation of conditional commitments. To see why this is the case, consider the following examples:

- Suppose an offer is made relative to a single specified commodity (e.g., an apartment), to the extent that the commodity will be transferred to a buyer within one week from the payment of the due price (e.g., 100,000 euros). Moreover, the offer is valid for the whole year 2004. This is an example of a *one-shot conditional commitment*, which can be described by the English sentence: "for all 2004, as soon as a payment for the commodity is made, the commodity is transferred to the buyer within one week";
- Suppose an offer is made relative to products of a specified type (e.g., a cellphone), to the extent that a product of the given type will be transferred to every buyer within one week from the payment of the due price (e.g., 100 euros). Moreover, the offer is valid for the whole year 2004. This is an example of a *standing conditional commitment*, which can be described by the sentence: "for all 2004, every time a payment for a product of the specified type is made, then a product of the specified type is transferred to the buyer within one week".

Both examples involve commitments whose content is best viewed as an event-driven structure. In the first case, the event described by the interval proposition "as soon as a payment for the commodity is made in year 2004" acts as a trigger that generates the interval proposition "the commodity is transferred to the buyer within one week". In the latter case, every event described by the instant proposition "a payment for a product of the specified type is made in year 2004" generates a new interval proposition "a product of the specified type is transferred to the buyer within one week". To express such contents, we introduce two event-driven propositional structures: *on* and *whenever*.

An *on proposition*, used to express one-shot conditional commitments, is an object with fields for:

- the *on condition*, which is an interval proposition, Q;
- the *statement*, which is an interval proposition, P;
- the *truth value*, representing the global truth value of the *on* proposition;
- the *time of change*, representing the time of change of the *on* proposition from $\perp$ to 1 or to 0.

For the sake of simplicity, in our examples (see Section 4.4) an *on* proposition will be represented by the expression P *on* Q.

Every *on* proposition has a truth manager that computes the truth value as follows:

- the interval proposition Q is created, with $Q.truth\_value = \perp$, and its truth manager is set up;
- as soon as $Q.truth\_value = 0$, the truth value of the *on* proposition is set to 1;

- as soon as $Q.truth\_value = 1$, the interval proposition P is created with $P.truth\_value = \perp$, and its truth manager is set up (the boundaries of P's interval may depend on Q's time of change). The truth value of the *on* proposition is then given by $P.truth\_value$.

To express interesting one-shot conditional commitments, it is important that the boundaries of the statement's time interval may depend on the *time of change* of the *on* condition. An example of a conditional commitment of this type is reported in Section 4.4.

A *whenever* proposition, used to express standing conditional commitments, is an object with fields for:

- the *whenever* condition, which is an instant proposition, q;
- the *reference interval*, which is the time interval, $[t_{start}, t_{end}]$, in which the truth value of the *whenever* condition has to be monitored;
- the *statement*, which is an interval proposition P;
- the *truth value*, representing the global truth value of the *whenever* proposition;
- the *time of change*, representing the time of change of the *whenever* proposition from $\perp$ to 1 or to 0.

In our examples (see Section 4.4), a *whenever* proposition will be represented by the expression P *whenever* q *in* $[t_{start}, t_{end}]$.

Every *whenever* proposition has a truth manager that computes the truth value as follows:

- as soon as the current system time reaches t_{start}, the instant proposition q is created and its truth manager is set up;
- every time that $q.truth\_value = 1$, an interval proposition object P_i is created ($i = 1, 2, ...$), with $P_i.truth\_value = \perp$, and its truth manager is set up (the boundaries of P_i's interval may depend on q's time of change);
- as soon as the current system time reaches t_{end}, the truth value of the *whenever* proposition is set to the Boolean conjunction of all the P_i's that have been created; given that the P_i's are interval proposition objects, it may be necessary to wait for all the corresponding intervals to expire before producing the final truth value.

The truth value of a *whenever* proposition may be computed more efficiently by noting that:

- as soon as one of the P_i's becomes false, the whole *whenever* proposition may be set to false;
- as soon as one of the P_i's becomes true, it may be deleted by the set of conjuncts that defines the truth value of the *whenever* proposition;
- if the set of conjuncts that defines the truth value of the *whenever* proposition becomes empty, the truth value of the *whenever* proposition may be set to true.

To summarize, a representation for the content of a commitment is an interval proposition, which may be:

- a simple interval proposition;
- a Boolean combination of interval propositions;
- an *on* proposition;
- a *whenever* proposition.

This completes the treatment of commitments and of their contents. We now proceed to another important aspect of agent communication, that is, the library of communicative acts.

4.3 A Library of Communicative Acts

The elementary operations on commitment (Section 4.1) should not be viewed as actions to be directly performed by agents; rather, they are low-level methods used to implement operations on commitment objects. Agents do not directly invoke these methods, but manipulate commitments through a library of communicative acts (see Section 4.3), according to their institutional powers. Such powers are defined by a set of institution-dependent *authorizations* which, in order to abstract from specific agents, are expressed in terms of *roles*. The Basic Institution has a role for registered agents, *RegAgt*, which is the role that every agent takes when it becomes part of the "society of agents."; moreover, every commitment implicitly defines two roles, *debtor* and *creditor*, which affect the institutional power of agents. Coherently with the prescriptions of the logical model, the authorizations of the Basic Institution are:

- a registered agent may create an *unset* commitment with any registered agent as the debtor and the creditor;
- the debtor of an *unset* commitment can set it to either *pending* or *cancelled*;
- the creditor of an *unset* or *pending* commitment can set it to *cancelled*.

Special institutions may enlarge or modify this basic set of authorizations according to need.

In our operational model, we have not yet defined a general mechanism to guarantee that actions are performed by authorized agents. While this is a topic for future research, for the time being we assume that all communicative acts are defined in a communicative act library in such a way that the authorizations of the Basic Institution are met.

We shall now define the meaning of the basic types of communicative acts as identified by Speech Act Theory [13]. We assume that the agents involved are registered as members of the Basic Institution. With the exception of declarations, that will be dealt with in a special way, all communicative acts defined are compatible with the authorizations of the Basic Institution. As a whole, the library of communicative acts can be regarded as the set of conventions (see Section 3.6) of the Basic Institution.

In the following definitions the symbol ":=" means that the act represented on the left-hand side is actually performed through the invocation of the methods listed on the right-hand side.

214   Marco Colombetti, Nicoletta Fornara, and Mario Verdicchio

Assertives. We consider the *inform* act as our prototypical assertive act. This act is used by agent a to inform agent b that proposition P holds. In a commitment-based approach, an act of informing can be defined as follows:

$$inform(a, b, P) := \{C_i().mc(a, b, P); C_i(unset, a, b, P).sc(pending)\}.$$

Directives. We treat *request* as our basic directive act, and define it as the creation of an unset commitment with the sender as the creditor and the receiver as the debtor. The request by agent a to agent b to bring about proposition P is defined as:

$$request(a, b, P, to) := \{C_i().mc(b, a, P, to)\}.$$

Questions (or queries) are requests to be informed about something (see [10] for a definition of *yes-no-question* and *wh-question*).

Commissives. Here we define the basic commissive act of *promising*. A promise by agent a to agent b to bring about proposition P is defined as:

$$promise(a, b, P) := \{C_i().mc(a, b, P); C_i(unset, a, b, P).sc(pending)\}.$$

Two main types of commissive acts can be performed only in connection with an unset commitment, namely *accept*, and *refuse*. These act have nontrivial *ontological possibility* preconditions (see Section 3.2), and can be defined as follows:

$$preconditions : \; \exists\, C_i(unset, b, a, P, to)$$
$$accept(b, a, C_i(unset, b, a, P, to)) := \{C_i(unset, b, a, P, to).sc(pending)\}$$

$$preconditions : \; \exists\, C_i(unset, b, a, P, to)$$
$$refuse(b, a, C_i(unset, b, a, P, to)) := \{C_i(unset, b, a, P, to).sc(cancelled)\}.$$

Declarations. The point of a declaration is to bring about a change in the world, obviously not in the physical or natural world but in an institutional world, that is, a conventional world relying on common agreement among the interacting agents [12]. Declarations actually change the institutional world simply in virtue of their successful performance.

Coherently with the logical model, it is necessary to identify what agents are authorized to perform a given declaration. Typically, authorizations are granted to agents in virtue of the role they play in an interaction, and thus authorizations are naturally associated to roles. A complete treatment of declarations will require an operational model of special institutions that, as we have already remarked, is a topic for future research. However, we suggest here a simplified treatment, that we have adopted elsewhere to deal with the special institution of English auctions [11].

Let us assume that the environment in which the agents interact contains a number of *institutional objects*, O_i, that represent aspects of institutional reality.

For example, certain institutional objects may represent states of ownership; such objects will at least include two fields, one for the *owner* and one for the *commodity* owned, and a method (*set_owner*) for setting the value of the owner field. In such an environment, institutional actions may be viewed as actions that modify the values of the fields of institutional objects. For example, to represent the action of transferring the ownership of commodity c from agent a to agent b we can use an institutional object O such that $O.commodity = c$; this object will have $O.owner = a$ before ownership is transferred to b, and $O.owner = b$ after such an action is performed. The action itself can be executed by a method call,

$$O(owner = a, commodity = c).set\_owner(b).$$

Like the methods for commitment manipulation, *set_owner* should not be viewed as an action that can be directly performed by agents, but as a low-level procedure used to implement an institutional action. To actually perform such institutional action, an agent needs to perform a suitable communicative act, which will succeed only if the agent has sufficient institutional powers. As it has been clarified in Section 3.8, only one communicative act type is sufficient to perform all kinds of institutional actions, namely *declarations*. However, it is necessary to specify *authorization* preconditions to perform any specific declaration. To do so, we then introduce a construct to express that an agent having a given role has the power to bring about an institutional change of a given kind:

$preconditions : x$ *has a given role*
$declare(x, O_j, "field_k", y) := \{O_j.set\_field_k(y)\}.$

Using a construct of this type it is possible, for example, to state that the owner of a commodity is authorized to transferring its ownership by declaration:

$preconditions : x = O.owner()$
$declare(x, O, "owner", y) := \{O.set\_owner(y)\}.$

4.4 Examples

Example 1. A common type of interaction is when a *seller* commits to delivering a specific product to a *buyer* within a given *deadline*, and the buyer commits to paying the price of the product to the seller within a given *delay* from its delivery. This situation involves two commitments, which can be described as follows:

- commitment 1: the seller commits, relative to the client, to delivering the specified product within the specified deadline;
- commitment 2: the buyer commits, relative to the seller, to paying the price of the product within the given delay from delivery.

In other words, the seller is unconditionally committed to delivering the product; when the product is actually delivered, the condition of the buyer's commitment becomes true, and then the buyer is unconditionally committed to paying its price. Note that the time interval of this second commitment is defined only after the associated condition becomes true.

To represent the two commitments, let us first define two instant propositions as follows:

- p means that "the product is delivered to the buyer";
- q means that "the product's price is paid to the seller".

We then define two interval propositions as follows:

- P is the interval proposition $P(p, [now, deadline], \exists)$;
- Q is the interval proposition
  $Q(q, [P.time\_of\_change(), P.time\_of\_change() + delay], \exists)$.

The seller can now make its commitment by performing the communicative act $promise(seller, buyer, P)$, which creates the commitment $C_1(pending, seller, buyer, P)$. In turn, the buyer can make its commitment by performing the communicative act $promise(buyer, seller, Q\ on\ P)$, which creates the commitment $C_2(pending, buyer, seller, Q\ on\ P)$.

Example 2. Consider an *employer* promising to an *employee* that for all year 2004, the employee's salary will be paid within one week from the end of each month. This case is similar to Example 1, but involves a standing conditional commitment.

To represent the commitment, let us first define two instant propositions as follows:

- p means that "it is the end of the current month";
- q means that "the employee's salary is paid".

We then define an interval proposition as follows:

- Q is the interval proposition
  $Q(q, [p.time\_of\_change(), p.time\_of\_change() + 7days], \exists)$.

We define $t_{start} = 00:00/01/01/2004$ and $t_{end} = 24:00/31/12/2004$. The employer can now make its commitment by performing the communicative act $promise(employer, employee, Q\ whenever\ p\ in\ [t_{start}, t_{end}])$, which creates the commitment $C_1(pending, employer, employee, Q\ whenever\ p\ in\ [t_{start}, t_{end}])$.

Example 3. Consider a situation where the *provider* of a service reserves a *resource* for a *client* (for example a room in a hotel, a place on a flight, a table at a restaurant, etc.) for a time interval from t_1 to t_2; more precisely, the provider commits, relative to the client, to giving the reserved resource to the client (within a maximum delay of $delta_1$ time units) if the client *claims* it during $[t_1, t_2]$.

This example is more complex that it may appear. From the point of view of Speech Act Theory, a *claim* is a directive act, and therefore is akin to a request. What distinguishes a claim from a plain request is that it has the additional precondition (or "preparatory condition," in Searle's terminology) that the sender has the right to have its claim accepted. In a commitment-based framework, a right of agent a can be represented in terms of a commitment of some other agent, b, relative to a. In our case, the simplest solution is to assume that the provider is committed to accepting an unset commitment of given form. This solution, however, introduces a further parameter, that is, the maximum delay, δ_2, for accepting the unset commitment (of course, δ_2 must be smaller than δ_1).

More precisely, let:

- p be the instant proposition meaning "the resource is given to the client";
- P be the interval proposition $P(p, [now, now + \delta_1], \exists)$, meaning "the resource is given to the client within δ_1 time units";
- q be the instant proposition meaning "a commitment of form $C(unset, provider, client, P)$ is made" (the time at which this commitment is created will set the *now* parameter in P);
- Q be the interval proposition $Q(q, [t_1, t_2], \exists)$, meaning "a commitment of form $C(unset, provider, client, P)$ is made during the interval from t_1 to t_2";
- r be the instant proposition meaning "the provider accepts the commitment $C(unset, provider, client, P)$";
- R be the interval proposition $R(r, [now, now + \delta_2], \exists)$, meaning "the provider accepts the commitment $C(unset, provider, client, P)$ within δ_2 time units".

The provider can now make its commitment by performing the communicative act *promise(provider, client, R on Q)*. To make its claim, the client has to create a suitable unset commitment, which can be done by performing the communicative act *request(client, provider, P)*.

5 Conclusions

In this paper we have presented a logical model and an operational specification of the social concepts necessary to specify the semantics of ACLs. Then, using such concepts, we have defined the meaning of a set of basic communicative acts that can be exploited by heterogeneous agents to interact in an open framework.

Our proposal is based on two main assumptions: (i) that language is the fundamental component of every communicative interaction, and (ii) that communication is an institutional activity, in that it is made possible by social institutions that exist thanks to the common agreement of the interacting agents (or, in the case of artificial agents, of their designers)(see [15]). We suggest that the basic components of an institution are: the ontology of a fragment of social reality, a set of authorizations to perform actions within the institution, the conventions to perform such actions, and a (possibly empty) set of norms that regulate the agents' behavior.

In our view, a social concept that is central to the treatment of communication is commitment. Therefore, we have defined what we call the Basic Institution, to define the concepts, authorizations and conventions related to commitment manipulation. We then view most types of communicative acts as conventions for the manipulation of commitments. We also remark that some kinds of communicative acts require more specific institutional settings. However, a detailed analysis of the special institutions required for agent interaction is a topic for future research.

Another aspect that deserves further research is content language, that is, the language used to represent the content of communicative acts. In this paper we have proposed no specific content language, and have adopted two different representations of contents. More specifically, contents have been represented as first-order terms in the context of the logical model, and as object structures in the context of the operational specification. However, we believe that the relationship between our representations and actual content languages has to be better clarified. In particular, if we want ACLs to reach the level of real applications it will be necessary to establish a standard treatment of time in content languages.

Acknowledgments

We thank Francesco Viganò for useful observations on the operational specification.

Appendix

Truth-Tables for Interval Propositions

Truth-tables of Boolean operators of classical propositional logic can be used to obtain the extended truth-tables of the same operators when the propositions can be true (1), false (0), or undefined($\perp$). The key move is to regard the undefined value as "either 0 or 1", that we represent as $\{0,1\}$.

As an example, the classical truth table of the *and* operator ($\wedge$) is shown in Table 1, and the extended truth table of the same operator is shown in Table 2.

Table 1. Truth table of the "and" operator

$\wedge$	0	1
0	0	0
1	0	1

Table 2. Extended truth table of the "and" operator

$\wedge$	0	1	$\{0,1\}$
0	0	0	0
1	0	1	$\{0,1\}$
$\{0,1\}$	0	$\{0,1\}$	$\{0,1\}$

The extended truth-table is obtained from the classical one by writing $\{0,1\}$ when it is impossible to write a single truth value. For example $\{0,1\} \wedge 0$ gives 0 because the 0 column in Table 1 contains only 0's, while $\{0,1\} \wedge 1$ gives $\{0,1\}$ because the 1 column in the same table has both 0's and 1's.

References

1. Cohen, P., Levesque, H.: Rational interaction as the basis for communication. In Cohen, P., Morgan, J., Pollack, M., eds.: Intentions in communication. MIT Press (1990) 221–156
2. Finin, T., Labrou, Y., Mayfield, J.: KQML as an agent communication language. In Bradshaw, J., ed.: Software agents. The MIT Press, Cambridge, MA (1995)
3. Foundation for Intelligent Physical Agents: FIPA 97 Specification Part 2: Agent Communication Language (1997)
4. Singh, M.P.: Agent communication languages: Rethinking the principles. IEEE Computer **31** (1998) 40–47
5. Singh, M.P.: A social semantics for agent communication languages. In: Proceedings of IJCAI-99 Workshop on Agent Communication Languages. (1999) 75–88
6. Colombetti, M.: A commitment–based approach to agent speech acts and conversations. In: Proc. Workshop on Agent Languages and Communication Policies, 4th International Conference on Autonomous Agents (Agents 2000), Barcelona, Spain (2000) 21–29
7. Pitt, J., Mamdani, A.: A protocol-based semantics for an agent communication language. In Thomas, D., ed.: Proceedings of the 16th International Joint Conference on Artificial Intelligence (IJCAI-99-Vol1), Morgan Kaufmann Publishers (1999) 486–491
8. Jones, A., Parent, X.: Conventional signalling acts and conversation. In Dignum, F., ed.: Advances in Agent Communication. LNAI. Springer Verlag (to be published)
9. Verdicchio, M., Colombetti, M.: A logical model of social commitment for agent communication. In Rosenschein, J.S., Sandholm, T., Wooldridge, M., Yokoo, M., eds.: Proc. Second International Joint Conference on Autonomous Agents and Multiagent Systems (AAMAS 2003), Melbourne, Australia, ACM Press (2003) 528–535
10. Fornara, N., Colombetti, M.: Operational specification of a commitment-based agent communication language. In Castelfranchi, C., Johnson, W.L., eds.: Proc. First International Joint Conference on Autonomous Agents and MultiAgent Systems (AAMAS 2002), Bologna, Italy, ACM Press (2002) 535–542
11. Fornara, N., Colombetti, M.: Defining interaction protocols using a commitment-based agent communication language. In Rosenschein, J.S., Sandholm, T., Wooldridge, M., Yokoo, M., eds.: Proc. Second International Joint Conference on Autonomous Agents and MultiAgent Systems (AAMAS 2003), Melbourne, Australia, ACM Press (2003) 520–527
12. Colombetti, M., Verdicchio, M.: An analysis of agent speech acts as institutional actions. In Castelfranchi, C., Johnson, W.L., eds.: Proc. First International Joint Conference on Autonomous Agents and Multiagent Systems (AAMAS 2002), Bologna, Italy, ACM Press (2002) 1157–1166
13. Searle, J.R.: Speech Acts: An Essay in the Philosophy of Language. Cambridge University Press, Cambridge, United Kingdom (1969)

220   Marco Colombetti, Nicoletta Fornara, and Mario Verdicchio

14. Alberti, M., Gavanelli, M., Lamma, E., Mello, P., Torroni, P.: Modeling Interactions Using *Social Integrity Constraints*: A Resource Sharing Case Study. In this volume.
15. Searle, J.R.: The construction of social reality. Free Press, New York (1995)
16. Jones, A., Sergot, M.J.: A formal characterisation of institutionalised power. Journal of the IGPL **4** (1996) 429–445
17. Emerson, E.A., Halpern, J.Y.: 'Sometimes' and 'Not Never' Revisited. Journal of the ACM **33** (1986) 151–178
18. Esteva, M., Rodríguez-Aguilar, J.A., Sierra, C., Garcia, P., Arcos, J.L.: On the formal specification of electronic institutions. In Dignum, F., Sierra, C., eds.: Agent Mediated Electronic Commerce, The European AgentLink Perspective (LNAI 1991). Springer (2001) 126–147
19. Vasconcelos, W.W.: Logic-based electronic institutions. In this volume.
20. Reichenbach, H.: Elements of Symbolic Logic. MacMillan, New York (1947)
21. Searle, J.R., Vanderveken, D.: Foundations of illocutionary logic. Cambridge University Press, Cambridge, UK (1985)
22. Foundation for Intelligent Physical Agents: FIPA Content Language (CL) Specifications. http://www.fipa.org (2003)
23. Ferguson, G., Allen, J., Fikes, R., Hayes, P., McDermott, D., Niles, I., Pease, A., Tate, A., Tyson, M., Waldinger, R.: A DAML ontology of time. http://www.cs.rochester.edu/~ferguson/daml/ (2002)
24. Harnad, S.: The symbol grounding problem. Physica D **42** (1990) 335–346

Logic-Based Electronic Institutions

Wamberto W. Vasconcelos

Department of Computing Science, University of Aberdeen
Aberdeen AB24 3UE, UK
wvasconcelos@acm.org

Abstract. We propose a logic-based rendition of electronic institutions – these are means to specify open agent organisations. We employ a simple notation based on first-order logic and set theory to represent an expressive class of electronic institutions. We also provide a formal semantics for our constructs and present a distributed implementation of a platform to enact electronic institutions specified in our formalism.

1 Introduction

In this paper we propose a logical formalism that allows the representation of a useful class of protocols involving many agents. This formalism combines first-order logic and set theory to allow the specification of interactions among agents, whether an auction, a more sophisticated negotiation or an argumentation framework. We introduce and exploit the logic-based formalism within the context of electronic institutions: these are means to modularly describe open agent organisations [1]. As well as providing a flexible syntax for interactions, we also formalise their semantics via the construction of models.

Current efforts at standardising agent communication languages like KIF and KQML [2] and FIPA-ACL [3] do not cater for dialogues: they do not offer means to represent relationships among messages. Work on dialogues (*e.g.* [4], [5] and [6]), on the other hand, prescribe the actual format, meaning and ultimate goal of the interactions. Our effort aims to provide engineers with a notation for specifying interactions among the components of a Multi-Agent System (MAS, for short), but which allows *relationships* to be established among the interactions. A typical interaction we are able to express in our formalism is "all seller agents advertise their goods; after this, all buyer agents send their offers for the goods to the respective seller agent". In this interaction, it is essential that the buyer agents send offers to the appropriate seller agents, that is, each seller agent should receive an appropriate offer for the good(s) it advertised.

This paper is structured as follows. In Section 2 we describe the syntax and semantics of our proposed logic-based formalism to describe protocols. In Section 3 we introduce a definition of electronic institutions using our logic-based notation for protocols giving their formal meaning; in that section we illustrate our approach with a practical example and we describe how we implemented a platform to enact electronic institutions expressed in our formalism. In Section 4 we discuss related work and in Section 5 we draw conclusions and give directions for future work.

J. Leite et al. (Eds.): DALT 2003, LNAI 2990, pp. 221–242, 2004.

2   A Set-Based Logic $\mathcal{L}$ for Protocols

In this section, we describe a set-based first-order logic $\mathcal{L}$ with which we can define protocols. Our proposed logic provides us with a compact notation to formally describe relationships among messages in a protocol. Intuitively, these constructs define (pre- and post-) conditions that should hold as agents follow a protocol.

We aim at a broad class of protocols in which many-to-many interactions (and, in particular, one-to-one, one-to-many and many-to-one) can be formally expressed. The protocols are *global* in the sense that they describe any and all interactions that may take place in the MAS. One example of the kind of interactions we want to be able to express is "an agent x sends a message to another agent y offering an item k for sale; agent y replies to x's message making an offer n to buy k" and so on. We define $\mathcal{L}$ as below:

Definition 1. $\mathcal{L}$ *consists of formulae Qtf (Atfs $\Rightarrow$ SetCtrs) where Qtf is the quantification, Atfs is a conjunction of atomic formulae and SetCtrs is a conjunction of set constraints.*

Qtf provides our constructs with universal and existential quantification over finite sets; *Atfs* expresses atomic formulae that must hold true and *SetCtrs* represents set constraints that are made to hold true. We define the classes of constructs *Qtf*, *Atfs* and *SetCtrs* in the sequel. We refer to a well-formed formulae of $\mathcal{L}$ generically as *Fml*.

We shall adopt some notational conventions in our formulae. Sets will be represented by words starting with capital letters and in this type font, as in, for example "S", "Set" and "Buyers". Variables will be denoted by words starting with capital letters in *this type font*, as in, for example, "*X*", "*Var*" and "*Buyer*". We shall represent constants by words starting with non-capital letters in *this font*; some examples are "*a*" and "*item*". We shall assume the existence of a recursively enumerable set *Vars* of variables and a recursively enumerable set *Consts* of constants.

In order to define the class *Atfs* of atomic formulae conjunctions, we first introduce our *terms*:

Definition 2. *All elements from Vars and Consts are in Terms. If $t_1, \ldots, t_n$ are in Terms, then $f(t_1, \ldots, t_n)$ is also in Terms, f being a function symbol.*

The class *Terms* is thus defined recursively, based on variables and constants and their combination with functional symbols. An example of a term using our conventions is *enter(buyer)*. We can now define the class *Atfs*:

Definition 3. *If $t_1, \ldots, t_n$ are Terms, then $p(t_1, \ldots, t_n)$ is an atomic formula (or, simply, an atf), where p is any predicate symbol. A special atomic formula is defined via the "=" symbol, as $t_1 = t_2$. The class Atfs consists of all atfs; furthermore, for any Atf_1 and Atf_2 in Atfs, $Atf_1 \wedge Atf_2$ is also in Atfs.*

This is another recursive definition: the basic components are the simple atomic formulae built with terms. These components (and their combinations) can be put together as conjuncts.

We now define the class of *set constraints*. These are restrictions on set operations such as union, intersection, Cartesian product and set difference [7]:

Definition 4. *Set constraints are conjunctions of set operations, defined by the following grammar:*

$$SetCtrs \rightarrow SetCtrs \wedge SetCtrs \mid (SetCtrs) \mid MTest \mid SetProp$$
$$MTest \rightarrow Term \in SetOp \mid Term \notin SetOp$$
$$SetProp \rightarrow card(SetOp)\ Op\ \mathbb{N} \mid card(SetOp)\ Op\ card(SetOp)$$
$$\mid SetOp = SetOp \mid SetOp \neq SetOp$$
$$Op \rightarrow = \mid \neq \mid > \mid \geq \mid < \mid \leq$$
$$SetOp \rightarrow SetOp \cup SetOp \mid SetOp \cap SetOp \mid SetOp - SetOp$$
$$\mid SetOp \times SetOp \mid (SetOp) \mid \mathsf{Set} \mid \emptyset$$

MTest is a *membership test*, that is, a test whether an element belongs or not to the result of a set operation *SetOp* (in particular, to a specific set). *SetProp* represents the *set properties*, that is, restrictions on set operations as regards to their size (*card*) or their contents. $\mathbb{N}$ is the set of natural numbers. *Op* stands for the operators on the set properties. *SetOp* stands for the *set operations*, that is, expressions whose final result is a set. An example of a set constraint is $B \in$ Buyers $\wedge\ card(\mathsf{Buyers}) \geq 0 \wedge card(\mathsf{Buyers}) \leq 10$. We may, alternatively, employ |Set| to refer to the cardinality of a set, that is, $|\mathsf{Set}| = card(\mathsf{Set})$. Additionally, in order to simplify our set expressions and improve their presentation, we can use $0 \leq |\mathsf{Buyers}| \leq 10$ instead of the previous expression.

Finally, we define the quantifications *Qtf*:

Definition 5. *The quantification Qtf is defined as:*

$$Qtf \rightarrow Qtf'\ Qtf \mid Qtf'$$
$$Qtf' \rightarrow Q\ Var \in SetOp \mid Q\ Var \in SetOp, Var = Term$$
$$Q \rightarrow \forall \mid \exists \mid \exists!$$

Where Term $\in$ Terms and Var $\in$ Vars.

We pose an important additional restriction on our quantifications: either *Var* or sub-terms of *Term* must occur in $(Atfs \Rightarrow SetCtrs)$.

Using the typographic conventions presented above, we can now build correct formulae such as:

$$\exists B \in \mathsf{Ags}\,(m(B, adm, enter(buyer)) \Rightarrow (B \in \mathsf{Bs} \wedge 1 \leq |\mathsf{Bs}| \leq 10))$$

To simplify our formulae, we shall also write quantifications of the form *Qtf Var $\in$ SetOp, Var = Term* simply as *Qtf Term $\in$ SetOp*. For instance, $\forall X \in$ Set, $X = f(a, Z)$ will be written as $\forall f(a, Z) \in$ Set.

2.1   The Semantics of $\mathcal{L}$

In this section we show how *Fml* is mapped to truth values $\top$ (true) or $\bot$ (false). For that, we first define the *interpretation* of our formulae:

Definition 6. *An interpretation $\Im$ for Fml is the pair $\Im = (\sigma, \Omega)$ where σ is a possibly empty set of ground atomic formulae (i.e. atfs without variables) and Ω is a set of sets.*

Intuitively our interpretations provide in σ what is required to determine the truth value of $Qtf(Atfs)$ and in Ω what is needed in order to assign a truth value to $Qtf(SetCtrs)$.

We did not include in our definition of interpretation above the notion of *universe of discourse* (also called *domain*) nor the usual mapping between constants and elements of this universe, neither did we include the mapping between function and predicate symbols of the formula and functions and relations in the universe of discourse [8,9]. This is because we are only interested in the relationships between *Atfs* and *SetCtrs* and how we can automatically obtain an interpretation for a given formula. However, we can define the union of all sets in Ω as our domain. It is worth mentioning that the use of a set of sets to represent Ω does not lead to undesirable paradoxes: since we do not allow the formulae in $\mathcal{L}$ to make references to Ω, but only to sets in Ω, this will not happen.

The semantic mapping $\mathbf{k} : Fml \times \Im \mapsto \{\top, \bot\}$ is:

1. $\mathbf{k}(\forall\, Terms \in SetOp\; Fml, \Im) = \top$ iff $\mathbf{k}(Fml|_e^{Terms}, \Im) = \top$ for all $e \in \mathbf{k}'(SetOp, \Im)$
   $\mathbf{k}(\exists\, Terms \in SetOp\; Fml, \Im) = \top$ iff $\mathbf{k}(Fml|_e^{Terms}, \Im) = \top$ for some $e \in \mathbf{k}'(SetOp, \Im)$
   $\mathbf{k}(\exists!\, Terms \in SetOp\; Fml, \Im) = \top$ iff $\mathbf{k}(Fml|_e^{Terms}, \Im) = \top$ for a single $e \in \mathbf{k}'(SetOp, \Im)$
2. $\mathbf{k}((Atfs \Rightarrow SetCtrs), \Im) = \bot$ iff $\mathbf{k}(Atfs, \Im) = \top$ and $\mathbf{k}(SetCtrs, \Im) = \bot$
3. $\mathbf{k}(Atfs_1 \wedge Atfs_2, \Im) = \top$ iff $\mathbf{k}(Atfs_1, \Im) = \mathbf{k}(Atfs_2, \Im) = \top$
   $\mathbf{k}(Atf, \Im) = \top$ iff $Atf \in \sigma, \Im = (\sigma, \Omega)$
4. $\mathbf{k}(SetCtrs_1 \wedge SetCtrs_2, \Im) = \top$ iff $\mathbf{k}(SetCtrs_1, \Im) = \mathbf{k}(SetCtrs_2, \Im) = \top$
5. $\mathbf{k}(Terms \in SetOp, \Im) = \top$ iff $Terms \in \mathbf{k}'(SetOp, \Im)$
   $\mathbf{k}(Terms \notin SetOp, \Im) = \top$ iff $Terms \notin \mathbf{k}'(SetOp, \Im)$
   $\mathbf{k}(|SetOp|\; Op\; \mathbb{N}, \Im) = \top$ iff $|\mathbf{k}'(SetOp, \Im)|\; Op\; \mathbb{N}$ holds
   $\mathbf{k}(|SetOp_1|\; Op\; |SetOp_2|, \Im) = \top$ iff $|\mathbf{k}'(SetOp_1, \Im)|\; Op\; |\mathbf{k}'(SetOp_2, \Im)|$ holds
   $\mathbf{k}(SetOp_1 = SetOp_2, \Im) = \top$ iff $\mathbf{k}'(SetOp_1, \Im) = \mathbf{k}'(SetOp_2, \Im)$
   $\mathbf{k}(SetOp_1 \neq SetOp_2, \Im) = \top$ iff $\mathbf{k}'(SetOp_1, \Im) \neq \mathbf{k}'(SetOp_2, \Im)$

In item 1 we address the three quantifiers over Fml formulae, where $Fml|_e^{Terms}$ is the result of replacing every occurrence of $Terms$ by e in Fml. Item 2 describes the usual meaning of the right implication. Item 3 formalises the meaning of conjunctions $Atfs$ and the basic case for individual atomic formulae – these are only considered true if they belong to the associated set σ of the interpretation $\Im$. Item 4 formalises the meaning of the conjunct and disjunct operations over set constraints $SetCtrs$ and the basic membership test to the result of a set operation $SetOp$. Item 5 describes the truth-value of the distinct set properties $SetProp$. These definitions describe only one case of the mapping: since ours is a total mapping, the situations which are not described represent a mapping with the remaining value $\top$ or $\bot$.

The auxiliary mapping $\mathbf{k}' : SetOp \times \Im \mapsto \mathsf{Set}$ in $\Omega, \Im = (\sigma, \Omega)$, referred to above and which gives meaning to the set operations is thus defined:

1. $\mathbf{k}'(SetOp_1 \cup SetOp_2, \Im) = \{e \mid e \in \mathbf{k}'(SetOp_1, \Im)$ or $e \in \mathbf{k}'(SetOp_2, \Im)\}$
2. $\mathbf{k}'(SetOp_1 \cap SetOp_2, \Im) = \{e \mid e \in \mathbf{k}'(SetOp_1, \Im)$ and $e \in \mathbf{k}'(SetOp_2, \Im)\}$
3. $\mathbf{k}'(SetOp_1 - SetOp_2, \Im) = \{e \mid e \in \mathbf{k}'(SetOp_1, \Im)$ and $e \notin \mathbf{k}'(SetOp_2, \Im)\}$
4. $\mathbf{k}'(SetOp_1 \times SetOp_2, \Im) = \{(e_1, e_2) \mid e_1 \in \mathbf{k}'(SetOp_1, \Im)$ and $e_2 \in \mathbf{k}'(SetOp_2, \Im)\}$
5. $\mathbf{k}'((SetOp), \Im) = (\mathbf{k}'(SetOp, \Im))$
6. $\mathbf{k}'(\mathsf{Set}, \Im) = \{e \mid e \in \mathsf{Set}$ in $\Omega, \Im = (\sigma, \Omega)\}$, $\mathbf{k}'(\emptyset, \Im) = \emptyset$

The 4 set operations are respectively given their usual definitions [7]. The meaning of a particular set Set is its actual contents, as given by Ω in $\Im$. Lastly, the meaning of an empty set $\emptyset$ in a set operation is, of course, the empty set.

The semantic mapping above captures the intended meaning for the $\mathcal{L}$ formulae: we assign values to those variables using elements from the quantified sets and obtain candidate atomic formulae for σ, then in possession of a σ we can build the set Ω. For instance, the formula

$$\exists X \in \mathsf{SetA} \cup \mathsf{SetB}\ [m(X) \Rightarrow (X \in \mathsf{SetC} \wedge |\mathsf{SetC}| = 2)]$$

intuitively means "there are some elements X of $\mathsf{SetA} \cup \mathsf{SetB}$ for which $m(X)$ holds and we can build a set SetC with these elements, provided there are exactly 2 of them." For the sake of this example, let us assume the partial interpretation

$$\Im = (\{m(a_1), m(a_3), m(b_2)\}, \{\mathsf{SetA} = \{a_1, a_2, a_3\}, \mathsf{SetB} = \{b_1, b_2\}, \mathsf{SetC}\})$$

and we can use the semantic mapping to obtain SetC. Formally, we have:

$\mathbf{k}(\exists X \in \mathsf{SetA} \cup \mathsf{SetB}\ [m(X) \Rightarrow (X \in \mathsf{SetC} \wedge |\mathsf{SetC}| = 2)], \Im) = \top$ iff
$\mathbf{k}([m(X) \Rightarrow (X \in \mathsf{SetC} \wedge |\mathsf{SetC}| = 2)]|_e^X, \Im) = \top$ for some $e \in \mathbf{k}'(\mathsf{SetA} \cup \mathsf{SetB}, \Im)$ iff
$\mathbf{k}([m(X) \Rightarrow (X \in \mathsf{SetC} \wedge |\mathsf{SetC}| = 2)]|_e^X, \Im) = \top$ for some $e \in \{a_1, a_2, a_3, b_1, b_2\}$ iff
$\mathbf{k}([m(X) \Rightarrow (X \in \mathsf{SetC} \wedge |\mathsf{SetC}| = 2)]|_e^X, \Im) = \top$ for $e = a_3$ and $e = b_2$ iff
$\mathbf{k}([m(X) \Rightarrow (X \in \mathsf{SetC} \wedge |\mathsf{SetC}| = 2)]|_{a_3}^X, \Im) = \top$ and
$\qquad \mathbf{k}([m(X) \Rightarrow (X \in \mathsf{SetC} \wedge |\mathsf{SetC}| = 2)]|_{b_2}^X, \Im) = \top$ iff
$\mathbf{k}([m(a_3) \Rightarrow (a_3 \in \mathsf{SetC} \wedge |\mathsf{SetC}| = 2)], \Im) = \top$ and
$\qquad \mathbf{k}([m(b_2) \Rightarrow (b_2 \in \mathsf{SetC} \wedge |\mathsf{SetC}| = 2)], \Im) = \top$ iff
$\mathbf{k}(m(a_3), \Im) = \mathbf{k}((a_3 \in \mathsf{SetC} \wedge |\mathsf{SetC}| = 2), \Im) = \top$ and
$\qquad \mathbf{k}(m(b_2), \Im) = \mathbf{k}((b_2 \in \mathsf{SetC} \wedge |\mathsf{SetC}| = 2), \Im) = \top$ iff
$m(a_3) \in \sigma, m(b_2) \in \sigma, \Im = (\sigma, \Omega)$, and
$\qquad \mathbf{k}(a_3 \in \mathsf{SetC}, \Im) = \mathbf{k}(b_2 \in \mathsf{SetC}, \Im) = \mathbf{k}(|\mathsf{SetC}| = 2), \Im) = \top$ iff
$a_3 \in \mathbf{k}'(\mathsf{SetC}, \Im)$ and $b_2 \in \mathbf{k}'(\mathsf{SetC}, \Im)$ and $|\mathbf{k}'(\mathsf{SetC}, \Im)| = 2$ iff
$\Im = (\{m(a_1), m(a_3), m(b_2)\}, \{\mathsf{SetA} = \{a_1, a_2, a_3\}, \mathsf{SetB} = \{b_1, b_2\}, \mathsf{SetC} = \{a_3, b_2\})$

We are interested in *models* for our formulae, that is, interpretations that map *Fml* to the truth value $\top$ (true). We are only interested in those interpretations in which *both* sides of the "$\Rightarrow$" in the *Fml*'s hold true. Formally:

Definition 7. *An interpretation $\Im = (\sigma, \Omega)$ is a model for a formula Fml = Qtf(Atfs $\Rightarrow$ SetCtrs), denoted by $\mathbf{m}(Fml, \Im)$ iff σ and Ω are the smallest possible sets such that $\mathbf{k}(Qtf\ Atfs, \Im) = \mathbf{k}(Qtf\ SetCtrs, \Im) = \top$.*

The scenarios arising when the left-hand side of the *Fml* is false do not interest us: we want this formalisation to restrict the meanings of our constructs only to those desirable correct ones. The study of the anomalies and implications caused by not respecting the restrictions of a protocol, albeit, important is not in the scope of this work.

We now define the extension of an interpretation, necessary to build models for more than one formula *Fml*:

Definition 8. *$\Im' = (\sigma', \Omega')$ is an extension of $\Im = (\sigma, \Omega)$ which accommodates Fml, denoted by $\mathbf{ext}(\Im, Fml) = \Im'$, iff $\mathbf{m}(Fml, \Im''), \Im'' = (\sigma'', \Omega'')$ and $\sigma' = \sigma \cup \sigma'', \Omega' = \Omega \cup \Omega''$.*

3 Logic-Based Electronic Institutions

In the same way that social institutions, such as a constitution of a country or the rules of a club, are somehow established (say, in print or by common knowledge), the laws that should govern the interactions among heterogeneous agents can be defined by means of electronic institutions (e-institutions, for short) [1,10,11,12]. E-institutions are non-deterministic finite-state machines describing possible interactions among agents. The interactions are only achieved by means of message exchanges, that is, messages that are sent and received by agents. E-institutions define communication protocols among agents with a view to achieving global and individual goals.

Although different formulations of e-institutions can be found in the literature [1,10,11,12,13], they all demand additional informal explanations concerning the precise meaning of constructs. In an e-institution the interactions among agents are described as finite-state machines with messages labelling the edges between two states. A simple example is graphically depicted in Figure 1 where two agents x and y engage in a simple two-step conversation – to save space, we have represented messages as atomic formulae of the form $m(Sender, Addressee, Conts)$, meaning that $Sender$ is sending to $Addressee$ message $Conts$; alternative formats such as FIPA-ACL [3] could be used instead. Agent x informs agent y that it wants to sell item k and y replies with an offer n. In the example above we employed variables x, y, k and n but it is not clear what their actual meaning is: is x the same in both edges? is it just *one* agent x or can many agents follow the transition? It is not clear from the notation only what the meaning of the label is. While it is true that informal explanations could solve any ambiguity, nevertheless by tacitly assuming the meaning of constructs (*i.e.*, "hardwiring" the meaning to the syntax), variations cannot be offered. For instance, if we assume that the variables in Figure 1 are universally quantified, then it is not possible to express the existential quantification and vice-versa. Similar loss in expressiveness occurs when other assumptions are made.

$$w_1 \xrightarrow{\ m(x, y, sell(k))\ } w_2 \xrightarrow{\ m(y, x, offer(k, n))\ } w_3$$

Fig. 1. Protocol as a Finite-State Machine

We have incorporated our proposed logic $\mathcal{L}$ to the definition of e-institutions. In this combination, constructs of $\mathcal{L}$ label edges of finite-state machines. This allows for precisely defined and expressive edges, thus extending the class of e-institutions one can represent. Furthermore, by embedding $\mathcal{L}$ within e-institutions, we can exploit the model-theoretic issues in an operational framework.

3.1 Scenes

Scenes are the basic components of an e-institution, describing interactions among agents:

Definition 9. *A scene is* $\mathbf{S} = \langle R, W, w_0, W_f, WA, WE, f^{Guard}, Edges, f^{Label} \rangle$ *where*

- $R = \{r_1, \ldots, r_n\}$ *is the set of roles;*
- $W = \{w_0, \ldots, w_m\}$ *is a finite, non-empty set of states;*
- $w_0 \in W$ *is the initial state;*
- $W_f \subseteq W$ *is the non-empty set of final states;*
- *WA is a set of sets* $WA = \{WA_r \subseteq W \mid r \in R\}$ *where each* WA_r, $r \in R$, *is the set of access states for role r;*
- *WE is a set of sets* $WE = \{WE_r \subseteq W \mid r \in R\}$ *where each* WE_r, $r \in R$, *is the set of exit states for role r;*
- $f^{Guard} : WA_r \mapsto Fml$ *and* $f^{Guard} : WE_r \mapsto Fml$ *associates with each access state* WA_r *and exit state* WE_r *of role r a formula Fml.*
- $Edges \subseteq W \times W$ *is a set of directed edges;*
- $f^{Label} : Edges \mapsto Fml$ *associates each element of Edges with a formula Fml.*

This definition is a variation of that found in [13]. We have added to access and exit states, via function f^{Guard}, explicit restrictions expressed as formulae of $\mathcal{L}$. The labelling function f^{Label} is defined similarly, but mapping *Edges* to our formulae *Fml*.

3.2   Transitions

The scenes, as formalised above, are where communication among agents actually takes place. However, individual scenes can be part of a more complex context in which specific sequences of scenes have to be followed. For example, in some kinds of electronic markets, a scene where agents meet other agents to choose their partners to trade is followed by a scene where the negotiations actually take place. We define *transitions* as a means to connect and relate scenes:

Definition 10. *A transition is* $\mathbf{T} = \langle CI, w_a, Fml, w_e, CO \rangle$ *where*

- $CI \subseteq \bigcup_{i=1}^{n}(WE_i \times w_a)$, *is the set of connections into the transition,* $WE_i, 1 \le i \le n$ *being the sets of exit states for all roles from all scenes;*
- w_a *is the access state of the transition;*
- w_e *is the exit state of the transition;*
- *Fml, a formula of* $\mathcal{L}$, *labels the pair* $(w_a, w_e) \mapsto Fml$;
- $CO \subseteq \bigcup_{j=1}^{m}(w_e \times WA_j)$, *is the set of connections out of the transition,* $WA_j, 1 \le j \le m$ *being the sets of access states for all roles onto all scenes.*

A transition has only two states w_a, its access state, and w_e, its exit state, and a set of connections CI relating the exit states of scenes to w_a and a set of connections CO relating w_e to the access states of scenes. The conditions under which agents are allowed to move from w_a to w_e are specified by a formula Fml of our set-based logic, introduced above.

Transitions can be seen as simplified scenes where agents' movements can be grouped together and synchronised out of a scene and into another one. The roles of agents may change, as they go through a transition. An important feature of transitions lies in the kinds of formula Fml we are allowed to use. Unlike scenes, where there can only be references to constructs within the scene, within a transition we can make references to constructs of any scene that connects to the transition. This difference is formally represented by the semantics of e-institutions below.

3.3 $\mathcal{L}$-Based E-Institutions

Our e-institutions are collections of scenes and transitions:

Definition 11. *An e-institution is* $\mathbf{E} = \langle Scenes, \mathbf{S}_0, \mathbf{S}_f, Trans \rangle$ *where*
- *Scenes* $= \{\mathbf{S}_0, \dots, \mathbf{S}_n\}$ *is a finite and non-empty set of scenes;*
- $\mathbf{S}_0 \in Scenes$ *is the root scene;*
- $\mathbf{S}_f \in Scenes$ *is the output scene;*
- *Trans* $= \{\mathbf{T}_0, \dots, \mathbf{T}_m\}$ *is a finite and non-empty set of transitions;*

We shall impose the restriction that the transitions of an e-institution can only connect scenes from the set *Scenes*, that is, for all $\mathbf{T} \in Trans$, $CI \subseteq \bigcup_{i=0}^{n}(WE_i \times w_a), i \neq f$ (the exit states of the output scene can not be connected to a transition), and $CO \subseteq \bigcup_{j=1}^{n}(w_e \times WA_j)$ (the access state of the root scene cannot be connected to a transition).

For the sake of simplicity, we have not included in our definition above the *normative rules* [10] which capture the obligations to which agents become bound as they exchange messages. We are aware that this makes our definition above closer to the notion of *performative structure* [10] rather than an e-institution.

3.4 Models for $\mathcal{L}$-Based E-Institutions

In this section we introduce models for scenes, transitions and e-institutions using the definitions above.

A model for a scene is built using the formulae that label edges connecting the initial state to a final state. The formulae guarding access and exit states are also taken into account: they are used to extend the model of the previous formulae and this extension is further employed with the formula labelling the edge to the next state. Since there might be more than one final state and more than one possible way of going from the initial state to a final state, models for scenes are not unique. More formally:

Definition 12. *An interpretation* $\Im$ *is a model for a scene* $\mathbf{S} = \langle R, W, w_0, W_f, WA, WE, f^{Guard}, Edges, f^{Label} \rangle$, *given an initial interpretation* $\Im_0$, *denoted by* $\mathbf{m}(\mathbf{S}, \Im)$, *iff* $\Im = \Im_n$, *where:*
- $f^{Label}(w_{i-1}, w_i) = Fml_i, 1 \leq i \leq n, w_n \in W_f$, *are the formulae labelling edges which connect the initial state* w_0 *to a final state* w_n.
- *for* $w_i \in WA_r$ *or* $w_i \in WE_r$ *for some role* r, *that is,* w_i *is an access or exit state, then* $f^{Guard}(w_i) = Fml_{[WA,i]}$ *or* $f^{Guard}(w_i) = Fml_{[WE,i]}$, *respectively.*
- *for* $1 \leq i \leq n$, *then* $\Im_i = \begin{cases} \mathbf{ext}(\mathbf{ext}(\Im_{i-1}, Fml_{[WA,i]}), Fml_i), & \text{if } w_i \in WA_r \\ \mathbf{ext}(\mathbf{ext}(\Im_{i-1}, Fml_{[WE,i]}), Fml_i), & \text{if } w_i \in WE_r \\ \mathbf{ext}(\Im_{i-1}, Fml_i), & \text{otherwise} \end{cases}$

One should notice that the existential quantification allows for the *choice* of components for the sets in Ω and hence more potential for different models. In order to obtain a model for a scene, an initial model $\Im_0$, possibly empty, should be provided.

The model of a transition extends the models of scenes connecting to it:

Definition 13. *An interpretation $\Im$ is a model for a transition* $\mathbf{T} = \langle CI, w_a, Fml, w_e, CO \rangle$, *denoted by* $\mathbf{m}(\mathbf{T}, \Im)$, *iff*

- $\mathbf{S}_1, \ldots, \mathbf{S}_n$ *are all the scenes that connect with CI, i.e. the set WE_i of exit states of each scene $\mathbf{S}_i, 1 \leq i \leq n$, has at least one element $WE_{i,r} \times w_a$ in CI, and*
- $\mathbf{m}(\mathbf{S}_i, \Im_i), \Im_i = (\sigma_i, \Omega_i), \Im' = (\bigcup_{i=1}^n \sigma_i, \bigcup_{i=1}^n \Omega_i), 1 \leq i \leq n$, *and* $\mathbf{ext}(\Im', Fml) = \Im$

The model of a transition is an extension of the union of the models of all its connecting scenes to accommodate *Fml*. Finally, we define the meaning of e-institutions:

Definition 14. *An interpretation $\Im$ is a model for an e-institution* $\mathbf{E} = \langle Scenes, \mathbf{S}_0, \mathbf{S}_f, Trans \rangle$, *denoted by* $\mathbf{m}(\mathbf{E}, \Im)$, *iff*

- *Scenes* $= \{\mathbf{S}_0, \ldots, \mathbf{S}_n\}, \mathbf{m}(\mathbf{S}_i, \Im), 0 \leq i \leq n$; *and*
- *Trans* $= \{\mathbf{T}_0, \ldots, \mathbf{T}_m\}, \mathbf{m}(\mathbf{T}_j, \Im), 0 \leq j \leq m$.

3.5   Building Models for $\mathcal{L}$-Based E-Institutions

We can build a model $\Im$ for a formula *Fml* if we are given an initial value for the sets in Ω. We need only those sets that are referred to in the quantification of *Fml*: with this information we can define the atomic formulae that make the left-hand side of "$\Rightarrow$" true. If the conditions on the left-hand side of *Fml* are fulfilled then we proceed to *make* the conditions on the right-hand side true, by means of the appropriate creation of other sets.

Building a model $\Im$ is a computationally expensive task, involving combinatorial efforts to find the atomic formulae that ought to be in σ and the contents of the sets in Ω. An exhaustive approach consists of replacing variables that appear in the *Atfs* (left-hand side) with values from the quantified sets. This replacement should assign values to variables following their quantification. When all variables of the *Atfs* have values, then its atomic formulae are stored in σ. The universal quantifications require an exhaustive generation of atomic formulae with every possible value from the quantified sets. Since quantifications can be nested, finding all values of atomic formulae may involve a combinatorial effort.

After a σ is assembled, then we can build sets that satisfy the *SetCtrs*. If the sets that appear in *SetCtrs* are different from the ones that are quantified in

$Atfs^1$, then we attempt to build the sets in Ω with the existing σ. If this fails, we have to try another σ by changing the values given to variables in the atomic formulae. Because our sets are finite, there is only a finite number of values that can be given to the variables in the atomic formulae, and eventually we will run out of possible ways to build σ. The number of possible values for σ is, however, an exponential function on the number of elements in the quantified sets.

If, however, the formulae Fml of a scene have a simple property, $viz.$ the quantification of each formula Fml_i only refers to sets that appear on preceding formulae $Fml_j, j < i$, then we can build an interpretation gradually, taking into account each formula at a time. This property can be syntactically checked: we can ensure that all sets in the quantification of Fml_i appear on the right-hand side of a Fml_j which leads on to Fml_i in a scene. Only if all scenes and transitions of an e-institution fulfill this property is that we can automatically build a model for it in feasible time.

If this property holds in our e-institutions, then we can build for any formula Fml_i a model $\Im_i$ that uses the $\Im_{i-1}$ of the preceding formula (assuming an ordering among the edges of a path). The models of a scene are then built gradually, each formula at a time, via $\mathbf{ext}(\Im_{i-1}, Fml_i) = \Im_i$. The quantifiers in Fml assign values to variables in its body, following the semantic mapping $\mathbf{k}$ shown previously. The existential quantifiers $\exists$ and $\exists!$ introduce non-determinism: in the case of $\exists$ a subset of the elements of the quantified set has to be chosen; in the case of $\exists!$ a single element has to be chosen. Additional constraints on the choice to be made can be expressed as part of Fml.

Given an initial interpretation $\Im = (\emptyset, \Omega)$ in which Ω is possibly empty or may contain any initial values of sets, we can start building the models of the ensuing formulae. Given $\Im_{i-1}$ and Fml_i we can automatically compute the value $\mathbf{ext}(\Im_{i-1}, Fml_i) = \Im_i$. Since the quantifiers of Fml_i only refer to sets of the right-hand side of preceding Fml_j, then $\Im_{i-1}$ should have the actual contents of these sets. We exhaustively generate values for the quantified variables – this is only possible because all the sets are finite – and hence we can assemble the atomic formulae for a possible σ_i of $\Im_i$. With this σ and Ω_{i-1} we then assemble Ω_i, an extension of Ω_{i-1} which satisfies the set constraints of Fml_i.

This restriction on our $\mathcal{L}$-based e-institutions should not render our protocols trivial. We argue that if it is indeed necessary to make references to future points in a protocol then with some engineering it should be possible to $move$ the reference to the point in the future being referred to and to convert the reference to the event in the past. For instance, if we have the interaction "the

---

[1] Some formulae in which a set appears both in the quantification and in the *SetCtrs* have *infinite models*. For instance, $\forall X \in$ Set $p(X) \Rightarrow s(X) \in$ Set (assuming the left-hand side must be true, as we do in $\mathcal{L}$) can only be true if σ is infinite – any initial value for Set has to be expanded with $s(X)$ which always appear nested within $s(\ldots)$. To illustrate this, if we start with Set $= \{a\}$, then we have to augment it to accommodate $s(a)$, but $p(s(a))$ is also true, hence $s(s(a))$ should also be in Set and so on. This feature, however, is not exclusive to our logic $\mathcal{L}$ – the simple first-order logic formula $\forall x [(p(x) \lor \neg p(x)) \Rightarrow p(x + 1)]$ also requires an infinite set of numbers for its models.

seller agent advertises a number of goods – there should be one for each buyer that will send a message showing its intention to buy", then we could convert it to "the seller agent advertises a number of goods" and move the constraint to the point of the protocol when the buyer agents send a message showing their intention to buy – only as many buyer agents are allowed to send this message as there are advertised goods.

Clearly there are scenarios for which this re-engineering is not possible. For instance, an interaction such as "the seller agent sends a message to the buyer agents who will send a message showing their intention to buy" may pose serious difficulties. On the other hand, we doubt whether such description of an interaction is of any practical use as the participants will need the ability to "see the future" before it happens. More importantly, a protocol may progress considerably before it is noticed that it has been subverted.

3.6   Example: A Simple Agoric Market

We illustrate the definitions above with an example comprising a complete virtual agoric marketplace. We provide in Figure 2 a graphic rendition of an e-institution for our market – the same e-institution is, of course, amenable to different visual renditions. Scenes are represented as boxes with rounded edges; the root scene **Admission** has a thicker box and the output scene **Departure** has a double box. Transitions are represented as triangles. The arcs in our diagram connect exit states of a scene with the access state of a transition and the exit state of a transition with an access state of a scene. Agents have to be initially admitted in the e-institution (**Admission** scene) where their details are recorded; agents then may proceed to trade their goods in the **Agora Room** scene, after which they may (if they have bought or sold goods) have to settle any debts in the **Settlement** scene. Finally, agents leave the institution, via the **Departure** scene.

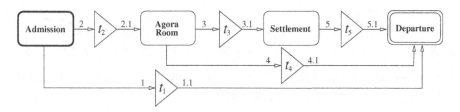

Fig. 2. E-Institution for Simple Agoric Market

We now focus on a specific scene in the e-institution above. In Figure 3 we "zoom in" on the **Agora Room** scene, in which agents willing to acquire goods interact with agents intending to sell such goods. This agora scene has been simplified – no auctions or negotiations are contemplated. The sellers announce the goods they want to sell and collect the replies from buyers (all buyers must reply). The simplicity of this scene is deliberate, so as to allow us to fully repre-

Fig. 3. Diagram for **Agora Room** Scene

sent and discuss it. A more friendly visual rendition of the formal definition is employed in the figure and is explained below.

The states $W = \{w_0, w_1, w_2\}$ are displayed in circles and $Edges = \{(w_0, w_1),$ $(w_1, w_2)\}$ are shown as arrows: if $(w_i, w_j) \in Edges$, then $w_i \longrightarrow w_j$. The initial state w_0 is shown enclosed in a thicker circle; the final state $W_f = \{w_2\}$ is enclosed in a double circle. We define the set of roles as $R = \{seller, buyer\}$. An access state $w \in WA$ is marked with a "▶" pointing towards the state with a box containing the role(s) of the agents that may enter the scene at that point and a set name. Exit states are also marked with a "▶" but pointing away from the state; they are also shown with a box containing the roles of the agents that may leave the scene at that point and a set name. We have defined the formulae $Fml_i, 0 \leq i \leq 3$, as:

$$Fml_0 : \exists B, S \in \mathsf{Ags} \left(\binom{m(B, adm, enter(buyer)) \wedge}{m(S, adm, enter(seller))} \Rightarrow \binom{B \in \mathsf{Bs} \wedge 1 \leq |\mathsf{Bs}| \leq 10 \wedge}{S \in \mathsf{Ss} \wedge 1 \leq |\mathsf{Ss}| \leq 10} \right)$$

$$Fml_1 : \forall S \in \mathsf{Ss}\, \forall B \in \mathsf{Bs}\, \exists I \in \mathsf{Is}\, (m(S, B, offer(I, P)) \Rightarrow \langle S, B, I, P\rangle \in \mathsf{Ofs})$$

$$Fml_2 : \forall \langle S, B, I, P\rangle \in \mathsf{Ofs}\, \exists! A \in \mathsf{As}(m(B, S, reply(I, P, A)) \Rightarrow \langle S, B, I, P, A\rangle \in \mathsf{Rs})$$

$$Fml_3 : \forall B \in \mathsf{Bs}\, \forall S \in \mathsf{Ss} \left(\binom{m(B, adm, leave) \wedge}{m(S, adm, leave)} \Rightarrow \binom{B \in \mathsf{OutBs} \wedge S \in \mathsf{OutSs} \wedge}{\mathsf{OutBs} = \mathsf{Bs} \wedge \mathsf{OutSs} = \mathsf{Ss}} \right)$$

The left-hand side of the Fml_i are atomic formulae which must hold in σ_i and the right-hand side are set constraints that must hold in Ω_i. The atomic formula stand for messages exchanged among the agents as they move along the edges of the scene. The above definitions give rise to the following semantics:

$$\mathbf{ext}\!\left(\left(\emptyset, \begin{Bmatrix} \mathsf{Ags,} \\ \mathsf{As,} \\ \mathsf{Is} \end{Bmatrix} \right), Fml_0 \right) = \Im_0 = \left(\begin{Bmatrix} m(ag_1, adm, enter(seller)), \\ m(ag_2, adm, enter(buyer)), \\ m(ag_3, adm, enter(buyer)) \end{Bmatrix}, \begin{Bmatrix} \mathsf{Ags, As,} \\ \mathsf{Is, Bs,} \\ \mathsf{Ss} \end{Bmatrix} \right)$$

Let us assume that $\mathsf{Ags} = \{ag_1, \ldots, ag_4\}$, $\mathsf{As} = \{ok, not\_ok\}$ and $\mathsf{Is} = \{car, boat, plane\}$, and we obtain $\mathsf{Bs} = \{ag_2, ag_3\}$ and $\mathsf{Ss} = \{ag_1\}$;

$$\mathbf{ext}(\Im_0, Fml_1) = \Im_1 = \left(\sigma_0 \cup \begin{Bmatrix} m(ag_1, ag_2, offer(car, 4)), \\ m(ag_1, ag_3, offer(boat, 3)) \end{Bmatrix}, \begin{Bmatrix} \mathsf{Ags, As, Is,} \\ \mathsf{Bs, Ss, Ofs} \end{Bmatrix} \right)$$

where $\mathsf{Ofs} = \{\langle ag_1, ag_2, car, 4\rangle, \langle ag_1, ag_3, boat, 3\rangle\}$;

$$\mathbf{ext}(\Im_1, Fml_2) = \Im_2 = \left(\sigma_1 \cup \begin{Bmatrix} m(ag_2, ag_1, reply(car, 4, ok)), \\ m(ag_3, ag_1, reply(boat, 3, not\_ok)) \end{Bmatrix}, \begin{Bmatrix} \mathsf{Ags, As, Is,} \\ \mathsf{Bs, Ss, Ofs,} \\ \mathsf{Rs} \end{Bmatrix} \right)$$

where $\mathsf{Rs} = \{\langle ag_2, ag_1, car, 4, ok\rangle, \langle ag_3, ag_1, boat, 3, not\_ok\rangle\}$;

$$\mathbf{ext}(\mathfrak{S}_2, Fml_3) = \mathfrak{S}_3 = \left(\sigma_3 \cup \left\{\begin{array}{l} m(ag_1, adm, leave), \\ m(ag_2, adm, leave), \\ m(ag_3, adm, leave) \end{array}\right\}, \left\{\begin{array}{l} \mathsf{Ags, As, Is, Bs, Ss, Ofs,} \\ \mathsf{Rs, OutBs, OutSs} \end{array}\right\}\right)$$

where $\mathsf{OutBs} = \{ag_2, ag_3\}$ and $\mathsf{OutSs} = \{ag_1\}$.

Intuitively, the σ_i provide "snapshots" of those messages that were sent up to a particular state: the record of the messages sent characterises the state of the scene. Each state is associated with a σ_i and Ω_i. We explicitly list the messages that should be sent at each state of the scene, indicating that the complete set σ_i is an extension of σ_{i-1}. The contents of the sets in Ω_i shown above represent information relevant for defining future steps in the global protocol. This information is gathered as the protocol is followed and it defines the subsequent steps.

The semantics of transitions is defined similarly. However, the sets over which the formulae Fml in $\mathbf{T}_i$ are quantified are built by merging the sets of all those scenes that are connected to the transition, as stated in definition 13 above.

3.7   Design Rationale of $\mathcal{L}$

The class of protocols we aim at require the unambiguous reference to details of previous interactions so as to determine the ensuing message exchanges among the participating agents. In the example above, the model is gradually built taking any such restrictions into account: the quantification of the formulae labelling each edge ensures that restrictions be taken into account. For instance, Fml_2 restricts the interaction and only permits that buyer agents send messages; these messages must be a reply to their respective offers. This is only possible because the semantics of $\mathcal{L}$ allows the reference to sets built – they store any relevant information as edges are followed. This information is then employed via the quantifiers to restrict ensuing steps of the protocol. We are thus able to capture dynamic aspects of the protocol in a generic and abstract fashion.

The atomic formulae depict messages that are sent and, assuming there is no loss of messages, received. Negation is not part of our syntax because our targeted protocols are the sequence of messages that are sent at each point: if there is a need to refer to a message that was not sent (and that should have been sent) then we simply represent the alternative messages sent instead. The set constraints appearing on the right-hand side of our $\mathcal{L}$ formulae all have negated forms (or offer complementary operations such as $>$ and $\le$) hence making negation superfluous.

The logic $\mathcal{L}$, a restricted form of first-order logic, has been engineered for our purposes of labelling connections of a finite-state machine. The set quantifications are just a notational variant of first-order quantification. It is easy to see that, for any arbitrary formula α, if $\forall X \in \mathsf{Set}. \alpha$ holds, then $\forall X.X \in \mathsf{Set} \wedge \alpha$ also holds. The same is true for the other quantifiers $\exists$ and $\exists!$. The set constraints are just first-order predicates whose intended meanings have been "hardwired" to the underlying semantics.

There are connections between $\mathcal{L}$ and many-sorted logics [8]. The sets employed in our quantifications can be viewed as explicit sorts. However, the set

```
roles(market,agora,[buyer,seller]).
states(market,agora,[w0,w1,w2,w3]).
initial_state(market,agora,w0).
final_states(market,agora,[w3]).
access_states(market,agora,[buyer:[w0],seller:[w0,w2]]).
exit_states(market,agora,[buyer:[w3],seller:[w1,w3]]).
edges(market,agora,[(w0,w1),(w1,w2),(w2,w3)])
guard(market,agora,w0,[exists(B,agents),exists(S,agents)],
      [m(B,adm,enter(buyer)),m(S,adm,enter(seller))],
      [in(B,buyers),1 =< card(buyers) =< 10,
      in(S,sellers),1 =< card(buyers) =< 10]).
label(market,agora,w0,w1,
      [forall(S,sellers),forall(B,buyers),exists(I,items)],
      [m(S:seller,B:buyer,offer(I))],
      [in([S,B,I],offers)]).
      ⋮
```

Fig. 4. Representation of **Agora Room** Scene

constraints do not have a counterpart in many-sorted logics since sets are not part of the allowed syntax. Set-based logics are not more powerful than standard first-order logic [8]. However, we have decided to employ a set-based logic to provide for a more disciplined design with a cleaner representation. Clearly, all the sets of an $\mathcal{L}$ formula can be put together as one single set (*i.e.* the union of all sets) but if we needed to differentiate among elements (say, agents that are of different roles) then we should provide extra means. Another advantage of set-based logics stems from the potential reduction in the search space for a model: if our universe of discourse is organised in sets, our search procedure can concentrate only on the sets concerned with the formulae, thus avoiding having to unnecessarily examine large numbers of spurious elements.

3.8   Representing and Checking $\mathcal{L}$-Based E-Institutions

$\mathcal{L}$-based e-institutions can be readily represented in many different ways. We show in Figure 4 a Prolog [14] representation for the **Agora Room** scene graphically depicted in Figure 3 above. Each component of the formal definition has its corresponding representation. Since many e-institutions and scenes may co-exist, the components are parameterised by the e-institution and scene names (first and second parameters, respectively). The f^{Guard} component is represented as a guard/6 term; to save space, we only show the first of them. Component f^{Label} is represented as label/7 – we only show the first of them to save space. Both guard/6 and label/7 incorporate the same representation for $\mathcal{L}$ formulae, in their last three arguments: a list for the quantifications *Qtf*, a list for the conjunction *Atfs* and a list for the set constraints *SetCtrs*. The actual coding of the logical constructs into a Prolog format is done in a simple fashion: "$\forall x \in$ Set" is coded as forall(X,set), "$\exists x \in$ Set" is encoded as exists(X,set), "$x \in$ Set" (set operation) is encoded as in(X,set) and so on.

The terms standing for the messages sent in the `labels` of our representation have been augmented with information on the *role* of the agents which sent them (and the roles of the agents the messages are aimed at). In our example above, the roles `seller` and `buyer` were added, respectively, to the first and second arguments of the message, that is, `m(S:seller,B:buyer,offer(I))`. We use this information when we automatically synthesise agents to enact our e-institutions, as explained in [13,15]. This information can be inferred from the scene specification, by propagating the roles adopted by the agents which entered the scene in access states. We have adopted the standard messages `enter(`*Role*`)` and `leave` in our scenes to convey, respectively, that the agent wants to enter the scene and incorporate *Role* and that the agent wants to leave the scene.

The representation above renders itself to straightforward automatic checks for well-formedness. For instance, we can check whether all `label/7` terms are indeed defined with elements of `states/3`, whether all `label/6` are defined either for `access_states/3` or `exit_states/3`, if all `access_states/3` and `exit_states/3` have their `guard/6` definition, whether all pairs in `edges/3` have a corresponding `label/7`, and so on. However, the representation is also useful for checking important graph-related properties using standard algorithms [16]. It is useful to check, for instance, if from the state specified in `initial_state/3` we can reach all other `states/3`, whether there are `states/3` from which it is not possible to reach an `exit_state` (absence of *sinks*), and so on.

The use of logics for labels in our e-institutions also allows us to explore logic-theoretic issues. Given a scene, we might want to know if the protocol it describes is feasible, that is, if it is possible for a number of agents to successfully enact it. This question amounts to finding out whether there is at least one path connecting the initial (access) state to a final (exit) state, such that the conjunction of the formulae labelling its edges is satisfiable, that is, the conjunction has at least one model. Since the quantified sets in our formulae are finite then the satisfiability test for conjunctions of $\mathcal{L}$ formulae has the same complexity of propositional logic: each atomic formula with variables can be seen as a conjunction of atomic formulae in which the variables are replaced with the actual values over which they are quantified; atomic formulae without variables amount to propositions (because they can be directly mapped to $\top$ or $\bot$). There are algorithms to carry out the satisfiability test for propositional logic which will always terminate [8,9]. Model-checking techniques (*e.g.*, [17] and [18]) come in handy here, helping engineers to cope with the exponential complexity of this problem.

Transitions are represented in a similar fashion. We show in Figure 5 how we represented transition $\mathbf{T}_1$ of our agoric market e-institution of Figure 2. Transition $\mathbf{T}_1$ guarantees that only those agents that successfully registered in the **Admission** scene (their identification being included in `registered_clients`) and that showed their interest in joining the **Agora Room** scene (by sending the message `m(C,adm,move(agora))`) will be able to move through it. We employed the same `label/7` construct as in the scene representation, but here it stores the *Fml* labelling the edge connecting `w0` and `w1` in the transition.

```
access_state(market,t1,w0).
exit_state(market,t1,w1).
connections_into(market,t1,[(admission,client:[w2])]).
connections_outof(market,t1,[(agora,buyer:[w0]),(agora,seller:[w0])]).
label(market,t1,w0,w1,[exists(C,registered_clients)],
                      [m(C,adm,move(agora))],
                      [in(C,agora_agents)]).
```

Fig. 5. Representation of Transition T_1

The above representation for transitions is also useful for performing automatic checks. We can automatically verify, for instance, that the scenes, states and roles referred to in connections_into/3 and connections_outof/3 are properly defined. A desirable property in transitions is that the connecting scenes have at least one model – this property, as explained above, can be automatically checked. E-institutions are collections of scenes and transitions in the format above, plus the extra components of the tuple comprising its formal definition.

3.9   Enacting $\mathcal{L}$-Based E-Institutions

We have incorporated the concepts above into a distributed platform for enacting our protocols. This platform, implemented in SICStus Prolog [19], uses the semantics of our constructs to perform a simulation of an e-institution. The platform relies on a number of administrative agents, implemented as independent processes, to overlook the enactment, building models and interacting with the agents partaking the enactment via a blackboard architecture, using SICStus Linda tuple space [20,19].

An enactment of an e-institution begins with the enactment of the root scene and terminates when all agents leave the output scene. Engineers may specify whether a scene can have many instances enacted simultaneously, depending on the number and order of agents willing to enter it. We did not include this feature in our formal presentation because in logic-theoretic terms instances of a scene can be safely seen as different scenes: they are enacted independently from each other, although they all conform to the same specification. The atomic formulae of the σ's specify the format of exchanged messages. The quantifiers assign values to any variables the messages may have. The set constraints are used to build sets with these messages and also to impose further restrictions that ought to be satisfied.

The platform starts up for each scene an administrative agent *admScene*. An initial model is available for all scenes, $\Im = (\emptyset, \Omega)$ where Ω (possibly empty) contains the values of any sets that need to be initially defined. Some of such sets are, for instance, the identity of those agents that may join the e-institution, the possible values for items and their prices, and so on. Agent *admScene* follows the edges of a scene, starting from w_0 and, using $\Im$, creates the set σ_0 of atomic formulae. Set σ_0 is assembled by evaluating the quantification of $\mathcal{L}_0$ over Ω sets.

Our platform takes into account the agents that will take part in it the e-institution. These are called the *performing agents* and are automatically synthesised from the description of the e-institution, as described in [13]. A performing agent sends a message by checking if the corresponding σ set contains the message it wants to send; if the message is available then the agent "sends" it by marking it as sent. This mark is for the benefit of the *admScene* agent: the *admScene* agent creates templates for *all* messages that can be sent, but not all of them may in fact be sent. The messages that have been marked as sent are those that were actually sent by the performing agents.

Similarly, a performing agent receives a message by marking it as received. However, it can only receive a message that has been previously marked as sent by another agent. Both the sending and receiving agents use the format of the messages to ensure they conform to the format specified in the edge they are following. To ensure that an agent does not try to receive a message that has not yet been marked sent but that may still be sent by some agent, the *admScene* agent synchronises the agents in the scene: it first lets the sending agents change state by moving along the corresponding edge, marking their messages as sent. When all sending agents have moved, then the *admScene* agent lets the receiving agents receive their messages and move to the following state of the scene.

The synchronisation among the agents of a scene is achieved via a simple semaphore represented as a term in the tuple space. The performing agents trying to send a message must wait until this semaphore has a specific value. Likewise, the agents that will receive messages are locked until the semaphore allows them to move. The performing agents inform the *admScene* agent, via the tuple space, about the state of the scene they are currently at. With this information the *admScene* agent is able to "herd" agents from one state to another, as it creates messages templates, lets the sending agents mark them as sent and then lets the receiving agents mark them as received (also retrieving their contents). Those agents that do not send or receive can move between states without having to wait for the semaphore. All agents, though, synchronise at every state of the scene, that is, there is a moment in the enactment when all agents are at state w_i, then after sending and receiving (or just moving) they are all at state w_{i+1}.

Transitions are enacted in a similar fashion. The platform assigns an agent *admTrans* to look after each transition. Transitions, however, differ from scenes in two ways. Firstly, we do not allow instances of transitions. This is strictly a methodological restriction, rather than a technical one: we want transitions to work as "meeting points" for agents moving between scenes and instances of transitions could prevent this. Secondly, transitions are *permanent*, that is, their enactment never comes to an end. Scenes (or their instances), once enacted (*i.e.* all the agents have left it at an exit state), cease to exist, that is, the *admScene* agent looking after it stops.

When a scene comes to an end, the *admScene* agent records in the tuple space the model it built as a result of the scene's enactment. The atomic formulae are only important during the enactment since they actively define the interpretations being built. However, only the sets in the Ω part of the interpretation are left as a record of the enactment. This is useful for following the dynamics of the e-institution, and it is also essential for the transitions. The *admTrans* agents looking after transitions use the sets left behind by the *admScene* agents to build their models.

A model is explicitly represented and is used to guide the distributed enactment of a $\mathcal{L}$-based e-institution. The model representation is shared by all administrative agents which use it instead of building its own (sub-)model. Variations of an enactment can additionally be explored by using *partially defined* models, in which variables are allowed as part of the atfs in σ_i. For instance, σ_1 of our previous agora room scene example, could be defined as $\sigma_1 = \{m(Ag_1, Ag_2, \text{offer}(I_1, P_1)), m(Ag_3, Ag_4, \text{offer}(I_2, P_2))\} \cup \sigma_0$ that is, the actual values of the agents' identification and items/price are not relevant, but there should be *exactly* two such messages. Restrictions can be imposed or relaxed by adequately using variables or specific values.

4   Related Work

Combining the expressiveness of logics with the operational model of finite state machines is not entirely new. In the late 70's, *communicating finite-state machines* [21] were introduced to specify low-level one-to-one protocols. In this proposal statements about messages being sent or received labelled the edges of machines. This formalism has been modified (e.g., [22] and [23]) to accommodate different message-passing primitives or to define classes of protocols with desirable properties. Communicating finite-state machines can only represent one-to-one interactions and the meaning of references to values of previous (or future) interactions is not part of the original proposal.

We find in [24] a more similar approach whereby full first-order logic is used to label the edges of finite-state machines. This approach, however, only addresses one-to-one interactions, although different protocols can be interleaved. It is not clear, though what the scope of the variables is and this impacts on the expressiveness of the formalism. More recently, our approach has connections with the work described in [25]: a set of first-order formulae represents a finite state machine annotated with illocutions. The formulae capture the ordering of the states of the machine and prescribe the sequence of moves each participant of the protocol may make. Quantification is implicit and the protocols are aimed at only 2 participants.

Another related work is [26] where protocols are represented as *social integrity constraints*. These are a restricted class of first-order logics of the form $\chi \rightarrow \phi$ which contain in χ a conjunction of atomic formulae and in ϕ a disjunction of conjunctions. Quantification is implicitly defined as universal or existential depending on where variables appear in different parts of a formula. Special social integrity constraints which refer to events in the past (backward expectations) give rise to interaction protocols. In this proposal, it is possible to temporally order formulae: by using an extra argument which refers to the point of time in which a formula holds true and adding constraints relating such arguments of different formulae, then a temporal ordering is established.

Work on electronic institutions [1,10,11,12,13] rely on additional informal explanations to describe the semantics of constructs. The meaning of the annotations on edges, that is, the messages sent/received, is particularly difficult to capture, depending on the notation employed. When variables are used in the annotation of edges, there is the inevitable problem of quantification and its scope. An interesting convergence between our work and [27] is the automatic creation of agents that can enact a protocol. Such agents are named *governors* in [27] and are offered to external entities wanting to take part in the electronic institution, guaranteeing that the protocol is followed and norms and obligations fulfilled. An altogether different approach is taken in [27] whereby e-institutions are formalised via process algebras.

5   Conclusions and Future Work

In this paper we present a formalism to represent global protocols, that is, all possible interactions among components of a multi-agent system, from a global perspective. The proposed formalism is $\mathcal{L}$, a set-based restricted kind of first-order logic that allows engineers to describe a protocol and to forge relationships among messages of one-to-one, one-to-many and many-to-many interactions. This paper lays out the theoretical foundations of the work depicted in [28,13,15] and provides an original complete formalisation of electronic-institutions.

We have put our formalism to work by embedding it within the definition of electronic institutions [10], giving rise to $\mathcal{L}$-based electronic institutions. Existing formulations of electronic institutions, *e.g.* [10,1,12,13], resort to informal explanations when defining the meaning of their constructs. Our rendition, on the other hand, has its syntax and semantics formally defined using $\mathcal{L}$. We have also presented an implementation of a platform to enact e-institutions represented in our formalism. Our proposal has been exploited for rapid prototyping of large multi-agent systems [15]: we successfully modelled and simulated auctions in a supply-chain scenario [29] whereby hundreds of synthesised software agents interacted to sell and buy goods.

Our platform is a proof-of-concept prototype, engineered with two principles in mind: a minimum number of messages should be exchanged and a maximum distribution and asynchrony among processes should be achieved. Its distributed implementation allows its scale-up: more machines can be used to host its agents. Starting from an e-institution description in our formalism, represented as a sequence of Prolog constructs, the platform starts up a number of administrative agents to overlook the scenes and transitions. The same e-institution formulation is employed to synthesise the agents that will perform in the e-institution, following our approach described in [13]. The specification of the e-institution is used to guide the synthesis of the performing agents and also to control the execution of the administrative agents.

The e-institutions are represented as Prolog terms, in a declarative fashion. We have noticed that this representation is suitable for many different sorts of manipulation. We have used it, for instance, to synthesise agents [28,13] – these are guaranteed to conform to the e-institution they were synthesised from – and also to guide the execution of general-purpose administrative agents. However, the declarative representation also allows for desirable properties to be checked before we run the e-institution, as explained above.

We do not explicitly address temporal aspects in our logic $\mathcal{L}$, for two reasons. First, the underlying finite-state machine of our e-institutions provides a temporal ordering among the formulae labelling its edges – this ordering is a major feature of temporal logics [30,31,32,33] which we can express at no additional costs, that is, no extra notation (nor its semantic counterpart!) has to be added to our formalism. Secondly, the expressive power of temporal logics for representing and checking properties can be recast as *accessibility* relationships in the finite-state machines comprising our e-institutions. For instance, a property $\Diamond\varphi$ (that is, *eventually* φ holds) can be recast as "is there a path starting from the current state in which φ holds?". More practical notions of time such as deadlines (how long do we have to wait for the agents to send their messages?) were dealt at an implementational level: a parameter sets the amount of time required for an event to occur after which we consider it did not happen.

Our implementation does not take into account message loss or delays. We also assume that there are no malignant agents intercepting messages and impersonating other agents. Our platform can be seen as an idealised correct version of a multi-agent system to be built, whereby the performing agents stands for "proxies" of foreign heterogeneous agents, guaranteed to follow an e-institution. The practical security issues that actual heterogeneous agents are prone to are not transferred to the e-institution platform. We are working on how agents synthesised from the e-institution specification [13] could be presented to foreign agents and customised as their proxy agents.

Acknowledgements

This work was partially sponsored by the European Union, under contract IST-1999-10208, research grant **Sustainable Lifecycles in Information Ecosystems** (SLIE). Thanks are due to the anonymous DALT 2003 reviewers and attendants for their constructive criticisms and suggestions which helped improving this paper. Any remaining mistakes and/or imprecisions are the author's fault only.

References

1. Esteva, M., Rodríguez-Aguilar, J.A., Sierra, C., Garcia, P., Arcos, J.L.: On the Formal Specification of Electronic Institutions. In Dignum, F., Sierra, C., eds.: Agent Mediated E-Commerce. Volume 1991 of LNAI., Springer-Verlag (2001)
2. Labrou, Y., Finin, T., Peng, Y.: Agent Communication Languages: the Current Landscape. IEEE Intelligent Systems **14** (1999) 45–52
3. FIPA: The Foundation for Physical Agents. http://www.fipa.org (2002)
4. Hulstijn, J.: Dialogue Models for Inquiry and Transaction. PhD thesis, University of Twente (2000)

5. McBurney, P., van Eijk, R., Parsons, S., Amgoud, L.: A Dialogue-Game Protocol for Agent Purchase Negotiations. Journal of Autonomous Agents and Multi-Agent Systems **7** (2003) 235–273

6. Wagner, T., Benyo, B., Lesser, V., Xuan, P.: Investigating Interactions between Agent Conversations and Agent Control Components. In Dignum, F., Greaves, M., eds.: Issues in Agent Communication. Springer-Verlag: Heidelberg, Germany (2000) 314–330

7. Halmos, P.R.: Naive Set Theory. Van Nostrand, Princeton, New Jersey (1960)

8. Enderton, H.B.: A Mathematical Introduction to Logic. 2nd edn. Harcourt/Academic Press, Mass., USA (2001)

9. Manna, Z.: Mathematical Theory of Computation. McGraw-Hill Kogakusha, Ltd., Tokio, Japan (1974)

10. Esteva, M., Padget, J., Sierra, C.: Formalizing a Language for Institutions and Norms. Volume 2333 of LNAI. Springer-Verlag (2001)

11. Rodríguez-Aguilar, J.A.: On the Design and Construction of Agent-mediated Electronic Institutions. PhD thesis, IIIA-CSIC, Spain (2001)

12. Rodríguez-Aguilar, J.A., Martín, F.J., Noriega, P., Garcia, P., Sierra, C.: Towards a Formal Specification of Complex Social Structures in Multi-Agent Systems. In Padget, J., ed.: Collaboration between Human and Artificial Societies. Volume 1624 of Lect. Notes in Art. Intell. Springer-Verlag (2000) 284–300

13. Vasconcelos, W.W., Sabater, J., Sierra, C., Querol, J.: Skeleton-based Agent Development for Electronic Institutions. In: Proc. 1st Int'l Joint Conf. on Autonomous Agents & Multi-Agent Systems (AAMAS 2002), Bologna, Italy, ACM, U.S.A (2002)

14. Apt, K.R.: From Logic Programming to Prolog. Prentice-Hall, U.K. (1997)

15. Vasconcelos, W.W., Sierra, C., Esteva, M.: An Approach to Rapid Prototyping of Large Multi-Agent Systems. In: Proc. 17th IEEE Int'l Conf. on Automated Software Engineering (ASE 2002), Edinburgh, UK, IEEE Computer Society, U.S.A (2002) 13–22

16. Cormen, T.H., Leiserson, C.E., Rivest, R.L.: Introduction to Algorithms. MIT Press, USA (1990)

17. Holzmann, G.J.: The SPIN Model Checker. IEEE Trans. on Software Engineering **23** (1997) 279–295

18. Holzmann, G.J., Najm, E., Serrhrouchni, A.: SPIN Model Checking: an Introduction. Int. Journal of Software Tools for Technology Transfer **2** (2000) 321–327

19. SICS: SICStus Prolog User's Manual. Swedish Institute of Computer Science, available at http://www.sics.se/isl/sicstus2.html#Manuals (2000)

20. Carriero, N., Gelernter, D.: Linda in Context. Comm. of the ACM **32** (1989) 444–458

21. Bochman, G.V.: Finite State Description of Communications Protocols. In: Procs. Computer Network Protocols Symposium. (1978) F3.1–F3.11

22. Brand, D., Zafiropulo, P.: On Communicating Finite-State Machines. Journal of the ACM **30** (1983) 323–342

23. Boigelot, B., Godefroid, P.: Symbolic Verification of Communication Protocols with Infinite State Spaces using QDDs. Formal Methods in System Design (1997) 1–2

24. Lin, H.P.: Modeling a Transport Layer Protocol using First-Order Logic. In: Procs. of the ACM SIGCOMM Conf. on Comm. Architectures & Protocols, ACM Press (1986) 92–100

25. Endriss, U., Maudet, N., Sadri, F., Toni, F.: Protocol conformance for logic-based agents. In Gottlob, G., Walsh, T., eds.: Proceedings of the 18th International Joint Conference on Artificial Intelligence (IJCAI-2003), Morgan Kaufmann Publishers (2003) 679–684
26. Alberti, M., Gavanelli, M., Lamma, E., Mello, P., Torroni, P.: Modeling Interactions using Social Integrity Constraints: a Resource Sharing Case Study. In this volume.
27. Esteva, M.: Electronic Institutions: from Specification to Development. PhD thesis, Universitat Politècnica de Catalunya, Spain (2003)
28. Vasconcelos, W.W., Robertson, D., Sierra, C., Esteva, M., Sabater, J., Wooldridge, M.: Rapid Prototyping of Large Multi-Agent Systems through Logic Programming. Accepted in *Annals of Mathematics and Artificial Intelligence*, special issue on Logic-Based Agent Implementation (2004)
29. Harland, C.M.: Supply Chain Management: Relationships, Chains and Networks. British Journal of Management **7** (1996) 63–80
30. Barringer, H., Fisher, M., Gabbay, D., Gough, G., Owens, R.: MetateM: an Imperative Approach to Temporal Logic Programming. Formal Aspects of Computing **7** (1995) 111–154
31. Manna, Z., Pnuelli, A.: How to Cook a Temporal Proof System for your Pet Language. In: Proc. 10th POPL-ACM. (1983) 141–154
32. Rescher, N., Urquhart, A.: Temporal Logic. Springer-Verlag, Wien (1971)
33. Vasconcelos, W.W.: Time as a Model: The Application of Temporal Logics in the Formal Specification of Distributed Systems. MSc Dissertation, COPPE – Federal University of Rio de Janeiro; Rio de Janeiro, Brazil (1989) In Portuguese.

Modeling Interactions Using *Social Integrity Constraints*: A Resource Sharing Case Study

Marco Alberti[1], Marco Gavanelli[1], Evelina Lamma[1],
Paola Mello[2], and Paolo Torroni[2]

[1] Dipartimento di Ingegneria, Università degli Studi di Ferrara
Via Saragat, 1 - 44100 Ferrara, Italy
{malberti,mgavanelli,elamma}@ing.unife.it
[2] DEIS, Università degli Studi di Bologna
Viale Risorgimento, 2 - 40136 Bologna, Italy
{ptorroni,pmello}@deis.unibo.it

Abstract. *Computees* are abstractions of the entities situated in global and open computing environments. The *societies* that they populate give an institutional meaning to their interactions and define the allowed interaction protocols. *Social integrity constraints* represent a powerful though simple formalism to express such protocols. Using social integrity constraints, it is possible to give a formal definition of concepts such as violation, fulfillment, and social expectation. This allows for the automatic verification of the social behaviour of computees. The aim of this paper is to show by way of a case study how the theoretical framework can be used in practical situations where computees can operate. The example that we choose is a resource exchange scenario.

1 Introduction

Global Computing [1] is a European Union initiative which aims at obtaining technologies to harness the flexibility and power of rapidly evolving interacting systems composed of autonomous computational entities. Among the assumptions made on the application domain there are the following: activity is not centrally controlled, the computational entities can be mobile, the configuration may vary over time, and the systems operate with incomplete information about the environment.

The problems that such an ambitious objective poses can be tackled from different perspectives: along with aspects such as efficiency and scalability, there are also other ones like formal soundness, possibility to prove properties and to reason on the behaviour of the system, predictability, verifiability, semantics. Declarative methods and formalisms can be used to face the problem from this second perspective. Logic programming in particular is a suitable tool to model the reasoning capabilities of autonomous entities, to give semantics to their interaction, and to throw a bridge between formal specification and operational model.

J. Leite et al. (Eds.): DALT 2003, LNAI 2990, pp. 243–262, 2004.
© Springer-Verlag Berlin Heidelberg 2004

SOCS [2] is a Global Computing project that aims at providing the tools for specifying and verifying computational entities, called *computees*, which can be seen as abstractions of the entities that populate global and open computing environments. Computees have a declarative representation of knowledge, capabilities, resources, objectives and rules of behaviour. Each computee typically has only a partial, incomplete and possibly inaccurate view of the society of the environment and of the other computees, and it might have inadequate resources or capabilities to achieve its objectives. Computees are a specialization of software agents, characterized by exhibiting reasoning abilities, based on a declarative representation of knowledge and on computational logic-based functionalities (e.g. abduction, learning, planning, and so forth). These entities can form complex organizations, which we call *societies of computees*.

By using a computational logic based approach it is possible to specify the set of allowed interaction patterns among computees in the society. In general, such patterns are expressed as protocols, which we model by means of *social integrity constraints*.

By using social integrity constraints, it is possible to give a formal definition of concepts such as social expectation, violation, and fulfillment. The use of social integrity constraints is twofold. In fact, through them the society – equipped with a proper proof procedure – can automatically verify the compliance of its members to the protocols, and can actively suggest to its members what are possible conforming behaviours, thus guiding them in their social life.

Our idea is to exploit abduction for checking the compliance of the computation at a social level. Abduction captures relevant events and hypotheses about future events, which we call *expectations*. The social infrastructure, based on a suitably extended abductive proof procedure, will dynamically consider socially relevant events as they happen. Its activity, which includes checking of social integrity constraint, will result in an evolution of the social expectations, and in a proof of compliance of events to protocols or of their violation.

In this work, we explain our ideas with a focus on protocols: we provide an intuitive understanding of the semantics of social integrity constraints, and we show how they can be used to verify protocol compliance. We will not discuss about the reasoning activity of the individual computees that makes them take certain actions rather than other ones. We will observe instead their behaviour from the outside, in relationship with the protocols imposed by the society, focussing on the evolution of social expectations, making no assumptions on their internal architecture, nor on their social attitude.

We adopt as a running example a resource sharing problem, inspired by the work done by Sadri et al. [3], where the authors propose a multi-agent solution to the problem, based on a logic programming framework. In such a framework, agents initiate negotiation dialogues to share resources along time, adopting one among several protocols, depending on how much information they wish to disclose in order to achieve some missing resources.

Drawing inspiration from [3], in our example the society of computees defines as interaction protocols those for resource sharing. As the interaction proceeds, we show the evolution of social expectations and their possible fulfillment, or the raising of a violation if some expectations are disregarded.

The paper is structured as follows. In Section 2, we introduce the idea of social integrity constraints. In Section 3, we explain the resource exchange scenario. In Section 4, we give an example of social integrity constraints in the proposed scenario and we show how social expectations are generated as the computees interact with each other. In Section 5, we show how the formalism that we propose can be used to verify the conformance of computees to social interaction protocols. In Section 6, we relate our work to other proposals in the literature and to our past and current work within the SOCS project. Conclusions follow.

2   Social Integrity Constraints

We envisage a model of society, tolerant to partial information, which continues to operate despite the incompleteness of the available knowledge. In such a model, the society is time by time aware of social events that dynamically happen in the social environment. Moreover, the society can reason upon the happened events and the protocols that must be followed by its members, and therefore define what are the *expected social events*. These are events which are not yet available (to the society), but which are expected if we want computees to exhibit a *proper* behaviour, i.e., conforming to protocols.

Such expectations can be used by the society to behave pro-actively: suitable social policies could make them public, in order to try and influence the behaviour of the computees towards an ideal behaviour.

Indeed, the set of expectations of the society are adjusted as soon as it acquires new knowledge from the environment on social events that was not available while planning such expectations. In this perspective, the society should be able to deal with unexpected social events from the environment, which possibly violate the previous expectations.

This can be the case in an open environment where "regimentation" [4] cannot be assumed. In an open society, where computees are autonomous, unexpected events can bring to a state of *violation*, from which it could be necessary to recover by taking appropriate measures (e.g., sanctions), in order to bring the society back to a consistent state.

In the proposed model, the knowledge in a society is composed of three parts: organizational knowledge, environmental knowledge, and Social Integrity Constraints to express the allowed interaction protocols. Organizational knowledge is about roles, membership, and possibly about society goals. Environmental knowledge is about events that happened within the society, and that have a socially relevant meaning for its members. For instance, messages exchanged among computees having certain roles. We will refer to the set of happened events as *event record*, or *history*. Social Integrity Constraints (IC_S, for short) express what is expected to happen or not to happen, given some event record. For example, an IC_S could state that the manager of a resource should give an answer to whomever has made a request for that resource.

In this paper, we will focus on this last part of the society knowledge. In particular, we will see how IC_S can be used to specify protocols. IC_S relate socially significant happened events to *expectations* about the behavior of computees. They are used to check if a computee inside the society behaves in a permissible way with respect to its "social" behavior.

IC_S are forward implications

$$\chi \rightarrow \phi$$

which contain in χ a conjunction of social events and expectations, and in ϕ a disjunction of conjunctions of expectations. Expectations can be of two kinds: positive (**E**) and negative (**EN**), and their variables can be constrained to assume some values.

Happened events are denoted by **H**. Intuitively, an **H** atom represents a socially significant event that happened in the society.

Being the focus of this paper on the motivation of the use of social integrity constraints in a declarative agent programming setting, we will not give here more detail about IC_S. In a companion paper [5] we define the full syntax of social integrity constraints, the scope of variables, quantification, and we give some results about the conditions for a proper behaviour of the framework. Also, we give a formal semantic characterization of concepts such as coherence and consistency of sets of expectations and their fulfillment. Instead, in [5] we do not discuss how the framework can be used to prove properties of interactions. The aim of this paper is to show by a concrete example how the theoretical framework can be used in practical situations where computees can operate. We will therefore give below a flavour of the operational behaviour of the framework.

In our approach, computees autonomously perform some form of reasoning, and the society infrastructure is devoted to ensuring that in performing their tasks they do not violate the established rules and protocols.

H events, **E**/**EN** expectations, and society knowledge and protocols can be smoothly recovered into an abductive framework, so to exploit well-assessed abductive proof-theoretic techniques in order to check the compliance of the overall computation with respect to the expected social behavior.

We represent the knowledge available at the social level as an Abductive Logic Program (ALP) [6], since we want to deal with incomplete knowledge. In particular, in order to model interactions, the incompleteness of their knowledge includes ignorance about communicative acts that have not been made yet. The idea of modelling communicative acts by abduction is derived from [7], where the abducibles are produced within an agent cycle, and represent actions in the external world. Here, we adopt an approach where abduction is used to generate expectations. The dynamic knowledge available at a social level grows up along with the computees' social activity.

Along with with **H** events and raised expectations, **E** and **EN**, we have *negated* expectations ($\neg$**E** and $\neg$**EN**), also represented as abducible atoms, in accordance with the usual way abduction can be used to deal with negation [6]. Positive and negative expectations and their negation are collected into **EXP** sets, which can be seen as sets of hypotheses. Since there can be several alternative sets of expectations, given a history, we will represent **EXP** as a set of disjunctions of atomic hypotheses [8,9]. We will adopt the notation $\mathbf{EXP}_j^i$, indicating that $\mathbf{EXP}_j^1, \mathbf{EXP}_j^2, \ldots \mathbf{EXP}_j^n$ are alternative to each other, where j denotes the time at which **EXP** is given.

At the society level, knowledge can be represented as an abductive logic program, i.e., the triple: $\langle KB, \mathcal{E}, IC \rangle$ where:

- KB is the knowledge base of the society. It contains the organizational and environmental knowledge, including happened events (we denote by **HAP** the event record: $KB \supseteq \mathbf{HAP}$);
- $\mathcal{E}$ is a set of *abducible predicates*, standing for the set **EXP** of positive and negative expectations, and their negation;
- IC is the set of social integrity constraints, IC_S.

The idea is to exploit abduction for checking the compliance of the computation at a social level. Abduction captures relevant events (or hypotheses about future events), and a suitably extended abductive proof procedure can be used for integrity constraint checking. **EXP** is an *admissible* set of expectations if and only if:

$$KB \cup \mathbf{EXP} \models IC_S \tag{1}$$

An admissible set of expectations **EXP** is coherent (2) and consistent (3) if and only if:

$$\forall p.\{\mathbf{E}(p), \mathbf{EN}(p)\} \notin \mathbf{EXP} \tag{2}$$

$$\begin{cases} \forall p.\{\mathbf{E}(p), \neg\mathbf{E}(p)\} \notin \mathbf{EXP} \\ \forall p.\{\mathbf{EN}(p), \neg\mathbf{EN}(p)\} \notin \mathbf{EXP} \end{cases} \tag{3}$$

Finally, conformance to rules and protocols is guaranteed by:

$$\mathbf{HAP} \cup \mathbf{EXP} \models \{\mathbf{E}(p) \to \mathbf{H}(p)\} \cup \{\mathbf{EN}(p) \to \neg\mathbf{H}(p)\} \tag{4}$$

In this last condition, expectations are put in relationship with the events, which gives a notion of fulfillment. If (4) is not verified, then a *violation* occurs.

In [5] we provide a declarative semantics. A suitable proof procedure is currently under development. In fact, a first version of the proof, handling social integrity constraints written in a restricted syntax, has already been developed, and allowed us to test all the examples shown in Section 4. Such a proof features an incremental fulfillment check, in order to detect violations as soon as possible.

3 Negotiation for Resource Sharing

In this section we briefly recall the resource exchange scenario defined in [3]. Let us consider a system where computees have *goals* to achieve, and in order to achieve them they use plans. Plans are partially ordered sets of activities. Activities have a duration and a time window in which they have been scheduled by the computee. In order to execute the activities, computees may need some resources during the scheduled time window.

An activity that requires a resource r is said to be *infeasible* if r is not available to the computee that intends to execute it. Similarly, infeasible is also a *plan* that contains an activity which is infeasible, and so is the *intention* of a computee, containing such plan[1]. The resources that computees *need* in order to perform an action in a plan but that they do not possess are called *missing* resources.

In fact, what we mean when we say *resource* is only an abstract entity, identified by its *name*, which possibly symbolizes a physical resource, such as a bike or a scooter. We do not explicitly model the actual delivery of physical resources.

The *resource exchange problem* is the problem of answering to the following *question*: Does there exist a resource distribution, which is possible to obtain as a result of a negotiation process, and such that each computee has the resources it requires for time periods that would allow it to perform the activities in its intention, within their specified time windows?

In [3], the authors propose a framework for resource exchange, where the computees can interact following different protocols. Without loss of generality, resources are assumed to be non consumable. The protocols are ordered into stages, each characterised by an increased chance of a mutually agreeable deal but at the price of disclosing more and more information. In the sequence of stages, the computees may agree to move on to the next stage if the previous one fails to produce a deal amongst them.

In particular, the authors define two different stages of negotiation, each characterized by the degree of flexibility of the computees and the amount of information disclosed and used by them:

> Stage 1: Request/flexible schedule
> Stage 2: Blind deal

The first stage implements a two-step request/accept/refuse protocol. The policy that a computee may adopt upon receival of a request is to try and give the resource in question. This may require a change in its own activity schedule. The second stage implements a more elaborate protocol, where the computee who answers to a request can either accept or refuse the request, as in Stage 1, but can also propose a series of deals. The allowed sequences of steps in the two stages are pictured in Figure 1 for a pair of agents y (requesting a resource) and x (answering to y's request).

In this paper, we do not suggest any ordering in the usage of these protocols, but we still refer to the protocols using the word "stage", as in [3], for easy of reference. We choose the multi-stage negotiation architecture because it was originally defined based on abductive logic programming, which makes it easy to

---

[1] In [3], *plans* are modeled as part of the computee *intentions*.

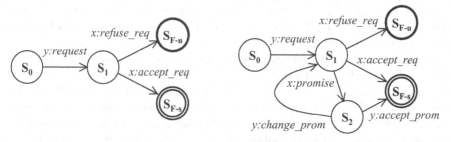

Fig. 1. Protocols for Stage 1 and Stage 2 (taken from [3])

(IC_{S1}) **H**($tell(Y, X, \textbf{request}(R, (Ts, Te)), d(st1, D), T)$)
$\quad\quad \rightarrow \textbf{E}(tell(X, Y, \textbf{accept\_req}(R, (Ts, Te)), d(st1, D), T')) : T < T'$
$\quad\quad \lor\ \textbf{E}(tell(X, Y, \textbf{refuse\_req}(R, (Ts, Te)), d(st1, D), T')) : T < T'$

Fig. 2. *Stage 1* protocol

translate the protocols into social integrity constraints, and because it presents a variety of protocols, which suggests interesting observations about society engineering and the advantage of having a formal definition of interaction protocols, and an operational framework to reason upon.

Negotiating computees will use the protocols based on some internal policies. The policies adopted by the negotiating peers at Stage 1 and Stage 2, as they are defined in [3], implement a very collaborative behaviour. But in an open society, where computees are free to choose their own policy, the only thing that we can look at, from a social (verification) perspective, are the exchanged messages, and the interaction protocols that they follow.

In the next section, we will define the protocols that are followed when negotiating at Stage 1 and at Stage 2, and show how expectations evolve as the negotiation proceeds.

4   Social Expectations for a Resource Sharing Scenario

The protocol followed at Stage 1 is shown in Figure 2, for two generic computees X and Y: once Y makes a *request* to X, concerning a resource R during a time window $[Ts - Te]$, X can either *accept* or *refuse* it. Note that there is no mention of the policies adopted by the computees (for instance, a computee could well refuse all requests and not be collaborative at all, whatever the request and its actual resource allocation are: it would still be compliant to the protocol).

H, **E** and **EN** enclose *tell* terms, which represent communicative acts, and whose parameters are: sender, receiver, subject, dialogue context, and time of the communicative act. In particular, since in this work we are presenting different protocols, we use the context field to specify both the instance of dialogue among the two computees, and the protocol that they are adopting: $d(ProtocolID, DialogueID)$. We will use $st1$ to denote Stage 1 protocol, $st2$ to denote Stage 2 protocol.

Social integrity constraints can encode extra knowledge about this protocol: in particular, in Figure 2 there is nothing saying how a protocol starts or terminates. In Figure 3, we see how by IC_S we can express the fact that some moves are "final", in the sense that they mean to put an end to a conversation, while some others are "initial", i.e., they are meant not to be preceded by other moves in the same conversation. We refer to the language $\mathcal{L}_{1-TW}$ defined in [3], where $request(\ldots)$ is the only allowed initial move, and $accept\_req(\ldots)$ and $refuse\_req(\ldots)$ are final moves. We use a generic $d(S, D)$ dialogue context because we will use these IC_S also in other protocols. We see here another use of integrity constraints, different from that in Figure 2: IC_S are used in fact to generate *negative* expectations, which tell what should not happen, given a certain course of events.

(IC_{S2}) $\mathbf{H}(tell(\_, \_, \mathbf{request}(Req), d(st1, D), T))$
$\rightarrow \mathbf{EN}(tell(\_, \_, \_, d(st1, D), T')) : T' < T$

(IC_{S3}) $\mathbf{H}(tell(\_, \_, \mathbf{accept\_req}(Req), d(S, D), T))$
$\rightarrow \mathbf{EN}(tell(\_, \_, \_, d(S, D), T')) : T' > T$

(IC_{S4}) $\mathbf{H}(tell(\_, \_, \mathbf{refuse\_req}(Req), d(S, D), T))$
$\rightarrow \mathbf{EN}(tell(\_, \_, \_, d(S, D), T')) : T' > T$

Fig. 3. Negative expectations following from the semantics of the negotiation language

By IC_{S2}, a *request* is expected to be the first move of a dialogue. We express this by expecting no prior move in the same context. In [10] we call *backward* this kind of expectations, i.e., those about some events in the past but raised by events happening at the current time. By IC_{S3} and IC_{S4}, *accept_req* and *refuse_req* are expected to be final moves (no moves are expected to follow in the same context).

In Figure 4 we define the protocol for Stage 2 negotiation. By IC_{S5}, after a *request* the expected moves are those of Stage 1, plus *promise*, which stands for a deal proposal: X will give R to Y for the requested time window, $[Ts - Te]$, provided that in exchange Y gives R to X for a different time window, $[Ts'-Te']$. By IC_{S6}, after *promise* one expects either an *accept_prom*$(\ldots)$, which means that the deal is accepted, or a *change_prom*$(\ldots)$, asking for a different deal proposal. By IC_{S7}, after a *change_prom*$(\ldots)$ one expects either another *promise* or a *refuse_req*, rejecting in the latter case the original request and thus terminating the dialogue. By IC_{S8}, one does not expect the same *promise* to be made twice. Finally, IC_{S9} states that *accept_prom*$(\ldots)$ is a final move.

(IC_{S5}) $\mathbf{H}(tell(Y, X, \mathbf{request}(R, (Ts, Te)), d(st2, D), T))$
$\rightarrow \mathbf{E}(tell(X, Y, \mathbf{accept\_req}(R, (Ts, Te)), d(st2, D), T')) : T < T'$
$\lor\ \mathbf{E}(tell(X, Y, \mathbf{refuse\_req}(R, (Ts, Te)), d(st2, D), T')) : T < T'$
$\lor\ \mathbf{E}(tell(X, Y, \mathbf{promise}(R, (Ts', Te'), (Ts, Te)), d(st2, D), T')) :$
$T < T'$

(IC_{S6}) $\mathbf{H}(tell(X, Y, \mathbf{promise}(R, (Ts', Te'), (Ts, Te)), d(st2, D), T))$
$\rightarrow \mathbf{E}(tell(Y, X, \mathbf{change\_prom}(R, (Ts', Ts'), (Ts, Te)), d(st2, D), T')) :$
$T < T'$
$\lor\ \mathbf{E}(tell(Y, X, \mathbf{accept\_prom}(R, (Ts', Te'), (Ts, Te)), d(st2, D), T')) :$
$T < T'$

(IC_{S7}) $\mathbf{H}(tell(Y, X, \mathbf{change\_prom}(R, (Ts', Te'), (Ts, Te)), d(st2, D), T))$
$\rightarrow \mathbf{E}(tell(X, Y, \mathbf{promise}(R, (Ts'', Te''), (Ts, Te)), d(st2, D), T')) :$
$T < T'$
$\lor\ \mathbf{E}(tell(X, Y, \mathbf{refuse\_req}(R, (Ts, Te)), d(st2, D), T')) : T < T'$

(IC_{S8}) $\mathbf{H}(tell(X, Y, \mathbf{promise}(R, (Ts', Te'), (Ts, Te)), d(st2, D), T))$
$\rightarrow \mathbf{EN}(tell(X, Y, \mathbf{promise}(R, (Ts', Te'), (Ts, Te)), d(st2, D), T')) :$
$T < T'$

(IC_{S9}) $\mathbf{H}(tell(\_, \_, \mathbf{accept\_prom}(Prom), d(st2, D), T))$
$\rightarrow \mathbf{EN}(tell(\_, \_, \_, d(st2, D), T')) : T' > T$

Fig. 4. *Stage 2* protocol

If we look at both protocols, for Stage 1 and Stage 2, we understand that $IC_{S1} \Rightarrow IC_{S5}$, in the sense that, abstracting away from the protocol identifier, IC_{S1} is more restrictive than IC_{S5} (all that is compliant to IC_{S1} is also compliant to IC_{S5}, but not vice-versa).

From this example it is possible to see a first achievement of the use of social integrity constraints to formally define protocols: we are able to formally reason on the protocols and adopt a modular approach to society engineering. For instance, it could be interesting to know that if we put Stage 1 constraints and Stage 2 constraints together, without any protocol identifier, then the resulting protocol is a more restrictive protocol than the two original ones. The study of tools to automatically prove some relationships among integrity constraints or protocols is subject for current investigation.

We would now like to show how social expectations are created and evolve as computees exchange requests and reply to each other. For the sake of the example, we consider a system composed of three computees: *david*, *yves*, and *thomas* (denoted by the letters *d*, *y*, and *t*). The resource that they share is a *scooter* (denoted by the letter *s*). *david* is normally entitled to have the scooter in the afternoon, while *yves* in the morning.

Let us assume that at time 1 *david* makes a request to *yves*, because he needs the scooter from 10 to 11 in the morning[2]. This request is recorded by the society and put into **HAP**:

$$\mathbf{H}(tell(d, y, request(s(10, 11)), d(st2, d), 1))$$

By looking at the history, the society modifies its set of expectations. Such a set could be initially empty. After the event at time 1, due to IC_{S5}, the society grows with expectations. Since IC_{S5} has a disjunction as a consequence of ah **H** term, the expectations will also be disjunctions of terms. In general, since we have disjunctions in the heads of IC_S, we will have a collection of alternative sets **EXP**. At time 2, we have

$$\mathbf{EXP}_2^1 = \{ \ \mathbf{E}(tell(y, d, accept\_req(s, (10, 11)), d(st2, d), T) : T > 1$$
$$\wedge (\ \mathbf{EN}(tell(\_, \_, \_, d(st2, d), T') : T' < 1) \}$$
$$\mathbf{EXP}_2^2 = \{ \ \mathbf{E}(tell(y, d, refuse\_req(s, (10, 11)), d(st2, d), T) : T > 1$$
$$\wedge (\ \mathbf{EN}(tell(\_, \_, \_, d(st2, d), T') : T' < 1) \}$$
$$\mathbf{EXP}_2^3 = \{ \ \mathbf{E}(tell(y, d, promise(s, (10, 11), (Ts, Te)), d(st2, d), T) : T > 1$$
$$\wedge (\ \mathbf{EN}(tell(\_, \_, \_, d(st2, d), T') : T' < 1) \}$$

Let us assume that at time 3 *yves* proposes a deal to *david*:

$$\mathbf{H}(tell(y, d, promise(s, (10, 11), (20, 23)), d(st2, d), 3))$$

The expectations **EXP** change. At time 4, we have:

$$\mathbf{EXP}_4^1 = \{ \ \mathbf{E}(tell(y, d, accept\_req(s, (10, 11)), d(st2, d), T) : T > 1$$
$$\wedge (\ \mathbf{EN}(tell(\_, \_, \_, d(st2, d), T') : T' < 1)$$
$$\wedge (\ \mathbf{E}(d, y, accept\_prom(s, (10, 11)), d(st2, d), T) : T' > 3)$$
$$\wedge (\ \mathbf{EN}(tell(y, d, promise(s, (10, 11), (20, 23)), d(st2, d), T') : T' > 3) \}$$
$$\mathbf{EXP}_4^2 = \{ \ \mathbf{E}(tell(y, d, refuse\_req(s, (10, 11)), d(st2, d), T) : T > 1$$
$$\wedge (\ \mathbf{EN}(tell(\_, \_, \_, d(st2, d), T') : T' < 1)$$
$$\wedge (\ \mathbf{E}(d, y, accept\_prom(s, (10, 11)), d(st2, d), T) : T' > 3)$$
$$\wedge (\ \mathbf{EN}(tell(y, d, promise(s, (10, 11), (20, 23)), d(st2, d), T') : T' > 3) \}$$

$$\dots$$

$$\mathbf{EXP}_4^6 = \{ \ \mathbf{E}(tell(y, d, promise(s, (Ts', Te'), (10, 11)), d(st2, d), T) : T > 1$$
$$\wedge (\ \mathbf{EN}(tell(\_, \_, \_, d(st2, d), T') : T' < 1)$$
$$\wedge (\ \mathbf{E}(d, y, change\_prom(s, (10, 11)), d(st2, d), T) : T' > 3)$$
$$\wedge (\ \mathbf{EN}(tell(y, d, promise(s, (10, 11), (20, 23)), d(st2, d), T') : T' > 3) \}$$

The disjunction **EXP** will keep evolving along with the social events. In [5] the authors give a declarative semantics to expectations and social integrity constraints. They define a notion of fulfillment of expectations. For instance, in our example, we can see that an expectation which is present in **EXP**$_1$ at time 2 is then fulfilled by *yves*' message to *david* at time 3. Similarly, we have a

---

[2] We make the simplifying assumption that the time of communication acts is centrally assigned, e.g. by the "social infrastructure", and that all computees are able to cope with this. We can then consider the time of the society as a transaction time.

violation if at a later time something happens which is expected not to happen, e.g., *yves* repeats the same promise for a second time.

Finally, if at time 7 *david* accepts *yves*'s *promise*:

$$\mathbf{H}(tell(d, y, accept\_prom(s, (10,11), (20,23))), d(st2, d), 7),$$

it is easy to see that the extensions of $\mathbf{EXP}_4^1$ and $\mathbf{EXP}_4^2$ will never be fulfilled, because they will contain an expectation (generated by IC_{S5}) which can only be fulfilled if it happens that *yves* accepts ($\mathbf{EXP}_4^1$) or refuses ($\mathbf{EXP}_4^2$) *david*'s request: but in that case IC_{S9} would be violated, since *accept_prom*(...) is expected to be a final move.

We have seen how in our framework it is possible to define a protocol as a sequence of states, as it is done with finite state machines. We can define initial and final moves by way of integrity constraints such as $IC_{S2}, IC_{S3}, IC_{S4}$, and IC_{S9}. We can define the expected moves given a certain state, such as we did for instance with IC_{S1}. In this way, we can achieve an exhaustive description of the graph representing a given protocol. But we can go beyond this. In line with Yolum and Singh's approach [11], we could define a protocol in a more flexible way, which minimally constrains the actions of the participants, allowing a better exploitation of opportunities, and exception handling. Let us consider the following situations:

(i) *david* often asks *yves* for the scooter; whenever *yves* does not need his scooter for a certain period of time, he could pro-actively offer *david* the scooter, without waiting for a request; conversely, whenever *yves* knows that he needs the scooter for some period of time, he could tell this to *david*, before *david* makes any request;

(ii) along the dialogue, *david*'s knowledge and needs may change. Taking this into account, *yves* could propose the same deal twice, hoping that the second time *david* accepts it;

(iii) a third agent might get involved or take over: after receiving *david*'s request, *yves* could forward the request to *thomas*, and *thomas* could continue the dialogue with *david*;

(iv) *yves* might need the scooter but he might have a spare bicycle, and he could answer to *david*'s request by accepting a request for a bicycle (and not for a scooter);

(v) *david* might not want to wait too long for an answer.

IC_S can easily give semantics to all these kinds of situation in a compact and simple way. For instance, the IC_S that we defined for Stage 1 and Stage 2 already allow the behaviour depicted in (i) (in fact, no constraint says that an *accept_req* must be preceded by a *request*). But we could prevent it, by adding the following constraint:

$$\mathbf{H}(tell(X, Y, \mathbf{accept\_req}(Req), d(S, D), T))$$
$$\rightarrow \mathbf{E}(tell(Y, X, \mathbf{request}(Req), d(S, D), T')) : T' < T.$$

This is a backward expectation, as well as IC_{S2}.

(ii) could be allowed by dropping IC_{S8}. (iii) could be allowed by changing IC_{S5} in the following way:

$$\mathbf{H}(tell(Y, \_, \mathbf{request}(R, (Ts, Te)), d(st2, D), T))$$
$$\rightarrow \mathbf{E}(tell(\_, Y, \mathbf{accept\_req}(R, (Ts, Te)), d(st2, D), T')) : T < T'$$
$$\vee \ \ldots,$$

i.e., by eliminating the binding between the recipient of the *request* and the computee who will answer. Similarly, (iv) could be allowed by relaxing the binding between the object of the *request* and the object of the answer to the *request*.

Finally, (v) could be achieved by imposing a constraint on the time variable of the expected answer:

$$(IC_{S10}) \ \ \mathbf{H}(tell(Y, X, \mathbf{request}(R, (Ts, Te)), d(st2, D), T))$$
$$\rightarrow deadline(request, T_d), T_{max} = T + T_d,$$
$$\mathbf{E}(tell(X, Y, \mathbf{accept\_req}(R, (Ts, Te)), d(st2, D), T')) :$$
$$T < T', T' < T_{max}$$
$$\vee \ \ldots,$$

where $deadline(request, T_d)$ is a predicate defined in the organizational part of the social knowledge.

For instance, assuming $deadline(request, 10)$, the following history is compliant to IC_{S10}:

$$\mathbf{HAP} = \{ \ \mathbf{H}(tell(d, y, \mathbf{request}(s, (10, 11)), d(st2, d), 1))$$
$$\mathbf{H}(tell(y, d, \mathbf{accept\_req}(s, (10, 11)), d(st2, d), 6))\},$$

whereas the following one is not:

$$\mathbf{HAP} = \{ \ \mathbf{H}(tell(d, y, \mathbf{request}(s, (10, 11)), d(st2, d), 1))$$
$$\mathbf{H}(tell(y, d, \mathbf{accept\_req}(s, (10, 11)), d(st2, d), 13))\}.$$

Clearly, each of those modifications of the initial protocol has its advantages and disadvantages, and to discuss them goes beyond the scope of this paper. On the other hand, the resource exchange scenario allowed us to exemplify some advantages of our formalism. Social integrity constraints enable us to:

- express allowed communication patterns inside a society (e.g., the protocols for Stage 1 and Stage 2). This is done independently of the computees' internal policies and implementation;
- fine-tune the flexibility of such communication patterns, in line with Yolum and Singh's approach;
- use the protocol definitions and the history of socially relevant events to generate at run-time the possible combinations of future events that represent a "proper" behaviour of the computees (e.g., $\mathbf{EXP}_1$ and $\mathbf{EXP}_2$);
- formally reason on the composition of protocols, and adopt a modular approach to society engineering (e.g. the composition of Stage 1 and Stage 2 defines a new, more restrictive protocol);

— verify at run-time the correct behaviour of some computees, with respect to the protocols, without having access to their internals (e.g., if *yves* repeats the same promise for a second time we enter, at Stage 2, a violation state).

As future extensions, we intend to investigate the issue of protocol composition, and the notion of violation, particularly about how to recover from a state of violation, and possibly — given such a state — how to identify one or more "culprits" and generate appropriate sanctions. Having all these elements in a unified declarative framework would be an important achievement.

5   Social Integrity Constraints for Verification

In [12,13], F. Guerin and J. Pitt propose a classification of properties that are relevant for e-commerce systems, in particular with respect to properties of protocols and interactions. In this setting, they propose a formal framework for verification of properties of "low level computing theories required to implement a mechanism for agents" in an *open* environment, where by open the author mean that the internals of agents are not public.

Verification is classified into three types, depending on the information available and whether the verification is done at design time or at run time:

Type 1: verify that an agent will always comply;
Type 2: verify compliance by observation;
Type 3: verify protocol properties.

As for *Type 1* verification, the authors propose using a model checking algorithm for agents implemented by a finite state program. As for *Type 2* verification, the authors refer to work done by Singh [14], where "agents can be tested for compliance on the basis of their communications", and suggest policing the society as a way to enforce a correct behaviour of its inhabitants. As for verification of *Type 3*, the authors show how it is possible to prove properties of protocols by using only the ACL specification. They construct a fair transition system representing all possible observable sequences of states and prove by hand that the desired properties hold over all computations of the multi-agent system. This type of verification is demonstrated by an auction example.

The formal framework that we propose for modelling interactions in an open society of computees lends itself very well to all these kinds of verification. In fact, both (public) protocols and (internal) policies are expressed in the same formalism, which makes it possible to relate social aspects with individual aspects in a static verification. We believe that all the above three types of verification can be *automatically* done in a computational logic setting.

Verification that a computee will always comply cannot be done by externally monitoring its behaviour. Quoting Hume, "we are in a natural state of ignorance with regard to the powers and influence of all objects when we consider them a priori" [15]. For verification of Type 1, we need to have access to the computees' internals, or to its specifications. We would be advantaged in this task if we could express the computee program and policies by means of an abductive logic programming based formalism, as it is done in [16]: in that case, specification and implementation coincide.

The proof that a given computee c will always comply with a set $\mathcal{IC}_S$ of integrity constraints representing a protocol, based on the agents' specifications, could be the following. We show that for all the integrity constraints in $\mathcal{IC}_S$, if in the head of an integrity constraint there is a social expectation about an event generated by c, then, the history of events that from a social viewpoint leads to such expectation, leads by that computee's viewpoint to producing an event that fulfills it (or prevents the computee from producing any event that violates it, in the case of negative expectations).

In the scooter example, if $yves'$ specifications are such that the constraint:

$$\mathbf{H}(tell(C, y, request(give(s, (10, 11)))), d(st2, d), T))$$
$$\rightarrow \mathbf{H}(tell(y, C, accept(request(give(s, (10, 11))))), d(st2, d), T') : T' > T)$$

is never violated, then $yves$ is compliant with the protocol, because the event that raises the expectation

$$\mathbf{E}(tell(y, C, accept(request(give(s, (10, 11))))), d(st2, d), T))$$

in the society also makes $yves$ generate an event which fulfills that expectation.

The study of a mechanism to automatically obtain such a proof (or its failure) is subject for current investigation.

For verification of Type 2 we need to be able to observe the computees' social actions, i.e., the communicative acts that they exchange. As in [13], we can assume that this can be achieved by policing the society. In particular, "police" computees will "snoop" the communicative acts exchanged by the society members and check at run time if they comply with the protocols specifications (given, in our case, by means of social integrity constraints).

This kind of run-time verification is theoretically already built in our framework and we do not need to provide additional formal tools to achieve it. Alberti et al. [10,17] show two implementations of two different fragments of social integrity constraints based on the CHR language [18].

Verification of Type 3 is about protocol properties. In order to prove them we do not need to access the computees' internals, nor to know anything about the communication acts of the system, because it is a verification which is statically done at design time. As we already mentioned in Section 4, we are working on the design of a logic-based formalism to automatically detect inconsistencies of combinations of protocols. In general, one of the main motivations behind our formal approach is to be able to prove properties that can be formally defined, e.g. by means of an invariant or an implication, as they are defined in [13].

6   Discussion

Computees are abstractions of the entities that populate global and open computing environments. The intuition behind a computee is very similar to that behind an agent. The reason why we adopt a different name is because we want to refer to a particular class of agents, which can rely on a declarative representation of knowledge, and on reasoning methods grounded on computational logic.

Within SOCS, we advocate that the use of the computee model for individuals and societies makes it easier to understand, specify, verify, and prove properties of the overall computational system, compare to other agent and agent system models. However, this work about societies can be applied to any kind of sociable agent. The availability of a declarative representation of the agent knowledge is a plus, which paves the way to proving results about specific instances of computees, within a social context. In this way, a declarative representation of the society knowledge and of social categories such as expectations, as we defined them in this work, can be smoothly integrated with the knowledge of its inhabitants, and similar techniques can be used by them to reason upon either knowledge base or upon a combination of them.

Esteva et al. [19] give a formal specification of agents societies, focussing on the social level of electronic institutions. In that model, each agent in a society plays one or more *roles*, and must conform to the pattern of behavior attached to its roles. The *dialogic framework* of a society defines the common ground (ontology, communication language, knowledge representation) that allows heterogeneous agents to communicate. Interactions between agents take place in group meetings called *scenes*, each regulated by a communication protocol; connections between scenes (for instance, an agent may have to choose between different scenes, or its participation in a scene may be causally dependent on its participation in another) are captured by the *performative structure*. *Normative rules* specify how agents' actions affect their subsequent possible behavior, by raising obligations on them.

In our framework, agents are only required to perform their communicative acts by a given computee communication language; they are not required to share an ontology (which, strictly speaking, need not even be specified). Possible interactions are not organized in separate (although inter-connected) scenes; agents' interactions are supposed to take place in one shared interaction space. For this reason, we do not distinguish, as in [19], between intra-scene (possible interaction paths *inside* a scene) and inter-scene (possible paths of an agent *through* scenes) normative rules. Without this distinction, normative rules are strictly related to our social integrity constraints, in that both constrain agents' future behavior as a consequence of their past actions. We would like to stress that Esteva et al., based on the analysis presented by Dellarocas and Klein [20], start from the same requisites as we do, considering as major issues heterogeneity, trust and accountability, exception handling and societal changes, and provide in their work a basis for a verified design of electronic marketplaces, by giving a very detailed formal specification of all the aspects of their electronic institutions, and graphical tools to make such a specification easy to understand. However, the focus of their work is not on a direct and automatic specification-verified implementation relationship, as in ours.

Vasconcelos [21] presents a very neat formalization based on first order logics and set theory to represent an expressive class of electronic institutions. As in our work, the use of variables and quantification over finite sets allow to express significant protocols patterns. The definition of allowed interaction patterns is based on the concept of scene, similarly to what is done in [19]. How expressive is the formalism proposed in [21] with respect to ours, and what are the differences in terms of verification, are issues that we would like to address in the future.

Moses and Tennenholtz [22] focus on the problem of helping interacting agents achieve their individual goals, by guaranteeing not only mere achievability of the goals, but also computational feasibility of planning courses of actions to realize them. Since an agent's behavior can affect the achievability of other agents' goals, the agents' possible actions are restricted by means of *social laws*, in order to prevent agents from performing actions that would be detrimental to other agents.

In our work, we aim more at verifying sound social interaction, rather than at guaranteeing properties of individual computees. Moreover, computing appropriate social laws requires a (correct) modelling of individual agents in terms of states, state-actions relations and plans, thus assuming reliable knowledge about agents' internals, which we do not require.

Gaia is a methodology in software engineering developed by Wooldridge et al. for agent-oriented analysis and design [23]. The developer of a MAS has to define *roles* that agents will then embody. Each role is defined by its *responsibilities*, *permissions*, *activities* and *protocols*. In particular, responsibilities explain how an agent embodying the corresponding role should behave in terms of *liveness* expressions (good things that should happen) and *safety* expressions (bad things that should not happen)[3]. These expressions can be seen as abstractions of our expectations, or, in a sense, social integrity constraints could be seen as a further refinement and a formalization of the concepts of responsibilities. Moreover, we use Social Integrity Constraints also to model *protocols*, i.e., interaction with other agents.

Our framework does not specifically cater for roles (very little we said about the structure of the knowledge related to the society). However, our aim is to propose a declarative framework where roles can indeed be expressed, but do not represent a first class entity in the definition of agent interactions in general. For instance, in a semi-open society [25] roles could be assigned to incoming computees by "custom officer" computees, or they could be statically defined in the society knowledge base, or else dynamically acquired along the time. It is not difficult to imagine social integrity constraints that define the protocols for role management.

Considerable work has been done about the formal definition and verification of properties of multi-agent systems, but to the best of our knowledge there is not yet a reference paper with a formal classification and definition of properties that are considered interesting in a general setting. In Section 5, we referred to the work by Guerin and Pitt because it neatly pins down the main requisites and

---

[3] This distinction is due to Lamport [24].

characteristics of a multi-agent system verification process (run-time verification vs. static-verification, and visibility of agents's internals). Although it is specially oriented to electronic commerce applications, we believe that its main ideas can be extended to a more general case of agent interactions.

Among other work that proposes list of properties of agent systems, more or less formally defined and related to particular domains, we cite work done by Mazouzi et al. [26], Yolum and Singh [11], Hewitt [27], Artikis et al. [28], and Davidsson [25].

Küngas and Matskin [29] propose a method for solving a resource sharing problem using a collaborative problem solving approach and a linear logic based formalism. Although we have a common application domain, that of negotiation for resource sharing, [29] does not refer to any particular social infrastructure, and makes a strong hypothesis on the collaborative behaviour of agents. The kind of interaction used by agents in [29] is richer than the one of [3], in that it involves the exchange of knowledge about capabilities. It could be interesting to investigate how to integrate [29] in a social framework which includes the notion of capabilities and gives a social semantics to the notion of collaboration.

We conclude this section by putting this work in relationship with our past and current activity within the SOCS project. In [30] a layered architecture for societies of computees has been proposed, where at the bottom level a platform is used to implement the system and give support to computees' communication, and a communication language layer defines syntax and semantics of communicative acts, while society and protocols are in a higher layer. The purpose the higher layers is to determine the set of allowed interaction patterns among computees in the society. A social semantics for communicative acts has been presented [31], along with a discussion about the advantages and motivation of a social semantics of communication with respect to other approaches, and in [10] an implementation of a restricted class of Social Integrity Constraints is proposed, based on the CHR language [18]. In [5] we define the full syntax of social integrity constraints, the scope of variables, quantification, and we give some results about the conditions for a proper behaviour of the framework, along with a formal semantic characterization of concepts such as coherence and consistency of sets of expectations and their fulfillment.

With respect to the work that we have been doing and that we have briefly reviewed above, this is the first paper which aims at showing the practical use of our theoretical framework, by means of a simple though realistic case study. The protocols that we used for our example are taken from the literature, and could be used to solve resource sharing problems among agents. We also contributed in showing how the framework can be the basis for the automatic proof of properties of interactions and protocols.

7   Conclusion

In this work, we have shown how a logic programming based framework is a suitable tool to give semantics to the interactions of autonomous entities populating a global computing environment. We illustrated the framework by means of a resource sharing example. The main idea is that of social integrity constraints, and of a correspondence with abductive frameworks of logic programming to provide a semantics to such constraints.

The main motivation of our approach is in its declarative nature, which has the potential to aiding a user's understanding of a system's specification, and in its solid formal basis, which puts together, under the same formalism, specification, implementation, and verification for multi-agent systems.

This paper wants to give a motivation to a formal approach by showing a concrete example of the expected operation of the framework.

The use of social integrity constraints could be twofold. In fact, through them the society can automatically verify the compliance of its members to the protocols, and ideally it could actively suggest to its members what are possible conforming behaviours, thus guiding them in their social life. The paper does not cover the last issue, which is subject for future work.

Acknowledgements

This work is partially funded by the Information Society Technologies programme of the European Commission under the IST-2001-32530 SOCS project.

References

1. Global Computing: Co-operation of Autonomous and Mobile Entities in Dynamic Environments http://www.cordis.lu/ist/fetgc.htm.
2. Societies Of ComputeeS (SOCS): a computational logic model for the description, analysis and verification of global and open societies of heterogeneous computees http://lia.deis.unibo.it/Research/SOCS/.
3. Sadri, F., Toni, F., Torroni, P.: Minimally intrusive negotiating agents for resource sharing. In Gottlob, G., Walsh, T., eds.: Proceedings of the 18th International Joint Conference on Artificial Intelligence, Morgan Kaufmann Publishers (2003)
4. Krogh, C.: Obligations in multiagent systems. In Aamodt A., Komorowski J., eds.: Proceedings of the 5th Scandinavian Conference on Artificial Intelligence, Trondheim, Norway. ISO Press, Amsterdam (1995) 19–30
5. Alberti, M., Gavanelli, M., Lamma, E., Mello, P., Torroni, P.: An Abductive Interpretation for Open Societies. In Cappello, A., Turini, F., eds.: AI*IA 2003: Advances in Artificial Intelligence, Proceedings of the 8th Congress of the Italian Association for Artificial Intelligence. Lecture Notes in Artificial Intelligence, Vol. 2829. Springer-Verlag (2003) 287–299
6. Eshghi, K., Kowalski, R.A.: Abduction compared with negation by failure. In Levi, G., Martelli, M., eds.: Proceedings of the 6th International Conference on Logic Programming, MIT Press (1989) 234–255
7. Kowalski, R.A., Sadri, F.: From logic programming towards multi-agent systems. Annals of Mathematics and Artificial Intelligence **25** (1999) 391–419
8. Poole, D.L.: A logical framework for default reasoning. Artificial Intelligence **36** (1988) 27–47
9. Fung, T.H., Kowalski, R.A.: The IFF proof procedure for abductive logic programming. Journal of Logic Programming **33** (1997) 151–165

10. Alberti, M., Ciampolini, A., Gavanelli, M., Lamma, E., Mello, P., Torroni, P.: Logic Based Semantics for an Agent Communication Language. In Dunin-Keplicz, B., Verbrugge, R., eds.: Proceedings of the International Workshop on Formal Approaches to Multi-Agent Systems (FAMAS), Warsaw, Poland (2003) 21–36

11. Yolum, P., Singh, M.: Flexible protocol specification and execution: applying event calculus planning using commitments. In Castelfranchi, C., Lewis Johnson, W., eds.: Proceedings of the First International Joint Conference on Autonomous Agents and Multiagent Systems (AAMAS), Part II, ACM Press (2002) 527–534

12. Guerin, F., Pitt, J.: Proving properties of open agent systems. In Castelfranchi, C., Lewis Johnson, W., eds.: Proceedings of the First International Joint Conference on Autonomous Agents and Multiagent Systems (AAMAS), Part II, ACM Press (2002) 557–558

13. Pitt, J., Guerin, F.: Guaranteeing properties for e-commerce systems. Technical Report TRS020015, Department of Electrical and Electronic Engineering, Imperial College, London, UK (2002)

14. Singh, M.P.: A social semantics for agent communication languages. In Dignum, F., Greaves, M., eds.: Issues in Agent Communication. Springer-Verlag (2000) 31–45

15. Hume, D.: An Enquiry Concerning Human Understanding. (1748)

16. Sadri, F., Toni, F., Torroni, P.: An abductive logic programming architecture for negotiating agents. In Greco, S., Leone, N., eds.: Proceedings of the 8th European Conference on Logics in Artificial Intelligence (JELIA). Lecture Notes in Computer Science, Vol. 2424. Springer-Verlag (2002) 419–431

17. Alberti, M., Daolio, D., Gavanelli, M., Lamma, E., Mello, P., Torroni, P.: Specification and verification of agent interaction protocols in a logic-based system. In: Proceedings of the 19th ACM Symposium on Applied Computing (SAC). Special Track on Agents, Interactions, Mobility, and Systems (AIMS) (2004) 72–78

18. Frühwirth, T.: Theory and practice of constraint handling rules. Journal of Logic Programming **37** (1998) 95–138

19. Esteva, M., Rodriguez-Aguilar, J.A., Sierra, C., Garcia, P., Arcos, J.L.: On the formal specification of electronic institutions. In Dignum, F., Sierra, C., eds.: Agent-mediated Electronic Commerce (The European AgentLink Perspective). Lecture Notes in Artificial Intelligence, Vol. 1991. Springer-Verlag (2001) 126–147

20. Dellarocas, C., Klein, M.: Civil agent societies: Tools for inventing open agent-mediated electronic marketplaces. In Moukas, A., Sierra, C., Ygge, F., eds.: Agent Mediated Electronic Commerce II, Towards Next-Generation Agent-Based Electronic Commerce Systems, IJCAI 1999 Workshop. Lecture Notes in Computer Science, Vol. 1788. Springer-Verlag (2000) 24–39

21. Vasconcelos, W.W.: Logic-based electronic institutions. In this volume.

22. Moses, Y., Tennenholtz, M.: Artificial social systems. Computers and AI **14** (1995) 533–562

23. Wooldridge, M., Jennings, N.R., Kinny, D.: The gaia methodology for agent-oriented analysis and design. Autonomous Agents and Multi-Agent Systems **3** (2000) 285–312

24. Lamport, L.: What Good Is Temporal Logic? In Mason, R.E.A., ed.: Information Processing, Vol. 83. Elsevier Sciene Publishers (1983) 657–668

25. Davidsson, P.: Categories of artificial societies. In Omicini, A., Petta, P., Tolksdorf, R., eds.: Engineering Societies in the Agents World II, 2nd International Workshop (ESAW), Prague, Czech Republic, 7 July 2001, Revised Papers. Lecture Notes in Artificial Intelligence, Vol. 2203. Springer-Verlag (2001) 1–9

26. Mazouzi, H., El Fallah Seghrouchni, A., Haddad, S.: Open protocol design fo complex interactions in multi-agent systems. In Castelfranchi, C., Lewis Johnson, W., eds.: Proceedings of the First International Joint Conference on Autonomous Agents and Multiagent Systems (AAMAS), Part II, ACM Press (2002) 402–409

27. Hewitt, C.: Open information systems semantics for distributed artificial intelligence. Artificial Intelligence **47** (1991) 79–106

28. Artikis, A., Pitt, J., Sergot, M.: Animated specifications of computational societies. In Castelfranchi, C., Lewis Johnson, W., eds.: Proceedings of the First International Joint Conference on Autonomous Agents and Multiagent Systems (AAMAS), Part III, ACM Press (2002) 1053–1061

29. Küngas, P., Matskin, M.: Linear logic, partial deduction and cooperative problem solving. In this volume.

30. Torroni, P., Mello, P., Maudet, N., Alberti, M., Ciampolini, A., Lamma, E., Sadri, F., Toni, F.: A logic-based approach to modeling interaction among computees (preliminary report). In: UK Multi-Agent Systems (UKMAS) Annual Conference, Liverpool, UK. (2002)

31. Alberti, M., Ciampolini, A., Gavanelli, M., Lamma, E., Mello, P., Torroni, P.: A social ACL semantics by deontic constraints. In Mařík, V., Müller, J., Pěchouček, M., eds.: Multi-Agent Systems and Applications III. Proceedings of the 3rd International Central and Eastern European Conference on Multi-Agent Systems (CEEMAS). Lecture Notes in Artificial Intelligence, Vol. 2691. Springer-Verlag (2003) 204–213

Linear Logic, Partial Deduction and Cooperative Problem Solving

Peep Küngas[1] and Mihhail Matskin[2]

[1] Norwegian University of Science and Technology
Department of Computer and Information Science
Trondheim, Norway
peep@idi.ntnu.no
[2] Royal Institute of Technology
Department of Microelectronics and Information Technology, Kista, Sweden
misha@imit.kth.se

Abstract. In this paper we present a model of cooperative problem solving (CPS). Linear Logic (LL) is used for encoding agents' states, goals and capabilities. LL theorem proving is applied by each agent to determine whether the particular agent is capable of solving the problem alone. If no individual solution can be constructed, then the agent may start negotiation with other agents in order to find a cooperative solution. Partial deduction in LL is used to derive a possible deal. Finally proofs are generated and plans are extracted from the proofs. The extracted plans determine agents' responsibilities in cooperative solutions.

1 Introduction

It is quite usual in multi-agent systems that an agent needs a help of another agent for performing its tasks and this situation has been considered in works on cooperative problems solving (CPS). Several attempts have been made in order to formalise CPS (see Section 5). Most of them are based on classical or modal logics. In particular, Wooldridge and Jennings [1] provide a formalisation of CPS process where a multi-modal logic is used as a formal specification language. However, since the multi-modal logic lacks a strategy for generating constructive proofs of satisfiability, the formalisation does not lead to direct execution of specifications. Moreover, since modal logics (like classical logic) lack the mechanism for keeping track of resources, it is not possible for agents neither to *count* nor dynamically update the number of instances of the same object belonging to their internal states.

In order to overcome the mentioned shortages of classical and modal logics we use a fragment of Linear Logic (LL) [2] for CPS. LL provides a mechanism for keeping track of resources (in LL one instance of a formula is distinguished from two or more instances of the formula) and this makes possible more natural representation of dynamical processes and agents' internal states.

The cooperative problem solving has been considered to consist of four steps [1]: recognition of potential for cooperation, team formation, plan formation and plan execution.

J. Leite et al. (Eds.): DALT 2003, LNAI 2990, pp. 263–279, 2004.
© Springer-Verlag Berlin Heidelberg 2004

An important feature of our approach is that we do not separate team and plan formation into different processes and that negotiation is embedded into the reasoning. Although this approach does not preserve the accepted structure of CPS, we think that it may be more natural for representing computational aspects of CPS, where team and plan formation processes interact with each other.

Basically, we are applying LL theorem proving for generating a constructive proof summarising the first 3 steps of CPS: recognition, team and plan formation. Negotiation is reformulated as distributed proof search. Then a solution, summarising the first 3 steps of CPS process, is extracted from a proof and is executed.

In CPS models it is often implicitly expected that agents have knowledge about sequences of actions, whose execution leads them to their goals, while the sequence construction process is not explicitly explained. Our CPS model is more planning-centric. Initially an agent tries to find a plan that allows achieving its goals. Then the agent may discover that either this is not possible or it is more efficient to involve other agents into problem solving process. Since other agents may be self-interested, they may propose their offers and start a negotiation process. The process lasts until a (shared) plan has been found. The plan determines agents' commitments and takes into account requirements determined during the negotiation.

In order to stimulate cooperation, agents should have a common goal [1]. We assume that all agents have a common *meta*-goal: as much agents as possible should become satisfied during run-time. All agents ask for minimum they need and provide maximum they can, during negotiation. This is biased with distributed theorem proving strategies. During negotiation the offers are derived using Partial Deduction (PD) in LL. PD allows determining missing links between proof fragments.

The rest of the paper is organised as follows. In Section 2 we present a general model of distributed problem solving and illustrate it with a working example. Section 3 gives an introduction to LL and PD. Section 4 proceeds with the working example from Section 2 by applying LL theorem proving and PD for CPS. Section 5 reviews related work and Section 6 concludes the article.

2   General CPS Model and a Working Example

2.1   A CPS Model

We define an agent $\mathcal{A}_i$ as a triple

$$\mathcal{A}_i = (\Gamma_i, S_i, G_i),$$

where:

- S_i is a set of literals representing the current state of the agent.
- G_i is a set of literals representing the goal state of the agent.

- Γ_i represents a set of agent's capabilities in form $Delete \mapsto Add$. $Delete$ and Add are sets of formulae, which are respectively deleted from and added to the agent's current state S_i, if the particular capability is applied. The capability can be applied only if $Delete \subseteq S_i$.

By agent's capabilities we mean actions that an agent can perform. While performing a capability $X \mapsto Y$, an agent consumes resources denoted by X and generates resources referred by Y. The word "state" is used herein instead of "beliefs" to emphasise that our approach is planning-centric. Moreover, it expresses explicitly that our approach is not related directly to BDI theory. We write S_i' and G_i' to denote modification of S_i and G_i respectively. Similarly we write S_i'' and G_i'' to denote modifications of S_i' and G_i', and so forth. While representing states and goals of agents we write A^n to specify that there are n instances of object A in a particular state or a goal.

While planning, an agent may discover that a plan, whose execution would lead it from state S_i to goal G_i, could not be found. If this is the case, the agent determines subproblems (missing links), which it cannot solve alone. A missing link with respect to S_i and G_i is a pair (S_i', G_i'), which is achieved by applying agent's capabilities to its initial state S_i in forward chaining and to its goal G_i in backward chaining manner. This is denoted by $S_i \longmapsto_* S_i'$ and $G_i' \longmapsto_* G_i$, where $\longmapsto$ represents application of a capability from Γ_i and $\longmapsto_*$ denotes that 0 or more capabilities are applied in sequence.

For illustrating detection of missing links let us consider the case where $S_1 = \{A\}$, $G_1 = \{D\}$ and $\Gamma_1 = \{A \mapsto B, C \mapsto D\}$. Possible missing links in this case are $(\{B\}, \{C\})$, $(\{B\}, \{D\})$, $(\{A\}, \{C\})$ and $(\{A\}, \{D\})$. If, for example, agent $\mathcal{A}_1$ decides that the most relevant missing link is $(\{B\}, \{C\})$, it sends a message with $S_1' = \{B\}$, $G_1' = \{C\}$ to another agent $\mathcal{A}_2$. Additionally $\mathcal{A}_1$ may send a list of its capabilities Γ_1 (or a fragment of Γ_1) that might help $\mathcal{A}_2$ in reasoning about possible offers.

Our general CPS model is depicted in Figure 1. Communication between agents goes via a Communication Adapter (CA), whose purpose is:

- to provide translations between agents' communication languages and
- to change the viewpoint of proposals

Usage of Communication Adapter will be explained in details in Section 3.5. A typical interaction sequence in the CPS model is as follows:

1. Agent $\mathcal{A}_1$ tries to generate such a plan from elements of Γ_1, that its execution would lead $\mathcal{A}_1$ from state S_1 to G_1. However, $\mathcal{A}_1$ fails to construct such a solution.
2. Agent $\mathcal{A}_1$ identifies possible missing links for achieving a complete solution. Every missing link derived from S_1 and G_1 is presented with a pair (S_1', G_1').
3. Agent $\mathcal{A}_1$ informs other agents about its missing links and asks them to solve the missing links. If no answer is received, the problem is not solvable.
4. If some agent $\mathcal{A}_2$ finds a solution for the link (S_1', G_1'), then S_1'' and G_1'' are just copies of S_1' and G_1', respectively, and $\mathcal{A}_2$ generates a solution for

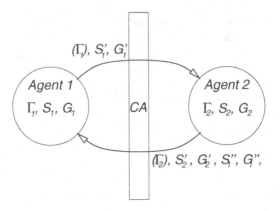

Fig. 1. General CPS model.

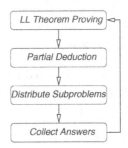

Fig. 2. Iterative CPS process.

the missing link. Otherwise, $\mathcal{A}_2$ may produce a new missing link S_1'' and G_1'' based on S_1' and G_1' and $\mathcal{A}_2$ generates a partial solution to the initial problem.

5. $\mathcal{A}_2$ delivers (S_1'', G_1'') and a solution (complete or partial) back to $\mathcal{A}_1$.

6. Additionally, $\mathcal{A}_2$ may require that $\mathcal{A}_1$ helps to solve a missing link (G_2', S_2') in return to the solution and the missing link (S_1'', G_1''). The link (G_2', S_2') is achieved by applying CA to the link (S_2', G_2').

7. Agent $\mathcal{A}_2$ may also send the new missing link (S_1'', G_1'') to other agents for solving. In this case $\mathcal{A}_2$ acts as a mediator agent.

Negotiation proceeds until the set of possible missing links will be exhausted or a solution satisfying both agents is found. In an extreme case all agents may be explicitly aware of each other capabilities and goals a priori. In this case there are less messages sent during negotiation, however, agents' privacy is less supported. For implementing our model we apply LL theorem proving for planning and PD for determining subtasks, which have to be solved by other agents. The iterative CPS process is depicted in Figure 2.

2.2   Working Example

Taking into account the general CPS model, our working example is described as follows. Let us assume that two students, John and Peter, are looking for ways to relax after long days of studying and a final successful examination. John has a CD and he wants to listen music:

$$G_{John} = \{Music\}.$$

Unfortunately, his CD player is broken and this makes his goal unachievable. John has to visit also a library to return books and this gives him possibility to return also books of other students when this may be useful for him. John has 10 USD for covering all his expenses, related to relaxing. Considering that he has a broken CD player and a CD, his initial state is as follows:

$$S_{John} = \{Dollar^{10}, CD, BrokenCDPlayer\}$$

and his capabilities are:

$$\Gamma_{John} = \begin{array}{l} Books \mapsto BooksReturned, \\ CDPlayer \& CD \mapsto Music. \end{array}$$

Peter is skilled in electronics and can repair the CD player. He has decided to spend his day in a park with his girlfriend. However, he has to return books to the library. Since he has to take a taxi to reach the library, he has to spend 10 USD to cover his transportation expenses. This does not match well with his goals, because of he has only 15 USD while he needs 25 USD for food, drinks and attractions in the park. Therefore he lacks 20 USD to achieve his goals. Peter's initial state, goal and capabilities are described as follows:

$$S_{Peter} = \{Dollar^{15}, Books\},$$

$$G_{Peter} = \{BooksReturned, Beer\},$$

$$\Gamma_{Peter} = \begin{array}{l} Dollar^{10} \& Books \mapsto BooksReturned, \\ BrokenCDPlayer \mapsto CDPlayer, \\ Dollar^{25} \mapsto Beer. \end{array}$$

Taking into account Γ_{John}, G_{John} and S_{John}, John constructs a new state and a goal and asks Peter whether he can repair his CD player:

$$S'_{John} = \{BrokenCDPlayer\},$$

$$G'_{John} = \{CDPlayer\}.$$

Peter decides to take advantage of the situation. He agrees to repair the CD player and asks 20 USD for performing this task:

$$S'_{Peter} = \{\},$$
$$G'_{Peter} = \{Dollar^{20}\},$$
$$G''_{John} = G'_{John},$$

and

$$S''_{John} = S'_{John}.$$

However, John has only 10 USD. Therefore he discloses additional information about his capabilities to Peter:

$$\Gamma''_{John} = \{Books \mapsto BooksReturned\}.$$

Peter discovers that John has decided to visit a university library and agrees to decrease a fee for repairing the CD player by 10 USD, if John delivers his books to the library. John agrees and negotiation is successfully finished. During the negotiation agents' plans have also been determined.

3   Formalisation of CPS Process

3.1   Linear Logic

LL is a refinement of classical logic introduced by J.-Y. Girard to provide means for keeping track of "resources". In LL two assumptions of a propositional constant A are distinguished from a single assumption of A. This does not apply in classical logic, since there the truth value of a fact does not depend on the number of copies of the fact. Indeed, LL is not about truth, it is about computation.

Although LL is not the first attempt to develop resource-oriented logics, it is by now the most investigated one. Since its introduction LL has enjoyed increasing attention both from proof theorists and computer scientists. Therefore, because of its maturity, LL is useful as a declarative language and an inference kernel.

In the following we are considering intuitionistic multiplicative additive fragment of LL (IMALL or MAILL) consisting of multiplicative conjunction ($\otimes$), additive disjunction ($\oplus$), additive conjunction (&) and linear implication ($\multimap$). In terms of resource acquisition the logical expression $A \otimes B \vdash C \otimes D$ means that resources C and D are obtainable only if both A and B are obtainable. After the sequent has been applied, A and B are consumed and C and D are generated.

The expression $A \vdash B \oplus C$ in contrary means that, if we have resource A, we can obtain either B or C, but we do not know which one of those. The expression $A\&B \vdash C$ on the other hand means that while having resources A and B we can choose, which one of them to trade for C. Therefore it is said that $\oplus$ and & are representing *external* and *internal* choice.

In order to illustrate the above-mentioned features we can consider the following LL sequent from [3] – $(D \otimes D \otimes D \otimes D \otimes D) \vdash (H \otimes C \otimes (O\&S) \otimes !F \otimes (P \oplus I))$, which encodes a fixed price menu in a fast-food restaurant: for 5 dollars (D) you can get an hamburger (H), a coke (C), either onion soup O or salad S depending, which one *you* select, all the french fries (F) you can eat plus a pie (P) or an ice cream (I) depending on availability (restaurant owner selects for you). The formula $!F$ here means that we can use or generate a resource F as much as we want – the amount of the resource is unbounded.

To increase the expressiveness of formulae, we use the following abbreviation $a^n = \underbrace{a \otimes \ldots \otimes a}_{n}$, for $n \geq 0$.

Lincoln [4] summarises complexity results for several fragments of LL. Propositional MALL is indicated to be PSPACE-complete, whilst first-order MALL is at most NEXPTIME-hard. If we would discard additives $\oplus$ and $\&$ from MALL, we would get multiplicative LL (MLL). Both, propositional and first-order MLL, are NP-complete. It is also identified that these complexity results do not change, if intuitionistic fragments of LL are considered. These results hint that for practical computations either MLL or propositional MALL (or their intuitionistic variants MILL and MAILL (IMALL), respectively) could be used. The complete set of IMALL inference rules is given in Appendix A.

3.2   Partial Deduction and LL

Partial Deduction (PD) (or partial evaluation of logic programs first introduced in [5]) is known as one of optimisation techniques in logic programming. Given a logic program, partial deduction derives a more specific program while preserving the meaning of the original program. Since the program is more specialised, it is usually more efficient than the original program, if executed. For instance, let A, B, C and D be propositional variables and $A \multimap B$, $B \multimap C$ and $C \multimap D$ computability statements in LL. Then possible partial deductions are $A \multimap C$, $B \multimap D$ and $A \multimap D$. It is easy to notice that the first corresponds to forward chaining (from initial states to goals), the second to backward chaining (from goals to initial states) and the third could be either forward or backward chaining.

Lloyd and Shepherdson [6] formalised PD for normal logic programs and showed its correctness with respect to Clark's program completion semantics. PD in logic programming is often defined as unfolding of program clauses.

Although the original motivation behind PD was to deduce specialised logic programs with respect to a given goal, our motivation for PD is a bit different. We are applying PD for determining subtasks, which cannot be solved by a single agent, but still are possibly closer to a solution than an initial task. This means that given a state S and a goal G of an agent we compute a new state S' and a new goal G'. This information is forwarded to another agent for further inference. Similar approach has been applied by Matskin and Komorowski [7] in automatic software synthesis. One of their motivations was debugging of declarative software specification.

The main problem with PD in LL is that although new derived states and goals are sound with respect to an initial specification, they may not preserve completeness anymore. This is due to resource-consciousness of LL – if a wrong proof branch is followed, initial beliefs may be consumed and thus further search becomes more limited. Therefore agents have to search, in the worst case, all possible PDs of an initial specification to preserve completeness of distributed search mechanism. In [6] completeness and soundness issues of PD are considered for classical logic programs. Issues of complexity, completeness and soundness of PD in LL will be considered within another paper.

We define the following LL inference figures as PD steps for backward and forward chaining:

Backward chaining step $\mathcal{R}_b(L_i)$:

$$
\cfrac{
\cfrac{S \vdash A \otimes C \qquad \cfrac{}{\vdash (A \multimap_{L_i} B)} \; Axiom}{S \vdash A \otimes C \otimes (A \multimap_{L_i} B)} \; R\otimes
\qquad
\cfrac{
\cfrac{C \vdash C}{} \; Id \qquad
\cfrac{
\cfrac{
\cfrac{A \vdash A}{} \; Id \qquad \cfrac{B \vdash B}{} \; Id
}{A, (A \multimap_{L_i} B) \vdash B} \; L\multimap
}{A \otimes (A \multimap_{L_i} B) \vdash B} \; L\otimes
}{
\cfrac{C, A \otimes (A \multimap_{L_i} B) \vdash B \otimes C}{A \otimes C \otimes (A \multimap_{L_i} B) \vdash B \otimes C} \; L\otimes
} \; R\otimes
}{S \vdash B \otimes C} \; Cut
$$

Forward chaining step $\mathcal{R}_f(L_i)$:

$$
\cfrac{
\cfrac{B \otimes C \vdash B \otimes C \; Id \qquad \cfrac{}{\vdash (B \multimap_{L_i} A)} \; Axiom}{B \otimes C \vdash B \otimes C \otimes (B \multimap_{L_i} A)} \; R\otimes
\qquad
\cfrac{
\cfrac{
\cfrac{C \vdash C}{} \; Id \qquad
\cfrac{
\cfrac{B \vdash B \; Id \qquad A \vdash A \; Id}{B, (B \multimap_{L_i} A) \vdash A} \; L\multimap
}{B \otimes (B \multimap_{L_i} A) \vdash A} \; L\otimes
}{C, B \otimes (B \multimap_{L_i} A) \vdash A \otimes C} \; R\otimes
}{B \otimes C \otimes (B \multimap_{L_i} A) \vdash A \otimes C} \; L\otimes
\qquad A \otimes C \vdash G
}{
\cfrac{B \otimes C \otimes (B \multimap_{L_i} A) \vdash G}{} \; Cut
}
}{B \otimes C \vdash G} \; Cut
$$

L_i in previous inference figures is a labelling for a particular LL axiom representing an agent's capability. PD steps $\mathcal{R}_f(L_i)$ and $\mathcal{R}_b(L_i)$, respectively, apply clause L_i to move the initial state towards the goal state or vice versa. A, B and C are multiplicative conjunctions. In $\mathcal{R}_b(L_i)$ inference figure formulae $B \otimes C$ and $A \otimes C$ denote respectively G and G'. Thus the inference figure encodes that, if there is an extralogical axiom $\vdash A \multimap B$, then we can change goal $B \otimes C$ to $A \otimes C$. Analogously, in the inference figure $\mathcal{R}_f(L_i)$ formulae $B \otimes C$ and $A \otimes C$ denote respectively S and S'. And the inference figure encodes that, if there is an extralogical axiom $\vdash B \multimap A$, then we can change initial state $B \otimes C$ to $A \otimes C$.

3.3 Agents in LL

An agent is presented with the following LL sequent:

$$\Gamma; S \vdash G,$$

where Γ is a set of extralogical LL axioms representing agent's capabilities, S is the initial state and G the goal state of an agent. Both S and G are multiplicative conjunctions of literals. Every element of Γ is in form

$$\vdash I \multimap O,$$

whereas I and O are multiplicative conjunctions of formulae, which are respectively consumed and generated when a particular capability is applied. It has to be mentioned that a capability can be applied only, if conjuncts in I form a subset of conjuncts in S.

3.4   Encoding Offers in LL

Harland and Winikoff [8] presented the first ideas about applying LL theorem proving for agent negotiation. The main advantages of LL over classical logic is its resource-consciousness and existence of two kinds of nondeterminism. Both internal and external nondeterminism in negotiation rules can be represented. In the case of internal nondeterminism a choice is made by resource provider, whereas in the case of external nondeterminism a choice is made by resource consumer. For instance, formula $Dollar^5 \multimap Beer \oplus Soda$ means that an agent can provide either some $Beer$ or $Soda$ in return for 5 dollars, but the choice is made by the provider agent. The consumer agent has to be ready to obtain either a beer or a soda. The formula $Dollar \multimap Tobacco \& Lighter$ in contrary means that the consumer may select which resource, $Tobacco$ or $Lighter$, s/he gets for a $Dollar$.

In the context of negotiation, operators & and $\oplus$ have symmetrical meanings – what is $A \oplus B$ for one agent, is $A\&B$ to her/his partner. This means that if one agent gives to another agent an opportunity to choose between A and B, then the former agent has to be ready to provide both choices, A and B. When initial resources owned by agents and expected negotiation results have been specified, LL theorem proving is used for determining the negotiation process.

We augment the ideas of Harland and Winikoff by allowing trading also services (agent capabilities) for resources and vice versa. This is a step further to the world where agents not only exchange resources, but also work for other agents in order to achieve their own goals. We write $A \vdash B \multimap C$ to indicate that an agent can trade resource A for a service $B \multimap C$.

3.5   Communication Adapter

In [9] bridge rules are used for translating formulae from one logic to another, when agents exchange offers. We adopt this idea of Communication Adapter (CA) for two reasons. First, it would allow us to encapsulate agents' internal states and, second, while offers are delivered by one agent to another, viewpoint to the offer is changing and internal and external choices are inversed. By viewpoint we mean agent's role, which can be either receiver or sender of an offer.

The CA rule is described in the following way. As long as formulae on the left and the right hand side of sequents consist of only $\otimes$ and $\multimap$ operators, the left and the right hand sides of sequents are inversed. However, if formulae contain additives, their types have to be inversed. This has to be done because there are 2 additives in LL – one with internal and another with external choice. Since internal and external choices are context-dependent, they have to be inversed, when changing viewpoints. For instance, sequent $A \otimes (A \multimap B) \vdash C \oplus D$ is translated to $C \& D \vdash A \otimes (A \multimap B)$ by the CA rule:

$$\frac{\underset{j}{\&} B_j \vdash \underset{i}{\bigoplus} A_i}{\underset{i}{\&} A_i \vdash \underset{j}{\bigoplus} B_j} \ CA$$

In the CA rule A and B consist of multiplicative conjunctions and linear implications. We allow $\&$ only in the left hand side and $\oplus$ only in the right hand side of a sequent. Due to LL rules $R\&$ and $L\oplus$ (see Appendix A) the following conversions are allowed:

$$D \vdash \underset{j}{\&} D_j \implies \bigcup_j (D \vdash D_j)$$

$$\bigoplus_j D_j \vdash D \implies \bigcup_j (D_j \vdash D)$$

Therefore we do not lose in expressive power of LL, when limiting places where disjunctions may occur.

Although our bridge rule is intended for agents reasoning in LL only, additional bridge rules may be constructed for communication with other non-LL agents. However, it should be mentioned that there is no one-to-one translation between most of logics and therefore information loss may occur during translation.

4   Running Example

Let us consider encoding of the working example from Section 2 in LL and explain how to represent agents' capabilities (actions they can perform), negotiation arguments, agents' states and goals with LL formulae. In order to keep the resulting proof simple, we take advantage of propositional MILL (a fragment of MAILL) only.

The initial scenario is described formally as follows:

$$\Gamma_{John} = \begin{array}{l} \vdash_{John} Books \multimap_{returnBooks} BooksReturned \\ \vdash_{John} CDPlayer \otimes CD \multimap_{playMusic} Music \end{array}$$

$$\Gamma_{Peter} = \begin{array}{l} \vdash_{Peter} Dollar^{10} \otimes Books \multimap_{returnBooks} BooksReturned \\ \vdash_{Peter} BrokenCDPlayer \multimap_{repairCDPlayer} CDPlayer \\ \vdash_{Peter} Dollar^{25} \multimap_{buyBeer} Beer \end{array}$$

The sets of extralogical axioms Γ_{John} and Γ_{Peter} represent capabilities of John and Peter, respectively. We write $\vdash_X$ to indicate that a capability is provided by X, $\multimap_Y$ labels a capability with name Y. The internal state of John is described by the following sequent:

$$\Gamma_{John}; Dollar^{10} \otimes CD \otimes BrokenCDPlayer \vdash_{John} Music$$

This means that John has 10 USD, a CD and a broken CD player. His goal is to listen music. Peter's state and goal are described by another sequent:

$$\Gamma_{Peter}; Dollar^{15} \otimes Books \vdash_{Peter} BooksReturned \otimes Beer$$

We write B, BR, BE, CD, P, BP, M and D to denote $Books$, $BooksReturned$, $Beer$, CD, $CDPlayer$, $BrokenCDPlayer$, $Music$ and $Dollar$ respectively. Given John's and Peter's capabilities and internal states, both agents start individually with theorem proving. Initially they fail, since they are unable to reach their goals individually. Then PD in LL is applied to the same set of formulae and new subtasks are derived. These subtasks indicate problems, which could not be solved by agents themselves and need cooperation with other agents. In particular, John has to ask help for solving the following sequent, which is derived by PD:

$$D^{10} \vdash_{John} BP \multimap P$$

The sequent is produced by applying the backward chaining PD step as follows (to allow shorter proof, we write here $\vdash$ instead of $\vdash_{John}$):

$$
\cfrac{
  \cfrac{
    \cfrac{
      \cfrac{\overline{CD \vdash CD}\ Id \quad \cfrac{D^{10} \vdash_{John} BP \multimap P}{D^{10} \otimes BP \vdash P}\ Shift}{CD, D^{10} \otimes BP \vdash CD \otimes P}\ R\otimes
    }{D^{10} \otimes BP \otimes CD \vdash CD \otimes P}\ L\otimes
  }{D^{10} \otimes BP \otimes CD \vdash_{John} M}\ \mathcal{R}_b(playMusic)
}{}
$$

where $Shift$ is another inference figure:

$$
\cfrac{\overline{C \vdash A \multimap B}\ Axiom \quad \cfrac{\overline{A \vdash A}\ Id \quad \overline{B \vdash B}\ Id}{A, A \multimap B \vdash B}\ L \multimap}{C \otimes A \vdash B}\ Cut
$$

The purpose of the inference figure above, is to transform sequents of the form $C \otimes A \vdash B$ to the form $C \vdash A \multimap B$, which is our sequent representation for agents' capabilities. It has to be mentioned that C can be possibly an empty formula.

Peter sees the offer as follows:

$$BP \multimap P \vdash_{Peter} D^{10}$$

Changing a viewpoint for offers is done by Communication Adapter (CA, see Section 3.5).

Since Peter can repair the CD player, he agrees partially with the proposal. However, because he needs 20 USD instead of the proposed 10 USD, he increases the number of dollars required. In addition, assuming that John may not have the asked amount of money, Peter provides him with information about tasks (Γ_{Peter}), which may be traded for money:

$$\Gamma_{Peter}; BP \multimap P \vdash_{Peter} D^{20}$$

This is viewed by John as follows:

$$\Gamma_{Peter}; D^{20} \vdash_{John} BP \multimap P$$

By exploring Γ_{Peter} John discovers that both his and John's goals would be reached, if he delivers Peters' books to the library for 10 USD and Peter repairs the CD player for 20 USD. Peter accepts the offer.

Another possible solution could be that Peter repairs the CD player for 10 USD and John delivers his books. However, while the former solution makes it possible to introduce binding contracts between agents, the latter expects that both agents trust each other. Depending on the proof strategy, we can represent different solutions to cooperation problem solving.

The final proposal from John is presented as the following sequent:

$$\Gamma_{Peter}; D^{20} \otimes (D^{10} \otimes B \multimap BR) \vdash_{John} BP \multimap P$$

After applying CA it is perceived by Peter as follows:

$$\Gamma_{Peter}; BP \multimap P \vdash_{Peter} D^{20} \otimes (D^{10} \otimes B \multimap BR)$$

During communication agents can send information about their capabilities (Γ_{Peter} in the current case). This provides their partners with hints about possible counteroffers. The following proof is constructed for John during the above-described series of message exchange (we omit Γ_{John} and Γ_{Peter} in the proof for simplicity):

John's plan can be extracted from the proof and then executed. In the proof action *returnBooks* occurs twice. While *returnBooks* means that John has to execute it, *returnBooks$_{Peter}$* explicitly represents that Peter has to be charged with 10 dollars for performing previous action. A proof for Peter can be constructed in a similar way.

The proof above does not present the whole negotiation process. It rather demonstrates the *result* of negotiation and team and plan formation. The proof

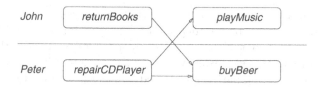

Fig. 3. Interdependent plans.

also indicates how John and Peter have joined efforts to achieve their goals. The interdependency of plans for John and Peter is shown in Figure 3.

Arrows in Figure 3 indicate a partial order of actions to be executed (or capabilities applied) and the line separates actions performed by different agents (actions above the line are executed by John and actions below the line are executed by Peter).

5   Related Work

As it has been indicated in [10] negotiation is the most fundamental and powerful mechanism for managing inter-agent dependencies at run-time. Negotiation may be required both for self-interested and cooperative agents. It allows to reach a mutually acceptable agreement on some matter by a group of agents.

Kraus et al [11] give a logical description for negotiation via argumentation for BDI agents. They classify arguments as threats and promises, which are identified as most common arguments in human negotiations. In our case only promises are considered, since in order to figure out possible threats to goals of particular agents, agents' beliefs, goals and capabilities should be known in advance to the persuader. We assume, that our agents do not explicitly communicate about their internal state.

Fisher [12] introduced the idea of distributed theorem proving in classical logic as agent negotiation. In his approach all agents share the common view to the world and if a new clause is inferred, all agents would sense it. Inferred clauses are distributed among agents via broadcasting. Then, considering the received information, agents infer new clauses and broadcast them further again. Although agents have a common knowledge about inferred clauses, they may have different sets of inference rules. Distribution of a collection of rules between agents means that different agents may have different capabilities and make different inferences. The latter implies that different agents contribute to different phases of proof search. Our approach differs from that work mainly in 2 aspects (in addition to usage of another logic): our agents do not share a common view of a world and inference results are not broadcasted.

Parsons et al [9] defined negotiation as interleaved formal reasoning and arguing. Arguments and counterarguments are derived using theorem proving while taking into consideration agents' own goals. While Parsons et al [9] perform reasoning in classical logic, it is possible to infer missing clauses needed for achieving a goal. The situation gets more complicated, when several instances of formulae are available and, moreover, the actions performed by agents or resources they spend can be interdependent. Thereby, inference in LL is not so straightforward, since some clauses are "consumed" while inferring other clauses. Due to the aforementioned reasons we apply PD to determine missing parts of a proof. Then the missing part is announced to other possibly interested agents.

Sadri et al [13] propose another logical approach to automated negotiation, which is built on work of Amgoud et al [14] on argumentation. The work of Sadri et al is more specialised and detailed than the work by Amgoud et al. That allows deeper analysis of the reasoning mechanism and the knowledge required to build negotiation dialogues.

Our approach could be viewed as distributed planning similarly to the work in [15]. Case-based planning has been used for coordinating agent teams in [16]. The planner generates a so called shared mental model of the team plan. Then all agents adapt their plans to the team plan. This work is influenced by the joint intentions [17,18] and shared plans [19] theory.

In [20] agent coordination is performed via task agents by planning. First, problem solving goals are raised and then solutions satisfying those goals are computed. Finally, these plans are decomposed and coordinated with appropriate tasks of other agents for plan execution, monitoring and result collection.

The joint intentions theory [18] determines the means of how agents should act to fulfill joint goals, when they should exchange messages, leave the team, etc. It also determines when the joint goal is considered to be achieved or when and how to break up commitment to it (for example, if it turns out that one agent is not able anymore to perform its task(s)). Decision making about whether a goal has been achieved, is not achievable or there is no need to achieve it anymore, is based on consensus. Then everybody acts as stated by the consensus. However, it is not stated how joint goals are formed via negotiation or other processes.

One of the first formalisations of cooperative problem solving is given by Wooldridge and Jennings [1] (other approaches presented so far are also reviewed there). One of the earliest *implemented* general models of teamwork is described in [21], which is based on joint intentions theory and on shared plans theory.

In [22] LL has been used for prototyping multi-agent systems at conceptual level. Because of fixed semantics of LL, it is possible to verify whether a system functions as intended at conceptual level. Although the prototype LL program is executable, it is still too high level to produce a final agent-based software. Thus another logic programming language is embedded to compose the final software.

Harland and Winikoff [23] address the question of how to integrate both proactive and reactive properties of agents into LL programming framework. They use forward chaining to model the reactive behaviour of an agent and backward chaining to model the proactive behaviour. This type of computation is called as mixed mode computation, since both forward and backward chaining are allowed.

6   Conclusions

We presented a computational model of CPS, where the main emphasis is set to negotiation and planning. Need for cooperation emerges, when an agent is unable to find a plan for achieving its goals alone. Agent teams are formed on basis of interdependent plans.

For formalising our general CPS model we use LL. Planning is implemented on top of LL theorem proving. Initially a planning problem is encoded in terms of LL sequents and theorem proving is applied for generating constructive proofs. Then plans are extracted from the generated proofs. We specified negotiation as distributed LL theorem proving, whereas PD is used for generating offers. Offers are generally in form – I can grant you X if you provide me with Y, where X and Y can be both resources and capabilities of agents.

We have implemented a planner on top of a theorem prover for first-order MILL and performed initial experiments. The planner is available at RAPS homepage http://www.idi.ntnu.no/~peep/RAPS.

Acknowledgements

This work is partially supported by the Norwegian Research Foundation in the framework of Information and Communication Technology (IKT-2010) program – the ADIS project. We would like to thank the anonymous referees for their useful comments.

References

1. Wooldridge, M., Jennings, N.R.: The cooperative problem-solving process. Journal of Logic and Computation **9** (1999) 563–592
2. Girard, J.Y.: Linear logic. Theoretical Computer Science **50** (1987) 1–102
3. Lincoln, P.: Linear logic. ACM SIGACT Notices **23** (1992) 29–37
4. Lincoln, P.: Deciding provability of linear logic formulas. In Girard, J.Y., Lafont, Y., Regnier, L., eds.: Advances in Linear Logic. London Mathematical Society Lecture Note Series, Vol. 222. (1995) 109–122
5. Komorowski, J.: A specification of an abstract prolog machine and its application to partial evaluation. PhD thesis. Technical Report LSST 69, Department of Computer and Information Science, Linkoping University, Linkoping, Sweden (1981)
6. Lloyd, J.W., Shepherdson, J.C.: Partial evaluation in logic programming. Journal of Logic Programming **11** (1991) 217–242
7. M. Matskin, J.K.: Partial structural synthesis of programs. Fundamenta Informaticae **30** (1997) 23–41
8. Harland, J., Winikoff, M.: Agent negotiation as proof search in linear logic. In: Proceedings of the First International Joint Conference on Autonomous Agents and Multi-Agent Systems (AAMAS 2002), Bologna, Italy. (2002)
9. Parsons, S., Sierra, C., Jennings, N.: Agents that reason and negotiate by arguing. Journal of Logic and Computation **8** (1998) 261–292

10. Jennings, N.R., Faratin, P., Lomuscio, A.R., Parsons, S., Sierra, C., Wooldridge, M.: Automated negotiation: Prospects, methods and challenges. International Journal of Group Decision and Negotiation **10** (2001) 199–215
11. Kraus, S., Sycara, K., Evenchik, A.: Reaching agreements through argumentation: A logical model and implementation. Artificial Intelligence **104** (1998) 1–69
12. Fisher, M.: Characterising simple negotiation as distributed agent-based theorem-proving – a preliminary report. In: Proceedings of the Fourth International Conference on Multi-Agent Systems, Boston, IEEE Press (2000)
13. Sadri, F., Toni, F., Torroni, P.: Logic agents, dialogues and negotiation: An abductive approach. In: Proceedings of the Symposium on Information Agents for E-Commerce, Artificial Intelligence and the Simulation of Behaviour Convention (AISB-2001), York, UK. (2001)
14. Amgoud, L., Parsons, S., Maudet, N.: Arguments, dialogue and negotiation. In: Proceedings of 14th European Conference on Artificial Intelligence, Berlin, Germany. (2000) 338–342
15. Fisher, M., Wooldridge, M.: Distributed problem-solving as concurrent theorem proving. In: Proceedings of 8th European Workshop on Modelling Autonomous Agents in a Multi-Agent World, Ronneby, Sweden. Lecture Notes in Computer Science, Vol. 1237. Springer-Verlag (1997) 128–140
16. Giampapa, J.A., Sycara, K.: Conversational case-based planning for agent team coordination. In Aha, D.W., Watson, I., eds.: Case-Based Reasoning Research and Development: Proceedings of the Fourth International Conference on Case-Based Reasoning, ICCBR 2001. Lecture Notes in Artificial Intelligence, Vol. 2080. (2001)
17. Levesque, H.J., Cohen, P.R., Nunes, J.H.T.: On acting together. In: Proceedings of the Eighth National Conference on Artificial Intelligence, AAAI-90. (1990) 94–99
18. Cohen, P.R., Levesque, H.J.: Teamwork. Nous **25** (1991) 487–512
19. Grosz, B., Kraus, S.: Collaborative plans for complex group actions. Artificial Intelligence **86** (1996) 269–357
20. Sycara, K., Zeng, D.: Coordination of multiple intelligent software agents. International Journal of Intelligent and Cooperative Information Systems **5** (1996) 181–211
21. Tambe, M.: Towards flexible teamwork. Journal of Artificial Intelligence Research **7** (1997) 83–124
22. Bozzano, M., Delzanno, G., Martelli, M., Mascardi, V., Zini, F.: Logic programming & multi-agent systems: a synergic combination for applications and semantics. In: The Logic Programming Paradigm: a 25-Year Perspective, Springer-Verlag (1999) 5–32
23. Harland, J., Winikoff, M.: Language design issues for agents based on linear logic. In Dix, J., Leite, J.A., Satoh, K., eds.: Proceedings of the Third International Workshop on Computational Logic in Multi-Agent Systems (CLIMA-02), 1st August, Copenhagen, Denmark. Electronic Notes in Theoretical Computer Science 70(5), Elsevier (2002)

A   Propositional IMALL Rules

Logical axiom and Cut rule:

$$A \vdash A \;\; (Axiom) \qquad \frac{\Gamma \vdash A, \Delta \quad \Gamma', A \vdash \Delta'}{\Gamma, \Gamma' \vdash \Delta, \Delta'} \;\; (Cut)$$

Rules for the propositional constants:

$$\vdash 1 \qquad \frac{\Gamma \vdash A}{\Gamma, 1 \vdash A}$$

$$\frac{\Gamma, A, B \vdash \Delta}{\Gamma, A \otimes B \vdash \Delta} \ (L\otimes) \qquad \frac{\Gamma \vdash A, \Delta \quad \Gamma' \vdash B, \Delta'}{\Gamma, \Gamma' \vdash A \otimes B, \Delta, \Delta'} \ (R\otimes)$$

$$\frac{\Sigma_1 \vdash A \quad B, \Sigma_2 \vdash C}{\Sigma_1, (A \multimap B), \Sigma_2 \vdash C} \ L \multimap \qquad \frac{\Sigma, A \vdash B}{\Sigma \vdash (A \multimap B)} \ R \multimap$$

$$\frac{\Gamma, A \vdash \Delta \quad \Gamma, B \vdash \Delta}{\Gamma, A \oplus B \vdash \Delta} \ (L\oplus) \qquad \frac{\Gamma \vdash A, \Delta}{\Gamma \vdash A \oplus B, \Delta} \ (R\oplus)(a) \qquad \frac{\Gamma \vdash B, \Delta}{\Gamma \vdash A \oplus B, \Delta} \ (R\oplus)(b)$$

$$\frac{\Gamma, A \vdash \Delta}{\Gamma, A\&B \vdash \Delta} \ (L\&)(a) \qquad \frac{\Gamma, B \vdash \Delta}{\Gamma, A\&B \vdash \Delta} \ (L\&)(b) \qquad \frac{\Gamma \vdash A, \Delta \quad \Gamma \vdash B, \Delta}{\Gamma \vdash A\&B, \Delta} \ (R\&)$$

Rules for quantifiers:

$$\frac{\Gamma, A[a/x] \vdash \Delta}{\Gamma, \forall x A \vdash \Delta} \ L\forall \qquad \frac{\Gamma \vdash \Delta, A[t/x]}{\Gamma \vdash \Delta, \forall x A} \ R\forall$$

$$\frac{\Gamma, A[t/x] \vdash \Delta}{\Gamma, \exists x A \vdash \Delta} \ L\exists \qquad \frac{\Gamma \vdash A[a/x], \Delta}{\Gamma \vdash \exists x A, \Delta} \ R\exists$$

where t is not free in Γ and Δ.

Author Index